THE EXCELLENT BENJAMIN KEACH

THE IMPACT OF Benjamin Keach on a young Baptist denomination for good should not be forgotten. His doctrinal clarity and coherence, his careful examination and courageous admonitions concerning ecclesiological issues, his searching and sound preaching and his well-chosen polemical engagements sent Baptists on a very healthy trajectory; a recovery of his influence would be pleasantly invigorating and strengthening. Austin Walker's treatment of *The Excellent Benjamin Keach* embraces all these qualities and sets them forth in a manly and robust style of writing. The thoroughness of his research, the accuracy of his organizational instincts and the engaging clarity of his style make this book a pleasant, educational and edifying experience. I welcome this re-issuing and encourage anyone zealous for the church's growth in purity, truthfulness, zeal and holiness to read it and encourage others to do the same.

TOM J. NETTLES

Baptist historian, author, professor, Louisville, Kentucky, USA

THE BAPTIST STALWART, Benjamin Keach is to be remembered as a leading pastor-theologian among seventeenth-century Baptists. A prominent nonconformist leader and a prolific writer, he helped shape the theological development of the Particular Baptists as they struggled through severe persecution. This second edition of *The Excellent Benjamin Keach* should be welcomed by any who desire to emulate Keach's statesmanship, productivity and pastoral leadership in their own ministry.

STEVEN J. LAWSON

President, OnePassion Ministries and professor of preaching, The Master's Seminary, Sun Valley, California, USA

IN THE LATE seventeenth century, when Baptist views often attracted derision and sometimes invited oppression, Benjamin Keach stoutly defended their position against a variety of opponents. At an early stage in his life, a book of his was condemned and ordered burned by the public hangman; and, later on, he engaged in verbal battle with a variety of adversaries. Against members of his own body of Christians, he asserted the legitimacy of hymn singing and the rightness of the laying on of hands at baptism. Austin Walker's thorough biography, which has already proved its worth, illuminates Keach's thought as well as his life, bringing out its firm theological foundations.

DAVID BEBBINGTON

Professor of History, University of Stirling, Scotland

ONE DOES NOT have to agree with Benjamin Keach's views on infant baptism to recognize that this book is an essential guide to understanding the life and teachings of one of the premier early Baptists. Austin Walker mines the seventeenth-century sources to let Benjamin Keach speak for himself. No student of the Calvinistic Baptist movement should be without it.

JOEL R. BEEKE

President, Puritan Reformed Theological Seminary, Grand Rapids, Michigan, USA

Comments about the first edition

"This book plugs a significant gap in the history of English Dissent."

ROBERT OLIVER

Lecturer in Church History and Historical Theology at London Theological Seminary and pastor of Old Baptist Chapel, Bradford-on-Avon, UK

"Surprisingly, no full-length biography has previously been attempted of this mighty figure from the golden age of Baptist church expansion. From his portrait in oils hanging in the Tabernacle, we have grown to 'know' him, or we imagine so, and this substantial and compelling account of his life and times has been a voyage of discovery for us. ...In this day of endless book production and surfeit of history, Austin Walker has selected a really worthwhile subject and created a book to be remembered."

PETER MASTERS

Pastor, The Metropolitan Tabernacle, London, UK

"In *The Excellent Benjamin Keach*, Austin Walker has given Reformed Baptists (and, of course, all of his readers) a wonderful gift, providing us with a carefully researched and thoroughly presented biography of one of the...great leaders of the earliest days of our movement. ...the first easily accessible book-length treatment of this notable and noble man."

JAMES M. RENIHAN

Academic Dean and Associate Professor of Historical Theology, The Institute for Reformed Baptist Studies, Westminster Theological Seminary, California, USA

"This is an important book. ...Benjamin Keach was under God one of the founders of the Particular Baptist denomination—as a preacher, a voluminous writer and a stalwart contender for the truth, in belief and order. ...We are delighted that Keach has been rediscovered, and we wholeheartedly agree with the title of the book, *The Excellent Benjamin Keach*."

B.A. RAMSBOTTOM

Editor of The Gospel Standard *and pastor of Bethel Chapel, Luton, UK*

"Austin Walker writes in a fluent and interesting style and sets before us a fascinating portrait, 'warts and all', of this brave, passionate and committed minister."

EDWARD DONNELLY

Principal, Reformed Theological College, Belfast, N. Ireland

"The English preacher Benjamin Keach was a proto-nonconformist; it is rare to find such an important figure largely untreated before the twenty-first century. An unusual man has been brought out from the gloom to speak to us, and for this we are indebted to the excellent Austin Walker."

GEOFF THOMAS

Pastor, Alfred Place Baptist Church, Aberystwyth, Wales

I. Surmans Delin:
M. Vandergucht Sculp.
Benjamin Keach
Ætatis 60. Anno. 1701

THE EXCELLENT

BENJAMIN KEACH

AUSTIN WALKER

SECOND REVISED EDITION

www.joshuapress.com

Published by
Joshua Press Inc., Kitchener, Ontario, Canada
Distributed by
Sola Scriptura Ministries International
www.sola-scriptura.ca

First published 2004. This Second Revised Edition published 2015.

Cover and book design by Janice Van Eck
Set in *17thC Print OT* and *Whitman*. *17thC Print OT* is a typeface taken from a book published in 1686. It incorporates not only the imperfections but also the art of seventeenth-century printing.

Cover portrait of Benjamin Keach from a portrait in the Metropolitan Tabernacle, London. Reproduced with permission.

Frontispiece © National Portrait Gallery, London. Artist: Michael Vandergucht. Used with permission.

The publication of this book was made possible by the generous support of
The Ross-Shire Foundation

Library and Archives Canada Cataloguing in Publication

Walker, Austin, 1946–, author
The excellent Benjamin Keach / Austin Walker. — Second revised edition.

Includes bibliographical references and index.
ISBN 978-1-894400-63-3 (pbk.)—ISBN 978-1-894400-64-0 (bound)

1. Keach, Benjamin, 1640–1704. 2. Baptists—England—History—17th century. 3. Baptists—England—Clergy—Biography. 4. Dissenters, Religious—England—Biography. I. Title.

BX6495.K42W34 2015 286'.1092 C2014-907513-8

To the members of
Maidenbower Baptist Church, Crawley, UK

CONTENTS

	Foreword to the second edition	xiii
	Foreword to the first edition	xv
	Preface to the second edition	xvii
	Acknowledgements	xix
	Abbreviations	xxv
	Chronology	xxvii
	Introduction: "Another manner of Character"	1
1	"Converted by the power of God's Word"	13
2	"One that is a teacher in their new fangled way"	43
3	"Great Troubles and Sorrows"	61
4	"The mysteries of the Gospel"	83
5	"The times of the Ten hot Persecutions"	105
6	"To learn to Read, good Child, give heed"	139
7	"A man of considerable parts and experience"	171
8	"The long'ed for presence"	197
9	"The ornament of my poor ministry"	223
10	"Entrusted with the Word"	249
11	"The hardest Dispensation of late"	279
12	"An orderly true constituted visible church of Jesus Christ"	311
13	"Law and Work-mongers"	343
	Epilogue: "The excellent Benjamin Keach"	375

Appendix 1: The will of Benjamin Keach 389
Appendix 2: The twenty-eight witnesses to Keach's character collected by Joseph Stennett, 1703 391
Appendix 3: "Keach's Covenant"— The solemn covenant of the church of Christ 395
Appendix 4: Of Laying on of Hands & Of Singing of Psalms 399

Bibliography 401
Index 439

FOREWORD TO THE SECOND EDITION

The interest shown in the first edition of this life of the Baptist pioneer Benjamin Keach has been immensely gratifying. Doing a second edition enables us to correct the all-too-numerous typographical errors of the first edition, add an index—which will make the work even more valuable—make some changes in design and a few substantial changes to the text, and include extracts from some book reviews. It is the publisher's sincere hope that all of these changes will—to paraphrase the King James Version translators—only serve to make a very good work better.

Michael A.G. Haykin
Dundas, Ontario, Canada

Very sweetly did Mr. Keach preach the great fundamental truths of the gospel, and glorify the name and work of Jesus.... [He was] one who loved the whole truth in Jesus, and felt its power.... He was very solid in his preaching, and his whole conduct and behaviour betokened a man deeply in earnest for the cause of God. In addressing the ungodly he was intensely direct, solemn and impressive, not flinching to declare the terrors of the Lord, nor veiling the freeness of divine grace.

CHARLES HADDON SPURGEON

FOREWORD TO THE FIRST EDITION

For students of seventeenth-century Calvinistic Baptist history, these are exciting days. The recovery of the doctrines of grace in various sectors of the English-speaking world since the 1950s opened the way for the emergence of numerous Reformed Baptist congregations. This, in turn, led to the appearance of a number of Baptist historians within these congregations who shared the theological convictions of their Calvinistic Baptist forebears. This deep interest in one of the most fascinating eras of Baptist history has continued to grow. And today, it can be rightly said that not since the Victorian era have there been so many Baptist historians who delight in the same biblical truths that lay deep in the hearts of such seventeenth-century Baptist leaders as Hanserd Knollys, William Kiffin, Abraham Cheare and Hercules Collins.

A good example of the fruit of this interest and delight is this book, which is a major study of the life and thought of Benjamin Keach, the most important Baptist thinker of his day. Keach produced a number of important biblical studies, one of which, *Tropologia*, was in print for much of the twentieth century. He also wrote extensively against the errors of the charismatic Quakers as well as those of the Roman Church. He was not afraid to point out the erroneous teaching of Richard Baxter and others on the doctrine of justification. Some of his works also defended the biblical convictions of his community against the polity of the Established Church of England. And Keach's pioneering defence of the singing of hymns has proven to be extremely important for later Baptist and other Christians.

For a few hundred years after his death, Keach was remembered as a notable pastor in the history of one of the most important congregations in Calvinistic Baptist history—what would become known as the Metropolitan Tabernacle in the nineteenth century. In more recent days, though, much of his story and thought have lain neglected. I am personally thrilled, therefore, that Austin Walker has undertaken this study and heartily recommend this book to fellow Baptists and others interested in a most important figure of early Baptist history.

Michael A.G. Haykin
Dundas, Ontario, Canada
September 23, 2004

PREFACE TO THE SECOND EDITION

I am particularly grateful to Joshua Press for deciding to republish *The Excellent Benjamin Keach*. It has provided an opportunity to correct the printing errors in the first edition, and it has also provided me with the opportunity to make minor revisions to the text, correct some of my own errors in dates and place names and update the book. The format of this second edition owes a great deal to the expertise of Janice Van Eck. I would like to express my appreciation to her for all her work. She is responsible for the new design and layout of the book and has not only typeset the entire text but also added an index and borne patiently with me, processing my several lists of corrections and additions.

Since the appearance of *The Excellent Benjamin Keach* in 2004, there have been significant developments. Interest in, and appreciation for, our Baptist forefathers has deepened. More research on them is now being undertaken than perhaps at any time since they were alive. Historical research is now carried out in a very different way, due largely to the Internet. Many of Keach's works are presently available online, saving hours of travel to specialist libraries and pouring over books that cannot be borrowed. In particular, Early English Books Online (EEBO) makes primary source material available to download from the Internet.

Keach also finds his rightful place in the panoramic coverage of Baptist history and theology provided by Tom Nettles and James

Leo Garrett in their publications.[1] Furthermore, significant research has also been done by others on various aspects of Keach's theology, his preaching and the hymn singing controversy. Two extensive studies have been produced by David Riker and Jonathan Arnold, and I have tried to take into account some of Arnold's comments, in particular, in this new edition. Other important studies of Keach's contemporaries have appeared, such as, Dennis Bustin's volume on Hanserd Knollys, and smaller works on Abraham Cheare and Hercules Collins. It would be wonderful if information on Keach was discovered, similar to that unearthed by Dr. Larry Kreitzer on William Kiffin,[2] but nothing has been forthcoming in the extensive records now available online.

The first edition was kindly received and reviewed favourably by a good number of people, and it is my hope and prayer that not only Reformed Baptists, but many other Baptists and Paedobaptists, will read and enjoy this new edition. Benjamin Keach, even with his strong views on believer's baptism, stood in the mainstream of historic biblical Christianity. He was Trinitarian, he understood the covenant of grace and he defended the biblical doctrine of justification by faith. Above all, Keach loved and served the Lord Jesus Christ and was a faithful preacher of his gospel.

Austin Walker
Crawley, West Sussex, UK
November 2014

---

1 Tom Nettles, *The Baptists: Key People Involved in Forming a Baptist Identity*. 3 vols. (Fearn: Christian Focus Publications, 2005, 2007); James Leo Garrett, *Baptist Theology: A Four-Century Study* (Macon: Mercer University Press, 2009).

2 Larry J. Kreitzer, *William Kiffin and his World (Part One); (Part Two); (Part Three); (Part Four)*; Resourcing Baptists History: Seventeenth Century Series, 4 vols. (Oxford: Regent's Park College, 2010, 2012, 2013, 2014).

ACKNOWLEDGEMENTS

As far as I am aware, no full-length biography of Benjamin Keach has ever been written. Biographies exist for his seventeenth-century Particular Baptist contemporaries, William Kiffin and Hanserd Knollys, but not for Keach.[1] Thomas Crosby, Keach's son-in-law who wrote some thirty years after Keach's death, noted the scarcity of many of his books. When he wrote an account of his father-in-law in *The History of the English Baptists* he was struggling to provide very much biographical material. Very few letters written by Keach survive, and there is scant information available either on his upbringing in Buckinghamshire in the 1640s and 1650s, or on the full extent of his sufferings after the restoration of the monarchy in 1660. Of his works, only his books on the parables of Christ and the types and metaphors of the Bible are currently in print. Many other books are scarce and very expensive and difficult to obtain. However,

1 Michael A.G. Haykin, *Kiffin, Knollys and Keach: Rediscovering our English Baptist Heritage* (Leeds: Reformation Today Trust, 1996). On Hanserd Knollys, see William Kiffin, *The Life and Death of That Old Disciple of Jesus Christ and Eminent Minister of the Gospel, Hanserd Knollys* (London, 1692); James Culross, *Hanserd Knollys: A Minister and Witness of Jesus Christ* (London: Alexander and Shepheard, 1895); Muriel James, *Religious Liberty on Trial: Hanserd Knollys—Early Baptist Hero* (Franklin: Providence House Publishers, 1997). On William Kiffin, see William Orme, ed., *Remarkable Passages in the Life of William Kiffin* (London, 1823); Joseph Ivimey, *The Life of Mr William Kiffin* (London, 1833); B.A. Ramsbottom, *Stranger than Fiction: The Life of William Kiffin* (Harpenden: Gospel Standard Trust, 1989).

with the advent of microfilm and computerization, material has become more widely obtainable.

It has now been over three-hundred years since Keach's death. *The Excellent Benjamin Keach* was written as an attempt to provide an account of Keach's life and an examination of his teaching. Keach's fame is usually based on two things: his sufferings as a twenty-four-year-old preacher when he was pilloried in his native Buckinghamshire in 1664; and when he introduced hymn singing into congregational worship in the latter part of the seventeenth century. This biography sets out to show that Keach's significance far exceeds these two areas. I have drawn on almost all of Keach's available writings, especially his many printed sermons, in order to show why the term "excellent" may justly be applied to his name.

In citing primary sources I have changed nothing apart from occasional capitalized words. Therefore, grammatical errors, punctuation and spelling errors have been retained in quotations, together with variations in spelling from modern standardized forms. The same practice has been followed in citing bibliographical references. The habit of seventeenth-century writers of introducing capital letters for key words in the middle of sentences and in titles is well known. These capital letters have also been retained in the text.

In researching and writing this biography, I have become indebted to a large number of people whose help has proved indispensable. On numerous occasions, Sue Mills, the librarian of the Angus Library at Regent's Park College, Oxford, has come to my aid and cheerfully pursued source material and clarified bibliographical data on my behalf. Margaret Simmons, formerly an assistant in the Boyce Library, Southern Baptist Theological Seminary, Louisville, Kentucky, also rendered considerable help both directly and by email correspondence. Furthermore, I would like to thank the librarians and archivists at Dr. Williams's Library, London; The Evangelical Library, London; the Southwark Local Studies Library; the Public Record Office; the Corporation of London Records Office; the Greater London Record Office; the Guildhall Library; Lambeth Palace Library; the Surrey History Centre, Woking; and the Centre for Buckinghamshire Studies, Aylesbury. In particular, Sarah Charlton, an assistant archivist at the Centre for Buckinghamshire Studies, went to great lengths to provide valuable source material. In addition, I wish to thank Dr. Williams's Library for permission to reproduce the portraits of Elias Keach, Joseph Stennett and Daniel Williams and the National Portrait Gallery for permission to reproduce the portrait of Matthew Mead and Benjamin Keach.

A number of individuals have been of considerable encouragement and help, sometimes providing advice as well as important source material. In particular, I would like to thank Raymond Brown for helping to identify Matthew Mead as the instrument of Keach's conversion; Mark Goldie for a copy of his work on the Hilton Gang; Richard L. Greaves of Florida State University for allowing me to purchase from him the *Biographical Dictionary of British Radicals in the Seventeenth Century*; Ian Green of Queen's University, Belfast, for the long term loan of *Print and Protestantism in Early Modern England*, together with photocopies of relevant sections of this and *The Christian's ABC*; Neil Keeble of Stirling University for his advice about seventeenth-century literary studies and criticism; Jim Renihan of Westminster Theological Seminary, California, for his encouragement and photocopies of several of Keach's smaller works; Mike Renihan of Worcester, Massachusetts, for his help in understanding aspects of the debate about baptism in the seventeenth century; Kenneth Dix for photocopies of material by Elias Keach; Robert Oliver for his encouragement to write this biography and also inviting me, in 2002, to lecture on Keach to students at London Theological Seminary participating in a Westminster Theological Seminary module on English Nonconformity; Malcolm Watts and Norman Hopkins for the loan of books from their personal libraries; Rachel Perozzi and

Jonathan Norton for help in obtaining source materials; and Laurence Evans for photographing some of the portraits.

Michael Haykin, the editorial director of Joshua Press, and professor of church history and biblical spirituality at The Southern Baptist Theological Seminary in Louisville, Kentucky, has been the person primarily responsible for encouraging me to write this biography and has been a valued source of ideas and advice. My close friend, Jim Savastio, pastor of the Reformed Baptist Church of Louisville, Kentucky, has supplied practical help and, along with his wife Becky, have provided hospitality and a free taxi service to and from Southern on my numerous visits there during the writing of this book.

Several members of my family deserve a special word of appreciation. The contribution of my daughter, Dr. Rachel Bown, has been noteworthy. Her knowledge of late seventeenth-century politics, in particular the impact of the arrival in England of William of Orange, has been of peculiar value. My son, Jeremy, read through various versions of the text and made innumerable corrections and suggestions to improve the flow of the text, and also helped me to interpret and apply some of the complexities of *The Chicago Manual of Style*. To my wife, Mai, I owe more than I can say. Her continued patience and encouragement, her willingness to ensure I caught the early morning coach from Gatwick to Oxford, and her bearing with my frequent frustrations in completing the writing, are all particularly worthy of thanks.

I would also like to thank two groups of people for their help. First, Maidenbower Baptist Church, Crawley, UK, of which I have been a pastor since its founding in 1975. In the weekly adult Sunday School hour, they listened patiently to some of my earlier versions of the life and ministry of Keach and, in 2003, kindly allowed me a month's leave from the pulpit on two separate occasions so that I could devote myself to writing. Without those months, this biography could not have been completed. Second, I would like to acknowledge my indebtedness to a small group of pastors with whom I regularly meet in London: Achille Blaize, Andrew Coats, Reuben Danladi, Jack Hampshire, John Sherwood and Jeremy Walker. They have constantly spurred me on, prayed for me as I have undertaken the research and the writing, and some of them were kind enough to preach while I was on leave from the church. They do not really know how much their encouragements have helped me complete the task.

Finally, I want to acknowledge the grace and goodness of God. In reading the writings, and in particular the sermons, of Benjamin Keach, I have discovered that he was in many ways a kindred spirit. While I cannot pretend to his usefulness or greatness—he was the leading Particular Baptist theologian and preacher before John Gill and Andrew Fuller—I can nevertheless readily identify with Keach, although I trust at the same time that I am not blind to some of his failings. Because of God's grace, I too have come to believe on the same Lord Jesus Christ that subdued and captivated the heart of Keach over three hundred years ago. As I have read his sermons and his other works, he has ministered to my own heart and he has, I hope, helped me to become a better Christian, as well as a better theologian, preacher and pastor. Furthermore, I am persuaded that it is not possible to accurately evaluate Keach without understanding the impact that the sovereign saving grace of God in the Lord Jesus Christ has on the heart and life of a man.

Whatever shortcomings readers find in this book, I hope it will serve not only to fill an important gap in Particular Baptist biography, but also to be a means in God's hands of making Christians today stronger and more courageous, as well as providing a firmer basis for further investigation into the contribution made by "the excellent Benjamin Keach."

Austin Walker
Crawley, West Sussex, UK
July 2004 (the tercentennial year of Keach's death)

ABBREVIATIONS

All references to Keach are to Benjamin Keach unless otherwise indicated.

BDBR	Richard L. Greaves and Robert Zaller, ed., *Biographical Dictionary of British Radicals in the Seventeenth Century*, 3 vols. (Brighton: Harvester Press, 1982–1984).
BQ	*Baptist Quarterly* (The Journal of the Baptist Historical Society), 1922–present.
Crosby, *History*	Thomas Crosby, *The History of the English Baptists*, 4 vols. (London, 1738–1740). Facsimile copy published by The Baptist Standard Bearer, Arkansas, n.d.
CSPD	*Calendar of State Papers, Domestic Series 1603–1714*.
Ivimey, *History*	Joseph Ivimey, *A History of the English Baptists*, 4 vols. (London, 1811–1830).
Keach, *Types and Metaphors*	Benjamin Keach, *Preaching from the Types and Metaphors of the Bible* (Grand Rapids: Kregel, 1972). This was originally published by Keach as *Tropologia, a Key to open Scripture Metaphors, together with Types of the Old Testament* (London, 1681).
Keach, *Parables One/Two*	Benjamin Keach, *Exposition of the Parables, Series One, Series Two* (Grand Rapids: Kregel, 1991). This was originally published by Keach as *Gospel Mysteries Unveil'd: Or, Exposition of all the Parables, and many express similitudes* (London, 1701).
PRO	Public Record Office, The National Archives, Kew, London.

Regester	*A perfect and Complete Regester of Marrages, Nativities and Burials belonging to the Congregation that Meeteth on Horselydown, over whom Benjamen Keach is Overseer*, PRO, RG4/4188.
TBHS	*Transactions of the Baptist Historical Society*, 1908–1921. *Transactions* became the *Baptist Quarterly* in 1922.

CHRONOLOGY

Age	Events related to Keach's life	Year	Other national events
	February 29: Benjamin Keach is born in Stoke Hammond, Buckinghamshire, and baptized six days later in the local parish church.	1640	Charles I is king (since 1625).
2		1642	First civil war between king and Parliament breaks out (1642–1646).
4	*First London Baptist Confession of Faith* signed by seven London Particular Baptist churches	1644	
6		1646	*Westminster Confession of Faith* is published.
8		1648	Second civil war
9		1649	Trial and execution of Charles I
10		1650	England becomes a Commonwealth under Oliver Cromwell. Attendance at parish churches is no longer compulsory.
12	A General Baptist church is founded in Southwark, London, with William Rider as pastor. The church later invited Keach to succeed Rider.	1652	

Age	Events related to Keach's life	Year	Other national events
15	Keach is converted through the ministry of Matthew Mead and is baptized by immersion among the General Baptists.	1655	
18	Begins to preach among General Baptists	1658	Oliver Cromwell dies; *Savoy Declaration of Faith*
		1659	Richard Cromwell resigns.
20	Marries Jane Grove (1639–1670) of Winslow	1660	Declaration of Breda issued on April 4 and Charles II restored to the throne on May 8
22		1662	The Act of Uniformity is declared, resulting in the Great Ejection (ejection of Nonconformists from the Anglican church).
23	Mary Keach is born.	1663	Gilbert Sheldon becomes Archbishop of Canterbury.
24	Twelve General Baptists (not Keach) are sentenced to death in Aylesbury, but saved by William Kiffin's plea. Keach is pilloried in Aylesbury and Winslow for publishing *A New Primer.*	1664	First Conventicle Act
25	Elias Keach is born.	1665	Five Mile Act (forbade clergymen from living within five miles of a parish from which they had been expelled); outbreak of the Great Plague (killed an estimated 100,000 Londoners)
26	Writes first version of *Sion in Distress: Or, the Groans of the Protestant Church*	1666	September 2–5: Great Fire of London destroys more than 2/3 of the city
27	Hannah Keach is born.	1667	

Age	Events related to Keach's life	Year	Other national events
28	Because of persecution, Keach moves with his wife and family to London and is soon ordained pastor of a church in Southwark.	1668	
29		1669	Future James II converts to Catholicism.
30	October: Keach's wife, Jane, dies at the age of thirty one leaving three young children.	1670	Second Conventicle Act (imposed a fine on anyone who attended a religious service other than the Church of England or allowed their home to be used for such); secret treaty between Charles II and Louis XIV
32	April: Keach marries the widow Susannah Partridge (1641–1727); he adopts Calvinistic theology; the Horselydown congregation erects a building.	1672	Charles II issues the Declaration of Indulgence, which is abandoned within a year.
33	Elizabeth Keach is born; Keach publishes his "best-seller" *War with the Devil.*	1673	
35	Susannah Keach is born.	1675	
36	Preaches at John Norcott's funeral in Wapping	1676	New secret treaty between Charles II and Louis XIV
37	*Second London Confession of Faith* drawn up and adopted by the Assembly in 1689	1677	Marriage of Princess Mary to William of Orange; William Sancroft becomes the new Archbishop of Canterbury
38	John Bunyan's *Pilgrim's Progress* is published.	1678	"Popish plot" uncovered creates panic in London
39	Rachel Keach is born; publishes epic poem, *The Glorious Lover*	1679	

Age	Events related to Keach's life	Year	Other national events
41	Publishes *Tropologia*	1681	From now until 1686, the "hottest" persecution of Dissenters
42	Rebecca Keach is born.	1682	
43	Publishes *The Travels of True Godliness;* Thomas Crosby is born (he later marries Keach's daughter Rebecca and becomes a historian of Baptists).	1683	Rye House plot is uncovered; savage repression of Scottish Covenanters begins.
44	Publishes *The Progress of Sin*; suicide of John Child; son Elias Keach leaves home for the American colonies	1684	
45		1685	Charles II dies; James II becomes king; Monmouth uprising fails; "Bloody Assizes" results in 300 executed for rebellion; James II begins to promote Catholicism; Edict of Nantes revoked by Louis XIV.
48		1688	Birth of a son to James II, succession crisis reaches a head; William of Orange invited to intervene in England by force, he invades and James II eventually flees to France.
49	Publishes *Distressed Sion Relieved;* First London Assembly of Particular Baptists; publishes *Gold Refin'd*—first of ten books to appear on baptism in the 1690s.	1689	William and Mary become joint sovereigns; Act of Toleration allows freedom of worship to Nonconformists.
50	Elizabeth Keach marries Thomas Stinton; beginning of the hymn singing controversy in Horsely-down and controversy with Isaac Marlow	1690	War with France

Age	Events related to Keach's life	Year	Other national events
50	Beginning of the Neonomian controversy with Richard Baxter, Daniel Williams and Samuel Clarke	1690	
51	His friend Hanserd Knollys dies, aged 93; publishes *The Counterfeit Christian* and *The Breach Repaired in God's Worship*	1691	
52	Elias Keach returns to London; publishes *Spiritual Melody*—the first of 3 hymn books; publishes *The Marrow of True Justification*	1692	Threat of French invasion removed
53	His friend Henry Forty dies; publishes funeral sermon called *The Everlasting Covenant*	1693	
54	Publishes A *Golden Mine Opened*	1694	Death of Queen Mary
56		1696	Plot to assassinate William III thwarted
57	Publishes *The Glory of a True Church*	1697	Peace congress at Ryswick, Holland
58	Publishes *The Display of Glorious Grace, A Short Confession of Faith, Christ Alone the Way to Heaven* and *Laying on of Hands on Baptized Believers*	1698	
59	Susannah Keach marries Benjamin Stinton; death of his son Elias	1699	
60	Publishes *The covenant and catechism of the church…meeting…in Southwark* and *The Jewish Sabbath Abrogated*	1700	
61	His friend William Kiffin dies, aged 85; publishes *Gospel Mysteries Unveil'd*—his last major work to be published in his lifetime	1701	

Age	Events related to Keach's life	Year	Other national events
62		1702	Death of William III, accession of Queen Anne
63	David Russen's attack on Keach	1703	
64	July 18: Keach dies at his home in Southwark; Benjamin Stinton (1676–1719) succeeds his father-in-law as pastor.	1704	

INTRODUCTION

"Another manner of Character"

It is midsummer in the year 1704. Queen Anne has recently come to the throne of England, Scotland and Ireland, following the death of William III in 1702. In his house in Southwark, on the south bank of the Thames in London, a sixty-four year old "gentleman, infirm and weak," aware that his days on earth are rapidly coming to an end, is engaged in conversation with a man over twenty years his junior.[1] The older man asks the younger to preach a memorial sermon at his funeral from 2 Timothy 1:12, on the words "for I know whom I have believed, and am persuaded that He is able to keep what I have committed to Him until that Day."[2] The older man is Benjamin

---

1 "The Will of Benjamin Keach," Surrey Will Abstracts, Vol. 26, 2001. Archdeaconry Court of Surrey 1700–1708, No. 820. See Appendix 1.

2 B.A. Ramsbottom, "The Stennetts." In *The British Particular Baptists 1638–1910*, 3 vols., ed. Michael A.G. Haykin (Springfield: Particular Baptist Press, 1998), 1:133. Stennett was providentially hindered from preaching this sermon at the funeral, although he did subsequently deliver it. Sadly, the sermon was never printed. See also Crosby, *History*, 4:308–309.

Keach (1640–1704), for over thirty years pastor of the largest Particular Baptist church south of the river in London. The man he has asked to preach is his younger ministerial colleague, Joseph Stennett (1663–1713), pastor of the Particular Baptist congregation meeting at Pinners' Hall, London, on the north bank of the Thames.[3]

These men had been good friends for a number of years. Only a few months previously, Stennett had responded to an accusation levelled at his friend Keach by an Anglican layman called David Russen. Russen had blackened the good name of Keach. Firstly, he had labelled him as an Anabaptist teacher and secondly, and far more seriously, he had reported that Keach had recently been accused of immoral behaviour when baptizing women in water:

> It hath been observ'd that the Anabaptist Teachers have fall'n more of them under one particular Sin, viz. Uncleanness, than any other vice, and these not only young Men but Men of Years. One hath publish'd it to the World that one Mr. Row of Bristol, confess'd to a great many Ministers, and to him in particular, and one Mr Fairclough, that the first Dipper there at Baptist Mill, the usual place of Dipping, lay with the woman he Dipt, and particularly with her self. Russel, who was at the Portsmouth Conference, hath been charged with the same Vice. *Benjamin Keach, another noted Writer and Teacher of theirs, hath been lately Accus'd of the same....* May this inclination be ascrib'd to the Temptations arising from Embracing the Fairer Sex in the Water?[4]

---

3 Ramsbottom, "The Stennetts." In *The British Particular Baptists*, 1:136–138. Ramsbottom provides a survey of the life and ministry of Joseph Stennett.

4 David Russen, *Fundamentals without Foundation: or, a True Picture of the Anabaptists, in their Rise Progress and Practice. Written for the Use of such that take 'em for Saints, when they are not so much as Christians* (London, 1703), 31, emphasis added.

Russen's book was a particularly bitter and prejudiced attack on Baptists. For nearly two centuries the label "Anabaptist" had often been associated with fanaticism.[5] His own prejudices lay on the surface: in the Epistle Dedicatory he referred to Anabaptists as "base-born brats," and further expressed his opinion of them by stating that

> when Men turn Anabaptists, despising the Ministry of the Gospel then, they become Antinomians, rejecting the rule of Law, then Enthusiasts, making their Phanatick Revelations to out-vie God's Word, then Libertines, casting off all Magistracy and Government, and then Ranters, destroying the very Being of Human Society: for the next step from Anabaptism is Quakerism.[6]

It would be difficult to find more derogatory terms than those used by Russen to describe those who became Anabaptists. His attack on Baptists has been described as a "compilation of truths, half-truths, errors and innuendoes...a sample of the hostile propaganda against which Baptists were reacting in the early seventeenth century."[7]

Russen did not attempt to distinguish between different kinds of Baptists, but rather lumped them all together under one label.

---

5 This legacy followed events like the Münster rebellion in 1535, in Germany of Luther's day. J.F. McGregor, noting this long-standing association, comments that Münster and John of Leiden were "potent images of anarchy; vivid examples of the danger of popular religious heresy and justification for the stern suppression of all its manifestations." J.F. McGregor, "The Baptists: Fount of all Heresy." In *Radical Religion in the English Revolution*, eds. J.F. McGregor and B. Reay (Oxford: Oxford University Press, 1994), 25. The tone of Russen's book shows that the passing of almost 200 years had not eradicated those images and examples.

6 Russen, preface to *Fundamentals without Foundation*.

7 Murdina D. MacDonald, "London Calvinistic Baptists 1689–1727: Tensions within a Dissenting community under Toleration" (Ph.D. dissertation, Regent's Park College, Oxford, 1982), 136.

Keach, as a Particular Baptist, would have been very unhappy to have the label "Anabaptist," attached to his name. In 1644, sixty years before this attack by Russen, the first generation of Particular Baptists were very aware of the abuse that was heaped on any group regarded as Anabaptist and took care to disassociate themselves from the name. They wanted to distance themselves from the fanaticism that claimed new revelations and from the errant view that Jesus Christ did not derive his human nature from the body of Mary. This latter teaching was derived from Dutch Mennonite teaching.[8] Seven London churches published their confession of faith in 1644, and they invited others to make a candid assessment of their claims on the basis of Scripture. It was entitled *The confession of faith of those churches which are commonly (though falsly) called Anabaptists; Presented to the view of all that feare God, to examine by the touchstone of the Word of Truth: As likewise for the taking off those aspersions which are frequently both in Pulpit and Print, (although unjustly) cast upon them.*[9]

Russen's slanderous rumors about Keach were far from the truth and Stennett had therefore quickly risen to the defence of his friend. He sent three men of good reputation to visit Russen, in order to confront him with the false nature of the accusation and obtain the source of his information. Stennett sought a retraction, but the visit proved to be a complete disappointment. The three men began by asking Russen why he had inserted the scandalous story. At first, Russen tried to deny ever having written anything against Keach. When shown the evidence from his own book, Russen said that a third party had reported the information to him, but he refused to identify the source.[10]

---

8 See H. Leon McBeth, *The Baptist Heritage* (Nashville: Broadman Press, 1987), 53.

9 William L. Lumpkin, *Baptist Confessions of Faith* (Valley Forge: Judson Press, 1959), 153.

10 Joseph Stennett, *An Answer to Mr David Russen's Book entituled Fundamentals without a foundation or a true picture of Anabaptists etc.* (London, 1704), 140–142.

Unable to vindicate his friend by obtaining a retraction from Russen, Stennett took up his own pen. He immediately answered Russen's attack, addressing the whole issue of believer's baptism raised by Russen.[11] Embedded in his reply was a vindication of Benjamin Keach. Stennett asserted that Mr. Keach had "another manner of Character," for he said,

> 'tis strange that a Man of his public Character should have been lately under such a Charge, and yet his Neighbours and Acquaintances entirely ignorant of it, till Mr R[ussen] who lives very distant from him, and perhaps never saw him, can furnish the World with an account of the matter. Since Mr Keach has lived in and near the City of London, which is more than 30 years, he has had *another manner of Character*, than what this Gentleman would fasten on him; and whatever Mischief he designs his Name among those that know him not, I can assure him his own Credit is likely to suffer by the Calumny, wherever Mr Keach is known; who desires Mr R. to name the Person if he can, that ever accus'd him either formerly or lately, of any such Crimes as he suggests.[12]

Furthermore, Stennett secured the signatures of twenty-eight neighbours and friends of Keach as his character witnesses. Some were paedobaptists and some Anglicans, but all were united in their conviction that the accusation against Keach was "false, groundless and malicious," and they testified of "his good Conversation as a Christian and as a Minister."[13]

---

11 Stennett, *An Answer to Mr David Russen's Book*.

12 Stennett, *An Answer to Mr David Russen's Book*, 141. Emphasis added.

13 Stennett, *An Answer to Mr David Russen's Book*, 250–251. For the entire statement relating to Keach, see Appendix 2.

Stennett affirmed in his book that Keach was so well known in London for his integrity and blameless reputation that he "could easily obtain many hundreds of hands in and about the City of London, to certify the Clearness of his Reputation, as to that Crime which Mr R[ussen] would fasten on him, or anything like it."[14]

Keach died on July 18, 1704, his reputation untarnished and his name clear of reproach. However, this final attack on his character had been only the last skirmish in a life that was often characterized by persecution, suffering, trials and controversy of various kinds. Uprooted from Buckinghamshire, he had first come to London in 1668, aged twenty-eight, with a wife and young family. In his native county, some forty-five miles northwest of London, he had been branded as "a Seditious, Heretical, and Schismatical Person," and had patiently endured fines, imprisonment and the pillory.[15] The harassment by the authorities in London did not cease until 1689 when the House of Orange, in the persons of William III and Mary II, secured the throne of England from the waning Stuart dynasty.

Controversies and trials of a different kind then followed Keach. He became engaged in a heated debate about the legitimacy of congregational hymn singing within the London Particular Baptist community. Keach described his experience then as the "hardest Dispensation...that ever I met withal since I have been in the World."[16] Furthermore, in the 1690s, and on a wider front, he was involved in a different theological controversy, defending what he and many others believed to be the biblical doctrine of justification by faith. Despite these and other controversies in which he was engaged, Keach was clearly a

---

14 Stennett, *An Answer to Mr David Russen's Book*, 142.

15 *CPSD*, 1663–1664, 595. The pillory was a wooden framework erected on a post, with holes for securing the head and hands, and used for public humiliation.

16 Keach, addressed "To all the Baptized Churches and faithful Brethren in England and Wales," written "from my house by Horselydown, June 27, 1692."

man who had earned a long-standing reputation for his moral integrity. It would have been a tragedy if Keach had died with Russen's accusation still hanging over his head and this final controversy unresolved. Stennett's actions on behalf of his friend prevented that from happening.

Why was his life so full of trials and difficulties? Benjamin Keach was not alone in his suffering. Other Calvinistic Baptists such as John Bunyan (1628–1688), Hanserd Knollys (c.1599–1691), Hercules Collins (d.1702), Abraham Cheare (1626–1668), Francis Bampfield (1615–1684) and Thomas Delaune (d.1685) suffered for their biblical convictions and believer's baptism.[17]

---

17 John Bunyan was twice imprisoned (from 1660 to 1672) for illegally preaching, and imprisoned again for six months in 1677. The first time he was prosecuted under the old Elizabethan Conventicle Act. Asked to give assurances that he would not preach again he refused and was sent to the county jail for his pains. Bunyan was a Baptist but his church in Bedford was not a Particular Baptist church. They practiced open communion, unlike the church associated with Keach.

Hanserd Knollys was a leader among the London Particular Baptists from the mid-1640s, and a pastor of a church in East London. He had renounced his Anglican ordination as early as 1631. He came into conflict with the authorities for preaching believer's baptism in 1644 and endured a short imprisonment. In 1661, he was imprisoned for suspected Fifth Monarchy sympathies following Thomas Venner's uprising. He suffered again as a result of the Second Conventicle Act in 1670, nearly dying as a result of his imprisonment.

Hercules Collins was a pastor of a Particular Baptist church in Wapping from 1677 until 1702. He suffered imprisonment in Newgate Prison for three years until he was released when James II issued an indulgence in 1687.

Abraham Cheare was a Particular Baptist in Plymouth, Devon, and—like Keach—possessed poetical gifts. After 1660, he was imprisoned three times. He was placed in Exeter jail for three months in 1661, then for three years, from 1662 to 1665. Refusing to stop preaching cost him dearly. He was arrested again and finally banished to Drake's Island in Plymouth Sound, where he died after a long illness.

Francis Bampfield was a Seventh-Day Baptist (like Joseph Stennett) and former Anglican; he was ejected in 1662. His ministry in Sherborne, Dorset, was interrupted when he endured almost nine years of imprisonment in Dorchester for refusing to take the oath of allegiance to the king. A short imprisonment then followed in Salisbury before he went to London. Arrested there in 1683, he again refused to take the oath and was sent to Newgate Prison where he died twelve months later.

Some of them died as a result of the persecutions they endured. Cheare died incarcerated on Drake's Island, Plymouth Sound; Bampfield and Delaune died in prison in London.[18] Their lives were profoundly affected by the changes resulting from the return of Charles Stuart in 1660 and the restoration of Anglicanism. Repressive legislation and rigid censorship were imposed on men like Keach, who, for conscience sake, would neither cease writing, nor stop preaching the Word of God to their congregations.

Why was it that Stennett pursued the vindication of his friend with such earnestness? Did he want to clear Keach's name simply because over the years this man had become his friend? Much more was at stake. After his arrival in London in 1668, Keach had emerged as a man of proven integrity, and during the last fifteen years of his life he had become the foremost theologian of the Particular Baptists and one of their acknowledged leaders. David Copeland has described him as the most influential Baptist at the turn of the century.[19] Murdina MacDonald said of Keach that

---

Thomas Delaune was originally from Ireland and brought up as a Catholic. Converted there, he had to leave because of persecution. Arriving in London in 1683, he published *A Plea for the Nonconformists*, and was promptly arrested and placed in Newgate Prison. At his trial he was accused of false, seditious and scandalous libel against the king and *The Book of Common Prayer*. The judge was Sir George Jeffreys. Delaune died in Newgate in 1685. He had worked closely with Keach and a part of his labours was published as the first section in Keach's *Tropologia*.

Keach knew all these men (although there is no record of any contact with Bunyan, Keach greatly admired him) and was a fellow-sharer in their sufferings. More detailed portraits of these men may be found in Ivimey, *History*. Bunyan, Knollys, Cheare and Bampfield are also found in *BDBR*.

18 There were, of course, others of different denominations: Presbyterians, Independents and General Baptists, who suffered in similar fashion for the faith and truths they held dear. The Quakers, with whom Keach fundamentally disagreed, also suffered severely for their convictions.

19 David A. Copeland, *Benjamin Keach and the Development of Baptist Traditions in Seventeenth Century England* (Lewiston: The Edwin Mellen Press, 2001), 5.

> for a man reputed to be in chronic ill-health, [he was] seemingly indefatigable. He was clearly the single most important apologist for Calvinistic Baptist views in the period 1689–1702. He not only published on congregational hymn singing, but on ministerial maintenance, laying on of hands on baptized believers, first day worship, enthusiasm, eschatology, the church of Rome, believer's baptism and justification. He produced a confession of faith, a church order, a catechism, a political poem dedicated to William and Mary, a hymn book and many sermons. Hercules Collins, John Piggott, Joseph Stennett and others also wrote in defence of believer's baptism, but neither the scope nor extent of their works matched Keach's production.[20]

During his lifetime Benjamin Keach was a prolific writer, but above all else he was a preacher of the gospel of the Lord Jesus Christ for forty-six years, thirty-six of them in London. A man of bold spirit and intense energy, he saw many people converted under his ministry and was instrumental in helping plant a number of churches.

Thomas Crosby, Keach's son-in-law, records that

> preaching the Gospel was the very pleasure of his soul, and his heart was so engaged in the work of the ministry, that from the time of his first appearing in public, to the end of his days, his life was one continued scene of labour and toil. His close study and constant preaching did greatly exhaust his animal spirits, and enfeeble his

20 MacDonald, "London Calvinistic Baptists 1689–1727," 77. Keach's role in the confession of faith is very questionable. He certainly was a signatory of *The Second London Baptist Confession of Faith*, but he did not have a hand in drawing it up in 1677. See chapter 8.

> strength, yet to the last he discovered a becoming zeal against the prevailing errors of the day; his soul was too great to recede from any truth that he owned, either from the frowns or flatteries of the greatest.[21]

Crosby clearly did not believe that Keach was a man-pleaser. Furthermore, it would be a caricature to present Keach simply as a controversialist, a man who simply loved to argue his opinions. He became involved in controversy because he was a man of conviction and felt compelled to defend the truths that were dear to his heart. His convictions were forged on the anvil of God's Word, the Bible. He held them with warm passion and zeal, and his conscience was bound to that same book. Keach cannot be appreciated until his convictions and conscience are understood. Like the apostle Paul before him, he could say, "I myself always strive to have a conscience without offense toward God and man" (Acts 24:16, NKJV). Herein lies the secret of his energies spent for God and the courage he displayed while suffering for the sake of Christ. It was his convictions and conscience that brought him into conflict with the civil authorities during the years 1660 to 1689. It was those same convictions and conscience that sometimes brought him into disagreement with other Protestant believers whom he believed to be in error. Equipped with these convictions and motivated by a conscience bound to the Word of God, he proved to be a faithful pastor to his large flock in Southwark, not only by his example but also by his teaching, confirming them in the truth of the Scriptures and defending the great truths of the gospel.

He was also the first of four notable preachers in Southwark in the seventeenth, eighteenth and nineteenth centuries associated with what became the Metropolitan Tabernacle. Keach's ministry in Southwark began shortly after 1668 and continued until his death in 1704. He was to be followed as pastor of the

---

21 Crosby, *History*, 4:304.

Southwark congregation by John Gill (1697–1771), John Rippon (1751–1836) and finally Charles Haddon Spurgeon (1834–1892). Spurgeon had no hesitation in tracing the ancestry of the church that met in the Metropolitan Tabernacle back to Keach, and was firmly of the opinion, as was Joseph Stennett, that Benjamin Keach was a man worthy of honour.[22]

Benjamin Keach is, therefore, a man whose life and ministry deserves careful study. Several modern writers have expressed regret that no biography of Keach exists. Biographies exist for William Kiffin (1616–1701) and Hanserd Knollys, who (together with Keach) were the best-known and most respected leaders of London Particular Baptists.[23] Keach outlived his friends by a few years: Knollys died in 1691 and Kiffin in 1701. This biography is an attempt to fill the gap left by previous generations and to begin to put together the story of his life.

In broad compass, the life of Keach can be divided up into three main periods. There is the period from 1640 to 1668 when he lived in north Buckinghamshire. Born into the Anglican Church, he joined the General Baptists in 1655 and soon began

---

22 C.H. Spurgeon, *The Metropolitan Tabernacle: Its History and Work* (Pasadena: Pilgrim Publications, 1990), 18–34. Keach was not the first pastor; that honour goes to William Rider.

23 See Michael A.G. Haykin, *Kiffin, Knollys and Keach: Rediscovering Our English Baptist Heritage* (Leeds: Reformation Today Trust, 1996). On Hanserd Knollys, see William Kiffin, *The Life and Death of That Old Disciple of Jesus Christ and Eminent Minister of the Gospel, Hanserd Knollys* (London, 1692); James Culross, *Hanserd Knollys: A Minister and Witness of Jesus Christ* (London: Alexander and Shepheard, 1895); B.R. White, *Hanserd Knollys and Radical Dissent in the Seventeenth Century* (London: Dr. Williams Trust, 1977); Muriel James, *Religious Liberty on Trial: Hanserd Knollys—Early Baptist Hero* (Franklin: Providence House Publishers, 1997); Dennis Bustin, *Paradox and Perseverance: Hanserd Knollys, Particular Baptist Pioneer in Seventeenth-Century England*, Studies in Baptist History and Thought, vol. 23 (Milton Keynes: Paternoster, 2006). On William Kiffin, see William Orme, ed., *Remarkable Passages in the Life of William Kiffin* (London, 1823); Joseph Ivimey, *The Life of Mr William Kiffin* (London, 1833); B.R. White, "William Kiffin—Baptist Pioneer and Citizen of London," *Baptist History and Heritage* 2 (1967): 91–103; B. A. Ramsbottom, *Stranger than Fiction: The Life of William Kiffin* (Harpenden: Gospel Standard Trust, 1989).

to preach and write. At the same time, he began to experience the intense heat of persecution. The second period runs from 1668 to 1689, when Keach lived in London and became the pastor of a congregation in Southwark. Persecution continued until the Act of Toleration was passed in 1689, but Keach carried on preaching and writing, gradually growing in stature and reputation. The third and final period of his life, the fifteen years from 1689 to 1704, saw the great flurry of published material from his hand. In these books he was able, for the first time, to express his teaching freely, without fear of repression. His pen only came to rest with his death in 1704.

CHAPTER 1

"Converted by the power of God's Word"

When one is Baptized he ought to be dead to sin, that is converted by the power of God's Word to Gospel truth, which always makes the soul loathe and detest sin; and then that soul may be said indeed to be dead to sin.[1]

"If you really want to understand the period, go away and read the Bible." This was the answer given by a history tutor to a pupil pressing him for a reading list on sixteenth- and seventeenth-century English economic history. Christopher Hill who related the story concluded that, "The Bible was central to the whole of the life of the society: we ignore it at our peril."[2] During that time in English history, the Holy Scriptures were regarded as the unique source of all wisdom covering every subject. In all matters political and religious, every party appealed to the

1 Keach, "Baptism a burial," *Types and Metaphors*, 630.

2 Christopher Hill, *The English Bible and the Seventeenth-Century Revolution* (London: The Penguin Press, 1993), 4.

Bible for support. During the civil wars, the Commonwealth and the Restoration, each side, party and faction made constant appeals to the Bible. Since William Tyndale's translation of the Bible into English a century before, God's Word had been available to be read by all—not just the educated elite—and it had a great impact on the life of the nation.

The Bible is central to understanding and appreciating Benjamin Keach's life and ministry. It is because Keach believed the Bible to be the Word of God that he displayed such strong convictions—and persevered in those convictions to the end of his life. He expressed his mature attitude to the Bible in a sermon on the parable of the rich man and Lazarus, by stating that "there is nothing needful for us to know or be instructed in, but is contained in the written Word of God, though they are not understood by any without the Holy Spirit opens them to us, and works faith in our souls."[3]

In the same sermon he states,

> of all the writings in the world, the sacred Scriptures assume most unto themselves, telling us, they are the Word of God, the words of eternal life, and given out by the inspiration of the Holy Ghost, the testimony of Jesus, the faithful witness, Rev. 1:9; and that they shall judge the world, John 12:48; that they are able to make men wise unto salvation, 2 Tim. 3:15; they are the immortal seed, 1 Pet. 1:23; their tenor is, "Thus saith the Lord"...and no conclusion but "the Lord hath spoken," "hear the word of the Lord," and "He that hath an ear let him hear."[4]

Neither can Keach be understood fully unless we grasp the great change that takes place in the life of a person when they

---

3 Keach, "The Rich Man and Lazarus," *Parables Two*, 402–403.

4 Keach, *Parables Two*, 405.

become a Christian, putting their faith in Jesus Christ as a direct result of the powerful regenerating work of the Holy Spirit. Faith in Jesus Christ is the first and fundamental effect of God's grace. Keach writes,

> Believing in Christ, coming to Christ, looking to Christ, leaning, trusting, or staying on Christ, receiving of Christ and eating of Christ, imply one and the same thing. It is the going out of ourselves to him, or feeding by faith on him, or resting and relying on his merits, on his obedience in his life, and in his death, for justification and eternal life, without any works done by us, or any righteousness wrought in us, as the Apostle speaks, 'But to him that worketh not, but believeth on him that justifies the ungodly, his faith is counted for righteousness' (Rom. 4:5).[5]

In order to understand Keach, we must understand how and when he reached that point of conversion to Christ in his own life, how he came to believe justification by faith and how he came to be persuaded that infant baptism was not biblical baptism.

Early life

Benjamin Keach began his life as a son of the Church of England. He was born in Stoke Hammond, in the county of Buckinghamshire, England, on February 29, 1640, the sixth of seven children born to John and Joyce Keach.[6] Each of the Keach's children was

---

5 Keach, "The Fan in his Hand," *Parables One*, 42.

6 Today, the village of Stoke Hammond lies a few miles south of the new town of Milton Keynes. The parish church where Keach was baptized is still standing, having been substantially restored in 1852. The church boasts a twelfth-century stone baptismal font. It is therefore possible that Keach would have been baptized using this font. There is some doubt over the identity of his mother. In the records of the church at Horselydown (Keach's Southwark congregation), Keach lists his parents as John and Joyce. In

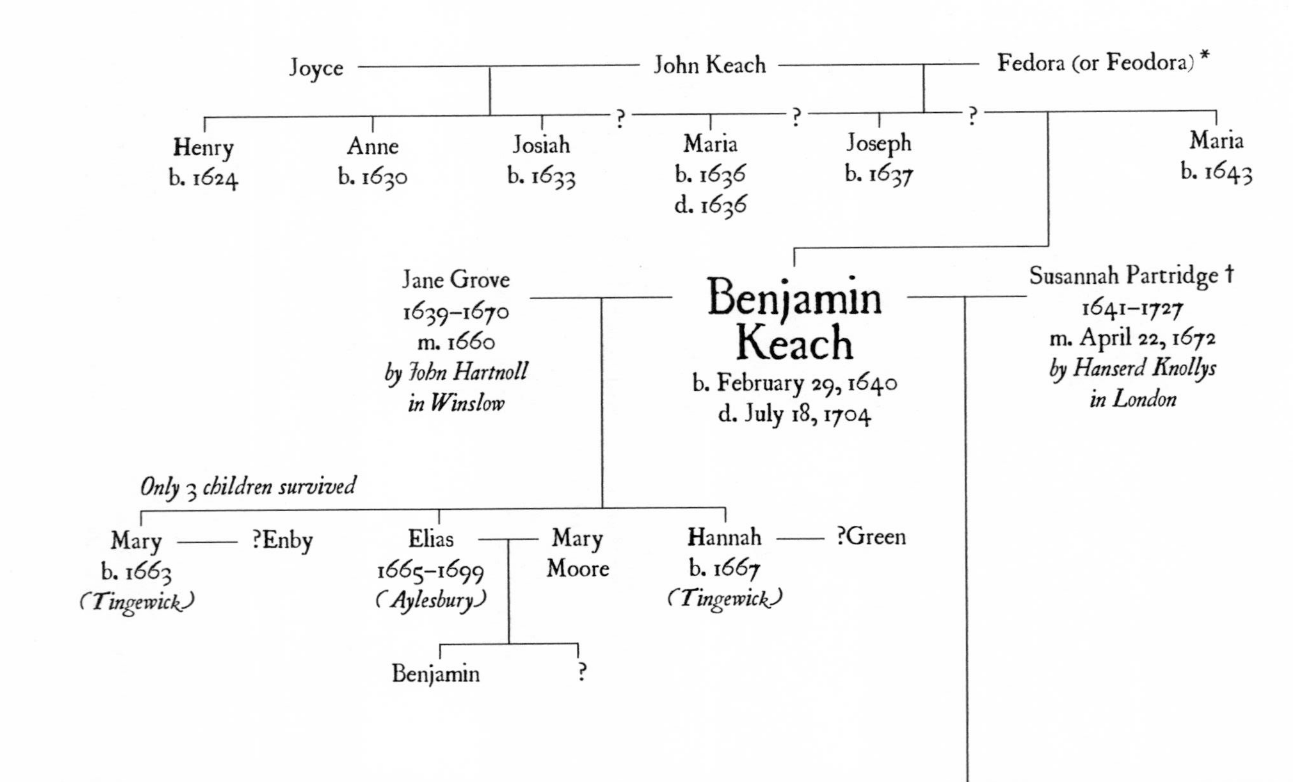
FAMILY TREE OF BENJAMIN KEACH
Joyce
John Keach
Fedora (or Feodora) *
Henry
b. 1624
Anne
b. 1630
Josiah
b. 1633
?
Maria
b. 1636
d. 1636
?
Joseph
b. 1637
?
Maria
b. 1643
Jane Grove
1639–1670
m. 1660
by John Hartnoll
in Winslow
Benjamin
Keach
b. February 29, 1640
d. July 18, 1704
Susannah Partridge †
1641–1727
m. April 22, 1672
by Hanserd Knollys
in London
Only 3 children survived
Mary
b. 1663
(Tingewick)
?Enby
Elias
1665–1699
(Aylesbury)
Mary
Moore
Hannah
b. 1667
(Tingewick)
?Green
Benjamin
?

Elizabeth — Thomas Stinton
- Elizabeth, b. 1673 *(Shadwell)*
- Thomas Stinton, b. 1668, m. May 29, 1690 *by George Barrett*

Benjamin Stinton — Susannah
- Benjamin Stinton, 1676–1719, m. 1699 *by Richard Adams (succeeded his father-in-law at Horselydown 1704–1719)*
- Susannah, b. 1675 *(Shadwell)*

Rachel, b. 1679 *(Shadwell)*

Thomas Crosby — Rebecca
- Thomas Crosby, 1683–1751 *Deacon in Goat St., schoolmaster, Baptist historian, after 1719 with John Gill*
- Rebecca, b. 1682 *(Cripplegate)*

Children of Benjamin Stinton and Susannah:

Tychicus	Samuel	Benjamin	John	Anne	Joshua	Timothy
b. 1700	b. 1703	b. 1704	b. 1705	b. 1707	b. 1710	b. 1710
d. 1700					d. 1710	d. 1712

Principal sources
- The will of Benjamin Keach
- Crosby, *History*
- Stoke Hammond Parish Register
- *Regester*
- W.T. Whitley, "Benjamin Stinton and his Baptist friends," *THBS* 1, 193.

Records are incomplete and must be gleaned from different sources. No one source is complete and sometimes correlation is difficult (variant spelling of names).

* In the Stoke Hammond Parish Register only Henry Keach is listed as the son of John and Joyce Keach. For Anne and Josiah only John's name appears. The name Fedora (or Feodora) appears in connection with Benjamin and Maria. (John Keach is listed as church warden for Stoke Hammond in 1627 and again in 1640.) *Regester* records Keach's mother as Joyce. There appears to be no extant record that indicates that Joyce died before Keach was born or that his father remarried.

† Variant spelling: Susanna.

Stoke Hammond Parish Church, Buckinghamshire, where the Keach family worshipped and Benjamin Keach was baptized in 1640

baptized in the local parish church: Henry was baptized on December 22, 1624, Anna on November 7, 1630, Josiah on October 6, 1633, Maria on July 31, 1636 (she died in infancy), Joseph on September 21, 1637 and Benjamin was baptized on March 6, 1640. His youngest sister, Maria, followed on June 4, 1643.[7] There is also evidence in the same records that John Keach was church warden in 1627 and again in 1640.[8]

Little is known of Keach's childhood and education. He appears to have had the trade of a tailor according to a letter written about him by Thomas Disney (1605–1686) in 1664.[9] Disney had become the new rector of the parish of Stoke Hammond in 1646. The letter indicates that several of the children of John Keach, along with other friends of Benjamin Keach, were well known to Thomas Disney. He complained that a number of them were no longer attending the parish church. Keach was at that point living in Winslow, but he had been moving in different circles for almost a decade. In 1655, when Keach was fifteen, he professed his faith in Jesus Christ and was baptized as a believer by immersion by John Russell, a General Baptist pastor.[10] However, as we

---

the Stoke Hammond church parish registers, his mother's name is listed as Fedora or Feodora. Joyce is clearly the name in the register only for his oldest brother, and the mother's name is omitted in two entries. Then there is a clear change to Fedora. There is no indication anywhere that John Keach's first wife died and he remarried. Was Mrs. Keach known by both names? It is unlikely that Benjamin Keach has listed the wrong name for his own mother even after fifty years. Detail on this issue can be gleaned from the *Regester* kept by Keach's church; *Parish Registers 1537–1758* (Stoke Hammond, Bucks Record Office, PR195); and James Barry Vaughn, "Public Worship and Practical Theology in the Work of Benjamin Keach (1640–1704)" (Ph.D. dissertation, University of St Andrews, 1989), 6. Vaughn suggests that Joyce died. We have no way of being certain.

7 *Parish Registers 1537–1758*.

8 *Parish Registers 1537–1758*.

9 *CSPD*, 1663–1664, SP29/98, 116, Thomas Disney to Luke Wilkes.

10 Crosby, *History*, 4:269. General Baptists inherited many convictions from the Separatists. John Smyth (c.1570–1612) and Thomas Helwys (c.1575–1616) were the founding fathers. They became convinced that Christian baptism should be for believers only and adopted the Mennonite practice they had seen in Amsterdam while in exile

The fourteenth-century baptismal font at Stoke Hammond Parish Church, Buckinghamshire, where Benjamin Keach was baptized as an infant.

shall see later, the General Baptists were probably not the only ones to shape the early religious convictions of Benjamin Keach.

Two related convictions seem to have been forged in Keach's mind before he had reached the age of twenty. The first concerned the illegitimacy of infant baptism, for Keach concluded that the Bible taught baptism was only for those who professed their faith in Jesus Christ and gave evidence of this by living a holy life. Some twenty-five years after his own conversion he wrote, "when one is Baptized he ought to be dead to sin, that is converted by the power of God's Word to Gospel truth, which always makes the soul loathe and detest sin."[11] He was persuaded that baptism was only for believers long before he wrote those words as is evidenced in the indictment read out at his trial in 1664 when he was charged with, among other things, rejecting the teaching of the Church of England about infant baptism.[12]

The second conviction concerned the nature of salvation, namely, that it was the result of God's free grace and that sinners were justified by faith in Jesus Christ and not by their own works. He was like a child learning to walk, and although Keach had

---

from 1608. Initially, though, baptizing was not by immersion but by sprinkling. They also began to adopt the teachings of James Arminius while in Holland, teachings that were rejected by the Synod of Dordt (1618–1619). This was to distinguish the General Baptists very clearly from the Particular Baptists who remained Calvinistic. In England, the main congregation of General Baptists was in London. For the best introduction to the General Baptists, see B.R. White, *The English Baptists of the Seventeenth Century* (Didcot: Baptist Historical Society, 1996), 15–58. See also *BDBR*, s.v. "Helwys, Thomas" and "Smyth, John."

11 Keach, *Types and Metaphors*, 630.

12 The first full account of Keach's trial appears as "The Tryall of Mr Benja. Keach who was prosecuted for Wrighting against Infant Baptism with an Account of ye Punishment inflicted upon him for ye same: Anno 1664." This is to be found in Benjamin Stinton, *A Repository of Divers Historical Matters Relating to the English Antipaedobaptists, Collected from Original Papers of Faithful Extracts* (Angus Library, Oxford, 1712), No. 21, 93–104. Stinton adds that this document was "taken from a mss. found among Mr Keach's papers after his death, which as he informed me when he was alive, was sent him from one in ye country who was present both at his tryall and punishment and took what passed in writing." Crosby used this evidence for his account in Crosby, *History*, 2:187–204. See also Ivimey, *History*, 1:340–351.

taken the first important steps and his convictions were beginning to take shape, at this point in his life he held to Arminian views about free will. Later on, Keach became much clearer about the ways in which God's free grace worked and, in particular, about the regenerating power of the Holy Spirit. He came to believe that "a child may as easily beget itself in the womb before itself was, as a man can form Christ in his own soul, or regenerate himself; 'tis God that doth it, the Holy Spirit that begets us."[13]

It is vital to consider by what means Keach came to adopt these related convictions, and where someone like him would have heard or been able to read something new and different. To leave the Anglican Church and insist on rebaptism for those who now possessed a personal faith in Jesus Christ was radical teaching to traditional ears, teaching that was believed by some to threaten the very stability of society. To answer these questions, we must consider what had happened in the nation as a whole at this time.

The years from 1640 to 1660 were those of unprecedented political and religious ferment that shook the foundations of British society. Three elements in particular are important:

1. There was a change in the status of the Church of England.
2. There was a new freedom to publish.
3. There was the development of religious toleration.

Oliver Cromwell himself was one of the principal advocates of liberty of conscience, especially after he became the Lord Protector in 1653. These three elements provide the background to the major reasons for the changes in Keach's thinking.

---

13 Keach, "The Blessedness of Christ's Sheep: Or, No final Falling from a State of true Grace. Demonstrated in Several Sermons, lately Preached, and now for general Good Published. Wherein all the grand Objections usually brought against the Saints final Perseverance, are fully answered," *A Golden Mine Opened; or, The Glory of God's Rich Grace Displayed in the Mediator to Believers: and His Direful Wrath against Impenitent Sinners. Containing the Substance of near Forty Sermons upon several Subjects* (London, 1694), 212.

Changes in the Anglican Church and Keach's conversion

The changes in the Church of England date back to the Reformation of the previous century.[14] Since the Reformation, separatism had been gathering momentum, though its development was not a smooth upward growth. Before 1640, it had survived either by going into exile on the Continent, usually in Holland, or to New England, or by going underground and meeting in secret. After 1650, men and women were no longer under legal obligation to attend the parish church every Sunday, although this was reasserted after 1660. Hill reminds us that "in 1640 the traditional Church of England collapsed, and with it the censorship which the Church had controlled."[15] The effects of this were massive both for the religious fabric of society and the practice of the population. Among the vast changes in the religious practices, there were two that are most relevant to Keach's religious development. Now Keach was no longer obliged to go and listen to Thomas Disney, his local clergyman, in whose selection he had had no choice and whose teaching and practice he could reject. Furthermore, unlicenced preachers began to minister to dissenting congregations springing up in many parts of the country. Keach himself became a General Baptist preacher in 1658, when he was only eighteen years old, and when he was probably based in the small Buckinghamshire market town of Winslow.[16]

---

14 Before the Reformation, the church in England had been part of a much larger international church, under the direction of the pope in Rome. At the Reformation, the link with Rome was severed. The English monarch became the head of the Church of England and everyone in England was regarded as a member of the national church. Attendance at church within the parish system was compulsory.

15 Christopher Hill, *England's Turning Point: Essays on 17th Century English History* (London: Bookmarks, 1998), 261.

16 There is no evidence that Keach became pastor of a church in Winslow in 1658. It appears that he simply preached there. We know that he married in 1660 and that his wife was from Winslow. Disney, in his letter to Wilkes (*CSPD*, SP29/98,116), mentions that Keach was living in Winslow in 1664. John Bunyan, twelve years older than

The most significant person in Keach's conversion however was not Thomas Disney or one of the General Baptists. Keach was baptized as a believer in 1655 when he was fifteen, but in the preceding two or three years before his baptism he had come under the influence of a man who was seeking to become rector in Great Brickhill, a neighbouring parish to Stoke Hammond. Keach may have learned about faith in Christ from this man but not believer's baptism. Keach never mentions by name the man who, under God, was responsible for his conversion. However, this man was still alive in the 1690s and was then preaching in Stepney. When replying to a Mr. Gyles Shute of Limehouse over the matter of the proper subjects of baptism, and lamenting the tone of Shute's writings, Keach made the following statement:

> I hope His Reverend Pastor (whom I have more cause both to love and honour than ten thousand Instructors in Christ, he being the blessed Instrument of my Conversion all most forty Years ago) gave no encouragement to him thus to write and abuse his Brethren.[17]

This "blessed Instrument," whom Keach held in such high esteem, was Matthew Mead (1629–1699). Gyles Shute and his wife Hannah were members of the Independent congregation meeting at Stepney, having joined in 1684 and 1683 respectively.[18]

Keach, began preaching about the same time in the county town of Bedford, some twenty miles northeast of Winslow.

17 Keach, *A Counter-Antidote to Purge out the Malignant Effects of a Late Counterfeit, Prepared by Mr. Gyles Shute, an Unskilful Person in Polemical Cures: being An Answer to his Vindication of his Pretended Antidote, to prevent the Prevalency of Anabaptism* (London, 1694), 3.

18 Stepney Meeting Church Book (1644–1894). See the entries in Mead's own handwriting for April 13, 1684 and February 17, 1683. These records are held by Tower Hamlets Local History and Archive Library, 277 Bancroft Road, London E1 4DQ. I am indebted to Raymond Brown for identifying Matthew Mead as the "blessed Instrument" of Keach's conversion.

Matthew Mead (1629–1699), that "blessed Instrument" in Benjamin Keach's conversion

Mead was about ten years older than Keach, and was born in the nearby town of Leighton Buzzard.[19] He had come to Great Brickhill in 1653, but after a considerable amount of legal wrangling with John Dunscombe, the patron of Great Brickhill, he was prevented from becoming the rector there.[20]

When Mead married in 1655, he was described as being "of Solber," which was the village of Soulbury, just two or three miles from Great Brickhill and Stoke Hammond, indicating that he was regarded as a resident of the area, even if he had not secured the living at Great Brickhill.[21] It is possible that Keach (and perhaps other members of his family) heard Mead preach in Great Brickhill or perhaps at some other meeting in the locality and having been affected by what he heard, spoke to him privately about what it meant to come to Christ. Because Keach was no longer obliged to attend the parish church in Stoke Hammond, he was free to go and hear whomever he liked. Mead was only in this area of Buckinghamshire a short while, for in 1656, he moved to London to become lecturer at St Dunstan's parish church in Stepney.[22]

---

19 *BDBR*, s.v. "Meade, Matthew."

20 George Lipscomb, *The History and Antiquities of the County of Buckingham* (London, 1847), 4:63. This account does not present Mead's attempts to secure the living of Great Brickhill in a good light. Mead alleged delinquency on the part of the local patron, John Dunscombe, Esquire, involved Cromwell in the dispute and, at one point, used force in order to try and secure the living. Incidents like this would have added fuel to the fires of Anglican reaction against Dissenters after the monarchy was restored in 1660.

21 Mead married Elizabeth Walton on January 3, 1654/5. He was described as being "of Solber." See Guildhall Library, London, Parish Register for St. Mary Woolnoth. Ms. 7635/2, 3 January 1654/5. The entry reads "The third day of this month were lawfully married Matthew Mead of the parish of Solber in the County of Bucks and Elizabeth Walton of the parish of All Hallows in Lombard Street, London." I am also indebted to Raymond Brown for this information. "Solber" is without doubt the modern Soulbury.

22 John Howe confirmed that Mead was associated with Buckinghamshire in a reference found in the funeral sermon Howe preached following Mead's death on October 16, 1699. He spoke of "his early labours in preaching the Gospel of Christ in his native country, in the city, and in this place," and also "consider (as I doubt not

This means that during the short period between 1653 and 1655 (the year Keach was baptized), Matthew Mead became Keach's instructor in Christ and showed him the way of salvation. Mead became famous for his book, *The Almost Christian Discovered*, which was a series of sermons preached in London a few years after his contact with Keach. In those sermons, Mead shows his warm evangelicalism, focusing on the Lord Jesus Christ. Phrases such as "the fullness of Christ," "the righteousness of Christ" and a "perfect and compleat Mediator," are found throughout the sermons.[23] He was not tinged with the antinomianism that characterized some writers on justification by faith, but believed that the Christian's obedience to the commands of Christ was "evangelical, universal and continual," and that this obedience was "sure proof of our Christianity and friendship to Christ."[24] Even after forty years, Keach recalled the event of his conversion to Christ with gratitude and, although there is no written evidence, it is difficult to believe that Keach did not have contact with Mead once Keach moved to London in 1668 and came to live in nearby Shadwell.

In the mid-1650s, Mead was operating within the Anglican Church, but once he moved to London, and following his ejection in 1662, he became a prominent Independent. As an Independent, he did not practice believer's baptism. On the basis of Mead's first published work (sermons that he preached in London in 1661), subsequent connections in London and his

---

many a soul will bless God for him for ever) how glorious a sight it will be to see him one day appear in the head of a numerous company of saved ones; and say,—as a subordinate parent in the apostle's sense,—'Lord, here am I, and the children thou hast given me.'" See John Howe, *The Works of John Howe* (London: Religious Tract Society, 1863), 6:339, 343.

23 Matthew Mead, *The Almost Christian Discovered; or, the False Professor Tried and Cast* (London, 1675). These sermons were preached in 1661 at St. Sepulchre's, Holborn, London.

24 Mead, *The Almost Christian Discovered*, 123.

own ministry there, it is also reasonable to conclude that he was already a Calvinist in his theology.[25] The fifteen-year-old Keach did not, at this point in his life, appear to appreciate the significance of Mead's Calvinism. Instead, being persuaded that believer's baptism was biblical, he identified himself with the General Baptists and imbibed their Arminian teaching.

However, the coming of Matthew Mead to a neighbouring Anglican parish, the "blessed Instrument" which led to Keach's conversion, played a key role in the providence of God in Keach's life. Mead was unsuccessful in his attempt to secure the living of Great Brickhill but was instrumental in the conversion of a man who was to become, like him, a leading Nonconformist preacher in London in the last quarter of the seventeenth century.

The freedom to publish, Keach and justification by faith

Throughout the first twenty years of Keach's life (encompassing the civil wars and the Commonwealth period under Oliver Cromwell), there was a new freedom to publish in England. Books and pamphlets were now printed and sold, disseminating new—and sometimes radical—religious and political views. This followed the abolition of the Star Chamber and the High Commission, the normal means available to the Established Church to exercise censorship. Now, radical Protestants had "an unparalleled opportunity to spread their ideas."[26]

---

25 *BDBR*. In 1656, Mead became assistant to William Greenhill at the Independent Stepney Meeting. He held other posts in London before being ejected from all of them in 1660. Having found a place as lecturer at St. Sepulchre's, Holborn, for two years, he was later ejected from his living in 1662 under the Act of Uniformity, along with many other ministers who refused to compromise their consciences. In 1671, Greenhill died and Mead succeeded him, becoming one of London's leading Independent Nonconformists.

26 John Coffey, *Persecution and Toleration in Protestant England, 1558–1689* (Harlow: Pearson Education Limited, 2000), 144. Coffey draws attention to two statistics: in 1640, only 22 pamphlets were published while in 1642 it was an astonishing 1,966; and, between 1640 and 1660, more pamphlets were published than in the century and a half before (1485 to 1640).

Buckinghamshire itself was divided by political and religious loyalties. The king and his army held the southern part of the county and had a garrison in an adjoining county at Oxford. The Parliamentary forces held Aylesbury and Newport Pagnell in the north.[27]

Cromwell's New Model Army was a major influence in spreading new views. For example, Captain Paul Hobson (d. 1666) was a soldier in Cromwell's army. In 1645, he came to Newport Pagnell (about ten miles from Keach's home) as part of his duties as a member of Thomas Fairfax's regiment.[28] He had proved himself to be an eloquent preacher, but he was a controversial figure, regarded by some as a dangerous sectary.[29] As he moved about the country, Hobson often preached, but when he came to the garrison at Newport Pagnell, the commander of the garrison had him arrested because he was a lay preacher and for expressing dangerous opinions. He and another were denounced as "Anabaptists, who cannot consent with magistracy or government."[30] Significantly, Fairfax, Hobson's own commander, dismissed the charges and took no action against him.

There is no evidence linking Keach with the garrison at Newport Pagnell, but the attitudes and opinions being expressed in Cromwell's army were a part of the environment in which he grew up. For the first time in their lives, people were faced with

---

27 The garrison was on the frontier of the Parliament's Eastern Association and changed hands more than once during the first two years of the Civil War. John Bunyan was a soldier in the army for a short period and was based at Newport Pagnell. See Christopher Hill, *A Tinker and a Poor Man: John Bunyan and his Church 1628–1688* (New York: Knopf, 1989), 45-46.

28 That same year, Thomas Fairfax (1612–1671) became Captain-General of the New Model Army. See *BDBR*, s.v. "Fairfax, Thomas."

29 Hill, *A Tinker and a Poor Man*, 53–55. Hobson had established one of the seven Particular Baptist churches in London and had signed their 1644 confession. But he was one of those characters—perhaps typical of this period of English history—who cannot be neatly fitted into any one category. See also *BDBR*, s.v. "Hobson, Paul."

30 Hill, *A Tinker and a Poor Man*, 50.

options depending on their religious and political sympathies. Opinions became divided over two issues, continued attendance at the local parish church and continued support for the monarchy and Charles I. The garrison at Newport Pagnell was a hotbed of radical religious and political discussion and events that took place in Buckinghamshire, close to Keach's home, illustrate the new freedom to discuss religious and political alternatives to the Church of England and rule by monarchy and Parliament.[31]

John Saltmarsh (c.1612–1647) was a chaplain in the Parliamentary army for a short period and did influence Keach.[32] Over thirty years later, in 1692, Keach was still able to recall the impact made on him by a book written by Saltmarsh. During a sermon, Keach said:

> Nothing renders a Man righteous to Justification in God's sight, but the imputation of the perfect Personal Righteousness of Christ, received only by the Faith of *the Operation of God*. When I was a Lad, I was greatly taken with a Book called, *The flowing of Christ's Blood freely to Sinners, as Sinners*. O my Brethren, that's the Case, that's the doctrine which the Apostle preaches; you must come to Christ, believe on Christ, as Sinners, as ungodly ones, and not as Righteous, not as Saints, and Holy persons.[33]

Keach was referring to *Free Grace: or the flowings of Christ's blood freely to sinners*, published in 1645 by Saltmarsh. He did not mention the author when he loosely quoted the title of the book in his sermon, probably because he did not want to give the impression that he was in any way sympathetic to Saltmarsh's

31 Hill, *A Tinker and a Poor Man*, 52.

32 *BDBR*, s.v. "Saltmarsh, John."

33 Keach, *The Marrow of True Justification: Or, Justification without Works* (London, 1692), 8.

Antinomianism.[34] Nevertheless, Keach regarded this book as being formative in his grasping the truth of the biblical teaching, that justification is based on the fact that the righteousness of Christ is imputed to sinners who believe in Christ and is due entirely to God's free grace. Whatever shortcomings there were in the book by Saltmarsh, it would appear that there was sufficient biblical truth in it for Keach to imbibe one of the principal teachings of Christian orthodoxy early on in his Christian life. There is no evidence that Keach adopted the Antinomian opinions of John Saltmarsh, and it may have been the case that he had already been protected from imbibing those opinions by the preaching of Matthew Mead. It appears that Keach adopted a more biblical view of justification by faith—one that he was to maintain and defend all his life. One of his clearest and fullest statements on justification is found in the following statement, published in 1694:

> To be justified, is to be pronounced Just and Righteous in God's sight, through the perfect Righteousness of Jesus Christ, or to be actually acquitted upon Trial, or discharged from the Guilt and Punishment of Sins; not that we are not Sinners in ourselves, but as Christ was made Sin for us who knew no Sin (in himself) so we are made the Righteousness of God in him, who knew no Righteousness in ourselves. As our Sin was imputed unto Christ, so his Righteousness is imputed unto us, (as he doth in Pardon of Sin) but in a way of Justice and Righteousness also; we paid all that was due to vindictive Wrath and Justice in Jesus Christ, (I mean, Jesus Christ for us as our Surety hath done it).[35]

---

34 See *BDBR*, for an indication of Saltmarsh's Antinomianism. See also chapter 13 for further discussion of Saltmarsh.

35 Keach, "The Great Salvation," *A Golden Mine Opened*, 414.

It was Saltmarsh and not the General Baptists who made the most impression on Keach. The General Baptists did believe in justification by faith as *The Standard Confession* of 1660 shows, but the article on justification does not state the doctrine very fully.[36] Saltmarsh appears to be fuller than the 1660 confession in his statements, believing that Christ was the Mediator between God and man, that he died in the place of sinners and emphasizing that God imputed Christ's righteousness to those who believed in Christ.[37] Although Keach said he was "greatly taken" by Saltmarsh's book, we do not have any sermon of Keach's on justification from this period of his life and so we cannot state precisely Keach's own understanding of justification by faith when he began to preach among the General Baptists in and around Winslow in 1658.

Liberty of conscience and believer's baptism

In 1660, soon after the restoration of the monarchy in the person of Charles II, Keach published his first book, bringing down the wrath of the Buckinghamshire authorities on his head. Gone was the freedom enjoyed during the previous twenty years.

---

36 *The Standard Confession*, Article 6 (London, 1660). In Lumpkin, *Baptist Confessions of Faith*, 226–227. Compare Article 6 with Articles 28 and 30 of the 1644 *London Confession of Faith* (Lumpkin, *Baptist Confessions of Faith*, 164–165). The first generation of Particular Baptists made a clear statement on justification by faith.

37 John Saltmarsh, *Free Grace: or the Flowings of Christ's blood freely to Sinners* (London, 1645), 143, says, "All the grounds of a believers righteousnesse and salvation and exemption from the Law, Sin and Curse, is from the nature, office, and transaction or work of Christ, and God's accounting or imputing; Christ stood cloathed in our nature, betwixt God and man, and in that with all the sins of believers upon him, God having layd on him the iniquities of us all: In his Office he Obeyed, suffered, satisfied and offered up himself, and now fits as a Mediator to perpetuate or make his sacrifice, obedience, suffering, and righteousness everlasting: And thus bringing in everlasting righteousnesse: And God he accounts, reckons, or imputes all that is done in our own nature, as done by us, calling things that are not, as if they were: And in his person as in our person: And thus he is made sin for us, who knew no sin, that we might be made the righteousness of God in him."

However, by this time Keach's mind had been made up. He was no longer part of the Anglican Church. He had been converted to Christ though the influence of Matthew Mead somewhere between 1653 and 1655, and had joined the General Baptists in 1655. He had rejected infant baptism and had some understanding of what it meant to be justified by faith in Jesus Christ and had begun to preach to others. The return of repressive measures would test his mettle, but the strong convictions now formed in the mind of the young preacher were not about to be abandoned. Despite his youth, Keach was to prove that he was not a man for retracting his convictions, even if he had to suffer for them.

This is the third element that provides the background for understanding the changes in Keach's thinking. Toleration and liberty of conscience had been among the hotly debated issues during the years 1640 to 1660. Perhaps no one expressed them more clearly than Cromwell himself. At the conclusion of the Civil War, the "Rump" Parliament assumed supreme power.[38] A number of far-reaching events ensued. In January 1649, Charles I was tried and executed. The Rump Parliament abolished the monarchy and the House of Lords and, by May, England was declared to be a free commonwealth. In 1650, Cromwell became Lord General and, three years later, Lord Protector of England, Scotland and Ireland. Cromwell shared some of Keach's religious convictions, among them liberty of conscience. In the latter years of his life, Keach stated in a sermon that

> persecution upon the account of religion, is utterly unlawful, though men may hold grand errors, yet no magistrates have any power to persecute them, much less in

38 The Rump was the remnant of the Long Parliament following Pride's Purge in 1648, when troops under the command of Colonel Thomas Pride forcibly removed from the Long Parliament all those who were not supporters of the Grandees in the New Model Army and the Independents. Cromwell was not yet in control.

> the highest degree, so as to put them to death...because Jesus Christ is only the king and sovereign of the conscience. None ought to impose upon the consciences of men in matters of religion. They must stand and fall in such cases to their own master.[39]

The Lord Protector had expressed similar convictions in a very different arena when he had addressed Parliament in September 1654:

> In every Government there must be Somewhat Fundamental, Somewhat like a *Magna Carta*, which should be standing, be unalterable...is not Liberty of Conscience in Religion a Fundamental? So long as there is Liberty of Conscience for the Supreme Magistrate to exercise his conscience in erecting what Form of Church-Government he is satisfied he should set up—why should he not give the like liberty to others? Liberty of Conscience is a natural right; and he that would have it, ought to give it; having 'himself' liberty to settle what he likes for the Public.... All the money of this Nation would not have tempted men to fight upon such an account as they have here been engaged in, if they had not had hopes of Liberty 'of Conscience' better than Episcopacy granted them, or than would have been afforded by a Scots Presbytery—or an English either, if it had made such steps, and been as sharp and rigid, as it threatened when first set up![40]

---

39 Keach, *Parables One*, 219. Published in 1702, it was possibly preached much earlier than this. Keach had been preaching from the parables to his Southwark congregation for several years.

40 Thomas Carlyle, *Oliver Cromwell's Letters and Speeches* (New York: John B. Alden, 1885), 2:433–434. In this speech, Cromwell outlined four fundamentals: that a single person and Parliament should govern the country; that Parliaments should be elected

Oliver Cromwell (1599–1658) was an ardent proponent of toleration and liberty of conscience during Keach's early life

One of Cromwell's aims in fighting the civil wars was to secure liberty of conscience and thereby to promote religious toleration. Some in the 1640s did not swallow toleration easily, and some Puritans had advocated a national church (in this case Presbyterian) with the magistrate responsible for suppressing heresy. On the other hand, in 1654, Cromwell was effectively arguing not only for the legitimacy of Presbyterianism but also for the co-existence of other views, provided that those views did not threaten to overthrow law and order. It should be recognized that during the civil wars and the Commonwealth period, one of the loudest voices for toleration was Cromwell's own. He "towered over his contemporaries" in this regard.[41] So long as the related ideas of liberty of conscience and toleration remained on the religious and political agenda, it was possible for all kinds of groups (and, in particular, other branches of Separatism, such as Independents and Baptists) to flourish.[42]

The first twenty years of Benjamin Keach's life saw a severe reduction in the power and influence of the Church of England, new religious and political ideas spread by chaplains and preachers in the Parliamentary Army and attempts to promote toleration. A very different atmosphere prevailed in the country, compared to that which had existed prior to the civil wars. Separatist groups like General Baptists in north Buckinghamshire flourished during this period. In the new climate of freedom, Keach not only

---

and not permanent; that there should be liberty of conscience in matters of religion; and, that control of the army should be a shared by Protector and Parliament. For a fuller discussion and the context of this speech, see Barry Coward, *Oliver Cromwell* (London: Longman, 1991), 117–125.

41 Coffey, *Persecution and Toleration*, 147.

42 Separatists were those who began to organize "gathered churches" outside of the state church. They began as early as the reign of Mary I (1553–1558) and continued during the long reign of Elizabeth I (1558–1603). They objected to the parish system, believing it to be unbiblical. Rather, they believed a church should be comprised of those who had covenanted together. Membership should be voluntary and the members were free to choose their own officers.

had liberty to hear whomever he liked to hear and to read whatever he chose to read but he also had liberty to follow his own conscience. In doing so, he came to convictions that would bring him into collision with the civil authorities and with the Anglican Church, which, after 1660, made desperate attempts to reclaim lost territory.

We are now in a much better position to understand how Keach came to be baptized on profession of his faith in 1655 and begin to preach three years later, even though he was only eighteen years old and not licensed by the Anglican Church. He was living in days of religious toleration and free to follow his conscience. Crosby states that the church he joined thought it was fitting to ask him to preach the Word of God among them.[43] There is no indication that he was settled as a pastor in Winslow or anywhere else at this point in his life, simply that he began to preach publicly.[44]

John Russell baptized Keach as a believer. He was the pastor of a General Baptist church at Berkhamsted and Chesham in the southern part of the county.[45] He signed *The Orthodox Confession* in 1679 and was one of the leaders of General Baptists in Buckinghamshire.[46] General Baptists, rather than Particular Baptists, were strong in Buckinghamshire, especially in the Chiltern Hills area. By Keach's day, they had spread to the northern part of the county.[47] However, there is no evidence to show

---

43 Crosby, *History*, 4:270.

44 Evidence does exist to show that General Baptists were meeting not only in Winslow but also in outlying villages. Winslow would have served as the market town for the area. See Chapter 2.

45 Crosby, *History*, 4:269.

46 Arnold H.J. Baines, *The Signatories of the Orthodox Confession of 1679* (London: Carey Kingsgate Press, 1960), 31. Also in *BQ*, 17 (1957–1958), 171.

47 General Baptists in Buckinghamshire were linked to the Tudor Anabaptists and their predecessors, the Lollards. The Chiltern Hills in Buckinghamshire were one of the strongholds of Lollardy, together with the Weald of Kent and cloth-making towns of north Essex. This has been substantiated by Nesta Evans, "The descent of Dissenters

how Keach first came into contact with them and Keach made no mention of any indebtedness to Russell or any other individual. Crosby notes that Keach applied himself at an early age to the study of the Scriptures and suggests that he reached his own conclusions about the invalidity of the infant baptism he had received in the parish church at Stoke Hammond.[48]

Keach became persuaded that the Scriptures taught the necessity of a personal faith in Jesus Christ and believer's baptism. His understanding of faith and baptism deepened and he maintained and vigorously defended them until his death in 1704. In a sermon based on Matthew 15:13, first published in 1702, he states,

> baptism and the Lord's Supper are ordinances of mere positive right, and none but such who do believe, and make a profession of their faith, being regenerate persons, ought to be received or admitted to either of these ordinances, or be members of the church of Christ. Faith and repentance being required of all that ought to be baptized and planted in gospel congregations, by virtue of Christ's great commission, and the practice of apostolical churches.[49]

To what extent Keach came to understand liberty of conscience at this early stage in his life is less easy to define. What is clear, however, is that he expressed his liberty by choosing to leave the Church of England, parting company with the doctrine of infant baptism. Keach had been converted to Christ through

---

in the Chiltern Hundreds." In *The World of Rural Dissenters*, ed. Margaret Spufford (Cambridge: Cambridge University Press, 1994), 288–308. See also Michael R. Watts, *The Dissenters: From the Reformation to the French Revolution* (Oxford: Clarendon Press, 1978), 283–284. This evidence should persuade those who remain unconvinced about the continuity between General Baptists and Lollardy, e.g. H. Leon McBeth, *The Baptist Heritage* (Nashville: The Broadman Press, 1987), 55.

48 Crosby, *History*, 4:269.

49 Keach, "Every Plant God Has Not Planted," *Parables Two*, 364.

Mead's influence but began his preaching in a theological climate where Arminian doctrine prevailed. After 1668, he changed his views, having become persuaded that biblical teaching was much more fully and accurately represented in that system of theology called "Calvinism." Even before he adopted Calvinistic views, by rejecting infant baptism in particular, Keach was paving the way for what was to become a "Particular Baptist consciousness," although Keach obviously would not have recognized it as such in 1668 when he started preaching.

The baptism of believers was to become a cornerstone in Keach's theology. Over thirty years later, in 1690, after a long period when Nonconformists had been denied liberty of conscience and a new climate of religious toleration had become established, Keach and others expressed their convictions about believer's baptism. Keach was the man largely responsible for the preface to Philip Cary's book against William Allen, *A Solemn Call...or a Discourse Concerning Baptism*. The names of William Kiffin, John Harris, Richard Adams (c.1626–1698) and Robert Steed (d. c.1695) were included at the end of the short preface. Keach's name is given last of all. These men were all London Particular Baptists, although Philip Cary was from Devon, but they had the same basic perspective and shared a "Particular Baptist consciousness." The preface began by saying that they all believed that glorious biblical prophecies (such as Daniel 11:14) had just been fulfilled with the arrival of William of Orange. In their view, William had been the instrument God used to overthrow the anti-christian darkness that threatened England: Roman Catholicism that concealed the truths and ordinances of Christ. They were not alone in this persuasion. It was prevalent in Protestant thinking of the day and reflected in many sermons preached during this period.[50]

---

50 John Flavel, "Mount Pisgah: A Sermon preached at the Public Thanksgiving, February 14, 1668–9, for England's Deliverance from Popery, Etc." In *Works of John Flavel*,

Keach and his fellow Particular Baptists saw themselves as a "third wave"—following on from the Reformers and earlier Puritans. They described the first wave, associated with the Continental Reformers, Martin Luther (1483–1546) and John Calvin (1509–1564), exposing the corruptions of antichrist and bringing to light justification by faith, among other important truths. The second wave, they closely associated with the English Puritans and, in particular, those who became known as the Independents. They mentioned men like William Ames (1576–1633), Henry Ainsworth (1571–*c*.1622) and John Owen (1616–1683). They argued that these men demonstrated that "the true gospel visible church is to consist only of such as are saints by profession, and who give themselves up to the Lord and to one another by solemn agreement to practice the ordinances of Christ."[51] John Owen and others practiced infant baptism by sprinkling, but only for the children of believers.[52] For the authors of Cary's preface, the third wave consisted of men like Cary and themselves who exposed the error of paedobaptism. "Now latterly the Lord raised up learned and worthy men to detect the vanity of infant baptism."[53] In their minds, this meant that while on the one hand they were in disagreement with Independent paedobaptists, Presbyterians, Anglicans and Roman Catholics, on the other hand they were persuaded that they had moved beyond them in their understanding of the nature of the church of Jesus Christ, by the rejection of infant baptism and all that it implied.

---

6 vols. (London: Banner of Truth Trust, 1968), 4:307–335. Flavel's views on infant baptism were being criticized by Cary, but they agreed on the overthrow of popery.

51 Philip Cary, *A Solemn Call unto all that would be owned as Christ's Faithful Witnesses, speedily and seriously, to attend unto the Primitive Purity of the Gospel Doctrine and Worship: or, a Discourse Concerning Baptism* (London, 1690), preface. Matthew Mead would have been one of these Independents, but there is no evidence to show whether he was espousing these views in the early 1650s when he was in contact with Keach.

52 *The Savoy Declaration*, Chapter 29 "Of Baptism," Section 3, rejects immersion as the mode of baptism, and Section 4 asserts that "the infants of one or both believing parents are to be baptised, and those only."

53 Cary, *A Solemn Call*, preface.

Keach came to adopt a very uncompromising stand on believer's baptism. It was not simply that he was expressing his opposition to Catholicism. His concern was primarily pastoral. He was disturbed to think that people were deceived into thinking that they were Christians simply because they had been baptized as infants.

> I look upon Infant-Baptism to be one of the chief Pillars of the Romish Church, and of all National Churches and Constitutions in the European World; this is that Christendom that is so cried up, and the way of making and continuing the pretended Christian-Name; in the Anti-christian Church, and World, all are made Christian in their Infant-Baptism: And thus the inhabitants of the Earth are cheated, and deluded with a Shadow and empty Name that signifies nothing; and certain I am, until Christendom (as it is called) is Unchristianed of this pretended Rite, or Christendom, there will never be a thorough Reformation: I mean until they see that Christianity, or Christian-Name, which they received at their Infant-Baptism, signifies nothing, but throw it away as an Human Innovation, and labour after true Regeneration, or a likeness to Christ, and so believe and are baptized upon the profession of their Faith, according as in the Apostolical Primitive Church: 'Tis Infant-Baptism that tends to uphold all National Churches, and deceives poor People who think there were hereby made Christians.[54]

As Crosby points out, Keach was broadly Arminian in his theology in 1658.[55] He believed, for example, in the freedom of man's

54 Keach, *Light broke forth in Wales, expelling darkness: Or, The Englishman's love to the ancient Britains* [sic] *being an answer to a book, iutituled* [sic] *Children's baptism from Heaven, published in the Welsh tongue by Mr. James Owen* (London, 1693), 324.

55 Crosby, *History*, 4:270.

will and that Jesus Christ died for every man equally. Nevertheless, it is quite clear that the foundations of his convictions regarding conversion to Christ, justification by faith and believer's baptism were in place, at least in embryo. He became a genuine Christian and began to preach as a converted man. He appeared to have no doubts about the genuineness of his conversion to Christ and his experiences of the love of God. In a sermon he preached to his congregation in Southwark he reflects on his experiences of the love of Christ that he enjoyed in these early days:

> Brethren I have told you what choice experiences I had of the love of Jesus Christ unto my own soul, when first in my youthful days he manifested himself unto me; I was so raised and consolated with sweet tastes of God's love to me, that by the strength of those cordials I have been supported unto this very day.[56]

He was already a student of the Bible—it was increasingly to become his only rule of faith and practice. His writings show that he aimed to be a man of the Bible and to ensure his convictions were biblical convictions. In the matter of baptism, Keach did not make a gradual transition as some men did from ordination in the Church of England, through the varying streams of Separatism to become a Baptist. He began in the parish church at Stoke Hammond, at an early age was converted to Christ through an Anglican preacher from a neighbouring parish, but then came to imbibe believer's baptism. The die had been cast, and Benjamin Keach never looked back to the national Church of England.

---

56 Keach, "The Scribe," *Parables One*, 269.

CHAPTER 2

"One that is a teacher in their new fangled way"

> ...thou being a Seditious, Heretical, and Schismatical Person, evilly and maliciously disposed, and disaffected to his Majesty's Government, and the Government of the Church of England, dids't maliciously and wickedly ...write, print and publish, or cause to be written, printed and published one Seditious and Venomous Book, entitled, *The Child's Instructor*.[1]

In the early summer of 1664, Henry Keach, Benjamin Keach's eldest brother, received a visitor at his home, Stapleford Mill, in Soulbury, the adjoining parish to Stoke Hammond. Thomas Disney, the rector of the neighbouring parish of Stoke Hammond, had sent his man, George Chilton, to

1 Benjamin Stinton, "The Tryall of Mr Benja. Keach. who was prosecuted for Wrighting against Infant Baptism with an Account of ye Punishment inflicted upon him for ye same: Anno 1664." In A *Repository of Divers Historical Matters Relating to the English Antipaedobaptists, Collected from Original Papers of Faithful Extracts*, No. 21, 93–104 (Angus Library, Oxford, 1712). This is part of the indictment against Keach.

purchase a book by Benjamin Keach. This book was *The Child's Instructor: or, A New and Easy Primmer*. This primer was then sent with an accompanying letter to Luke Wilkes, "Chief Yeoman of the Removing of the Wardrobe of the King," in Whitehall, London, with a very specific request: "pray have some speedie course to acquaint my Ld. Archbishop with it."[2] Luke Wilkes was Disney's brother-in-law and, evidently, he made full use of his position in the royal household in the palace of Whitehall.[3] The full text of the letter is as follows:

> Honoured sir,
> and loving brother this primer owned by Benjamin Keach as the Author, and bought by my man George Chilton for five pence of Henry Keach of Stableford Mill, neare me, a miller; who then sayd that his brother Benjamin Keach is Author of it, & that there are fiveteene hundred of them printed. This Benjamin Keach is a Taylor, & one that is a teacher in their new fangled way, & lives at Winslow, a market towne in Buckinghamshire. Pray have some speedie course to acquaint my Ld. Archbishop

2 The inscription on the outside cover of the letter is: "These for the honoured friend Luke Wilkes [....] at Whitehall with spd pray present," *CSPD*, 1663–1664, 116, SP29/98. Luke Wilkes was from Leighton Buzzard in Bedfordshire. See *Victoria County History for Bedfordshire* (London: Constable, 1912), 3:411 and George Lipscomb, *History and Antiquities of the County of Buckingham* (London, 1847), 2:44. The Lord Archbishop was Gilbert Seldon, appointed Archbishop of Canterbury in 1663. The position of Luke Wilkes in the royal household is confirmed by *CSPD*, 1664–1665, 110, 157, 302, which records three letters from Wilkes underlining the fact that he and others were not receiving their royal household salaries and other allowances on time.

3 *Victoria County History for Bedfordshire*, 3:411, mentions Luke Wilkes as the son of Edward (d.1646) and Joan Wilkes (d.1657) of Leighton Buzzard, which lies just over five miles from Stoke Hammond. The stone burial inscription in memory of Thomas Disney and his wife Ioane Wilks in Stoke Hammond parish church records Disney's wife as "Ioane, the daughter of Mr Edw Wilks of Leighton Budesert in Bedfordshire and of Mrs Ioane Besouth of Corner Hall neare Hempstead in Hertfordshire." The inscription also mentions another brother-in-law, Marke, who died in 1673.

> his grace with it, whereby his Authoritie may issue forth that the impressions may be seized upon Before they be much more dispersed to ye possessing of people: they containing (as I conceive) factious, Schismatical & hereticall matter. Some are scattered in my parish, & perchance in noe place sooner because he hath a sister here & some others of his gang; two whereof I have b[r]ought up. Pray let me have your speedie account of it. I doubt not that it will be taken as acceptable service to God's church, & believe it a very thankful obligement to,
>
> Honoured sir,
> Your truly loving brother,
> Thomas Disney.
>
> Stoke Hamond in Bucks – 64. May 26th.[4]

Luke Wilkes was in the employment of Charles II at Whitehall and evidently had access to Gilbert Sheldon, the new Archbishop of Canterbury.[5] We know that Wilkes undertook Disney's request, acting with "some speedie course," for on October 8 and 9, 1664, Benjamin Keach appeared before Sir Robert Hyde, the Lord Chief Justice at the Buckinghamshire Assizes in Aylesbury.[6]

Keach could not expect any sympathy from Hyde. He was a thorough-going Royalist who had joined Charles I at Oxford, and later provided shelter in his own home for the future Charles II, on his flight from Worcester in 1651. Hyde's loyalty guaranteed him a knighthood in the restored regime of 1660. Hyde was a

4 *CSPD*, 1663–1664, 116, SP 28/98.

5 Sheldon was Archbishop from 1663 until 1677. Both he and his successor, William Sancroft (1677 to 1690), were zealous for a strict enforcement of the law especially the Conventicle Acts.

6 Sir Robert Hyde (1595–1665), Lord Chief Justice, not to be confused with Sir Edward Hyde, The Earl of Clarendon, the Lord Chancellor. Joseph Ivimey made that mistake and has been followed by some recent writers. Ivimey, *History* 1:359–360. The Hydes were cousins and Robert Hyde owed his promotion, to Lord Chief Justice in 1663, to the influence of his cousin.

member of the regicide trial team that successfully prosecuted those who were held responsible for the execution of Charles I in 1649. As a judge, Hyde found it almost impossible to conceal his bias. His attitude to Dissenters was one of total hostility. The outcome of Keach's trial, therefore, was a foregone conclusion.[7]

Before this court case, however, Benjamin Keach had also received visitors at his home in Winslow. Thomas Strafford, a justice of the peace, had visited him with a constable, and seized about thirty copies of the primer. Keach was taken and "bound over to answer for it at the next Assizes in a Recognizance of an hundred Pounds, and two Sureties with him in fifty Pounds each."[8]

Before the assizes

On the first day of the assizes, October 8, the Lord Chief Justice told the court that Keach's book contained at least two things that were contrary to the liturgy of the Church of England, (that is *The Book of Common Prayer*), and that they were in breach of the Act of Uniformity.[9] In particular, offending teachings were that infants ought not to be baptized and that laymen may preach the gospel. Hyde further suggested that Keach was a Fifth Monarchy man, because his book also stated that Christ would reign personally on the earth in the latter day.

The Judge displayed his impatience with and prejudice against Keach even before he was charged. Holding up the book before the prisoner, he accusingly asked, "What have you to do to take other men's trades out of their hands?" Quite clearly Hyde did not regard the contents of the book as matters fit for a layman to be writing. Keach was perceived to be transgressing into another

---

7 The sympathies and conduct of Hyde as a judge, especially in connection with the regicide trial, have been portrayed in Geoffrey Robertson, *The Tyrannicide Brief: The Story of the Man who sent Charles I to the Scaffold* (London: Vintage Books, 2006), 289, 291, 302, 350–351.

8 *CSPD*, 1663–1664, 595.

9 The Act of Uniformity was imposed in 1662, for details see later in this chapter.

man's field. Hyde went on to describe Keach's teaching as "damnable doctrine, to seduce and infect his Majesty's Subjects." He portrayed him to the grand jury as "a base and dangerous fellow; if this be suffered, Children by learning of it will become such as he is."[10] By making these kinds of statements Hyde was betraying not only his own sympathies, but also the fears of the authorities when confronted with religious and political sedition. The early 1660s were times of increased tension and the authorities were clamping down hard on offenders in an attempt to impose their own authority.

On the second day of the trial, the clerk of the court read out the charge.[11] The full indictment reads:

> Thou art here indicted by the Name of *Benjamin Keach* of the Parish of *Winslow*, in the county of Bucks: For that thou being a Seditious, Heretical, and Schismatical Person, evilly and maliciously disposed, and disaffected to his Majesty's Government, and the Government of the Church of *England*, did'st maliciously and wickedly, on the 1st day of *May*, in the 16th Year[12] of the Reign of our Sovereign Lord the King, write, print and publish, or cause to be written, printed and published one Seditious and Venomous Book, entitled, *The Child's Instructor: or, A New and Easy Primmer*; wherein are contained, by way of Question and Answer, these Damnable Positions,

10 *CSPD*, 1663–1664, 595.

11 There is nothing unique about the indictment for sedition drawn up against Keach. There was a certain formula used, and therefore, all similar cases would have contained the same preamble, reflecting the concerns of the state. For a brief summary of the laws regarding treason and sedition in this period see Rachel E. Walker, "Ordinary and Common Discourses: The Impact of the Glorious Revolution on Political Discussion in London 1688–1694" (Ph.D. dissertation, University of Sheffield, 1998), 157–158.

12 Calculated from the death of Charles I, so discounting the Commonwealth period.

contrary to the Book of Common Prayer, and the Liturgy of the Church of England: That is to say, in one Place you have thus written: Q. *Who are the right Subjects of Baptism?* A. *Believers, or godly Men and Women only, who can make Confession of their Faith and repentance.* And in another place, you have maliciously and wickedly written these Words; Q. *How shall it go with the saints?* A. *O very well. It is the Day that they have longed for: then they shall hear that Sentence,* Come ye Blessed of my Father, inherit the Kingdom prepared for you; *and so shall they reign with Christ on the earth a thousand Years, even on Mount Sion, in New Jerusalem; for there will Christ's Throne be, on which they must sit down with him.* Then follows this Question, with the Answer thereto, in these plain *English* Words; Q. *When shall the Wicked and the Fallen Angels, which be the Devils, be judged?* A. *When the Thousand Years shall be expired, then shall the rest of the Devils [Dead] be raised, and then shall be the general and last Judgment, then shall all the rest of the Dead and Devils be judged by Christ and his glorified Saints; and they shall be arraigned and judged, the Wicked shall be condemned, and cast by the Angels into the Lake of Fire, and there be burned for ever and ever.*

In another place thou hast wickedly and maliciously written these plain English words: Q. *Why may not infants be received into the Church now, as they were under the Law?* A. *Because the fleshly Seed is cast out: Tho God under that Dispensation did receive Infants in a lineal way by Generation, yet he that hath the key of David, that openeth and no Man shutteth, that shutteth and no Man openeth, hath shut up that Way into the Church; and hath opened the Door of Regeneration, receiving in none now but Believers.* Q. *What then is the State of Infants?* A. *Infants that die are Members of the Kingdom of Glory, tho they are not Members of the Visible Church. Q. Do they then that bring in Infants in a fleshly lineal way, err from the way of Truth?* A. *Yea, they do; for they make not God's Holy Word their Rule, but do presume to open the Door that Christ hath shut, and none ought to open.* And also in another place thou hast wickedly and maliciously composed *A Short Confession of the Christian Faith*; wherein thou hast affirm'd this concerning the second Person in the Blessed Trinity, in these plain English words: *I also believe that he rose again the third Day from the Dead, and ascended into Heaven above, and there now sitteth at the right hand of God the Father; and from thence he shall come again at the appointed time of the Father, to reign personally on the Earth, and to be the Judge of the Quick and the Dead.* And in another place thou hast wickedly and maliciously affirmed these things concerning true Gospel-Ministers, in these plain *English* words: *Christ hath not chosen the wise and prudent Men after the Flesh, nor great Doctors and Rabbies; Not many Mighty and Noble, saith Paul, are called: but rather the Poor and Despised, even Tradesmen and suchlike, as was Matthew, Peter, Andrew, Paul and others. And Christ's true Ministers have not their Learning and Wisdom from Men, or from Universities, or human Schools for human Learning. Arts and Sciences are not essential to the Making of a True Minister, but the Gifts of God, which cannot be bought with Silver and Gold; and also as they have freely received the Gift, so do they freely administer: They do not preach for Hire, for Gain and filthy lucre: They are not like the false Teachers, who look for Gain from their Quarter; who eat the Fat, and clothe themselves with the Wool, and kill them that are fed, those that put not into their mouths, they prepare War against: Also they are not Lords over God's Heritage they rule them not by Force and Cruelty,*

> *neither have they Power to force and compel Men to believe and obey their Doctrines, but are only to persuade and intreat; for this is the Way of the Gospel, as Christ taught them.*
>
> And many other things hast thou seditiously, wickedly, and maliciously written in the said Book, to the great Displeasure of Almighty God, the Scandal of the Liturgy of the Church of *England*, the Disaffection of the King's People to his Majesty's Kingdom, to the evil Example of others, and contrary to the Statute in that case made and provided. How say you, *Benjamin Keach* are you guilty, or not guilty?[13]

This indictment confirms that Keach was a resident in Winslow in 1664 and that he was a preacher of the gospel. It also indicates that all copies of the primer were destroyed after the trial (this is the only record we have of some of the precise contents). It reveals that Keach's convictions, as outlined in the previous chapter, had altered and developed since his early years. It also clearly shows that there had been a radical change in religious policy with the return of Charles II and the re-establishment of the Church of England as the only legitimate national church. The liberty of conscience and toleration promoted by Cromwell and others under the Commonwealth and Protectorate had given way to a new repressive regime. Finally, together with the letter of Thomas Disney to Luke Wilkes, it exhibits the new attitude on the part of the authorities, religious and civil, against Nonconformists like Keach. Religious authorities from the top to the bottom of the Anglican hierarchy, from the Lord Archbishop in London to the rector of Stoke Hammond, were now zealous in bringing the full force of the law down on anyone who refused to conform. This zeal was equalled among the civil authorities, and

13 Stinton, "The Tryall of Mr Benja. Keach," 1712.

Keach's conviction similarly involved the highest legal civil power, the Lord Chief Justice, as well as local officers of the legal system, the justices of the peace and constables.

Benjamin Keach pleaded "not guilty" to the charges laid against him. The surviving assize report also includes browbeating and intimidating words by the judge directed against Keach, before the witnesses were sworn in and their evidence received. *The Book of Common Prayer* was then produced for Sir Robert Hyde and a copy of the primer was given to the jury. The relevant pages of the primer were marked for them, having had the leaves turned down. These preparations completed, the clerk of the court then read out the offending passages from the book and at each point the Judge contradicted Keach's teaching from the Prayer Book. Keach was given very little opportunity to speak in his own defence; rather, he was cut off several times by Hyde. Keach asked, "Is my religion so bad, that I may not be allow'd to speak? He received a blunt reply, "I know your Religion, you are a Fifth-Monarchy Man; and you can preach, as well as write books; and you would preach here, if I would let you: but I shall take such order, as you shall do no more mischief."[14]

As the trial reached its close, the Lord Chief Justice impatiently summed up the evidence and gave his charge to the jury. His mind was already made up, and he was simply paving the way for the appropriate sentence to be passed once the inevitable verdict had been reached. It is quite clear from the evidence that the jury was not being asked to exercise their own judgement about Keach. The jury existed merely to "rubber-stamp" the decision already made by Hyde as to his guilt. The jury then withdrew to "consider" their verdict. They were unable to reach a unanimous decision and Hyde, in private discussion with one of the jurors, appeared to threaten him. However, there was still hesitation on the part of the jury, although now only over a

14 Stinton, "The Tryall of Mr Benja. Keach."

technicality. Any misgivings they had regarding quotations in the indictment not corresponding with the printed text were overruled. Hyde felt forced to threaten them publicly before they finally returned a verdict of guilty.

Pronouncing sentence, Hyde jailed Keach for two weeks. Bail was denied him, and he was in addition subjected to the public shame and humiliation of being placed in the pillory twice for two hours, once in Aylesbury and then again a few days later in Winslow. Furthermore, at Winslow the hangman was instructed to torch his primer publicly. Finally, he was fined twenty pounds and bound over to appear at the next assizes to renounce his doctrine.[15]

Despite his youth and inexperience, it is evident that Keach was not intimidated by the words and actions of the highest judge in England. The treatment that he received at the hands of Sir Robert Hyde was unjust, unnecessarily malicious and brutal. The mixture of scorn, derision and unsubstantiated allegations were all aimed at portraying the defendant in the worst possible light and establishing his alleged seditious and malicious intent. Though all Keach's attempts to defend himself were denied, he appears to have had the last word, stating that, "I hope I shall never renounce those Truths which I have written in that Book."[16] These were not empty words, for though he may have later modified some aspects of his understanding of the second coming of Christ, he never renounced his views on infant baptism or on gospel preachers, as will become clear in subsequent chapters. Surprisingly, the court records hold no account of Keach appearing at the next assizes. It seems likely, had he done so, he would have refused to recant. Keach was clearly a man who maintained the courage of his convictions, even if it meant a baptism of suffering.

---

15 Stinton, "The Tryall of Mr Benja. Keach."
16 Stinton, "The Tryall of Mr Benja. Keach."

His courage was further demonstrated in the midst of his punishment. Far from being humiliated in the pillory, he used it as an opportunity to preach, much to the consternation of the jailor and the sheriff, demonstrating his willingness to suffer for his faith and gladly confess the Lord Jesus Christ before men.

> It is no new thing for the servants of the Lord to suffer, and to be made a gazing-stock: and you that are acquainted with the Scriptures, know that the way to the crown is by the cross.... I do not speak out of prejudice to any person, but do sincerely desire, that the Lord would convert them, and convince them of their errors, that their souls may be saved in the day of the Lord Jesus. Good people, the concernment of souls is very great; so great, that Christ died for them: and truly a concernment for souls was that which moved me to write and publish those things, for which I now suffer, and for which I could suffer greater things than these.... Oh! Did you but experience...the great love of God, and the excellencies that are in him; it would make you more willing to go through any sufferings for his sake. And I do account this the greatest honour, that ever the Lord was pleas'd to confer upon me.[17]

These words not only illustrate Keach's willingness to suffer, but also show what motivated him to go through these troubles and sorrows. He had an evangelistic zeal. He wanted others, whom he was persuaded were in error, to share his biblical convictions and come to faith in Christ. He believed that the practice of infant baptism blinded people to their need to be converted. Furthermore, he had an overwhelming sense of his own unworthiness and the love of God toward him in Jesus Christ. Because

---

17 Crosby, *History*, 2:205–207.

Christ had suffered so much for him, Keach thought it was little, by comparison, for him to suffer for Christ. To know that God loved him, even if he was despised by men, sustained his spirit and gave him strength to endure persecution. His lion-like courage and willingness to undergo persecution were, therefore, the fruit of his love for God and his love for his fellow men.

A radical change in outlook

Why was a man like Keach now being persecuted for what he believed? What had happened to bring about these changes? In 1658, Keach had enjoyed liberty of conscience along with many others in England. He could preach, and if he had written his primer then, there would have been no fear of prosecution by the civil authorities.

The early 1660s had seen a dramatic change in the political and religious landscape. Cromwell's death in 1658 was followed by a brief period of uncertainty. Then, in April 1660, Charles II issued the Declaration of Breda. In it, he offered an olive branch:

> And because the passion and uncharitableness of the times have produced several opinions in religion, by which men are engaged in parties and animosities against each other; which, when they shall hereafter unite in a freedom of conversation, will be composed, or better understood; we do declare a liberty to tender consciences, and that no man shall be disquieted, or called into question, for differences of opinion in matters of religion which do not disturb the peace of the kingdom; and that we shall be ready to consent to such an act of parliament, as, upon mature deliberation, shall be offered to us, for the full granting that indulgence.[18]

---

18 Peter Bayne, "Declaration of King Charles II from Breda." In *Documents Relating to the Settlement of the Church of England by the Act of Uniformity of 1662 with an Historical Introduction* (London, 1862), 2–3.

Charles II (1630–1685) reigned from 1660 until his death in 1685. Under the Restoration, Nonconformists faced severe persecution, and many laws were enacted that restricted their movements, religious freedoms and prospects of employment. Heavy fines and imprisonment faced those who disobeyed the sweeping new laws.

Whether Charles was sincere or not is open to debate but, as many national leaders since have discovered, it is one thing to *make* a promise, but quite another thing to *deliver* that promise. The reign of Charles II showed that he was unable to deliver. The new king soon found himself confronted by the desires of many Anglicans. Their bitter memories recalled the expulsion of Anglican clergymen during the Puritan revolution in the 1640s and 1650s, some 2,780 in total, according to John Coffey.[19] Thoughts of a generous settlement were far from their minds, and in their resentment, they sought revenge. They wanted the restoration of the *Thirty-Nine Articles* and *The Book of Common Prayer* in an exclusively Anglican state church. The principal architect for this policy was Gilbert Sheldon, who was appointed Archbishop of Canterbury in 1663. His voice reverberated strongly in favour of the repressive measures against those who failed to conform.

Old fears of religious radicalism were reinvigorated on the return of Charles II as king. Feelings ran high against Puritans and broke out spontaneously in various parts of England, some of which were recorded by Henry Jessey (1601–1663).[20] Among these outbreaks of sometimes violent persecution, Jessey mentions a mob who made havoc of the meeting place of William Kiffin's congregation in London, Independent ministers and their people in Gloucestershire who were beaten up and had their homes looted by those who proclaimed themselves loyal to the king and leaders of the Abingdon Baptist Association jailed in Reading for refusing to take oaths.[21]

More seriously for those who held these beliefs, suspicions on the part of the government increased—former supporters of

---

19 John Coffey, *Persecution and Toleration in Protestant England, 1558–1689* (Harlow: Pearson Education Limited, 2000), 140–141.

20 Henry Jessey, *The Lord's Loud Call to England* (London, 1660). Jessey was a key figure among the early Separatists in Southwark, London, long before Keach came there in 1668. See also Benjamin Stinton's *Repository* for similar reports.

21 Jessey, *The Lord's Loud Call*, 8, 17–18, 24–26.

Cromwell, Baptists, Independents, Fifth Monarchists, Quakers and the like were not trusted. The government felt that such men represented the radical and revolutionary spirit of the previous two decades. Plots and rumours of plots that punctuated the Restoration period further increased the government's highly developed sense of insecurity.[22] The first significant uprising took place in London in January 1661, led by the Fifth Monarchist Thomas Venner (*c.* 1608–1661).[23] This was successfully put down, but the government reacted by filling the capital's prisons with suspects and issuing a proclamation prohibiting unlawful meetings and conventicles.[24] Though residents were allowed to meet in their private homes, public services were banned unless held in parish churches and chapels. Magistrates were alerted to search out conventicles and arrest those who attended them. This reaction was to prove only a foretaste of what was to become a more permanent series of measures.

An intolerant Anglicanism was effectively re-established after 1660. However, any attempt to establish a uniform national church was doomed to failure, because Nonconformity had put down deep roots in the previous twenty years. Nevertheless, repressive measures were enacted and "tender consciences" like Keach's suffered heavily for their convictions.[25]

---

22 Richard L. Greaves, *Deliver Us from Evil: the Radical Underground in Britain, 1660–1663* (Oxford: Oxford University Press, 1986), outlines the cultures of suspicion and resentment that emerged in Restoration Britain and details the various plots. See also companion volumes by Greaves, *Enemies Under His Feet: Radicals and Nonconformists in Britain 1664–1677* (California: Stanford University Press, 1990), and *Secrets of the Kingdom: British Radicals from the Popish Plot to the Revolution of 1668–89* (Stanford: Stanford University Press, 1992).

23 The Fifth Monarchy movement was not a denomination but had followers among several groups, including Baptists and Independents. They believed that Christ would return once the saints had seized civil and military power. See B.S. Capp, *The Fifth Monarchy Men: A Study in Seventeenth-Century English Millenarianism* (London: Faber and Faber, 1972).

24 Bayne, *Documents*, 104–106.

25 For the purposes of this book, only a sketch is given of the legislation. More

The first measure was the Corporation Act of December 1661. All municipal officers, including magistrates, had to swear loyalty to the king and take the sacrament of the Lord's Supper in the Anglican Church. However, it was a second measure, the Act of Uniformity, passed in May 1662, which determined the shape of acceptable religious practice on a national scale. Every minister was now required to be ordained by a bishop, to declare acceptance of the new *Book of Common Prayer*, and to denounce the Solemn League and Covenant, or be deprived of their livings.[26] Keach and many other Baptists had already left the Church of England, but hundreds of ministers with Puritan sympathies were driven out of the church to swell the ranks of Nonconformity. Nevertheless, Keach was prosecuted under the 1662 Act, as his trial at the assizes clearly shows. The Lord Chief Justice used *The Book of Common Prayer* to condemn Keach's teaching.

The severest laws were those that penalized people who continued to worship outside of the Church of England. The Corporation Act was aimed at magistrates, the Act of Uniformity at ministers. The new Conventicle Act of 1664 was aimed at the laity. Anyone over the age of sixteen attending a meeting for worship with five or more people outside the normal household, and not using the *Prayer Book*, would face punishment. Fines or imprisonment followed the first and second offences, and fines or transportation were threatened for a third. When the first Act expired, a new one was passed in 1670. The fines were moderated for those who attended conventicles, but preachers and those who owned the houses where meetings were held were subject to heavy fines: £20 for the first offence and £40 for subsequent offences. Finally, after the Great Plague of 1665,

---

details may be found in other sources. Bayne, *Documents*, provides the full text of the legislation. Watts, *The Dissenters*, 221–227, provides a comprehensive survey.

26 By denouncing the 1643 Solemn League and Covenant, ministers would be firmly rejecting a Presbyterian form of church government.

some ministers who had been deprived of their livings took up preaching in pulpits abandoned by churchmen. Parliament soon acted against this practice and one more piece of legislation was passed. The Five Mile Act of 1665 prohibited any former minister from residing within five miles of his former parish or of any corporate town.

During the early years of the Restoration, the religious and civil authorities combined their powers to apprehend and to punish Benjamin Keach, yet this "teacher in their new fangled way" stood firm. The new climate of religious intolerance, with its repressive laws, lay behind this persecution. Despite the injustice he endured at the hands of the Lord Chief Justice, twenty-four year old Benjamin Keach did not waver in his convictions. However, what happened to Keach in Aylesbury on October 8 and 9, 1664, was only one part of the persecution he suffered in Buckinghamshire. It became so severe for him and for others who shared his convictions that, in 1668, he concluded that the wisest course of action would be to leave his native county and head south to London.

CHAPTER 3

"Great Troubles and Sorrows"

Conscience is made a cloak for ignorance, wilfulness and treachery.[1]

By the end of May 1660, Charles II had arrived back in England. That same month was a memorable month for Keach, then twenty years old, because he married Jane Grove. She was a year younger than her husband and came from the small town of Winslow. In the records of Keach's church an entry marked for 1660 reads, "Benjamin Keach and [...] his wife were maried in may at winslow in ye county of Bucks by Mr. John Har[...] on ye day called holy Thursday."[2]

---

1 *CSPD*, 1668, 232. Richard Bower of Yarmouth to Joseph Williamson, secretary to Lord Arlington, Secretary of State.

2 The sections marked [...] are illegible. *Regester*, PRO, RG4/4183. The first refers to Jane Grove, the second probably to John Hartnoll. A General Baptist church was in existence in Winslow by 1654 and Hartnoll was sent as a messenger to their General Assembly. *Non-conformist Chapels and Meeting Houses, Buckinghamshire* (London: Her Majesty's Stationery Office, 1986), 27. Hartnoll also appears in the 1669 Episcopal Visitation returns for Bucks, being identified as a teacher in the Winslow area.

Crosby described her as "a woman of great piety and prudence."[3] Jane Keach bore five children, but only three survived: Mary, born in 1663; Elias, in the year of the Great Plague of 1665; and, Hannah, two years later in 1667.[4]

Also listed in this register are their children's places of birth. Mary and Hannah were born in Tingewick (modern spelling) in the county of Buckinghamshire, but Elias was born in Aylesbury. The Keaches are traditionally associated with Winslow and, as we have seen in the previous chapter, in May 1664 Keach was definitely living in Winslow. The very fact that he was forced to undergo a second session in the pillory at Winslow, and that while he suffered the pains of the pillory there, his primer was burned in front of his face, confirms this close association. Tingewick and Aylesbury are some twelve and fifteen miles respectively from Winslow, but lie in totally opposite directions, Tingewick to the northwest and Aylesbury to the south. Could it be that the changes in location are an indication of the fact that the Keaches had to move around in order to avoid detection by the authorities? Or perhaps Keach moved his wife and family there for their own safety while he remained in Winslow?[5]

Whatever the situation was, Jane Keach did not let her husband stand alone in his sufferings. She followed him from Winslow to Aylesbury in 1664, and when he was placed in the pillory a few days later, she stood stoutly alongside him and "frequently spoke in vindication of her husband, and the principles for which he suffered."[6] We cannot be certain of the reasons for the different places of birth, but this much is certain: in the eyes of the authorities in Buckinghamshire, Benjamin Keach became

---

3 Crosby, *History*, 4:271.

4 *Regester*, PRO, RG4/4188, 3.

5 This uncertainty over Keach's movements at this point is part of a larger problem that confronts anyone trying to compile his biography. There are a number of times when, because there is no evidence in existence, we have to leave a gap in the story.

6 Crosby, *History*, 2:206.

a marked man, especially after he published his primer. Daily life must therefore have presented many uncertainties for the young Keach family.

As we have already seen, Keach was willing to endure such hardship because of his love for God and for his fellow men. There was, however, one other event that must have strengthened his resolve. There seems to have been a reluctance to talk much about this event, yet it clearly left a vivid and indelible impression on him, one that remained with him for the rest of his life. There is only one reference to this experience, and Keach gives no precise date. He preached a sermon to his congregation that was published in 1698, just six years before his death, and in that sermon he says:

> I could tell you of one (dream) I had when I was Young; a discovery to me of those great Troubles and Sorrows I should meet with, I thought I was with the Lord Jesus, and he gave me a touch, and bid me follow him, (though I saw no form) and he spake to me, and told me, that I should suffer hard things for his Sake; and soon after my Trials began, which were known to many, tho this was between 30 and 40 years ago, yet is as fresh in my Memory as if not above a year hence.[7]

Keach is referring to a dream he had at some point before 1668. Given that he had already suffered considerably by then, a date soon after 1658, when he began to preach, or the early 1660s would be a reasonable conjecture. Keach did not believe that dreams were God's "normal" means of communication, for he was well aware of the Anabaptist abuses and claims of new revelation during the Reformation and had no time for such claims.

7 Keach, *Christ Alone the Way to Heaven; Or, Jacob's Ladder Improved* (London, 1698), 8.

He reminded his congregation on many occasions that God had finished his revelation when he spoke through his Son, and that the Bible was their only rule of faith and practice. Preaching from the parable of the rich man and Lazarus, he instructed them:

> Expect no new revelation from God, for God has established his Word for ever, he will not alter the thing that has gone out of his mouth; heaven and earth shall pass away, before one jot or tittle of God's Word shall pass away. Expect no new revelation, nor any other prophet to be raised up, to discover the mind of God to you, or to make void anything that is not written, or to teach you otherwise to believe, act, or do, that you may be saved.[8]

Keach was, therefore, very cautious and explained to his congregation that his sympathies lay with Martin Luther. He told them that because various Anabaptists in Luther's day had been deluded and carried away by their dreams, Luther had prayed that God would give him such a good understanding of the Scriptures that he would not need any dreams![9]

As has been seen, the new legislation introduced in the 1660s created grave difficulties for dissenting groups like the General Baptists. Men like Keach were placed in a difficult position. On the one hand, they wanted freedom of conscience and were prepared to suffer in order to obtain that freedom. On the other hand, the civil and religious authorities saw the General Baptists as part of a much wider problem. During Keach's trial at the Aylesbury Assizes, Sir Robert Hyde had told Keach, "I know your Religion, you are a Fifth-Monarchy-Man."[10] Like all the magistrates, Hyde would have sworn his loyalties to the king (the oaths of allegiance

---

8 Keach, "The Rich Man and Lazarus," *Parables Two*, 403.

9 Keach, *Christ Alone the Way to Heaven*, 10.

10 Stinton, "The Tryall of Mr Benja. Keach."

and supremacy) and to the Church of England. By identifying Keach in this manner, Hyde was only expressing what was, among those who had similarly sworn their loyalties, a widespread and deep-seated culture of suspicion and hatred toward those who refused to conform. Keach would not have been willing take up arms as Thomas Venner, the Fifth Monarchist, had done in 1661, but in the eyes of the authorities, Keach and others like him could not escape being associated with such men.

It is easy to see then why anyone arguing for liberty of conscience would be seen as a potential troublemaker. Richard Bower, complaining to Joseph Williamson in 1668 that "conscience is made a cloak for ignorance, wilfulness and treachery," was only expressing a view that was widely held among those who were loyal to the king and the church.[11] Treachery, in particular, was the main fear on the government side. Richard Greaves points out that the many plots and rumours of plots, and the actions of militants like Venner (continuing for nearly thirty years until 1689), provided—at least in the minds of the authorities—a rationale for the Conventicle Acts. These opponents were seen as potential revolutionaries bent on overthrowing law and order and therefore needed to be suppressed at all costs.[12] Greaves concludes: "The actions of the militants made it possible for advocates of an exclusive settlement to cast the opprobrium of sedition on even moderate Nonconformists, creating a legacy of distrust that lasted to 1689 and beyond."[13] So, Keach's opinions, expressed in his primer and in his preaching,

---

11 *CSPD*, 1668, 232. Bower sent regular reports to Williamson during this period, usually about religious and shipping matters. Here he was complaining that the people of Yarmouth were "high for liberty of conscience," inspired by the writings of Nathaniel Strange. Strange had died in 1665. During his life he was pastor of a Particular Baptist church in the West Country and in the 1660s was associated with the Fifth Monarchy Movement. See *BDBR*, s.v. "Strange, Nathaniel."

12 Richard L. Greaves, *Deliver Us from Evil: The Radical Underground in Britain 1660-1663* (Oxford: Oxford University Press, 1986), 227.

13 Greaves, *Deliver Us from Evil*, 227.

would have been considered a major threat and viewed with great suspicion. To the authorities, such publications and preaching were regarded as a legitimate target for prosecution, for they represented the radical revolutionary spirit associated with the civil wars and Commonwealth periods, which they were so anxious to crush.

Conventicles around Winslow

In the northern part of Buckinghamshire there seemed to be a particularly intense struggle between the authorities and different groups of Nonconformists, in this case principally the General Baptists and the Quakers. Besides the recent Conventicle Act, a law dating from the latter days of Elizabeth I entitled, Act to retain the Queen's subjects in their due obedience (1581), was also on the statute books. In the neighbouring county of Bedfordshire, John Bunyan had already fallen foul of its provisions and was arrested and imprisoned for preaching in the open-air in 1660.[14]

This same law was pressed into service against twelve General Baptists, ten men and two women, in Aylesbury in 1664 (prior to Keach's trial in October).[15] These men and women were arrested and then convicted at the Quarter Sessions for conventicling. They were required to either conform to the Church of England or go into exile, as this particular law prescribed. Their troubles were increased when they were told that should they refuse either to conform or to leave the country, sentence of death would be passed on them. Given only one afternoon to decide what to do, they cast themselves on the mercy of the court, saying that they could neither conform nor leave the country. The court then passed the sentence of death on them, ordered the prisoners back to jail to await execution and sent officers to the homes of the twelve in order to seize all their personal effects.

---

14 Watts, *The Dissenters*, 224.

15 A full account of the trial is to be found in Crosby, *History*, 2:180–185.

Thomas Monk, a son of one of the prisoners, rode to London to seek the help of another Baptist, William Kiffin.[16] Kiffin was a man of some standing who had access to those in authority, and so he immediately took him to see the Lord Chancellor, Edward Hyde, with a request that Charles II intervene and issue a reprieve thus saving the lives of the prisoners. With a great deal of haste, a much-relieved Monk rode back to Aylesbury with a copy of the king's reprieve in his hands.

Historians writing about the effects of the Conventicle Act point out that persecution was not continuous during this period and often depended on the attitudes of the local civil and religious authorities.[17] This incident in Aylesbury shows how determined some in Buckinghamshire were to stamp out dissent, even being prepared to use existing legislation with harsher penalties to do so. It represented a particularly vicious attempt on the part of some in authority to act against those who defied the law and continued to meet in illegal conventicles. The Baptist historian Thomas Crosby reports that on this occasion not all of the justices of the peace in Aylesbury were in agreement with these extreme measures, and some left the bench, disassociating themselves from the severity of the decision—and perhaps fearful of the consequences.[18]

This incident also shows us how vigorously conventicles were targeted by the authorities in Buckinghamshire. Why was this the case? It is not simply enough to say that it was "against the

---

16 William Kiffin was a rich cloth merchant who had become associated with the early Separatists in London in the late 1630s. He became the pastor of Devonshire Square Baptist Church and signed the 1644 Particular Baptist confession. He, together with Hanserd Knollys and Benjamin Keach, were the acknowledged leaders of the London Particular Baptists after the 1670s. Because of his integrity and wealth, he had contacts and influence among the leaders of the government. Charles II knew him personally. See *BDBR*, s.v. "Kiffin, William."

17 John Coffey, *Persecution and Toleration in Protestant England 1558–1689* (Harlow: Pearson Education Limited, 2000), 169–179.

18 Crosby, *History*, 2:182.

law." It is important to understand that "every conventicle or social gathering...was a potential cause for concern."[19] The government had a difficult task distinguishing between militants like Venner on the one hand and more peaceful and less threatening Nonconformists on the other. Given the climate of fear and suspicion—sometimes expressed with additional hatred and malice—it should not be surprising to find magistrates erring on what they regarded as the side of caution in their attempts to maintain law and order and so suppress illegal gatherings. Those who gathered in conventicles saw themselves as exercising liberty of conscience. If their opponents saw this as a "cloak for treachery" then the conventicles themselves came to be seen as one of the principal expressions of that same treachery.

Crosby informs us that Keach "had no small share in the suffering of these times. He was often seized while preaching, and committed to prison, sometimes bound, sometimes released on bail, and sometimes his life was threatened."[20] He would have been arrested when he was found preaching in conventicles. If a justice of the peace and local constables were seeking to carry out their public duties according to the law, where would they find people like Keach preaching and others gathered to hear them? A visit to Winslow today would uncover an old building with a notice board outside indicating that it was Keach's meeting-house. This was not built until 1695. A meeting-house would probably not have existed in 1660 and no licence for one was issued under the 1672 Indulgence.[21] In fact, it appears that at this time there were no purpose-built meeting-houses in north Buckinghamshire where the General Baptists met. Instead, there was a network of meetings that rotated irregularly, gathering in various homes of the members. Using evidence gleaned from

---

19 Greaves, *Deliver Us from Evil*, 228.

20 Crosby, *History*, 2:185.

21 *Nonconformist Chapels and Meeting-houses, Buckinghamshire*, 27.

William Kiffin (1616–1701) was one of the key leaders of the Particular Baptists in London.

the two Episcopal returns of 1665 and 1669, it is possible to reconstruct at least a partial picture of the meetings of the General Baptists with whom Keach was undoubtedly associated.[22] However, we cannot marry together the occasions when Keach was arrested with the meeting of any particular conventicle because that evidence does not exist.

Keach was born and raised in the parish of Stoke Hammond some miles from Winslow, but after 1655 he was no longer attending the parish church. By 1658, he was preaching, perhaps in Winslow, and had married Jane Grove of Winslow in 1660. Furthermore, Thomas Disney, in his letter to Luke Wilkes (his brother-in-law in London), identified Keach as living in Winslow and related how a man had been sent to Stapleford Mill in order to obtain a copy of Keach's primer from his brother Henry, the owner of the mill. Other members of Keach's family evidently remained in the vicinity of Stoke Hammond. Besides Henry Keach, Joseph Keach is also mentioned in the returns, being described as a teacher. Stapleford Mill was clearly a meeting-place for quite a large conventicle.[23] However, there is no available

---

22 G. Lyon Turner, *The Original Records of Early Nonconformity under Persecution and Indulgence*, 3 vols. (London: T. Fisher Unwin, 1911–1914). These are edited extracts from the Episcopal Returns for 1665 and 1669. The 1665 returns asked about the activities of ejected ministers following the Act of Uniformity and are very incomplete. The 1669 returns asked about dissenting meetings and their congregations, and provided evidence for implementing a Second Conventicle Act (1670).

23 Stapleford Mill was in an isolated spot by the River Ouzel—an ideal lcoation for a Baptist conventicle. The mill was in use until 1850. The two older brothers of Benjamin Keach were key figures: the group met in Henry's mill and Joseph, listed as a bricklayer, was one of the teachers. Thomas Mead, a blacksmith and John Hall, son of a husbandman, were the other teachers. The Keach brothers appear in the first returns for absenting themselves from parish services. In the 1669 returns, the curate of Soulbury reported that while there were no constant meetings in his parish, during the past three years there were often meetings of over 100 people at Stapleford Mill, many coming from outside the parish to attend. He concludes his return by expressing a desire that these meetings be suppressed by the power and assistance of the magistrate. See John Broad, ed., *Buckinghamshire Dissent and Parish Life, 1669–1712* (Bucks Record Society, 1993), 28:63.

evidence directly linking Keach with preaching or being arrested at a conventicle held in his brother's mill.

It is much more likely that the conventicles associated with Winslow are the ones where Keach was engaged in preaching, thus exposing himself to the risk of arrest by the authorities. From the 1669 returns, it is possible to reconstruct the several meeting places of one congregation. It a reasonable conjecture that this is the congregation, associated with Benjamin Keach, which he left in 1668 when he departed for London. In the returns, therefore, it is the name of John Hartnoll, rather than Benjamin Keach, that is associated with each location. The 1669 records for Winslow read:

> Winslow in Bucks. At the houses of Eliot, a carpenter, and Foster, a baker; John Holland of Greenborough, and at North Marston and Oving monthly by turnes. Sect: Anabaptist; number: 40; teacher: Hartnell, a thatcher of North Marston.[24]

The records for Oving report twenty meeting in a house, and for North Marston thirty or forty meeting in Hartnoll's own house.[25] John Hartnoll is also listed in connection with a meeting at Swanbourne.[26] All these tiny villages would have used Winslow as their local market town, each being no more than five miles away.

The authorities, aiming in particular at the preacher and the homeowner, targeted these meetings. Officers of the peace, sometimes assisted by local militia, had to track down these meeting places and actually be present when they were meeting

24 Arthur Clear, *The King's Village in Demesne or a Thousand Years of Winslow Life* (Winslow, 1894), 93–94.

25 Turner, *The Original Records*, 1:77–84, and Broad, ed., *Buckinghamshire Dissent*, 59–60, 62.

26 Turner, *The Original Records*, 2:837–841.

to apprehend the guilty parties. Crosby records how, on one occasion, the militia came across a meeting where Keach was preaching and, with considerable violence, threatened to kill him by trampling him under the feet of their horses. They had actually bound him and were ready to take the law into their own hands when their commanding officer, realizing what was about to happen, intervened and prevented them from carrying out their murderous threats. Nevertheless, Keach was still arrested, tied to a trooper's horse and carried off to the jail in Aylesbury where he endured considerable suffering before eventually being released.[27] This may well be the same incident described by a later writer, in which the meeting place is identified as being in Winslow.[28]

Sion in Diſtress

From the information available, it would seem that Keach was arrested at least three times, including his arrest and appearance at the Aylesbury Assizes in 1664, and was imprisoned on at least two other occasions.[29] Keach himself makes mention of his imprisonment in 1666 in his poem, *Distressed Sion Relieved*:

> For almost Thirty years past have I
> Seen Floods of Tears flowing continually
> From Sions Eyes, whose sad distressed state
> With Filial Sympathy I did relate.
> In Sixty Six a year of expectation
> Came no relief, but still fresh Lamentation;
> When she was told her sorrows would be o're,
> That year produc'd more sorrow than before,
> Which caus'd me who in Prison then did lye

---

27 Crosby, *History*, 2:185–186.

28 Margaret M. Verney, *Buckinghamshire Biographies* (Oxford: Clarendon Press, 1912), 146.

29 *CSPD*, 1663–1664, 116, SP29/98.

To sigh and sob, and weep most bitterly,
In prospect of what I saw coming on
Poor Sion, e're her miseries would be gone.[30]

In 1666, Keach also began to write another poem entitled, *Sion in Distress: Or, The Groans of the Protestant Church.*[31] Like *The Child's Instructor*, no copies of the original have survived but Keach expanded it and published the fuller edition in 1681 at the height of persecution in London.

From the poem's opening lines, it is apparent that Keach saw what was happening to him and others as the beginning of persecution against "Sion," not merely the Baptists but the Protestant church. As the new regime tried to tighten its grip, so "tender consciences" continued to feel the pain inflicted on them. At some point, Keach presumably had to ask himself whether it was time to leave Winslow. Perhaps he reflected on the words of his Saviour, the Lord Jesus Christ, in Matthew 10:23, "When they persecute you in this city, flee to another." Whatever his thoughts, it was not a decision to take lightly. By 1668, he had been preaching for ten years and also had to care for a wife and three young children. He would be leaving friends and family behind, and if he went to London there would be few there whom he would know. William Kiffin had perhaps heard of him following events in 1664. The fact remains, however, that Keach was a marked man so long as he remained in Buckinghamshire, for he had felt the fury of the authorities on all sides and his face was well known to friend and foe.

---

30 Keach, *Distressed Sion Relieved: Or, The Garment of Praise for the Spirit of Heaviness: wherein are discovered the grand causes of the churches trouble and misery under the late dismal dispensation. With a compleat history of and lamentation for those renowned worthies that fell in England by Popish rage and cruelty, from the year 1680 to 1688* (London, 1689), 1.

31 Keach mentions the 1666 edition in the section addressed "To the Reader." In *Distressed Sion Relieved*, and in the 1694 edition of *A Golden Mine Opened*, Keach lists the 1666 edition on the final page as part of his published works.

The stone inscription in the parish church of Stoke Hammond in memory of rector Thomas Disney (1605–1686)

A number of Church of England authorities were aware of his activities. None of them would have had any sympathy for a man of Keach's convictions, or for his irregular activities in preaching and for writing heretical books. Even before 1660, a gulf existed between Benjamin Keach and Thomas Disney. They came from very different backgrounds. On the one hand, Disney, the rector of Stoke Hammond, had been educated at Christ Church College, Oxford, and was from a Lincolnshire family of Anglican gentry. A stone inscription in the parish church of Stoke Hammond betrays his background, describing Disney as "the son of Sir Henry Disney Lord of Norton Disney and of Swinderby in Lincolnshire." On the other hand, Keach had little, if any, formal education and was a tailor by trade. After 1660, the gulf was driven wider and deeper. Disney conformed to the Act of Uniformity in 1662, and his letter to his brother-in-law in 1664 shows that he was very irritated with Keach and others among Keach's family and friends who had left the parish church.[32] Furthermore, Disney's brother-in-law, Luke Wilkes, was from a prominent family in Leighton Buzzard, and was in the employ of the king in Whitehall. As a member of the royal household, he would have taken an oath of allegiance to the king, and in his position would be able to pass on his brother-in-law's letter and Keach's primer to the Archbishop of Canterbury, Gilbert Sheldon. Sheldon himself was very eager to suppress dissent, and in this he was largely successful. One of his aims in the 1669 returns was to provide information and evidence to argue the case for renewing the Conventicle Act once it expired in 1670.

Furthermore, the civil authorities were also well acquainted with Keach and showed no sympathy for his dissenting views. Thomas Strafford of Tattenhoe was the local justice of the peace. He had been present at Keach's arrest, gave evidence against

---

32 *CSPD*, 1663–1664, 116, SP29/98.

him at the October 1664 assizes and had a reputation for harshness.[33] In addition, John Egerton, the Lord Lieutenant for Buckinghamshire from 1660 to 1686, actively persecuted all Dissenters. As Lord Lieutenant, he was the king's representative in the county, the head of the magistracy and had extensive powers with regard to the militia. He is described as

> a rigid churchman and strict disciplinarian, [who] gained a reputation for the severity with which he upheld the Act of Uniformity in cases of unlawful assembly, and the leaders of the Dissenters, particularly the Quakers, had cause to fear the harshness of some of his sentences.[34]

We do not know the precise reasons for Keach's decision to leave Buckinghamshire and go to London. One thing is certain: it was not because he lacked courage or because he had doubts about his convictions. There is no evidence that he thought of quitting because he was growing weary of the harsh and persistent persecution he endured at the hands of the authorities. Rather, he expected to suffer for his faith, and the changes that took place in 1660 did not alter his religion but rather strengthened it. He was not the kind of man who would hide away while the storm raged and come out only when the sun shone again. Keach was a man who had counted the cost of following his convictions and, in the period from 1660 to 1668, began to display a spiritual and emotional toughness evidenced by his patience, courage and constancy—characteristics that he continued to display after 1668. Later on, perhaps reflecting on his earlier experiences, he likened the work of a Christian to that of a soldier going to war:

---

33 A. Taylor, *The History of the English General Baptists*, 3 vols. (London, 1818), 1:225–229, and Broad, ed., *Buckinghamshire Dissent*, xvii.

34 Douglas Coult, *A Prospect of Ashridge* (London: Phillimore, 1980), 124.

> The work of a Christian is not easy, but a very hard and difficult work. What is a harder undertaking, or attended with greater trouble than that of a soldier? Moreover it may inform us, what the reason is, that so many professors who seemed zealous in times of peace and prosperity, have deserted in an hour of trial and persecutions. Alas, they did not sit down and consult what a mighty force, or what troops of temptation...troops of opposition from without, and from within, they should meet withal.[35]

As he thought of leaving his home county in 1668, Keach knew that he would face again in London the temptations he had already faced in Buckinghamshire.

It should not be imagined that Keach accepted his sufferings in a fatalistic manner or that, fuelled by these bitter experiences, he then turned on his persecutors to vilify them. As a man of the Bible, he sought to follow the injunction, "Repay no one evil for evil" (Romans 12:17), thus following the example of the Lord Jesus Christ. Instead, he began to pour out his grief and sorrows in poetry. The experience of persecution drove him to deeper reflection, and in *Distressed Sion Relieved* he began to express his concerns and prayers for the church of Christ. Such poetry was to become a dominant feature of his life, especially until 1689 when the Act of Toleration became law.

While Keach himself does not reveal his reasons for leaving Buckinghamshire, it is possible to provide the backdrop for his decision to uproot his family and leave for London. Winslow was a small market town with a population no larger than 1,000. Aylesbury only housed a population between 2,000 and 3,000 people.[36] It was far more difficult to remain concealed in such

35 Keach, "Going to War," *Parables One*, 104.

36 Broad, ed., *Buckinghamshire Dissent*, xl. Chesham and Newport Pagnell were the largest towns, being over 3,000, Aylesbury had between 2,000 and 3,000 and all the other market towns in Buckinghamshire between 1,000 and 2,000.

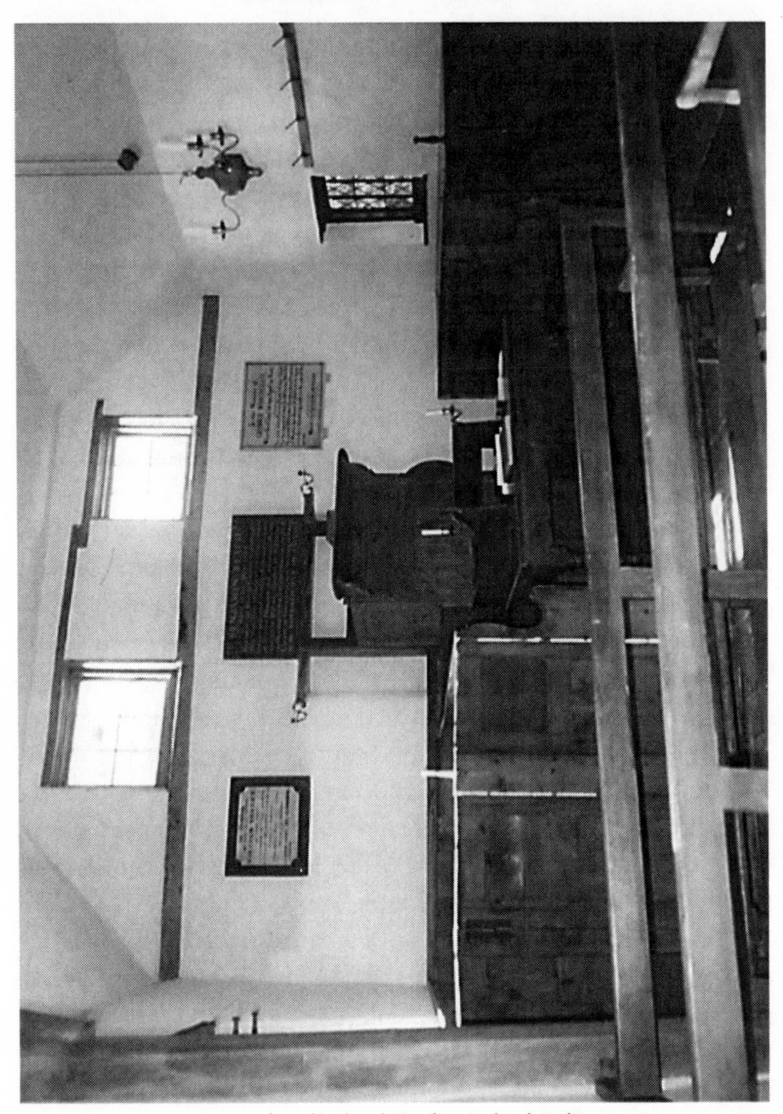

Interior of Keach's Chapel, Winslow, Buckinghamshire

Interior of Keach's Chapel, Winslow, Buckinghamshire (view from the pulpit)

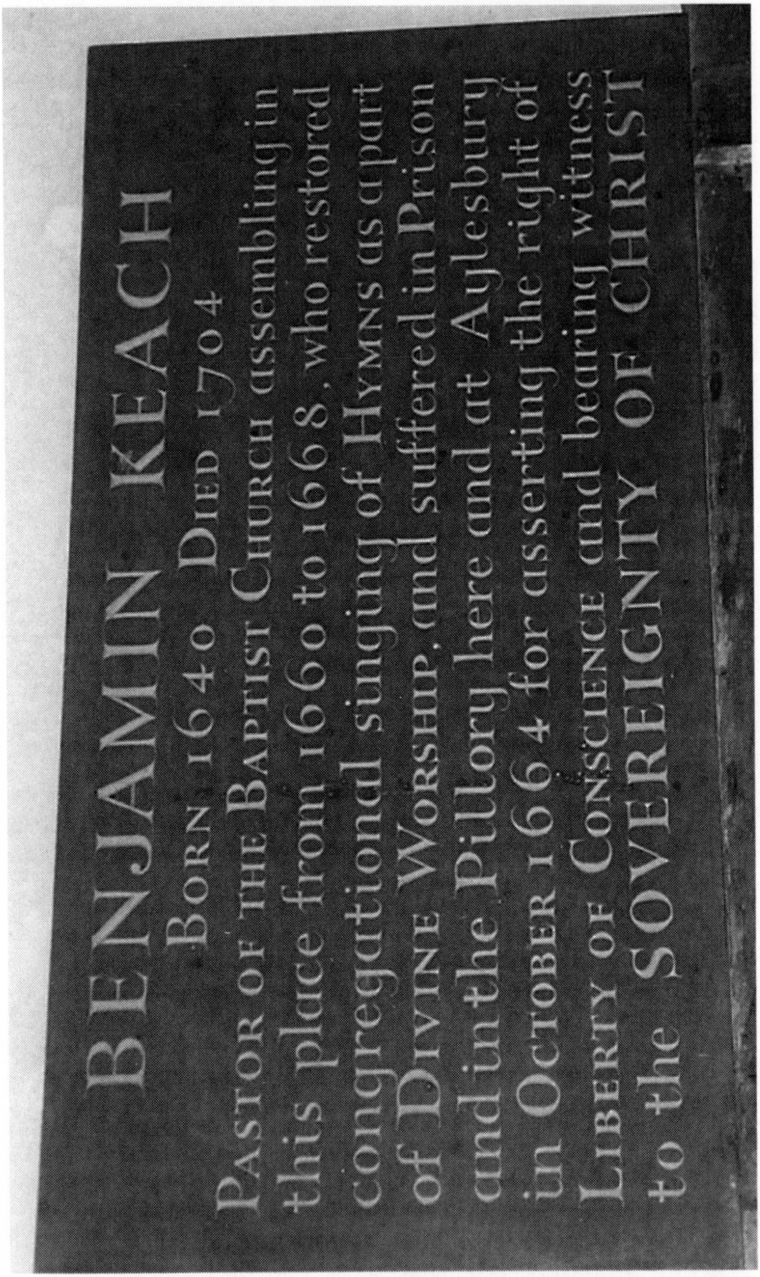

Commemorative plaque in Keach's Chapel, Winslow, Buckinghamshire

small communities—especially after his public trial in Aylesbury and being pilloried both there and in Winslow—than it would be in a larger centre. By 1668, Keach would have been a familiar face to everyone in the vicinity and easy prey for informers. In London, it would be easier to remain incognito. Keach would not have been able to live and carry on preaching and teaching with any degree of peace in Winslow, and he probably concluded he would have more and better opportunities in London for his work.

Yet, even his departure for London was not without incident. Having sold his possessions and turned them into money, Keach was then robbed by highwaymen as he and his family took the stagecoach to London.[37] This must have been a frightening experience for him and his young family. Later, with the rest of the passengers on the coach, he was able to sue the county of Buckinghamshire and recover his losses. Nevertheless, they arrived in London as penniless strangers.[38]

---

37 Thomas Delaune, *Angliae Metropolis, or the Present State of London with Memorials* (London, 1681), 401. In a list of carriers, waggoners and stagecoach operators, he shows that there was a daily service on weekdays to and from Aylesbury in the 1670s.

38 Crosby, *History*, 3:144.

Southwark, Hollars View, 1647 (Southwark Local Studies Library).
The Tower of London can be seen across the Thames on the far bank.

CHAPTER 4

"The mysteries of the Gospel"

When I was a Child, I thought as a Child, I understood as a Child, as the Apostle speaks. And let me intreat you to study the Nature of the Covenant of Grace; for until I had that opened to me, I was ignorant of the Mysteries of the Gospel.[1]

Keach arrived in London in 1668, coming to a city recovering from two major catastrophes—the Great Plague and the Great Fire. Michael Watts comments that in the minds of most sober Dissenters, such catastrophes could only be interpreted as God's judgements on an apostate nation.[2] Keach was no exception in seeing them as dreadful divine warnings:

1 Keach, "The Blessedness of Christ's Sheep," *A Golden Mine Opened*, 314–315.

2 Watts, *The Dissenters*, 238. For a specific example see Thomas Vincent, *God's Terrible Voice in the City* (Philadelphia: Soli Deo Gloria, 1997). Vincent first published his sermons in 1667.

Yet they proceed in foul Impenitence,
And aggravate their horrid Insolence;
Seeming to bid Defiances to Heaven,
Scorning to take the dreadful Warnings given.
The sweeping Plague (that Messenger of Wrath)
In such as 'scap'd, small Reformation hath
Produc'd! Nor has the desolating Fire
(A perfect Token of Gods flaming Ire)
Remov'd the City's Pride; 'twas great before,
And now it seems to multiply much more.[3]

The first catastrophe, the "sweeping Plague" of 1665, had accounted for the deaths of over 100,000 people in London, out of a total population of about half a million. Though few died as a result of the Great Fire, more than two-thirds of the city was destroyed. Estimates vary, but between 65,000 and 80,000 people were probably made homeless as a consequence.[4] In 1668, London was being extensively rebuilt following the "desolating Fire." It was also a year in which there was serious civil rioting in London, in the form of the "Bawdy house riots" of March 1668. These were attacks on London brothels, beginning in the east end of the city, in Poplar, and spreading to other districts in London, culminating with rioting in Moorfields. The forces of law and order successfully put down the protests but they represented strong feelings against the licentious court of Charles II and were linked to issues relating to the Dissenters. For the king to make a proclamation against conventicles and yet allow illegal brothels to continue unsuppressed seemed incongruous.[5] The protests gave the rioters opportunity to vent their anger against

3 Keach, *Sion in Distress: Or, The Groans of the Protestant Church* (London, 1681), 9.

4 Stephen Porter, *The Great Fire of London* (Godalming: Bramley Books, 1996), 71.

5 Timothy Harris, *London Crowds in the Reign of Charles II: Propaganda and Politics from the Restoration until the Exclusion Crisis* (Cambridge: Cambridge University Press, 1987), 82–91. See also Greaves, *Enemies Under His Feet*, 195–197.

this incongruity and attack the royal court, the Duke of York (the future James II) and the Anglican hierarchy, while at the same time making their demands for religious toleration heard.

London was the numerical stronghold of dissent when Keach came to live there.[6] Presbyterians, Independents, both General and Particular Baptists, together with Quakers and Fifth Monarchists, were to be found living and worshipping both within and without the walls of the city, especially in the east end of London and south of the Thames in Southwark, which lay immediately across London Bridge.

Benjamin Keach was soon to become associated with a church in Southwark. However, it was in the eastern part of London that the Keach family lived for a number of years, and it does not appear that he lived in Southwark until after 1689, perhaps because, by living in the same area where he regularly preached, he would have been more exposed to the possibility of arrest. Thomas Crosby suggests that when the penniless Keach family arrived in London, kind-hearted Baptists gave them hospitality.[7] The identity of these Baptists and their location remains unknown, but Keach himself tells us that he and his family came to settle in "S. Paul's, Shadwell."[8] Certainty

---

6 Greaves, *Enemies Under His Feet*, 151–153. Greaves assesses the reliability of Archbishop Sheldon's incomplete 1669 survey but points out that no accurate figures are available for this period, and if we are to gain a more accurate picture, it is necessary to project numbers back from the 1715–1718 list of Nonconformist congregations carried out by John Evans. Using Michael Watts' detailed analysis of this list, he shows that Middlesex and London (33,220), Essex (18,080), Surrey and Southwark (12,080) and Kent (11,150) contained the most Nonconformists, and even allowing for a growth in numbers, it probably reflects the pattern that existed for fifty years. He concludes, "one could hazard an estimate that Dissenters constituted no more than 4 percent of the English population in 1670."

7 Crosby, *History*, 3:144.

8 Keach, "A Trumpet Blown in Sion," *A Golden Mine Opened*, 48. W.T. Whitley identifies the street as Shakespeare's Walk but gives no evidence. W.T. Whitley, *The Baptists of London 1612–1928* (London: The Kingsgate Press, n.d.), 125.

exists, however, about the gift which Keach and his family received a decade or so later, in 1679, following another robbery. On being informed of this event, the Wapping church, pastored by Hercules Collins, responded. The minute book of the church for December 30, 1679, recorded, "Bro. Collings gave to Bro. Keach the Sum of three pound Eight Shillings which was gathered for him of the Church."[9]

The church register of births listing four daughters born to Keach once he came to London further confirms that he did not live in Southwark. The first three were born in 1673, 1675 and 1679, and in each case "S. Paul's, Shadwell," is given as the place of birth. A fourth daughter was born in White's Alley, Cripplegate in 1682, suggesting perhaps a further move for the family on the east side of London.[10]

Shadwell lies a few miles downstream from London Bridge on the north bank of the river. By choosing to live here, Keach would have had opportunity to be in contact with existing leaders in Particular or Calvinistic Baptist churches, men like William Kiffin, Hanserd Knollys, John Norcott and later Hercules Collins, all of whom lived in the area and became close friends of Keach.[11] These men were pastors of churches within a few miles of each other on the east side of London, north of the river Thames. Kiffin was a pastor of the church that met in Devonshire Square, Bishopsgate, while Knollys' congregation met in Whitechapel.

---

9 I am indebted to Steve Weaver for this information (http://pastorsteveweaver.wordpress.com/2012/01/26/christmas-1679-a-collection-for-benjamin-keach/: accessed January 26, 2012).

10 *Regester*, PRO, RG4/4188.

11 Hercules Collins succeeded John Norcott in Wapping. Keach would likely have had opportunity once again of meeting Matthew Mead, who was now based in Stepney, but I have found no evidence to substantiate this. For further information on Collins, see Michael A.G. Haykin and Steve Weaver, eds., *"Devoted to the Service of the temple": Piety, Persecution and Ministry in the Writings of Hercules Collins* (Grand Rapids: Reformation Heritage Books, 2007).

Arminian to Calvinist

In March 1676, Keach preached the funeral sermon for John Norcott, pastor of the Particular Baptist church in nearby Wapping. Previously, in 1674, Keach had joined with Norcott in commending a book by Josias Bonham of Byfield, Northamptonshire, encouraging believers to live a holy life.[12] Keach's contribution is characteristic of his later writings—his style is plain, direct and full of exhortations, but gives no indication of a recent change in thinking. Bonham was a Particular Baptist, and Keach was comfortable in commending his work, and Norcott was content to see his name placed alongside that of his younger friend. Although this commendatory epistle by Keach endorses Bonham's Calvinism, it does not shed any further light on how Keach came to adopt Calvinistic teaching. All it suggests is that Keach and Norcott were friends and that they were of one mind about the value of Bonham's book.

Keach had come to London from Buckinghamshire, where his roots were among the General Baptists. They held to Arminian teachings about salvation, suggesting that at the time of Keach's conversion in 1655, Matthew Mead may not have had much influence on Keach's own understanding of his conversion to Christ. By the early 1670s, Keach had come to regard these Arminian teachings as error and adopted what he believed were more biblical views of salvation, views that he was to believe, preach in his church and publish in his sermons for the rest of his life. The precise means that produced this change have never been entirely clear to subsequent generations, and nowhere does Keach give us the details of how he came to change his understanding. Thomas Crosby says it was the result of having

12 Josias Bonham, *The churches Glory: or, the Becoming Ornament: being a Seasonable Word, tending to the Provoking, Encouraging and Perfecting of Holiness in Believers* (London, 1674). Keach wrote a commendation and Norcott an epistle to the reader. It is possible that Keach knew Bonham before coming to London, as Byfield was but 20 to 25 miles from Winslow.

greater opportunity in London of "consulting both men and books," but never tells us which men and which books.[13] In a similar vein, Crosby is also tantalizingly vague about Keach's previous contacts in Buckinghamshire, relating that those "with whom he conversed...generally, tho' not all...went under the name of Arminians."[14] Crosby does not reveal the identity of the other men who were not Arminians, nor how they may have influenced him. However, Keach himself makes it clear that he had undergone a momentous change, and he attributed this change to the love of God toward him, and second only to his conversion in importance.

> Brethren, next unto the grace of God in my conversion, I have often said, I do look upon myself bound to admire the riches of God's love and goodness to me, in opening my eyes to see those Arminian errors, which when I was young, I had from some men of corrupt principles sucked in; nay, and when I was about 23 years old I wrote a little book for children, in which some of those errors were vindicated; which after my eyes were inlightened, and the book with alterations being again reprinted, I left out, and now do declare my dislike of the first impressions, and do disown what I there asserted: *When I was a child, I thought as a child, I understood as a child*, as the apostle speaks. And let me intreat you to study the nature of the covenant of grace; for until I had that opened to me, I was ignorant of the mysteries of the Gospel.[15]

13 Crosby, *History*, 4:271.

14 Crosby, *History*, 4:270. Crosby may have included here the preacher responsible for Keach's conversion. However Crosby nowhere identifies Matthew Mead as that particular preacher.

15 Keach, "The Blessedness of Christ's Sheep," *A Golden Mine Opened*, 314–315.

In this statement, Keach repudiates the errors he had included in *The Child's Instructor*, and tells us that when he rewrote it, he made a number of alterations that reflected these significant changes in his understanding. The most important statement here is the reference to the covenant of grace. The covenant of grace became the cornerstone of his theology, a conspicuous note repeated in many of his sermons and other writings. One such writing was published in 1698, a series of fourteen sermons based on Isaiah 54:10 called, *The Display of Glorious Grace: Or, the Covenant of Peace Opened.*

Before we consider the importance of the covenant of grace, it is necessary to trace some of the important events in Keach's life at this time, some of which had a bearing on his adoption of Calvinistic theology.

There is no real evidence from Keach's residence in Winslow to suggest that he had been a pastor with a church under his care, but when he came to London this changed. Fairly soon after his arrival, he was chosen and ordained as pastor of a congregation in Southwark that met in a private house in Tooley Street, a road that ran eastward, parallel to the river, immediately after crossing London Bridge. It was a small General Baptist congregation that had begun meeting in 1652, having separated from a larger church for some practices they judged to be disorderly. William Rider had been their recognized elder but had died some years earlier, perhaps in the plague.[16] In 1668, Keach was ordained as their pastor with prayer and the laying on of hands. W.T. Whitley claims that this was the first dissenting ordination in London, though this seems very unlikely.[17] Keach did not move to Southwark but journeyed from his home in Shadwell, perhaps walking the few miles, crossing by London Bridge, or paying the fare to one of the many watermen who provided crossings by boat across the River Thames.

---

16 Crosby, *History*, 4:272.

17 Whitley, *Baptists of London*, 110.

The Dutch cartographer Jacob de la Feuille first published this "novissima & accuratissima" (new and accurate) map of Angliae Regni Metropolis *(England's capital city) in Amsterdam in 1690.*

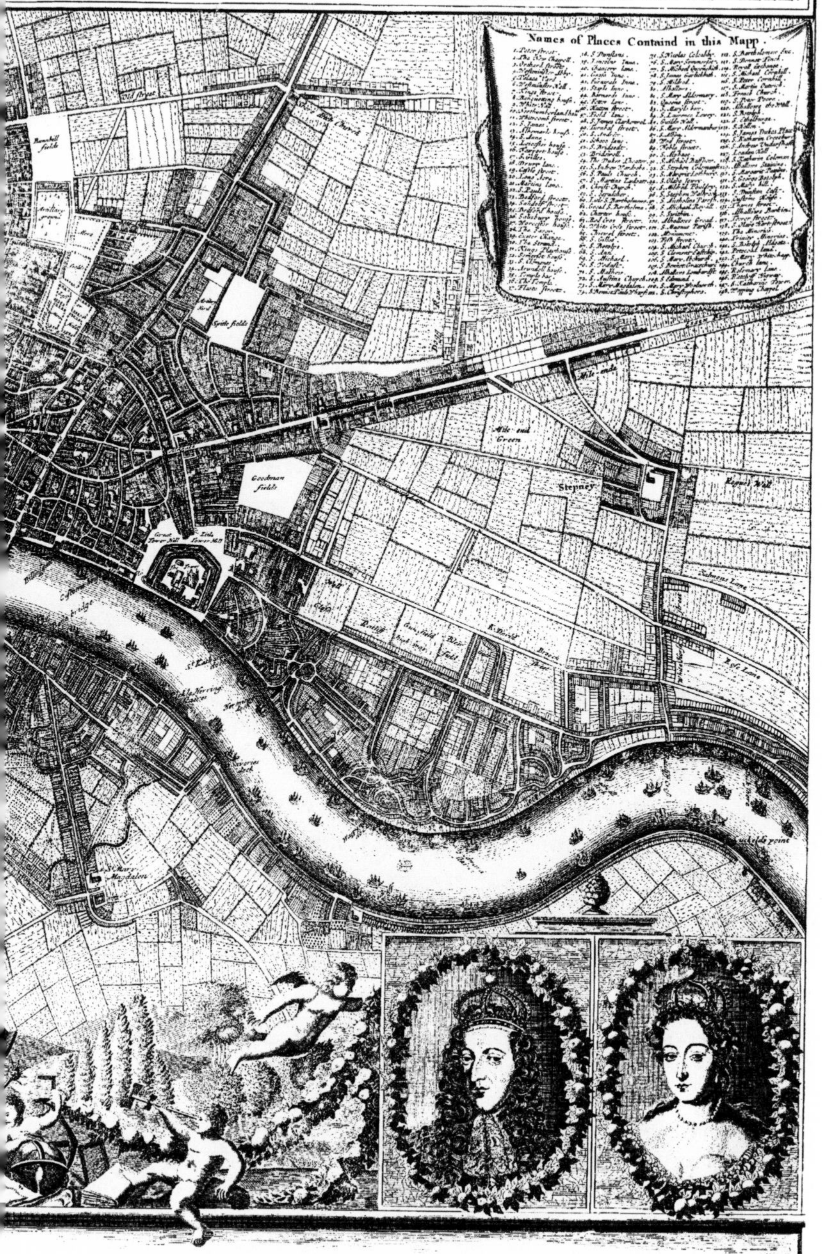

The map shows the sprawling metropolis of London, Westminster and Southwark during the joint reign of William III and Mary II (Southwark Council).

It is not clear precisely what happened to the congregation when Keach became a Particular Baptist. It is possible he persuaded the majority of them of the truth he had now come to believe, though Whitley says he split the church. However, there was a large enough congregation in 1672 to build a meeting-house in Horselydown, at the far end of Tooley Street. This was possible because there was a short lull in persecution when Charles II granted an Indulgence to Dissenters.[18] This group became the core of Keach's congregation for the remainder of his life, growing eventually into the largest Particular Baptist church south of the Thames. For Keach, the year 1668 was significant, for it marked the beginning of a ministry in Horselydown, Southwark, which was to last until his death thirty-six years later.

Keach had come to London with his wife Jane and three young children, Mary, Elias and Hannah. Mary, the eldest, was seven years old, but Hannah the youngest was only three when, in October 1670, Jane Keach died at the age of thirty-one, plunging the family into deep sorrows. Keach had come to London to find relief from the intensity of persecution, and now troubles from a very different source confronted him. Deeply moved by his loss, he took up his pen and composed a brief elegy as a memorial to his wife, called *A pillar set up*. He based this on Jacob's example recorded in Genesis 35:19–20, who—when his wife Rachel died—built a pillar of stones on her grave. The elegy has not survived, but Crosby has preserved the essence of the poem. It shows that Keach had a very high opinion of the Christian character of his wife and, in particular, keenly appreciated the

18 Charles II issued this Indulgence and all penal laws against Catholics and Dissenters were suspended. Many preachers took out licences and householders had their houses licenced for worship, and some, like Keach's church in Southwark, erected their own meeting-houses. Anglicans reacted strongly, and the king was forced to withdraw the Indulgence in 1673. For a summary of those who took out licences, see John Coffey, *Persecution and Toleration in Protestant England 1558–1689* (Harlow: Pearson Education Limited, 2000), 172.

faithful support she gave to him during his days of persecution in Buckinghamshire. In his poem, Crosby says, her husband:

> gave her a very great and noble character, commending her for her zeal for the truth, sincerity in religion, uncommon love to the saints, and her great content, in whatsoever condition of life, God was pleased to bring her to. He particularly observes, how great an help, and comfort she was to him, in his *suffering* for the cause of Christ, visiting, and taking all possible care of him, while in prison, instead of tempting him, to use any base means, for delivery out of his troubles, encouraging him to go on, and counting it an honour done them both, in that they are called to *suffer* for the sake of Christ. She was of an heavenly conversation, her discourse was savoury, and for the most part about divine things, seeking the spiritual good of those, with whom she conversed, and so successful was she herein, that some have acknowledged, that their conversion to God, was thro' the conversation they had with her.[19]

Now a widower and with three young children to raise, it is not altogether surprising that Keach married again eighteen months after the death of his first wife. The new Mrs. Keach was Susannah Partridge, herself only recently widowed. She was a year younger than Keach and was born in 1641 in Rickmansworth, Hertfordshire, a daughter of Henry and Elizabeth Skidmore.[20] It would seem that he met Susannah in London. One of the most interesting facts about the marriage is that it is recorded that they were married on April 22, 1672, by "Mr Han: Knowles."[21]

---

19 Crosby, *History*, 4:274.

20 *Regester*.

21 *Regester*.

This fact does not tell us whether Hanserd Knollys was the primary influence in moulding Keach's Calvinistic views, (i.e. whether he was one of those men Crosby mentioned, that Keach now had an opportunity to consult), or simply that he knew Keach well enough by 1672 to be responsible for marrying the new couple.[22] What it does confirm is that by 1672 Keach was moving in a much wider circle in London than just General Baptists. Keach and Knollys were to become close friends and worked together in London for many years until Knollys died in 1691. It has sometimes been suggested that Susannah herself was the catalyst for the change, but once again there is no clear evidence that this was definitely the case.[23]

Benjamin and Susannah Keach lived together as husband and wife for another thirty-two years, first in Shadwell, then perhaps in Cripplegate, before moving, probably after 1689, to a house in Freemans Lane in Southwark.[24] They lived together in great love and friendship and Thomas Crosby says of his mother-in-law that, "she was a woman of extraordinary piety, who had a good report of all; a most tender mother, and grandmother, and if she exceeded due bounds in anything, it was in her love and tenderness towards her children and grandchildren."[25]

---

22 Hanserd Knollys represented the mainstream of English seventeenth-century Particular Baptist thought and practice. See Barry H. Howson, *Erroneous and Schismatical Opinions: The Question of Orthodoxy Regarding the Theology of Hanserd Knollys (c. 1599–1691)* (Leiden: Brill, 2000) and Bustin, *Paradox and Perseverance: Hanserd Knollys, Particular Baptist Pioneer in Seventeenth-Century England.*

23 Alan Clifford, "Benjamin Keach and Nonconformist Hymnology." In *Spiritual Worship*, Westminster Conference, 1985, 72.

24 Keach sometimes put his address on the frontispiece of his books that were published after 1689, and occasionally signed a letter, "from my house in Freemans Lane." Freemans Lane can still be traced on early editions of Ordnance Survey maps but it was demolished to make way for the southern approach road for Tower Bridge in the 1890s.

25 Crosby, *History*, 4:275.

Susannah was to outlive her husband by twenty-three years, dying in February 1727 at the age of eighty-six. Besides becoming a mother to young Mary, Elias and Hannah, she bore her husband five daughters, four of whom survived: Elizabeth, born in 1673; Susannah, born in 1675; Rachel, born in 1679; and, Rebecca, born in 1682. It was the youngest daughter, Rebecca, who was to become the wife of Thomas Crosby.[26]

The significance of the covenant of grace

The covenant of grace assumed a central place in Keach's thinking, so much so that it is not possible to appreciate either Keach's Calvinism or the man himself without a right appreciation of his understanding of it. It is not possible to trace out the evolution of his thought throughout the 1670s and 1680s. Rather, we must focus on the maturer statements he made in sermons published in the 1690s, though some of them were first preached to his Southwark congregation at an earlier date. A comprehensive summary of Keach's teaching on the covenant of grace, gleaned from his works, provides a necessary introduction to this theme.[27]

The covenant of grace was not something theoretical to Keach, but rather immensely practical, something he firmly believed brought assurance, hope and comfort to those to whom he

---

26 *Regester*.

27 Keach, *The Everlasting Covenant, A Sweet Cordial for a drooping Soul: Or, The Excellent Nature of the Covenant of Grace Opened. In a Sermon Preached January the 29th. at the Funeral of Mr. Henry Forty, Late Pastor of a Church of Christ, at Abingdon, in the County of Berks. Who Departed this Life Jan. 25th 1693 and was Interr'd at Southwark* (London, 1693). This comprised two sermons on 2 Samuel 23:5. It began life as a sermon preached at the funeral of his friend Henry Forty, but by 1699 it was republished with a shorter title and the name of Forty excluded. Keach, "The Blessedness of Christ's Sheep," *A Golden Mine Opened*. This consists of sixteen sermons on John 10:27–28. Particular attention is drawn to 202–203 and 275–276. Keach, *The Display of Glorious Grace: or, the Covenant of Peace Opened. In Fourteen sermons lately preached in which the errors of the present day, about reconciliation and justification, are detected* (London, 1698). This contains fourteen sermons on Isaiah 54:10.

preached.[28] On a winter's day at the end of January 1693, he preached in Southwark at the funeral of a friend and fellow preacher Henry Forty (1625–1693), and chose to preach on the covenant of grace.[29] As he reached the climax of his sermon, he assured his hearers that the covenant of grace is a consolation to every Christian in whatever condition they find themselves:

> This Covenant stands firm, this Foundation of God is sure, it was established from all eternity by an Eternal act of God, that cannot be repeated, altered or changed: God is thine, Christ is thine, if thou hast Union with him, all is thine; and the Oath of God, the Truth and Faithfulness of God is engaged for the making good all the Blessings that are contained in this Covenant; God is thine and Christ is thine for ever.[30]

This brings us to the very heart of Keach's understanding of the covenant of grace. He laid great emphasis on this unbreakable and unchangeable covenant made in eternity between the Father and the Son—and through the Lord Jesus Christ, the Son—with the elect. This covenant could not be effective without the work of the Holy Spirit sealing all the blessings of the covenant to God's people in time. In detail, this meant that each person of the Trinity undertook to fulfill a distinct role in the covenant of grace. Keach believed that the Father took the initiative in establishing the covenant of grace. It was his eternal decree and electing love that underlay the sending of the Son and the Holy Spirit in order to bring salvation to this fallen

---

28 It should also be noted at this point that Keach's understanding of the covenant of grace profoundly influenced his treatment of baptism and justification by faith. Chapters 12 and 13 will cover these aspects of his theology.

29 Henry Forty spent twelve years in prison in Exeter for his faith and died in Abingdon, Oxfordshire. He had attended the 1689 National Assembly.

30 Keach, *The Everlasting Covenant*, 43.

sinful world, "The decree of God on his part is irrevocable...it is the high, unalterable and supreme law of heaven."[31]

The Son, Jesus Christ, said Keach, displays his glory in his deity and also in his love by undertaking to save sinners. It is the righteousness of the Son that provides the basis for the sinner's justification. And, it is the Son who continues to intercede for them in heaven so providing grace to persevere for all who believe in him. Finally, he taught that the Holy Spirit displays his glory by convincing sinners of their sin, by renewing them, by working God's image in them, by uniting them to Christ by faith, by sanctifying them and by working in them faith and love. All this, Keach concluded, was the result of the infinite wisdom and the inconceivable love and goodness of God. Therefore, any confidence of salvation was not founded on man but on God who had made an unbreakable and unchangeable covenant. And, it was the same God who took the initiative in salvation and undertook to ensure the salvation of all the elect.

Keach focused particular attention on Jesus Christ. He said that the covenant of grace was made primarily with him as the second person of the Trinity. He was the Mediator and was appointed as the root, the common head, the representative or surety in this covenant, for and on behalf of all that the Father has given to him, namely his elect.[32] The covenant between God, in the person of the Father, and Man, in the person of Christ, was the foundation of the covenant of grace.[33] As Mediator, in order to heal the breach caused by sin, Christ undertook to merit eternal life for his elect by his perfect obedience, to die in their place, to bear the wrath and curse due to their sin and bring them to glory, body and soul. Christ, as testator, confirmed and

---

31 Keach, "The Blessedness of Christ's Sheep," *A Golden Mine Opened*, 177.

32 "Surety" is a favourite term used by Keach. It means a guarantor.

33 Keach is here expressing what the *1689 London Baptist Confession of Faith* teaches, "This covenant...is founded in that eternal covenant transaction that was between the Father and the Son about the redemption of the elect," chapter 7, "Of God's Covenant."

ratified this covenant by the blood of the cross. The death of Christ was the price Christ paid to redeem his people:

> The Death of Christ was that Price by which all Grace is purchased for us...was the Pacifying, or Atoning Sacrifice, his Precious Blood quenched the fire of God's Wrath, and so it is the only way by which we come to be delivered from Hell: Our Jonah was cast overboard to make a Calm and caused the Storm of Divine Vengeance to cease.[34]

Finally, Keach says, it was the Holy Spirit who carries out and applies the covenant to God's people so that it is enjoyed in their experience. The Spirit's role is to ensure that all the legacies left in Christ's last will and testament are given to all believers. Therefore, it is his work to regenerate, sanctify and preserve, and to make the saints ready for their eternal inheritance, "the Holy Spirit is given to unite us to Christ, to quicken us, to illuminate our Minds, to renovate our Soul, to be our Guide, our Comforter, and to dwell in us for ever, and to seal all Covenant Blessings to us."[35]

Keach had his own vivid way of expressing the way in which the three persons of the Godhead fulfill their respective redemptive roles in the covenant of grace, using biblical metaphors:

> Salvation is called a garment...the Father may be said to prepare the matter which this robe is made of; the Son wrought it, he made the garment, and the Holy Spirit puts it on the soul; the garment of salvation is Christ's righteousness. Again, the Father sought out, or chose the bride, the Son espouses and marries her, but it is the

34 Keach, *Display of Glorious Grace*, 115–116.

35 Keach, *Display of Glorious Grace*, 238.

> Holy Ghost that inclines her heart and stirs up, nay that causes the soul to like and love this Blessed Lover, and brings it to yield and consent to accept heartily and willingly of Jesus Christ. We were sick of a fearful and incurable disease, and the Father found out the medicine; the blood of Christ is that medicine, and the Holy Spirit applies it to the soul. We were in debt, in prison, and bound in fetters and cruel chains, and the Father procured a Friend to pay all our debts; the Son was this our Friend, who laid down the infinite sum; and the Holy Spirit knocks off our irons, our fetters and chains, and brings us out of the prison-house. The Father loved us, and sent His Son to merit grace for us; the Son loved us and died, and thereby purchased that grace to be imparted to us; and the Holy Spirit works that grace in us. O what is the nature of this salvation; how great, how glorious! That the whole Trinity, both the Father, and the Son, and the Holy Ghost, are thus employed in and about it, that we might have it made sure to us for ever.[36]

Earlier it was pointed out that Keach was pre-eminently a man of the Bible. By adopting a Calvinistic theology Keach was, in his own appreciation of what was happening, coming to a fuller and clearer view of what the Bible actually teaches—what he referred to as "the mysteries of the Gospel."[37] At this point, we can better understand why Keach could say that while he remained ignorant of the covenant of grace he remained "ignorant of the mysteries of the Gospel." Keach identified the covenant of grace as lying at the heart of these "mysteries."

---

36 Keach, "The Great Salvation," *A Golden Mine Opened*, 382–383.

37 What has been described is a summary of what Keach believed, but the texts of Scripture that he expounded have been omitted for the sake of space and ease of reading.

Furthermore, we are now in a better position to appreciate Keach's Calvinism over against his former "Arminian errors," for he believed now in the sovereignty of God's grace in salvation. Keach came to the conviction that the Bible taught that it was God, through his Son Jesus Christ, who saved sinners from beginning to end, from election to glorification. He rejected such Arminian teachings as free will and universal redemption (the idea that Jesus Christ died to make possible the salvation of every man and woman). He would have concurred entirely with the *1689 London Baptist Confession of Faith* statements in chapter 8, sections 4 and 5 on "Christ the Mediator," and chapter 9, "Of Free Will."[38] Keach was one of the principal signatories of that *Confession* at the 1689 Assembly of Particular Baptists. Furthermore, he affirmed in another of his sermons that:

> It is no easy thing for a poor sinner to fall in love with Jesus Christ. It is not in the power of man's will, to tie this conjugal knot, or unite his heart to the Lord Jesus, but it must be by the agency of the mighty God, or by the power of the Holy Spirit; all moral persuasions, though never so strong and powerful, cannot do it any good, no, we must be drawn to Christ by the Father, and the effectual influences of the Holy Ghost, if ever we are united to Jesus Christ, the Spirit is the bond of this union.[39]

And to any who began to think that this made preaching the gospel a pointless exercise, or undermined the need for personal holiness of life, Keach was quick to aver as follows:

---

38 *Things most surely believed among us, The Baptist Confession of faith of 1689*. Nothing I have read of Keach would suggest any deviation from the teaching of the confession in these chapters.

39 Keach, "The Marriage Supper," *Parables Two*, 147–148.

> These men (those who say [there is] no point in preaching the gospel to sinners or pressing saints to holiness) dream of an election without the means, and of a salvation without faith and regeneration, and a preserving men to eternal life without a perseverance in grace and holiness: It is a perseverance in well-doing we plead for, and this we will say Christ will, in the use of means, not without it, enable all his people to do: He will help them, strengthen them and keep their souls alive.[40]

God has decreed not only the ends but also the means of salvation, and Keach preached the necessity of regeneration. He pleaded with sinners to believe on Christ and to repent of their sins and urged believers to pursue holiness of life.

Benjamin Keach was writing 300 years ago and our understanding of the covenant of grace has become more refined. The Bible does not use the term "covenant" to refer to an overarching "covenant of grace" that spans eternity and the whole of human history. It does not use the term "covenant" to describe the eternal counsels and agreements between the members of the Trinity. Rather, the Bible refers to covenants that God makes at certain points in history. There is a gradual unfolding of God's plan, as God made covenants with Abraham, with Israel through Moses and also with David before the promises of a new covenant, recorded in Jeremiah 31:31–34, all of which are fulfilled in the coming of the Lord Jesus Christ and the establishing of the new covenant.[41] Of course, none of this denies God's overarching

---

40 Keach, "Blessedness of Christ's Sheep," *A Golden Mine Opened*, 309.

41 For a contemporary Reformed Baptist understanding of the covenant of grace, see Samuel L. Waldron, *A Modern Exposition of the 1689 Baptist Confession of Faith* (Darlington: Evangelical Press, 1989), 105–122. See also: Alan Conner, *Covenant Children Today: Physical or Spiritual?* (Palmdale: Reformed Baptist Academic Press, 2007); Jeffrey D. Johnson, *The Fatal Flaw* (Conway: Free Grace Press, 2010); and *The Kingdom of God: A Baptist Expression of Covenant and Biblical Theology* (Conway: Free Grace Press,

plan of redemption and his decree to save sinners through his Son Jesus Christ. The terminology may differ today but this should not detract from Keach's presentation of the covenant of grace. His theology was essentially biblical, orthodox and Calvinistic. The covenant of grace was a subject that was very important to Keach. He was a preacher of God's gospel, consciously and prominently evangelistic in his thrust. He understood his Bible as meaning that preaching and the gospel ministry were essential parts of applying the reconciliation purchased by Jesus Christ. He was firmly persuaded that the salvation of sinners was found only in Jesus Christ and that this salvation came only because God, in his sovereign will and love, has been pleased to make a covenant of grace.

The notion of a "covenant of grace" did not originate with Benjamin Keach. It was a doctrine that came to be understood and expressed in the sixteenth century by the continental Reformers, in particular by Zacharias Ursinus (1534–1583) and Caspar Olevianus (1536–1587), who were developing the teachings of John Calvin.[42] It was Olevianus who expressed the idea of an eternal covenant between God the Father and God the Son for the salvation of man. The ideas of both the covenant of grace and the covenant of works made with Adam before the Fall were expressed in the *Westminster Confession of Faith* and the *Catechisms*, which were published in the 1640s when Keach was only a child.[43]

2014); W. Gary Crampton, *From Paedobaptism to Credobaptism: A Critique of the Westminster Standards on the Subject of Baptism* (Palmdale: Reformed Baptist Academic Press, 2010); Greg Nichols, *Covenant Theology: A Reformed and Baptistic Perspective on God's Covenants* (Birmingham: Solid Ground Christian Books, 2011); Earl M. Blackburn, ed., *Covenant Theology: A Baptist Distinctive* (Birmingham: Solid Ground Christian Books, 2013); and Pascal Denault, *The Distinctiveness of Baptist Covenant Theology* (Birmingham: Solid Ground Christian Books, 2013).

42 P.A. Lillback, "Covenant." In *New Dictionary of Theology*, eds. Sinclair B. Ferguson, David F. Wright, J.I. Packer (Leicester: InterVarsity Press, 1988), 173–175.

43 See *Westminster Confession of Faith*, chapters 7 and 8. Keach also taught the covenant of works. This spoke of a covenant of law between God and Adam in the

Those same ideas were expressed in the *Savoy Declaration* of the Independents and the *1689 London Baptist Confession* of the Particular Baptists.[44] Keach's contribution was not original, but there is no doubt that he was the single most important proponent of the covenant of grace among the Particular Baptists in the second half of the seventeenth century. Sometimes the impression is given that John Gill was the first Particular Baptist to formulate the doctrine of the covenant of grace, and to describe the different roles of the three persons of the Trinity.[45] However, this is clearly not the case.[46]

We will later take Keach's teaching a step further and examine how he understood the covenant with Abraham and the difference between the old and new covenants and how this had a direct bearing on his teaching and practice of believer's baptism and his doctrine of the church. Here, however, the covenant of grace as preached by Keach is summarized in order to explain what Keach regarded as the greatest change in his understanding of the gospel, second only to his conversion to Christ, and to show how he became a Particular or Calvinistic Baptist toward the beginning of his thirty-six-year ministry in Southwark.

---

garden of Eden that demanded perfect obedience on the part of Adam and promised life for obedience and threatened death for disobedience. Keach understood the covenant at Sinai and the giving of the law to be a republication of the covenant of works. In subsequent chapters, these matters will be considered in more detail. For understanding Keach more thoroughly in the sixteenth- and seventeenth-century context, and for Keach's exposition of the covenant of grace, see also Jonathan W. Arnold, *The Reformed Theology of Benjamin Keach (1640–1704)*, Centre for Baptist History and Heritage Studies, vol.11 (Oxford: Regent's Park College, 2013), 121–159.

44 *Savoy Declaration*, chapters 7 and 8, and *1689 London Baptist Confession of Faith*, chapters 7 and 8.

45 Richard A. Muller, "The Spirit and the Covenant: John Gill's Critique of the *Pactum Salutis*," *Foundations* 24, No.1 (January–March, 1981): 4–14.

46 This is not to say that Keach and Gill are identical in their formulation of the covenant of grace. The relationship between Keach's presentation and that of Gill is worthy of further consideration, but it is beyond the scope of this biography.

CHAPTER 5

"The times of the Ten hot Persecutions"

> Persecution is one of the ordinary trials of God's children ... is a thing common to the church in all ages then and now: therefore as they grow worse let us grow better; and let us be content to take the ordinary way, by the cross to come to the crown.[1]

When Benjamin Keach left Buckinghamshire in 1668, it was suggested that he left because he was a marked man and he would have greater opportunities for usefulness if he and his family moved to London. Being wedded to liberty of conscience and freedom to worship God, led to inevitable conflict with the civil and religious authorities, and Keach was prepared to break the law by meeting in forbidden conventicles and by publishing what was

1 Thomas Manton, *One Hundred and Ninety Sermons on the Hundred and Nineteenth Psalm*, 3 vols. (Edinburgh: Banner of Truth Trust, 1990), 3:366. Manton was a Presbyterian and was regarded as an outstanding Puritan preacher.

perceived to be seditious literature. In London, he followed a similar pattern of civil disobedience, together with other Dissenters, until the passing of the Act of Toleration in 1689. It thus follows that from the age of twenty until he was almost fifty Keach, endured persecution to some degree or other.

During the period of persecution that followed the new Conventicle Act in 1670, Keach expressed great fears and sorrows for what he perceived to be the true church of Christ not only threatened but actually under attack. Keach was also persuaded that the papacy—and all that was associated with it—was the underlying cause of the church's troubles and posed the main threat to her. At first sight, it may seem that Keach's position was extreme and without foundation, but there is evidence to show that his view was understandable and rational given the climate in which he lived.

It has already been noted that Keach regarded persecution by the state against a man or a woman because of their religion as unlawful—yet, at the same time, he *expected* to be persecuted. The Bible that he believed and lived by, told him that "...all who desire to live godly in Christ Jesus will suffer persecution" (2 Timothy 3:12). The view of Keach's Puritan contemporary, Thomas Manton (1620–1677), that "persecution is one of the ordinary trials of God's children," was a view shared by many Dissenters.[2] Keach himself adopted a very "positive" view toward persecution, stating that "persecution never does godly Christians any harm; they grow the more, not only in number but in goodness. It refines and purifies them, it purges and makes them white, they grow in faith, in patience."[3]

Persecution under the new Conventicle Act

In May 1670, the new Conventicle Act became law, leading to renewed struggles between the authorities and the Dissenters.

2 Manton, *One Hundred and Ninety Sermons*, 3:366.

3 Keach, *Types and Metaphors*, 755.

The new act was another attempt to tighten the noose around the neck of the Dissenters. It was more severe than the previous Conventicle Act.[4] Richard Greaves reports how Nonconformists poured into the capital in the spring of 1670, "knowing that if Conventicles may be prevented in London, they must of necessity lay downe in the Country."[5] The Lord Mayor reported that on one Sunday in May 1670, no less than 12,000 people attended conventicles.[6] Such vast numbers in attendance on this and similar Sundays made the implementation of the Conventicle Act by the justices of the peace a practical impossibility—no doubt that was the intent of those who gathered in this way. Notwithstanding this, several well-known London ministers were arrested in the weeks following the passing of the act, among them Thomas Manton, Richard Baxter, John Owen, Thomas Goodwin (1600–1680), William Kiffin, Hanserd Knollys and Edward Harrison (d.1689). The latter three were Particular Baptists, all of whom were soon to become close friends of Keach. However, Keach himself does not appear to have been arrested in the immediate wake of the new Conventicle Act.

It was not long, however, before Keach crossed swords with the authorities. Sometime after 1672, Crosby tells us that Keach was pursued for having printed another edition of his primer.[7]

---

4 The act prohibited conventicles of five or more persons, and one justice of the peace could convict without trial on the basis of a confession or sworn witnesses. A conventicler would be fined 5 shillings. for the first offence and 10 shillings for the second. For a minister, the fine was considerable: £20 for the first offense and £40 for the second. Anyone who allowed a meeting to take place in their house was subject to a £20 fine. Magistrates were authorized to use force to enter buildings where conventicles were being held. In order to ensure the law was being enforced, justices were liable to a £100 fine, and lesser magistrates to a £5 fine, for failing to prosecute conventiclers. The act also made provision for informers, who would be rewarded with a third of the fines levied.

5 Greaves, *Enemies Under His Feet*, 157.

6 Greaves, *Enemies Under His Feet*, 157.

7 Crosby, *History*, 3:146.

In 1664, all copies of his book, *The Child's Instructor*, had been destroyed, but it is clear Keach rewrote the book. Roger L'Estrange (1616–1704), Surveyor of the Press, implementing a policy of censorship against seditious literature on behalf of the king's government, was a staunch supporter of the Act of Uniformity and the subsequent legislation against Dissenters. He did not view his task of suppression as persecution, and John Coffey records his attitude to critics of the government's religious policy: "That which you call Persecution, I Translate Uniformity."[8] He had been operating a crusade against dissident printers and publishers since the early 1660s and was undoubtedly aware of Keach's activities in Buckinghamshire.[9] L'Estrange's campaign continued well into the 1670s and once again Keach fell foul of his efforts to suppress seditious literature, but this time in London. Crosby reports that Keach was actually a tenant of an informer named Cook, who on discovering the identity of Keach gave him protection from the authorities.[10] However, further efforts were made to prosecute Keach, and eventually he was forced to appear before Justice Glover, one of the local justices of the peace in Southwark. One of the members of Keach's church, John Roberts, a medical doctor, paid Keach's bail so that he did not have to go to prison. Eventually, Keach was fined £20, a sentence far lighter than the one he had received in 1664 for the same offence.[11]

Keach and his congregation were also pursued—along with many others—for continuing to meet in illegal conventicles. Once again Crosby records two instances, but gives no dates. Following a meeting in Jacob Street, and in another private

---

8 Roger L'Estrange, *Toleration Discuss'd* (London, 1663), 100, quoted in John Coffey, *Persecution and Toleration in Protestant England 1558–1689* (Harlow: Pearson Education, 2000), 27.

9 Greaves, *Enemies Under His Feet*, 167ff.

10 Was Keach using another name, or was he simply unknown to the informer?

11 Crosby, *History*, 3:146–147.

house down one of the numerous alleys in Southwark, the local constable came and seized six persons and brought them before Justice Reading, another justice of the peace operating in Southwark. He bound them over to appear at the next quarter sessions of the court.

On a second occasion, some of Keach's congregation were meeting in the house of a widow, Mrs. Colfe, in Kennington, two or three miles south of Southwark, in order to celebrate the sacrament of the Lord's supper. As the congregation were concluding their meeting by singing a hymn, the local officers of the peace burst in and all but one of the congregation escaped through the back door. The unfortunate individual was taken before a justice of the peace and imprisoned until his friends paid his bail. At the following quarter sessions, he was fined. However, attempts to arrest and fine Mrs. Colfe the permitted £20 for holding an illegal meeting in her home were not successful—probably as it was discovered that she was nursing someone with smallpox. Presumably the messenger was scared of catching the disease because he left rather rapidly, letting her be, and muttering oaths in the process.[12]

Persecution was neither continuous nor consistent in the 1670s and 1680s, but Keach himself likened persecution to the

---

12 Crosby, *History*, 3:145-146. Crosby gives no dates and a search through the Surrey Quarter Sessions records for these years confirms only the names of the justices of the peace concerned but not the appearance of Keach. This is a problem that I have faced constantly in trying to track down the actual prosecutions that Keach endured once he came to London. A search through the Quarter Sessions and the Surrey Assizes records for the period 1668–1689 has not produced the name of Keach. On the other hand, Southwark was clearly a hotbed of dissenting activity, and there are records of others such as Nathaniel Vincent (Presbyterian) and James Jones (who was, like Keach, a Particular Baptist) being prosecuted for meeting in the parish. At the time of writing, I have no answer to this perplexity. Crosby relates, "When the *indulgence* granted to *protestant* dissenters was removed, he was again very much harassed by his persecutors, and forced to remove from place to place for his security from their rage: and tho' the congregation, of which he was the pastor, were very careful to conceal themselves, yet they were twice disturbed."

scorching heat of the midday sun, referring to "the times of the Ten hot Persecutions," with the hottest of these being the last—from 1681 until 1686.[13] This period saw a return to excessive repression due to the further reinforcement of the second Conventicle Act. The Surrey Quarter Session records for these years show that Southwark was a favourite target for the authorities and that there were numerous convictions and fines by the justices of the peace.[14] We do know that Keach's name (spelled Mr Ceah) appears on a spy's list of London churches in connection with "about 350 pirtiler baptises" (presumably Particular Baptists).[15] His congregation is almost certainly included on a 1683 list of nearly seventy-five conventicles in London.[16] John Owen heads the list of dissenting ministers that includes Keach's friends, William Kiffin, Hanserd Knollys and Hercules Collins of Wapping.

Life was made even more difficult for the Dissenters during this period because of the intense activities of spies and

13 Keach, "The Sower," *Parables One*, 140. This assessment by Keach is confirmed by a modern historian. "The final years of Charles II's reign also saw the worst period of religious persecution in British history. In England, thousands of dissenters suffered heavy fines, imprisonment and even the loss of life (since not a few were to die in jail) for failing to conform to the Restoration Church." Tim Harris, *Revolution: The Great Crisis of the British Monarchy, 1685–1720* (London: Allen Lane, 2006), 28–29. Harris makes similar comments about the severity of persecution for Dissenters during the entire period of Charles II's reign. See Tim Harris, *Restoration: Charles II and his Kingdoms, 1660–1685* (London: Allen Lane, 2005), 424–425.

14 *Surrey Quarter Sessions* QS2/4-6 in Surrey History Centre, Woking. For example, at Southwark in December 1681, fines amounting to £9,680 were imposed on twenty-two dissenting ministers, *CSPD*, 1680–1681, 613. Among those fined were William Jenkins, Richard Steele, John Owen, Robert Ferguson. Thomas Watson, Thomas Doolittle, Samuel Annesley, Thomas Jacomb, Edmund Calamy and Matthew Mead. Benjamin Keach is conspicuous by his absence.

15 W.T. Whitley, "London Churches in 1682," *BQ*, 1 (1922–1923): 82–87.

16 W.T. Whitley, "London Conventicles in 1683" in *Transactions of the Congregational Historical Society*, III (1907–1908): 365–365. This was compiled around the time of the Rye House plot (intended to kill the king and the Duke of York).

informers. There was nothing new about spies and informers—they were active 1660 to 1689 as well—but the Second Conventicle Act rewarded their activities more generously.[17] The Hilton Gang was a notorious group of some forty people, including fifteen women, who monopolized London's informing trade in the early 1680s. The leader was the self-styled "Captain" John Hilton, a Catholic masquerading as a loyal Anglican, who has been described as "an odious thug...a bully, a liar, a drunk, a blackmailer and a rapacious fraudster."[18] Each Sunday, this gang disturbed meetings all over the City and Westminster from Wapping to the Strand and from Southwark to the Barbican. They targeted particular men, and particular meetings; they infiltrated meetings, used blackmail and extortion (those accused could pay the informer and avoid a court appearance), secured justice's warrants, were ready to give evidence in court and, if fines were not paid, turned to violence and broke down doors and shop hatches to secure and sell goods. They even managed to secure unofficial royal and church sanction. Hilton had an audience with Charles II and the Duke of York in May 1682 in which the king accepted the services of Hilton against Dissenters.[19] The Archbishop of Canterbury, William Sancroft (1617–1693), who had succeeded Sheldon in 1677, also seemed happy to promote their activities, telling the Quaker grocer, George Whitehead (who was instrumental in the downfall of the Hiltons) that "there must be some crooked timber in building a ship."[20]

---

17 Informers received one third of the offender's goods and chattels (personal property other than land and buildings).

18 Mark Goldie, "The Hilton Gang and the Purge of London in the 1680s." In *Politics and the Political Imagination in Later Stuart Britain*, ed. Howard Nenner (Rochester: University of Rochester Press, 1997), 43.

19 Goldie, "Hilton Gang," 46.

20 Goldie, "Hilton Gang," 43.

Keach's response to persecution

How did Benjamin Keach respond to this ongoing persecution? We have already pointed out that he endured persecution in varying degrees for nearly thirty years during the prime of his life. Furthermore, we should remember that during these years, in addition to his pastoral responsibilities for his flock in Southwark, he had family responsibilities to fulfill. With his re-marriage in 1672, his family continued to grow as four more children were born. His response to persecution was measured and sober, one of patient and prayerful perseverance. Persecution did not take him by surprise; rather, he regarded it as "normal" for a Christian—especially for a Christian who was also a preacher of the gospel of the Lord Jesus Christ. The events from 1660 to 1689 confirmed to him what the Scriptures taught about suffering for his faith, and they also served, in his mind, to confirm the dream he had as a young man. He understood that he must suffer hard things for the sake of Christ. This did not mean that he passively endured suffering. As we have seen, he continued to attend and to preach at illegal meetings and to publish his "seditious" books. Moreover, he longed for the day when the true church of God, as he understood it, would be delivered from her present troubles and enjoy liberty of conscience and freedom to worship according to that conscience.

Persecution was not the only matter that weighed heavily on the heart of the Southwark pastor, though it drew deep sighs from him. It was another subject, closely related, which drew a great deal of writing from his pen. Benjamin Keach possessed a tender and sensitive heart, one that genuinely grieved over the state of the nation. At the same time, he was filled with a desire for the honour of God. The precise content of Keach's 1666 edition of *Sion in Distress: Or, the Groans of the Protestant Church* cannot be recovered, but the second edition, published in 1681, had been enlarged to include commentary on events such as the "Popish plot" of 1678. Keach's dialogue in verse considered, in a broad way, the dangers threatening the church and did not focus exclusively on persecution.

Sion in Distress begins by taking the form of a conversation between grieving "Sion" (symbolizing the church of Christ) and "Sion's friend" and relations (representing those, like Keach, who were deeply concerned about the state of the church). Sion's friend asks questions about the condition of the church and these are then answered by Sion. "Sion's children" are then drawn in, expressing sympathy for their mother.

It is in this first section that we find Keach expressing his fears for the church and the nation. He was persuaded that the England of his day was a very favoured nation, privileged to hear many gospel preachers and sermons—yet he felt that so many of those sermons seemed ineffective in bringing their hearers to repentance, like a sword that had lost its cutting edge:[21]

> A General Heat did warm this Happy Nation,
> From its benign and pow'rful Operation:
> But now it falls! and from our Horizon
> Its vig'rous influence is almost gone.
> Thousands of Sermons lately have been preacht,
> But very few (if any) sinners reacht.
> How ineffectual is the quick'ning word!
> It shines, but warms not; its but like a Sword
> That's fair to sight, but has no Edge at all;
> Few prick'd at heart! and scarce do any fall

21 Keach did not set out primarily to write good poetry but rather to express the burden of his heart. However, he chose to write in the style similar to Dryden, and Swift, his contemporaries. The style is iambic pentameter, with rhyming couplets, in which sense and rhythm count more than rhyme. There are usually five "beats" to a line with the accent falling on the parts in bold print. For example:

> How **oft**/do **Par**/ents **Ill**/ Exam/ple **draw**
> Their **ten**/der **Chil**/dren **to**/ in**fringe**/ the **Law**.

Keach was not always consistent and at times the rhythm and rhyme is forced.

At Jesus feet! or have a sence of Sin,
Confessing how rebellious they have bin![22]

We have already drawn attention to Keach's grief over the way in which the dreadful divine warnings experienced in the plague and the fire in the second half of the 1660s had been scorned. He believed that sin had rendered the nation liable to God's judgements, both temporal and eternal. And, moved by compassion, he believed he should warn those who refused grace and slighted repentance, and call them to repentance, turning them away from their sins to find forgiveness from God through faith in Christ. Some years later, after the Glorious Revolution of 1689, he warned his congregation that:

> Gospel-Sins are the greatest Sins.... O what will they do in the Day of Judgement, that live in England, in London, in a Land and City of so great Light, and perish through their Sin, and Contempt or Neglect of Gospel-Grace![23]

It should not surprise us that Keach groans not only over the rejection of the gospel by so many but over the other sins of the nation. The debauched court of Charles II at Whitehall seemed to set the tone for the nation. Bishop Gilbert Burnet (1643–1715), who personally knew the king, summed up his character in three words, "wit, hypocrite and profligate."[24] Keach's dialogue does not mention the king in person but, nevertheless, it is part of what has been described as "a powerful nonconformist attack on libertinism."[25] Nonconformist sensitivities were offended, on the

---

22 Keach, *Sion in Distress*, 36.

23 Keach, "The Great Salvation," *A Golden Mine Opened*, 495.

24 Gilbert Burnet, *History of his own time: From the restoration of Charles II to the treaty of peace at Utrecht, in the reign of Queen Anne* (London, 1837), 61.

25 Timothy Harris, *London Crowds in the Reign of Charles II* (Cambridge: Cambridge University Press, 1987), 80.

one hand, by the declining moral standards found in the royal court and society as a whole and, on the other hand, by the oppression of "Sion":

> For Nonconformists, what was happening at Court was just symptomatic of a more widespread decline in public morals affecting society as a whole. There was an increase in brothels, in playhouses, in drunkenness and debauchery in general. In their eyes, all sorts of sins were being tolerated and even openly encouraged, whilst the godly, who merely wanted to worship God peacefully in their own way, were being victimized by harsh laws.[26]

For Keach it was time to call England to awaken out of its spiritual sleep. In his verse, he expresses his grief over the excesses of wealth, the sins of the tongue expressed in oaths and blasphemies, drunkenness and immorality among men and women, even though he does not at this point turn his pen against the court of Charles II.[27]

> Each Sex is bad, but Women seem to be
> The very Brokers of Immodesty;
> Which makes that passage to be born in mind,
> A wise and vertuous Woman who can find?
> Your City-Dames and Ladies are on fire
> With wanton passion, and unchaste desire;
> Providing Meats on purpose to inflame

---

26 Harris, *London Crowds*, 80.

27 Harris, *London Crowds*. 80. Others did rebuke the king and his court personally but were not well received. Harris relates two separate occasions when the sins of the court were condemned in sermons. The first was on Christmas Day, 1662, in a sermon by the Bishop of Winchester that drew laughter from his congregation and the second, in 1667, in a sermon by the Archbishop of Canterbury where he personally reproved the king's adultery and refused him holy communion on that account—costing him favour at court.

Their pamper'd Gallants to their wonted shame.
Bare Brests and Naked Necks, a Harlots Dress,
Are strong Temptations unto Wickedness.[28]

In addition, his soul was wearied over the "wretched atheists" and "Atheistick Sophistry" that seemed so prevalent.[29]

Domestic strife was another cause of grief to Keach. He observed that sometimes the homes of the godly are worse than those of heathens because the atmosphere was too often characterized by civil war and arguments:

Ah! why can't Saints in Familys eschew
That which meer Heathens are asham'd to do?
Their Houses are the Scene of Civil Wars,
Of Brawls, of Discord, and Domestick Jars.
In grace or comfort can they find increase,
Or Heavenly Blessings, who are void of Peace?[30]

He complains that parents are too often poor role models for their children to follow and that some ill-treat their children either by being too lenient or too severe:

How oft do Parents Ill Example draw
Their tender Children to infringe the Law
And Sanctions of the Everlasting God:
Do they not spoil them when they spare the Rod?
To strict Extremes some Parents do adhere,
Check not at all, or else are too severe:

---

28 Keach, *Sion in Distress*, 13.

29 Keach, *Sion in Distress*, 14–15. These are the words used by Keach, though it could be debated how widespread the philosophical position was in the 1680s. Keach appears to be using the terms with reference to the practical conduct of men and women contrary to the law of God.

30 Keach, *Sion in Distress*, 25.

On Back and Belly they bestow much Cost,
But care not if their Precious Souls be lost:[31]

In the professing church he finds hypocrisy; greed is sometimes discovered among pastors; many offer false worship to God; there are sad divisions among the saints:

Is there no Room for Love? or must that grace
Among my Children, have no proper place?
Why must one Saint be angry with his Brother
If not so tall as he? or with another,
Because his Face is not so white as his?
Or that his Habit not so gawdy is?
Alas! no Folly can be more absurd,
Nor more exploded in Gods Holy Word.
All should to Gospel-Purity adhere;
But to calumniate, villifie and jeer
All such as are not of their very pitch,
Is Anti-Gospel, and a practice which
The Lord abhors: If Causes of dissent
Evert not Truth, and shake the Fundament
Of True Religion, why such angry brawling?
Such Odious Nick-names? and such vile miscalling?[32]

As Keach develops his dialogue, he argues that the answer to all of Sion's troubles is to wait patiently on God. As her prayer is heard, Christ comes with comfort and with promises of deliverance.

The Roman Church, the real enemy

The dialogue moves on to consider the Roman Catholic Church and the pope as the greatest cause of Sion's distress. He outlines

31 Keach, *Sion in Distress*, 25.

32 Keach, *Sion in Distress*, 31.

the characteristic marks that identify "the beast": apostasy, the usurping of political power, the counterfeiting of true holiness, deception and false doctrine, claims to possess the keys of the kingdom, the practice of miracles and lying wonders and, finally, persecution of the true church.

> 'Tis He that aims at th' utter Dissolution
> Of precious Saints, by Bloudy Persecution,
> That does pronounce no Christian fit to live,
> Unless they do his Beastly Mark receive.[33]

Keach believed that Rome was the greatest cause of the church's troubles and lists what he believed to be the crimes of the Roman Church. He particularly identifies her persecution of the godly, before going on to describe her trial before "Justice" and the judgement seat of God and the final sentence that God passes against her. As will be seen, such a view of the Roman Church was typical of the Protestant dissenting opinion of these years.

> This Church herein hath driven such a trade,
> That thousands, broiling Martyrs she hath made.
> She sets the Pope above the holy one,
> The great Jehovah and his blessed Son.
> 'Tis she declares him Universal Head,
> 'Tis she forbids the Bible to be read.
> 'Tis she that first did from the Faith depart,
> 'Tis she that wounded Sion to the heart.
> 'Tis she hath been the occasion of all evil,
> 'Tis she advanc'd the Doctrine of the Devil.
> 'Tis she that taught her Sons to swear and lie,
> To vouch great falshdods,[34] and plain truths deny.

---

33 Keach, *Sion in Distress*, 61.

34 Falsehoods.

'Tis she that did forbid the Marriage Bed,
Whilst her vile Clergy such ill lives have led.
Was it not she that Canon did create,
Commanding plainly to abstain from meat,
Which God gave licence unto all to eat.
If from this charge she can her self defend,
Then may she make the Judge and Law her friend
Or if she can produce another tribe,
To whom we may this Character ascribe;
With greater clearness than we do to her,
We will consent her Sentence to defer.[35]

Why did Keach place the blame for the troubles of the Protestant church on the pope and the Roman Church? Were not their troubles caused by the reactionary measures adopted by a restored monarchy and a restored Church of England? We have noted that with the passing of the years, Charles II had not kept the promises he made to "tender consciences" in 1660. Why then should the blame be laid at the door of the Roman Church?

In 1689, Keach enlarged his poem again to take account of events in the 1680s, culminating in the 1689 Revolution. This new version was dedicated to William and Mary whom he viewed as deliverers from the twin monsters of popery and arbitrary government. Keach joined the chorus of voices who saw the events of 1688 and 1689 and, in particular, the coming of William of Orange, as a national deliverance from popery brought about by the providence of God. This final version contains several hymns of praise to God on this account. The full title for this third volume was, *Distressed Sion Relieved: Or, the Garment of Praise for the Spirit of Heaviness, wherein are discovered the grand causes of the churches trouble and misery under the late dismal dispensation. With a compleat history of and lamentation for*

35 Keach, *Sion in Distress*, 111–112.

those renowned worthies that fell in England by Popish rage and cruelty from the year 1680 to 1688. Together with an account of the late admirable and stupendous providence which hath wrought such a sudden and wonderful deliverance for this nation and God's Sion therein. In the dialogue, written in the same form as the earlier editions, Keach described the lot of Protestant Dissenters in the days of the hottest persecution, from 1681 to 1686:

> But to return; nothing for many years
> Is seen but Persecution, Blood and Tears
> No liberty at all Conscience it must have,
> But the Dissenters Prison proves his Grave,
> Where hundreds of them lay long buried,
> Whilst others of their Goods were plundered.
> Many in filthy Jayles so long did lye,
> That poisoned with the stench they there did dye.
> Law and Religion both were trampled down,
> And most good men term'd *Enemies to the Crown.*
> Charters of Towns and Cities ta'en away,
> That Popery and Slavery might bear sway.
> No stone was left unturn'd, whereby they might
> Bring on poor *England* an Eternal night
> Of Popish darkness: many therefore fled,
> Whilst others were strangely dis-spirited.
> Divers good Magistrates were laid aside,
> And wicked men for Judges they provide,
> Void of all fear of God, who any thing
> Would give for Law, they thought would please the King.
> Did a Dissenter Law or Justice crave?
> He's branded for a Rascal, Rebel, Slave.[36]

36 Keach, *Distressed Sion Relieved*, 18–19.

In the title, he mentions "popish rage and cruelty," and in these lines Keach refers to "an eternal night of Popish darkness," effectively equating popery with slavery. What grounds did Keach have for such concerns and fears? Was it rational for a man such as Keach to think in these terms? Was he looking for a scapegoat or was he suffering from a form of religious paranoia?

Christopher Hill points out that the identification of the pope as the "Antichrist" and of Rome as "Babylon" was not only deeply ingrained in the radical mind inherited by late seventeenth-century Dissenters from earlier generations of Protestants, but was also the conviction of many Church of England bishops—and no less a person than James I, the first Stuart king of England.[37] In the late Middle Ages, John Wycliffe and the Lollards had made that same link and, at the time of the Protestant Reformation, Martin Luther, John Calvin and others, reinforced this conviction. The great majority of the Dissenters were convinced that the Bible taught that the pope was Antichrist, and this found expression in their confessions of faith.[38] Furthermore, this conviction was reflected not only in the teaching of John Owen, the leading dissenting theologian of the period, but also in the sermons of a whole group of preachers who discoursed regularly in London, at Cripplegate and Southwark, during the days of persecution.[39] Furthermore, many of these men were convinced that

---

37 Christopher Hill, "Antichrist and his Armies," In his *The English Bible and the Seventeenth-Century Revolution* (London: Penguin, 1993), 315.

38 See Chapter 26, paragraph 4 of *The 1689 London Baptist Confession of Faith*. Similar statements are to be found in the *Westminster Confession of Faith* of the Presbyterians and the *Savoy Declaration of Faith* of the Independents.

39 W. Robert Godfrey, "Millennial Views of the Seventeenth Century and Beyond." In *God Is Faithful* (London: Westminster Conference, 1999), 8; *Puritan Sermons 1659–1689, Being the Morning Exercises at Cripplegate, St Giles in the Fields and in Southwark by seventy-five ministers of the Gospel in or near London* (Wheaton: Richard Owen Roberts, 1981), 5:547–727, 6:1–622. John Owen, the acknowledged leader of the Independents, believed that the persecuting nature and subsequent destruction of both the Roman Empire and the Roman Catholic Church were prophesied and depicted in the book of

the overthrow of the Roman Catholic Church was imminent.[40] Benjamin Keach was not a lone voice in this regard but one of the many voices of Protestant dissent in the 1670s and 1680s. Whereas others chose to preach and write against popery, Keach also expressed his convictions and concerns in his poetry. His assurance that popery was to be equated with evil is reflected in the sentence passed by God on Rome that Keach describes in one of the few parts of the dialogue that is written in prose:

> Rome! Thou hast been indicted by the Name of Mystery Babylon, Mother of Harlots, Scarlet-coloured Whore, False Church, and Pretended Spouse of Jesus Christ; and thou art found Guilty of all the Horrid and Prodigious Crimes following: That thou didst Apostatize from the Holy Religion of God and his Son Jesus Christ, and didst advance the Pope or Man of Sin, and hast Sacrilegiously

---

Revelation. He thought that the time for the prophecy to be fulfilled was close and that some of the first-fruits were being seen in England, where loyalty to Christ and his kingdom was replacing loyalty to prelates and tyrannical government. He looked therefore for the shattering of antichristian rule, government and worship. See John Owen, *The Works of John Owen*, 16 vols. (London: Banner of Truth Trust, 1965–1968). Volume 14 focuses particularly on the popish controversy, but volume 8 also contains a number of sermons related to popery.

40 Keach, *Sion in Distress*, 42–43. Keach adds explanatory notes at this point, saying that "the Beast" had been a mortal foe for 1,200 years and was identified with the "man of sin" in 2 Thessalonians 2:3. Drawing from several sources, but notably from Peter du Moulin (1568–1658), *The Accomplishment of the Prophecies* (1613), Keach believed that the Beast began his forty-two months or 1,250 prophetical days or years between A.D. 356 and A.D. 455, and therefore his end must soon come. Keach thus expected a glorious revolution in this present age, and du Moulin affirmed that the persecution of the church under the pope would end around 1689. The book of Revelation was interpreted by the majority of Dissenters as a prophecy of church history with a fulfillment of the events in Revelation 17–19. Earlier in the seventeenth century, there had been a consensus of opinion that Christ's return was to be expected between 1650 and 1656. The precise starting date, to which 1,250 was added, depended on the precise dating of Antichrist's power, namely the beginning of papal power in Rome. See Godfrey, "Millennial Views," *God Is Faithful*, 7–12.

> attributed and given to him those Names and Titles which belong only to God, and the Great Emanuel, magnifying his Decrees in wicked Councils above the Laws of God, and hast made void the Laws and Constitutions of the Gospel; making the Church National, and forming whole Kingdoms into one Universal Church.... Thou hast been guilty of shedding a mighty mass of innocent Blood, by cutting off Millions of Men, Women and Children without cause, and many other unspeakable Enormities hast thou committed. For all which horrid Crimes thou hast been Legally Indicted and Tryed, and against which thou hast made no defence: And therefore by the Laws of God, Nature and Nations, thou oughtest to be Punished....[41]

Was such a sentence justified? Were these the opinions of a religious bigot? It would be easy to dismiss Keach's understanding as irrational, but that would not do justice either to Keach or to his fellow Dissenters.[42] To dismiss this opinion out of hand, and to show no sympathy whatsoever for their interpretation, flies in the face of actual historical events and, as Coffey comments, "The idea of a Counter-Reformation design against English Protestantism was far from absurd, and we should resist the temptation to treat Protestant fear as irrational paranoia."[43]

The perceived threat of "popery"

We must therefore turn to consider the causes of the Protestant church's troubles and investigate the grounds for Keach's

41 Keach, *Distressed Sion Relieved*, 149.

42 Some modern Protestants still identify the pope with Antichrist. Others question that assertion, the present writer among them. I would share Keach's convictions about the apostate condition of the Church of Rome and reject entirely the false claims of the pope to be head of the church, for that title belongs to the Lord Jesus Christ alone. However, I would disagree with Keach on exegetical grounds and therefore would not identify the pope as *the* Antichrist, or *the* Man of Sin, but rather as *an* antichrist.

43 Coffey, *Persecution and Toleration*, 185.

contention that "popery" was the underlying cause. In doing so, it is important to bear in mind that Keach was writing not only as a Particular Baptist, but also as a Protestant Dissenter, and that the sorrows he expressed and the prayers that he uttered for the church concerned the Protestant Reformation cause. Richard Greaves has argued "perhaps no issue aroused more concern in British politics in the period 1673–1688 than James' Catholicism, particularly as it was a convenient symbol of court policies deemed by many to threaten traditional liberties and Protestant convictions."[44] Tim Harris has made the same point even more strongly than Greaves. He has concluded that "To all intents and purposes he [James II] did seek to establish Catholic absolute monarchy across his three kingdoms," and that the Glorious Revolution undoubtedly did save England, Scotland and Ireland from Catholic absolutism, "or, to put it in the contemporary parlance, it saved the three kingdoms from popery and arbitrary government."[45]

It is necessary at this point to provide the historical background to explain how James' Catholicism triggered fresh fears of popery in the minds of Englishmen, both Nonconformist and those within the Anglican Church. Attempts to prevent the future James II from becoming king became part of the political agenda in the late 1680s. It needs to be remembered that the 1688 invitation to William of Orange to intervene by force in the nation's affairs was not issued by Protestant Dissenters but by disaffected "notables," who were Anglicans, and included the Earl of Danby and Robert Compton, the Bishop of London.[46] The Protestant Dissenters rejoiced in the arrival of William and

44 Greaves, *Secrets of the Kingdom*, 1.

45 Harris, *Revolution: The Great Crisis of the British Monarchy*, 484–485.

46 Coffey, *Persecution and Toleration*, 190, and Greaves, *Secrets of the Kingdom*, 321. The seven disaffected notables were: Sir Henry Sidney; Edward Russell, Admiral; the Earl of Devonshire; Danby, the Earl of Shrewsbury; Lord Lumley; and Robert Compton, Bishop of London.

saw him, under God, as the deliverer of both the nation and the church. But, they were not instrumental in the actual events that surrounded his arrival at Torbay, England, in 1688, or in his eventual succession to the throne of England in April 1689.

By considering the historical background, one is able to see the precise context for Keach's analysis of the dangers facing the church. Whatever conclusions the reader might draw as to the rightness or wrongness of Keach's interpretation of events, one has to reckon with the fact that no historical figure can escape the context in which he or she lives. To some extent, all are coloured by the prevailing opinions of the day. The contemporary student of this era reads Keach with the benefit of 300 years of hindsight and has access to information and insights that were not available to him.

What was it that fuelled new fears of popery? In 1672, when Charles II issued the Declaration of Indulgence he had a "hidden agenda." The indulgence granted Dissenters the right to meet for worship and build meeting-houses providing they had a license. But, in addition, Catholics were also granted liberty to worship in private houses. His actions aroused suspicion and provoked opposition by members of Parliament. They forced the king's hand and secured the Test Act in 1673, excluding Catholics from holding public office. 1673 was a key turning point in events of this period, proving that anti-Catholic feelings in England were not dead but rather, like a dormant volcano, stirring and about to erupt. James, Duke of York, first in line to the throne, was a convert to Catholicism. When he married Mary of Modena, an Italian Catholic, English Protestants were confronted with a very disturbing prospect—a line of Catholic kings. These feelings were stirred in the exclusion crisis and then erupted when James II became king, following the death of Charles II in 1685.

Suspicions about Charles II's "hidden agenda" had arisen in 1670 when the Catholic king of France, Louis XIV, had signed the Treaty of Dover with Charles II. If the secret contents of that treaty had been revealed, the crisis would have erupted sooner. In the treaty, Charles had agreed with Louis XIV to go to war against Protestant Holland, grant toleration to Catholics (which he attempted to do in the 1672 Indulgence) and declare himself a Catholic when the time was ripe. Events in Catholic France did little to bolster confidence among English Protestants. They remembered only too well the St. Bartholomew's Day massacre of 1572 and the subsequent struggles of the Protestant Huguenots of France. The liberties of the Huguenots had been eventually secured in 1598 with the Edict of Nantes, but this security had been gradually stripped away over the course of the seventeenth century—and eventually ripped away in 1685 when Louis XIV revoked the Edict. This action created well over a quarter of a million refugees, driving the majority of the Huguenots out of France. Many of them came to England where they formed a visible representation of the effects of Catholic persecution. Many wondered whether what had happened in France could happen in England. Such events further fuelled Protestant fears of popery, arbitrary government and the threat of tyranny with absolute power now in the hands of a new Catholic king, James II.

English Protestant memories were long, not only in remembering events in France, but also in recalling what had happened the last time a Catholic sat on the throne of England. The persecutions of English Protestants by "Bloody" Mary (r.1553–1558) were etched into their consciousness and had been faithfully recorded by John Foxe (c.1516–1587) in his famous *Book of Martyrs*. Furthermore, other events were equally imprinted on English minds: Catholic Spain's attempt to overthrow Elizabeth I with an invading armada in 1588; the Gunpowder Plot of 1605; and, the massacre of Protestants in Ireland in 1641. Catholics were also suspected of being responsible for the Great Fire in 1666 that devastated so much of the city of London. In this environment, it is not surprising that the views of Keach and his Protestant contemporaries were shaped by these events and many other persecutions that Rome had perpetrated against "Sion."

Keach had written the second version of *Sion in Distress*, following "the uncovering" of the "Popish plot" in 1678.[47] He had hoped that a better day was dawning but was disappointed and could see only what he regarded as the ominous advance of Roman darkness. The plot of 1678 was actually hatched by Titus Oates and Israel Tong and purported to be a Catholic plot to assassinate Charles II and stamp out Protestantism. The justice of the peace who received Oates' deposition, Sir Edmund Godfrey, was mysteriously murdered and again Catholics were the prime suspects. Keach was in no position to judge the reliability of Oates' story, and, like many others, believed the whole account. He included it in his poem as evidence that Rome remained intent on the persecution and—if possible—the destruction of Protestantism. The announcement of a Catholic plot only served to promote rumours of Catholic invasions, of further fires in London and, eventually, led to severe reprisals against Catholics.[48] Charles II was in danger of losing control of the situation.

By 1681, though, Charles II had regained the lost ground and successfully resisted all attempts to have his brother excluded from succession to the throne. Furthermore, the Anglicans in power had time to regain a sense of perspective. Recalling that the nation had been drawn into civil war the last time Puritans had expressed anti-popish feelings in 1642, they believed Dissenters were actually the real troublemakers and engineered renewed and severe persecution under the terms of the Conventicle Act (1681 until 1686). All these events seemed to

---

47 A full assessment of the Popish plot and its significance can be found in Greaves, *Secrets of the Kingdom*, 5–52. Of the plot, he concludes, "...no serious historian now questions the fact that the Popish Plot was manufactured by Oates and Tong."

48 Coffey, *Persecution and Toleration*, 173, and Greaves, *Secrets of the Kingdom*, 8–9, 15–20.

increase the conviction of Keach and his dissenting friends that popery was the real enemy.

Moreover, further evidence soon came to light in the revengeful ways that Charles II responded to the Rye House Plot of 1683 and James II to the Monmouth uprising of 1685. Such events proved the threat of tyranny to be very real.

From 1681, Charles II could have been charged with acting "illegally," because from March 1681 until his death in 1685 he reigned without ever calling a Parliament. He thus left the Dissenters without any protection and exposed to the full force of royal vengeance. The Rye House Plot and the Monmouth uprising were really acts of desperation on the part of some Dissenters who could not see any way out of their dilemma. In particular, the cruel and vicious manner in which the Lord Chief Justice, Sir George Jeffreys (1645–1689), exercised his powers only served to confirm Keach's views about the dangers of arbitrary rule. Sympathetic readers of Keach's dialogue must have managed a wry smile of agreement when they read the following dart of sarcasm thrown at Jeffreys:

> But of my joys I must forbear to sing,
> A doleful noise seems in my Ears to ring,
> And still grows louder; sure 'tis from the West;
> What's that I see? a cruel savage Beast!
> A Man? no sure a Monster; though he came
> Of Humane Race, he don't deserve that name,
> A cursed Spirit of th' Infernal Legion.[49]

In his third and much-modified version of the poem, written in 1689, he chronicles the injustice following the Rye House affair and the Monmouth uprising. These events cost the lives of a significant number of men and women from 1681 to 1688,

---

49 Keach, *Distressed Sion Relieved*, 21.

though it was perhaps a little pretentious of him to refer to it as "a compleat history."[50] While one or two, like Stephen College (*c.*1635–1681), suffered for other reasons, Keach's poem contains laments and tributes to both men and women who suffered for the Protestant dissenting cause, many of them at the hands of Jeffreys, the "cursed Spirit of th' Infernal Legion."

Keach's catalogue begins in 1681 with Stephen College and Lord Essex. For 1683, it includes William Lord Russell and Algernon Sydney. Then, for 1684, James Holloway is included. Finally, for 1685, Colonel Abraham Holmes, Sampson Lark, Benjamin and William Hewling, Captain Thomas Walcott, Charles Bateman, John Ayliff, Richard Nelthrop, Lady Alice Lisle, Archibald Campbell, 9th Earl of Argyll (1629–1685), Captain Richard Rumbold, John Patchell, John Hicks, Alderman Henry Cornish and Mistress Elizabeth Gaunt are listed.[51] For Keach, this selection of names was a roll call of honour for those "renowned worthies who fell in England by Popish rage and cruelty."[52]

It is beyond the purpose of this chapter to describe in any detail the activities of these people and the ways in which they were involved or implicated in these events, but each of them came to be regarded as an enemy of the crown—and thus became victims of a royalist backlash. For example, Rumbold, Holmes and Walcott, all Baptists and former officers of Cromwell, suffered as a result of their involvement in the abortive Rye House Plot to kill Charles II and his brother, as they returned from the horse racing at Newmarket. Like so many of the plots during this period, it was a very tangled affair. But, it gave Charles II the opportunity to flex his muscles against Dissenters in particular and to brand

---

50 Greaves points out that the state tried nearly 1,300 Monmouth partisans, about 250 were executed and some 850 were transported to the West Indies. Greaves, *Secrets of the Kingdom*, 293.

51 For details of these men and women see Greaves, *Secrets of the Kingdom*, and also *BDBR*.

52 Keach, *Distressed Sion Relieved*, "To the Reader."

them as rebels.[53] The same label was attached to those involved in the Monmouth rebellion. Two of them were preachers: Sampson Lark was a Particular Baptist preacher in Lyme, Dorset, where Monmouth had first landed in England and John Hicks was a pastor, probably of Presbyterian persuasion, who joined the uprising at Shepton Mallett, in Somerset. The Hewling brothers were the young grandsons of Keach's close friend William Kiffin, and were hung in Taunton for their part in the Monmouth uprising. Lord Argyll had led the army supporting Monmouth in Scotland, while Alderman Cornish was the leading financial supporter of Monmouth in London. Lady Alice Lisle lost her life because she harboured John Hicks when he was on the run after the collapse of the uprising, and Jeffreys most cruelly treated Elizabeth Gaunt. He had her burnt at Tyburn for giving hospitality to an enemy of the crown, who then informed against her.[54]

At this point, we might ask whether Keach himself would have taken up arms and joined in the uprising. His answer is not clear-cut:

> Yet Non-resistance is our duty still,
> When Princes Rule by Law; but not by Will.
> When Magistrates pursue that gracious end,
> God by advancing of them did intend;
> Then to resist them is a horrid thing,
> And God to shame will all such Rebels bring.
> But must Superiors be submitted to,
> When they contrive to ruin and undo

53 Keach, *Distressed Sion Relieved*, 18–19. His poem picked up the labels given to the Dissenters, "Enemies of the Crown" and "branded as Rascals, Rebels, Slaves." Using modern-day parlance, Tim Harris has suggested that Charles and his supporters would have seen themselves as being "being engaged in a war on terrorism." Thus, they would have "justified their actions by claiming that they were merely defending the monarchy and the existing establishment in Church and state against those who wanted to bring both down again." See Harris, *Restoration: Charles II and his Kingdoms*, 425.

54 Watts, *The Dissenters*, 257.

Their faithful subjects, and o'return the State,
And their most sacred oaths do violate?[55]

Here he expresses real sympathy for the cause of those who, in the face of tyranny, joined the Monmouth uprising. He believed in non-resistance if the state ruled by law, but raised the question about the right to resist those who overturn the state by their tyranny. Keach was convinced that those who resisted acted with integrity, believing that they were involved in a just cause, but that they were misled:

To seek such ways to save your selves and me,
Which you thought Just, and hop'd would prosperous be
And though God did Success to you deny,
Yet you might act with all Integrity;
Which Heav'n doth seem to Crown now with Applause,
And to Assert the Justice of your Cause.
Since 'twas ordain'd that spot should be the Scene
Where the Cause dy'd, there to revive't agen:
And though for what you therein were misled
I did lament, and many tears have shed;
Yet I must vindicate you from the wrong
You suffer'd have by many a viperous Tongue;
And will more of your worthy names revive,
Though at your slips I never will connive.[56]

He wrote specifically about John Hicks, again pointing out that he believed Hicks was also mistaken:

But here's just cause of further Lamentation,
For one we scarce can equal in the Nation.

---

55 Keach, *Distressed Sion Relieved*, 31.
56 Keach, *Distressed Sion Relieved*, 32.

A worthy Preacher, who could not comply
With what his Conscience could not justifie.
But hark how th' Enemy doth scoff and jear,
That a Dissenter's taken in the snare.
A better Sacrifice there could not come,
To please the Canibals of Bloody Rome,
Who do believe there is no Dish so good,
As a John Baptist's Head serv'd up in Blood.
But he's a Rebel; Ay! that, that's the cry;
Now as to that, let's weigh impartially
His dying words, now printed, which relate
He did believe Monmouth Legitimate,
Or Lawful Son of Charles, or else that he
Would ne'er have acted in the least degree
In that design, and we may likewise find
The rest in general were of that mind;
And though they were mistaken, let's take care
Not to asperse what dying men declare.
But sober thoughts of them still to retain,
And not with Obloquy their Memory stain.[57]

In these passages from *Distressed Sion Relieved,* Keach makes four important observations about those involved in the Monmouth uprising. First, many of them were worthy men whose integrity should be defended. Second, many of them believed that Monmouth was a legitimate heir to the throne as the son of Charles II. Third, had they not believed he was the legitimate heir, many of them would not have taken up arms. Finally, they were mistaken in their belief that he was the legitimate heir (for the duke was the son of Lucy Walters, one of the king's mistresses, and thus unlike James II who was the rightful heir). Nevertheless, Keach refused to cast aspersions on them and their

57 Keach, *Distressed Sion Relieved*, 32.

memory because they were the victims of cruel injustice, an injustice that to Keach was characteristic and symbolic of popery. This then is the reason why he took up their lament and championed their cause. Keach did not hesitate to equate Jeffreys' conduct with that of Edmund Bonner during Queen Mary's reign:

> Swearing, He'd make examples of 'um all,
> Cry'd, On that Sign-post take and hang them up,
> The Rogues shall all taste of this bitter Cup:
> Whereby this bloody Wretch destroyed more
> In a few Weeks, than Bonner did before
> In full three years, many as faithful men
> As suffered by Popish fury then.
> He hang'd 'um up by two, by three, by seven,
> Whose Blood aloud for vengeance cries to Heav'n.[58]

The reasons why Keach identified popery as the main threat to the life and welfare of the true church of Jesus Christ are not to be regarded as a demonstration of irrational paranoia. The Protestant memory of previous Catholic-inspired persecution and efforts to take England back under Roman headship was central to Protestant fears. Renewed suspicions were aroused in the minds of English Protestants when Charles II signed a treaty with Louis XIV in 1670. Those suspicions turned to genuine fears when it became evident that the next king of England, in the person of James II, would be a Catholic. If the Catholic plots to remove Charles II—real or contrived—and the cruel treatment of those involved in the events of 1683 and 1685 are added to this, one can well see why Keach was convinced he had a valid case. Thus, although the opinions he expressed are characteristic of his age, they are certainly understandable.

---

58 Keach, *Distressed Sion Relieved*, 23. Bonner was the chief architect of persecution under Mary I.

The actions of James II when he succeeded to the throne in 1685 only served to compound Protestant fears and further validate the opinion of Keach and other Dissenters. James was the first Catholic monarch since Mary I. He quickly made it plain that he was going to make it his policy to secure civil and religious equality for all Catholics in his realm. He began to push Catholics into positions of power, as members of the Privy Council, as army officers, as fellows at Oxford and Cambridge and also as magistrates; he set up churches and chapels for the exercise of the Catholic religion, promoted the Jesuits, seized town charters and effectively suspended the administration of justice. In doing so, he succeeded in alienating Anglican royalists. However, attempting to be a shrewd politician, he turned to the Dissenters for support, offering them an indulgence.[59] His grand plans were to backfire spectacularly, as Coffey notes:

> Yet many Dissenters were suspicious of the intentions of a Catholic monarch who was introducing toleration through the use of his royal prerogative. They feared that James was introducing absolutist government and using toleration to prepare the ground for a restoration of Catholicism.[60]

James II was also implicated in and tainted by the cruelties associated with Jeffreys, as the executions associated with the Monmouth uprising continued into his reign. Since 1685 was also the year when the Edict of Nantes was revoked in France raising fresh fears of popery and arbitrary government, it is not difficult to see why men like Keach were alarmed and fearful.

---

59 Coffey, *Persecution and Toleration*, 188–189, and Greaves, *Secrets of the Kingdom*, 317.

60 Coffey, *Persecution and Toleration*, 189. Among those Particular Baptists who wrote an approving letter to James II were Nehemiah Coxe, William Collins, James Jones, Thomas Plant and Benjamin Dennis. Keach does not appear to have attached his signature to this letter. Ivimey, *History*, 1:462.

The arrival of the Protestant William of Orange (1650–1702) and his wife Mary, to England's shore in 1688, was seen as a great deliverance by the Dissenters.

When James' wife gave birth to a son, the threat of a line of Catholic despotic monarchs was brought a step nearer. It was then that many English eyes turned and looked across the waters of the North Sea to Holland—to William of Orange, married to Mary, the daughter of James II.[61]

The implementation of a second Conventicle Act in 1670, ushered in a painful period of persecution for Keach and other Dissenters. On three occasions—in 1666, 1681 and 1689—Keach had lamented over the state of the Protestant church in England, expressing his concerns for the future of the church in a poem he kept enlarging as events unfolded. His 1689 edition was different from the first two because it ended on a joyful and triumphant note with the arrival of William and Mary, offering the prospect of freedom to worship God according to conscience and a Protestant monarchy for years to come.

Keach's biggest fear had been popery. This author personally disagrees with identifying the pope as the Antichrist and the Roman Catholic Church as the whore of Babylon. Yet, it is eminently understandable why any English Protestant of the late seventeenth century would entertain those fears.[62] When he saw persecution threatening to extinguish the light of the church, he discerned the dark shadow of popery and the threat of tyranny and arbitrary government as the underlying reason. He contended that persecution had always been one of the "marks of the Beast."

Keach had some benefit of hindsight—it was nearly 200 years since Martin Luther had nailed his *Ninety-Five Theses* to the door of Wittenberg Castle church. He could observe the progress of both the Reformation and the Catholic Counter-Reformation,

---

61 Mary was the daughter of James II, but she had been brought up a Protestant.

62 Keach produced a fuller work in 1689 concerning the identity of Antichrist and Babylon in which he attempted to show from Scripture the rationale for identifying the pope with the Antichrist. Keach, *Antichrist Stormed: Or, the Mystery Babylon, the Great Whore, and Great City proved to be the present Church of Rome* (London, 1689).

and would surely have understood that, despite the passing of time, it was still very much the case that the religion of the king determined the religion of the people. The policies and decisions of kings like Charles II, James II and Louis XIV, invariably confirmed his fears for the church in England, particularly as they presented the prospect of a succession of Catholic monarchs and a return to popery.

In *Sion in Distress*, Keach wrote as a sensitive and faithful pastor and as a leader of the Protestant church seeking to defend and protect her from her enemies. His poetry provides a unique opportunity to listen to his heartbeat and to read his mind. It shows us that he was a man who, above all else, sought the glory of God. Though he was persecuted for nearly thirty years, he did not retaliate in a vengeful spirit, nor did he panic as some appeared to do in 1683 and 1685 (by taking matters into their own hands). While he believed some of them were mistaken in their actions, he did not disown them but grieved over their deaths and the loss they represented to the nation and to the churches and families to which they belonged. For himself, he continued to pray and wait on the Lord Jesus Christ to defend and deliver his church. And, Keach believed, his prayers were wonderfully answered in 1688 and 1689.

CHAPTER 6

"To learn to Read, good Child, give heed"

Consider the advantages of early age; religion now is most likely to make the deepest impression, and holy habits to be sooner acquired...that ground that hath long lain barren or unploughed, is hard to be broken up, or it not so easy to manure. A plant set but the last year, is sooner plucked up than an old tree; a colt is sooner broke than if you let him run wild til he becomes an old horse; you can bend a twig sooner than a great arm of a tree: also we put our children to learn any art or mystery when young, because youth can learn sooner than elder persons. And may not all these things convince you, that this is the best time to learn the mystery of religion and godliness?"[1]

Keach's *The Child's Instructor: or, A New and Easy Primmer*, had been branded as "a seditious and venomous book" in the indictment that was read out before the Lord Chief Justice, Sir Robert Hyde, when Keach was

1 Keach, "The Householder," *Parables Two*, 77.

brought before the assizes in Aylesbury, Buckinghamshire, in 1664. A few days later, when Keach was further punished and pilloried in Winslow, the hangman burned a copy of the book. The rector of Stoke Hammond, Thomas Disney (who had first alerted the authorities to the existence of the primer), claimed that some 1,500 copies of the offending book had been published and he was also anxious to suppress what he judged to be "factious, Schismatical, heretical matter." Such efforts on the part of the authorities tended to be short-lived successes. During the Restoration, from 1660 to 1688, the policy of censorship and suppression against Nonconformist writers like Keach, a policy that was led by the Surveyor of the Press, Sir Roger L'Estrange, proved in the end to be a failure:

> L'Estrange had his successes: printers were harassed and imprisoned; authors and booksellers were prosecuted. The final conclusion on his press campaign must, however, be that it was a failure. The Surveyor never came anywhere remotely near controlling the press. So far were he and the licensers from silencing dissenting voices, that they were hardly able even to mute them.[2]

This was certainly the case as far as Keach was concerned. He was not daunted by the repressive measures and, once he settled in London, he became a prodigious writer and publisher.

Keach was a major contributor to a particular kind of literature that came to characterize Nonconformity. Neil Keeble argues that by their extensive writings, Nonconformists produced a distinctive literary culture, and as a result they not merely survived but actually flourished.[3] A similar point has been made by

---

2 Neil H. Keeble, *The Literary Culture of Nonconformity in Later Seventeenth-Century England* (Leicester: Leicester University Press, 1987), 127.

3 Keeble's central theme is that the Nonconformist press was the chief means of their survival.

Sharon Achinstein, in which she speaks of a "vibrant culture" existing among the Dissenters, for whom "the prime challenge was to maintain commitment to God despite persecution."[4] Keach was one of those men who contributed to this "vibrant culture." He wrote and published a number of significant works during this period of suppression, including primers, poetry, hymns, funeral elegies, religious allegories, sermons and polemical works. He was one of many Dissenters who, although they were a persecuted religious minority in Restoration England, remained undaunted and faithful in their commitment to God and to the gospel of the Lord Jesus Christ.

When Keach picked up his pen to write, he had clear and specific aims in view. Focusing on what he believed were vital matters, Keach did so even though he was swimming against the tide of contemporary religious and political opinion. Keach cannot be properly understood without appreciating his convictions concerning how a person becomes a Christian and what is expected of them once they have professed their faith. His convictions were evangelical for he believed that the Bible taught the necessity of personal conversion to Christ, of faith in Jesus Christ and repentance for sin. He was not alone in this conviction as similar literature of the period demonstrates, such as John Bunyan's *The Pilgrim's Progress*, Joseph Alleine's *An Alarme to the Unconverted*, Richard Baxter's *A Call to the Unconverted* and Thomas Vincent's *God's Terrible Voice in the City*. Furthermore, Keach believed that once a person had professed their faith in Christ and had been baptized as a believer, that person ought to live a distinctive life, reflected in evangelical obedience to the law of God. Keach was happy to use the term "godliness" to summarize this distinctive pattern of life. Godliness, according to Keach, could be compared to following a trade and

---

4 Sharon Achinstein, *Literature and Dissent in Milton's England* (Cambridge: Cambridge University Press, 2003), 3.

> must be followed without intermission, it must be every day's work; the head, heart, hands, feet, time, strength, discourse, contrivance, must be taken up about it. No man can thrive in Godliness, if his heart be not in it. When thy hand is in the world, thy heart should be in heaven.[5]

Keach believed that a Christian was someone called to live to the glory of God and that this kind of life could be lived only by those in whom God had worked graciously and supernaturally, giving them a new heart and a new love for God and the Lord Jesus Christ. This belief is clearly reflected in a sermon preached probably in the 1680s:

> It is only the new nature, the renewed heart, that makes the soul delight in God as the chief good. Interest in God, adoption and regeneration, go always together in the same subject; he that is a child of God, hath the image of God stamped on his soul.[6]

Coming to know and love the Lord Jesus Christ was, for Keach, crucial both to conversion and to the life of godliness:

> Now the mystery of Godliness principally consists in the person of Christ, God manifest in the flesh.... When we know Christ better, we shall understand the mystery better: Christ is the mystery wrapt up in all the Gospel, he is the scope of all the Scripture, the pearl hid in the field; every line is drawn to him, as the proper center; all the types and shadows pointed to him, and all the promises run in him. Jesus Christ is really and truly God, and

5 Keach, "Godliness Compared to a Trade," *Types and Metaphors*, 936.

6 Keach, "The New Wine," *Parables One*, 117.

> yet very Man, God and man in one person, and is not this a mystery?[7]

An appreciation of how important these matters were to Keach provides a more informed basis for a consideration of Keach's contribution to this "vibrant culture" of Nonconformity at the end of the seventeenth century. Keach's writings during the 1670s and early 1680s aimed at promoting conversion to Christ and practical godliness, in particular among the second generation of persecuted Nonconformists. As we have already seen, apart from a brief lull following the 1672 Indulgence, the 1670s had been marked by continued persecution and the threat of Roman Catholicism had deeply coloured political and religious thoughts, words and actions.

During this period, Keach actively pursued his aims and produced two primers: *The Child's Delight: or, Instructions for Children and Youth* and *Instructions for Children*; and two poems in dialogue form: *War with the Devil: or, The Young Man's Conflict with the Powers of Darkness*, first published in 1673, and *The Glorious Lover: A Divine Poem, Upon the Adorable Mystery of Sinners Redemption*, first published in 1679. Two religious allegories followed: *The Travels of True Godliness*, published in 1683 and, in the following year, a companion volume entitled, *The Progress of Sin: Or, the Travels of Ungodliness*. These allegories were not only directed to young people but sought to embrace a wider readership. It should be remembered that he was now a father with a growing family, and a pastor of an increasing congregation, among whom were many young children. In both of these capacities, he was concerned to win young hearts and minds to Christ, and see their lives transformed by the power of the gospel of Jesus Christ. He sought to provide practical means for himself and his wife, and other parents, to teach their children. In so doing, he sought

7 Keach, "Godliness Compared to a Trade," *Types and Metaphors*, 934.

to lay a foundation for godliness and the building of a strong and faithful generation of Christians who would eventually take their place in the church and in the world and fulfill their various callings. Keach realized that the early years of life were years of opportunity not to be lost because "you can bend a twig sooner than a great arm of a tree."[8] Thus, Keach invested heavily in works for children and young people, believing that they provided the best hope for a better nation in the future.

Some of Keach's efforts were a publishing success. The two allegories together with *War with the Devil*, proved to be very popular and the allegories were still being published over 100 years after his death.[9] Indeed, so popular was *War with the Devil* that it rivalled John Bunyan's masterpiece, *The Pilgrim's Progress from this World to that which is to come*, and brought Keach considerable commercial success.[10] Ian Green's extensive study of over 700 volumes has established that these writings of Keach were steady sellers—if not among the bestsellers—of religious books in the seventeenth and early eighteenth century.[11] The primers, the dialogues and the allegories are now long forgotten, and thus the contribution of Benjamin Keach largely overlooked. Recent scholarship and interest in late seventeenth-century English dissenting literature has

8 Keach, "The Householder," *Parables Two*, 77.

9 Edward C. Starr, ed., *A Baptist Bibliography Being a Register of Printed Material By and About Baptists; Including Works Written Against the Baptists* (Rochester: American Baptist Historical Society, 1968), 21–22, 24–28.

10 Ian Green, *Print and Protestantism in Early Modern England* (Oxford: Oxford University Press, 2000), 377.

11 Green, *Print and Protestantism*, 168–238. In his Appendix I, "Sample of Best Sellers and Steady Sellers First Published in England c.1536–1700," Green lists at least 22 editions of *The Pilgrims Progress* for the period 1678–1727 and 19 editions of *War with the Devil* for the period 1673–1728. Green's conclusions establish even more firmly the earlier conclusions of C. John Somerville. Writing of the same books, Somerville said, "these were among the few dozen best-selling books in Restoration England, with total sales equivalent to bestsellers today in terms of the number of households." C. John Somerville, *The Discovery of Childhood in Puritan England* (Athens: University of Georgia Press, 1992), 132.

now brought his work to greater prominence.[12] Furthermore, the second half of the twentieth century saw a revival of interest in Puritan writings with several evangelical publishing houses republishing such works. Among those Puritan writings are the labours of Particular Baptists, including Benjamin Keach, although only two of his works have been republished.[13]

It needs to be emphasized that Keach was not aiming at producing best-selling books in order to make financial gain, though there is little doubt he would have appreciated the additional income from the sale of his books. There is no evidence to indicate whether or not his church in Southwark supported his ministry financially in the 1670s and 1680s.[14] His primary concerns were those of a Christian evangelist and pastor, anxious to bring the truth of the gospel of Jesus Christ to bear on the hearts and minds of his young hearers and readers, to place useful tools in the hands of parents and other Christian teachers and to promote godliness on as wide a scale as possible. The primers laid the foundations, the poems promoted conversion to Christ and the allegories were intended to further godliness.

---

12 Among the most important recent publications are Somerville, *The Discovery of Childhood in Puritan England*; Keeble, *The Literature of Nonconformity*; Ian Green, *The Christian ABC: Catechisms and Catechizing in England c.1530–1740* (Oxford: Clarendon Press, 1996) and *Print and Protestantism*; Achinstein, *Literature and Dissent in Milton's England*; and, Richard L. Greaves, *Glimpses of Glory: John Bunyan and English Dissent* (Stanford: Stanford University Press, 2002). Chadwyck-Healey Ltd have also published Keach's poetical works in *English Poetry Full-Text Database*.

13 They are Keach's *Preaching from the Types and Metaphors of the Bible* (Grand Rapids: Kregel, 1972) and *Expositions of the Parables*, 2 vols. (Grand Rapids: Kregel, 1991).

14 At some point in his life, Keach also derived profits "from selling (Dr) Roberts tincture elixir sugar plums and snuff over the cost of keeping the Dr and his wife Prudence Roberts." This is recorded in "The Will of Benjamin Keach," *Surrey Will Abstracts*, Vol. 26, 2001. Archdeaconry Court of Surrey 1700–1708, No. 820. See Appendix 1. John Roberts was a doctor and member of Keach's congregation. On one occasion, he had provided bail for Keach when he was prosecuted. Ivimey, *History*, 1:385. Whether these profits were sufficient to support Keach and his family, as well as Dr. Roberts and his wife, is unknown.

Laying the foundations: the primers

No copies of Keach's original 1664 primer are known to have survived. Presumably the Buckinghamshire authorities had managed to destroy most, if not all, of the offending copies. Therefore, when Keach rewrote the primer, he did so largely from memory but with significant modifications: now the new primer reflected the changes in his theological convictions. He spoke of "Arminian errors" which, "after my eyes were inlightened, and the book with alterations being again reprinted, I left out, and now do declare my dislike of the first impressions, and do disown what I there asserted."[15] When did Keach republish the primer? Starr lists a fifth edition of *The Child's Instructor* and dates it 1679, eleven years after Keach came to London.[16] It seems reasonable to suggest that he republished it after he left Buckinghamshire for London in 1668 and after he had left his "Arminian errors." To republish it while still living in his home county, where he was well-known, would have courted serious trouble, while in London he would have been much more difficult to track down and prosecute.

Keach set about producing two primers, *The Child's Delight* and *Instructions for Children*. These two works are similar in content, though the latter is almost twice as long as the former, and again it seems reasonable to assume that both primers expanded Keach's earlier original. *Instructions for Children* became a moderate bestseller in late seventeenth-century England and was still selling well into the eighteenth century.[17]

The importance of Keach's primers for the late seventeenth century needs to be emphasized. Some of his contemporaries realized the significance of his work. For example, later editions

15 Keach, "Blessedness of Christ's Sheep," *A Golden Mine Opened*, 314–315.

16 Starr, *Baptist Bibliography*, 14.

17 Green, *The Christian ABC*, 84, 672–673. He lists a fifteenth edition of *Instruction for Children* for 1723.

of this primer were to contain a commendatory preface by his friend Hanserd Knollys, who was also a schoolmaster:

> This little book, *Instructions for Children*, I have read and taught to scholars about 40 years in London...so I do commend it to all Religious Parents who are willing to catechize their children.... I could wish that all English schoolmasters in and about that city (nay throughout the nation) would make use of it for the Instruction of their Scholars.[18]

Knollys' preface indicates that the primer must have been in use by the 1670s at least, though his "about 40 years" seems to be an overstatement as Knollys died in 1691. Furthermore, it would seem that many took Knollys' words to heart, because a fifteenth edition was published in England in 1723, a twenty-fifth edition in 1738 and a thirtieth edition in 1763.[19] In addition, Keach's primer, particularly the catechisms, was influential in New England and Philadelphia as well. John Cotton used *Instructions for Children* as the foundation for *The New England Primer*, a book whose study was to become compulsory in Massachusetts.[20] Evidence from the minutes of the Philadelphia Baptist Association in the early eighteenth century shows that they encouraged churches to use Keach's primer to educate and catechize their children.[21]

Keach probably never envisaged his primers becoming so useful and successful when he first compiled them. Nevertheless, their success would have been of considerable encouragement to him because it would have been an indication that his aims

---

18 Keach, *Instructions for Children* (London, 1704), Preface.

19 Starr, *Baptist Bibliography*, 20.

20 Muriel James, *Religious Liberty on Trial, Hanserd Knollys—Early Baptist Hero* (Franklin: Providence House Publishers, 1997), 157.

21 David A. Copeland, *Benjamin Keach and the Development of Baptist Traditions in Seventeenth-Century England* (Lewiston: The Edwin Mellen Press, 2001), 30.

were being fulfilled. This success was also a vindication of his own determination to continue living by his convictions despite the opposition of the authorities.

It has been shown that Keach actively sought to promote the spiritual welfare and education of children as soon as he came to London. Keach recognized that for a child to acquire the ability to read was of first importance in furthering this aim:

> 'To learn to Read, good Child, give heed'
> For 'tis a precious thing:
> What may compare with learning rare!
> From hence doth virtue spring.[22]

Due to this emphasis on the ability to read, literacy rates among Nonconformists were higher than in other sections of society.[23] Keach was one of several Nonconformists who encouraged "all classes of society, and especially children, to learn to read and write and to be diligent practitioners of these skills."[24] However, Keach went a step further and linked the ability to read with the eventual acquisition of godliness. Keach thus used religious material as the basis for learning to read. His ultimate aim was to teach children to read the Bible for themselves. Some of his allegories were intended also to be the basis of religious instruction and to impress on children and their parents the grave dangers of spiritual ignorance and the importance of true religion based on the Bible. In *The Progress of Sin* he refers to the

---

22 Keach, *The Child's Delight* (London, n.d.) 8, and *Instructions for Children* (London, 1763), 6.

23 Keeble, *The Literary Culture of Nonconformity*, 166–167.

24 Keeble, *The Literary Culture of Nonconformity*, 166–167. Keeble mentions Bunyan's *A Book for Boys and Girls*, among other publications, advocating the benefits of literacy, and he could have equally given Keach as an example. He also notes that while it is impossible to assess the true size of the late seventeenth-century reading public, literacy rates were certainly higher than statistics alone suggest.

Hanserd Knollys (c. 1599–1691) was a friend of Benjamin Keach, a schoolmaster and one of the key leaders of the Particular Baptists in London.

Prince of Darkness keeping children in a state of blindness, through their parents, "so that they who should be as Eyes to the Blind, and Feet to the Lame, had no Eyes to see, nor Feet to go themselves."[25] How did the Prince of Darkness (Satan) accomplish this?

> He presented to many Parents the great Charge of putting their Offspring to school; persuading them (they being poor and low in the World) they could not be at the Cost, tho' they bestow'd a great deal more needlessly upon cloathing and feeding of them than their *Learning* would have come to. Now the reason why the enemy is so greatly set against *Learning*, is this: they should take to read the *Holy Bible*, which he dreads exceedingly; because when understood, it vanquisheth at once his Darling *Ignorance*.[26]

He was not alone among the Particular Baptists in his appreciation of the importance of learning. His close friends in London, Hanserd Knollys and Thomas Delaune, earned their livings largely as schoolmasters. Thomas Crosby, Keach's son-in-law, also became a schoolmaster.

The Child's Delight was in essence a reading primer, whereas *Instructions for Children* included more information and more extensive catechisms. Both contained the alphabet in Roman and italic forms, together with a list of vowels and consonants and words of one or more syllables. This rudimentary spelling was given to encourage the acquisition of reading skills and was combined with elementary biblical knowledge. This is developed more fully in *Instructions for Children*. Keach expected children as

---

25 Keach, *The Progress of Sin: Or, the Travels of Ungodliness*, 7th ed. (London, corrected 1781), 55.

26 Keach, *The Progress of Sin*, 55–56.

young as three or four to know the main characters and stories of the Bible. Furthermore, he expected even the youngest to be taught to pray for grace to believe for themselves.

Fundamental to the instruction were graded religious catechisms. His theology was Calvinistic, essentially the same as that taught in the *Westminster Confession of Faith*, approved in 1646, and *The Shorter and Larger Catechisms* and the *Savoy Declaration* of 1658. In order to teach children the fundamentals of the Christian faith, Keach provided parents—in particular, fathers—with an appropriate level of instruction for their children, thus breaking down the teaching into manageable portions. His aim was to ensure that as these children grew up, they would increase in their familiarity with and ability to understand the truths of the Bible. In *Instructions for Children* he provided three levels of catechetical instruction: for a little child (aged 3 to 4); a child (aged about 10); and the most advanced form, for youth (of "a mature age"). The latter he expected to be well versed in matters of doctrine and be able to make their own profession of faith. Each section is set out as a dialogue between father and son. There is also another section for daughters in which he warns them against imbibing worldly vanity. Keach was not averse to livening up his catechism, especially for those who were younger or found learning difficult. Among the questions and answers, he would insert interesting dialogue between children and fathers, sometimes of a humorous nature.

There was nothing unusual about catechisms and catechizing during the seventeenth century. Men such as Richard Baxter and John Owen wrote catechetical literature for Presbyterian and Independent Nonconformists respectively. The Anglicans also used catechisms. Thus, Keach followed a well-worn path. His significance lies in his emergence during the 1680s as one of the leaders among the Particular Baptists, and that he wrote with that constituency in mind. His catechism consciously reflected his theological convictions and was therefore both

Calvinistic and Baptistic. Believer's baptism was particularly stressed in *Instructions for Children* where Keach provided questions and answers identifying the proper subjects of baptism as "only such as believe" and denying sprinkling as the correct mode.[27] It is possible that he intended *The Child's Delight* for a wider Protestant use, as there is simply a broader statement on baptism that would be acceptable to both Baptist and paedobaptist alike.[28]

Catechizing was one of a number of methods of instruction and edification that Nonconformists like Keach promoted among their congregations and to a wider audience.[29] However, other methods, including reading the Bible, learning and singing hymns and repeating the contents of sermons while they were still fresh in the memory, were also encouraged.

Keach was a realistic man endowed with a good dose of common sense. Not all the teaching in his book was biblical; he also wanted children to acquire everyday practical skills. For example, Keach was concerned to equip young men to work in the world of trade and commerce and to enter apprenticeships. His primers included the units of time and money, explained how to write bonds, bills, receipts and wills, how to calculate interest, and how to use weights and measures. While this and all kinds of other information was available elsewhere (i.e. in almanacs), Keach was trying to ensure that young men and women with Nonconformist convictions would be able to earn a living in the world, particularly in a city like London.

Keach practiced what he preached by making provision for his fatherless grandson, also named Benjamin Keach. In his will, Keach left the younger Benjamin, "£5 to apprentice him and £5

---

27 Keach, *Instructions for Children*, 99, 101.

28 Keach, *The Child's Delight*, 38.

29 See Green's *The Christian ABC* for a comprehensive survey of the history of catechizing and the teaching of the catechisms.

more in book."[30] Keach made his will shortly before his death in 1704, and even though persecution of Dissenters had ceased in 1689, the Act of Uniformity was not repealed and Dissenters were excluded from certain professions. Thus, as H. Foreman has concluded,

> the inclusion of these documents (bond, will, etc.) is an indication of the type of career which the young Baptist, along with other Nonconformists, now found open to him after the English universities had been closed to him with the Act of Uniformity in 1662. The learned professions were debarred as far as he was concerned: the worlds of business and commerce were now his main avenue for a career.[31]

Nevertheless, the inclusion of such material should not detract from Keach's fundamental religious concerns. He clearly believed young children could become Christians. To encourage them to believe, he relates a number of instances of children of ten and eleven understanding what it means to be a Christian and demonstrating this by their faith in Jesus Christ, their prayers and their changed lives.[32]

Keach's primer was a banned and burned book in 1664. In its rewritten forms, it became immensely popular and in widespread

---

30 "The Will of Benjamin Keach," *Surrey Will Abstracts*, Vol. 26, 2001. Archdeaconry Court of Surrey 1700–1708, No. 820.

31 H. Foreman, "Some Seventeenth Century Baptist Educational Textbooks," *BQ*, 30 (1983), 113.

32 Keach's name has also been associated with another catechism, usually referred to as *Keach's Catechism*. It is very similar to the *Westminster Shorter Catechism*, though it has a distinctive Baptist flavour and is still in print today as *The London Baptist Confession of Faith of 1689 and Keach's Catechism* (Choteau: Gospel Mission, n.d.). There is some doubt whether this catechism is his work. We will leave discussion of the authorship of this catechism for a later chapter where we consider the publication of the *London Baptist Confession of Faith in 1689*.

use in England, across the Atlantic in New England and in the transatlantic British world.

Promoting conversion: the poetic dialogues

Keach wanted to convey the most important truths of biblical teaching to young people in an engaging way. For him, individual conversion to Christ was of first importance, and his poetic dialogues have that as the ultimate goal. *War with the Devil* begins with a young man far away from Christ, bent on following his own evil inclinations:

> I am resolved to search the World about,
> And I will suck the Sweetness of it out;
> No Stone I'll leave unturn'd, that I may find
> Content and Joy unto my troubled mind;
> No Sorrow shall, whilst I do live, come near me,
> Nor shall the Preacher with his Fancies scare me.[33]

Keach is not thinking of any one young man in particular, rather a representative youth. This young man's attitude sets the tone for the unfolding of the whole poem. As Keach exposes the sinful heart of any young man who is thinking this way, he shows him the nature of his sin and the condition of fallen man. He wants to awaken his conscience and show him the nature of true conversion. In her book, Sharon Achinstein reproduces the frontispiece from the 1683 edition of *War with the Devil*, comprising two pictures. The first, "The youth in his Natural State," depicts a young dandy, handsomely dressed in a doublet with a feathered hat, ruffles and curls, and dancing townspeople in the background. Inscribed at the foot of the picture are Christ's

33 Keach, *War with the Devil: Or, the Young Man's Conflict with the Powers of Darkness* (London, 1776), 8. This was first published in 1673. Quotations are from the 22nd edition in 1776.

words from Matthew 7:13, "Broad is the way &c." (The full biblical phrase is "...broad is the way that leads to destruction.") The second picture depicts "The youth in his converted State," with an inscription from Matthew 7:14, "Narrow is the way which leads to life." (The complete verse is, "Because narrow is the gate and difficult is the way which leads to life, and there are few that find it.") In this picture, the young man is more simply dressed and holds the Bible open in his hand, fighting the devil and his armed band by means of the Bible.[34] This woodcut summarized the message Keach was aiming to convey. Attempting to reach as wide an audience as possible, Keach evidently made use of pictures as well as words to make his point—something that was typical of the age.[35]

As the poem continues, a dialogue develops between Youth, Conscience, Truth (who comes and preaches to him), the Devil (who tries to disturb his listening to Truth and instead stirs up distracting interests) and, finally, a narrator called Vicinus, who links the dialogue together. Conscience begins by reproving the young man, and Truth comes to reason with Youth, urging him to taste of Christ's goodness:

> I with poor *Conscience* must a Witness bear;
> I am his Guide, his Rule, Tis by my Light
> He acts and does, and saith the Thing that's right.
> Art thou too young thy evil Ways to leave?
> And yet hast thou a precious Soul to save?
> Art thou too young to leave Iniquity,
> When old enough in Hell for Sin to lie?

---

34 Achinstein, *Literature and Dissent in Milton's England*, 20.

35 Rachel Walker, "Ordinary and Common Discourses: The Impact of the Glorious Revolution on Political Discussion in London, 1688–1694" (Ph.D. dissertation, University of Sheffield, 1998), 107–112. The 1776 edition of Keach's *War with the Devil* does not contain the frontispiece from the 1683 edition, and, like other eighteenth-century editions, it makes use of cheap woodcuts for illustrations throughout the dialogue.

This is, young Man, also thy choosing Time,
Whilst thou therefore dost flourish in thy Prime,
Place thou thy Heart upon the Lord above,
And with *Christ Jesus* fall in Love.[36]

By such means, Youth is gradually awakened and wishes he did not have a conscience. When the Devil comes, he brings wicked suggestions to Youth, telling him not to listen to the voice of Conscience. Then Youth's old companions appear briefly on the scene to follow up the Devil's suggestions.

Truth now begins to explain the true nature of conversion. Like all Puritan evangelists, Keach is quick to expose false foundations and to ensure that there is a thorough work of grace in the heart. Thus, Truth tells Youth that hypocrisy is not easy to detect. To be converted, prayer is not enough, reading and hearing sermons are not enough and the fear of hell is not enough to save him.

Before you have a Plaister for your Sore,
Your Wound must yet be search'd a little more:
If slightly heal'd, only for present Ease,
The Remedy's as bad as the Disease.[37]

Conscience continues to testify against Youth, telling him that he is not free but a slave to his sinful will, and that—although he may appear genuine among the godly—he is not yet converted. He cannot be because a true Christian is known by his godliness seen in a consistent life. Conscience points out to Youth the glaring inconsistency in his life, namely, that when he is among the ungodly he reverts to being like them. Conscience drives home the nature of sin and the reality of Youth's guilt before

36 Keach, *War with the Devil*, 20.
37 Keach, *War with the Devil*, 66.

God and that he deserves punishment in hell. Poor Youth is now brought low and begins to long for a Saviour. He is directed to pray to Jesus Christ for mercy:

> Thy counsel I resolve to take with Speed,
> If 'twas for me Christ on the Cross did bleed:
> I will send up a Sigh, a bitter Groan,
> And earnestly implore his gracious Throne.[38]

The reply of Christ brings assurance and forgiveness of sins:

> Look upon me, and see my Love descending;
> 'Tis from eternity, and has no Ending.
> Can'st thou have more, O Soul? Thou hast my Heart,
> Whate'er is mine, to thee I will impart.
> Thy Scarlet Sins are washed quite away,
> Nor one of them unto thy Charge I'll lay.[39]

The Devil threatens him again but now Youth has been soundly converted and believes that Christ will defend him. Youth is made confident in the knowledge of the covenant of grace, that Christ will complete the saving work that he has begun in his heart. The dialogue draws to a conclusion with Youth's hymn of praise to God.[40]

---

38 Keach, *War with the Devil*, 72.

39 Keach, *War with the Devil*, 77.

40 In many versions of *War with the Devil* there is a second part: *An Appendix, containing a Dialogue between an Old Apostate and a Young Professor. Worthy of the Perusal of All, but chiefly intended for the Instructions of the Younger Sort.* This is a sequel to *War with the Devil*. Youth is now making progress in the Christian life but is assaulted again by the Devil. Keach is acutely aware of the dangers to the church in the 1670s and 1680s, as we saw in chapter 5. This dialogue is concerned to expose the falsehood of Roman Catholicism and to show Youth how he might counter different arguments and remain faithful. Apostate is the mouthpiece of the world and Rome. We have already considered why Keach thought Rome the principal threat to the true church of his day.

War with the Devil clearly shows that Keach had embraced Calvinistic doctrine by the time he first composed it in 1673. For example, he believed God's grace conquers sin in a person who is converted to Christ. He also held that God's eternal love was the source of salvation, and that faith and repentance (conversion) were the result of God powerfully changing the human heart (divine regeneration). Thus, Youth speaks to this end:

> 'Tis I, blest Truth, the Conquest now is won;
> Grace has prevail'd, I am the conquered one.
> My Grief is turned to Joy; yea, and my Night
> Is also changed into eternal Light.
> Thy Power is great when Grace doth work with thee,
> You soon do then obtain the victory.
> Blest be the Day that ever thou wast sent
> To change my Heart and move me to repent.[41]

The Glorious Lover is a poem essentially about redemption accomplished and then applied to the soul by Jesus Christ. The same Calvinistic doctrines are reflected in this second poem but with a different emphasis. Here, Keach traces out the theme of the eternal love of God by focusing on his glorious plan to give his Son in marriage. Directed again to young people, it takes the form of a sacred romance. Yet it shows the same reasoning, persuading and pleading that is characteristic of his sermons. This sacred romance is about the heavenly Bridegroom seeking his bride. It expounds the love of God and the love of Christ in saving sinners with the same aim as *War with the Devil*, namely, the conversion of the reader. In "The Proem" Keach groans as he contemplates the seductive power of the world's amorous literature that so entices young men and women away from Christ:

---

41 Keach, *War with the Devil*, 80.

How many do their precious time abuse
On cursed products of a wanton muse;
On trifling fables, and romances vain,
The poison'd froth of some infected brain?
Which only tend to nourish rampant vice,
And to prophaneness easy youth entice;
Gilt o'er with wit, black venom in they take,
And 'midst gay flowers hug the lurking snake.[42]

Keach's aim, in contrast, is to present God's salvation in terms of the ultimate pattern of love: the love of God for his people and the love of Christ, the Bridegroom, for his church.

The Glorious Lover contains many biblical allusions, illustrations and references, and is rich in biblical doctrine. Indeed, behind the whole poem lies the Song of Solomon. Its echoes are found in the conclusion of the "Proem":

Read then, and learn to love truly by this,
Until thy soul can sing, raptur'd in bliss,
'My well-beloved's mine, and I am his.'[43]

It is a long, epic poem, containing over 8,400 lines and almost 61,500 words. It is considered Keach's most ambitious literary composition.[44]

In describing the love of the Bridegroom, Keach asks, "Did ever Lover go so far from Home to seek a Spouse?"[45] In Book I, the author unfolds God's eternal plan of salvation, describing how the Divine Lover, the Son of God, took human nature at the

42 Keach, *The Glorious Lover* (London, 1764), The Proem. This was first published in 1679.

43 Keach, *The Glorious Lover*, The Proem.

44 Vaughn, "Public Worship and Practical Theology in the Work of Benjamin Keach (1640–1704)," 283.

45 Keach, *The Glorious Lover*, 13.

incarnation. He describes the earthly life of Christ, culminating in his sufferings and death. He explains the reasons for Christ's coming, the fall of Adam into sin, its effects on the rest of the human race, together with man's subsequent blindness and rebellion. In the light of divine justice, atonement for sin lies at the heart of the redemptive work of Christ. Jesus speaks:

> I know not how to let this stroke be given,
> For I am come on purpose down from heaven,
> To make atonement, and to satisfy,
> For all her sins and foul iniquity.
> Tho' she to me doth no affection bear,
> Yet her I pity, and do love most dear.[46]

Book II begins to explain how redemption becomes the possession of Soul. The principal means is by the preaching of the gospel (Theologue is the godly preacher), but severe providences of God such as sickness may also be used to awaken the sinner. When Soul still refuses to turn back to God, the evil of her sin is explained. Keach makes plain the effects of sin on every human faculty, which prevents Soul from receiving the divine Lover, Jesus Christ:

> O wretched Soul! What thoughts dost thou retain
> Of thy dear Lord and blessed sovereign?
> Come, view thy choice, see how deprav'd thou art
> In judgment, will, affection, thy whole heart
> Is so corrupt, defiled, and impure
> Thou canst not Christ, nor godliness endure.[47]

---

46 Keach, *The Glorious Lover*, 95.

47 Keach, *The Glorious Lover*, 164. Further on in chapter 2, Keach shows very clearly that he had shed any notion of the freedom of the will, a doctrine that lays at the heart of Arminian teaching. Explaining why Soul will not "close" with Christ he says:

Keach portrays the Lover with imagery from the Song of Solomon:

> Look on his beauteous cheeks, and thoul't espy
> The Rose of Sharon deck'd in royalty.[48]

Christ, as the Lover, is described in his beauty, riches, bounty, power and wisdom, coming to court his bride. Keach depicts one attraction of the Lover after another, to draw the reluctant sinner to Christ. All the time, he is reasoning with his readers. Soul's conscience is awakened at last, and her thinking is enlightened. Satan is present seeking to keep Soul in her sin before the love of Christ is made the final plea, leading to her uniting with her Divine Lover. The epic ends with the same words as "The Proem,"

> Then let us sing on earth a song like this,
> My well-beloved's mine and I am his.[49]

> Two proud relations loftily stand off,
> Who urge her to reject him with a scoff.
> The one is will, a very churlish piece,
> Who all along for sin and Satan is.
> The other's judgment, once most grave and wise,
> But now with will both cursed enemies:
> To God and Christ true piety oppose,
> And lead the Soul with evil ways to close.
> 'Tis they who must dispose of her, if she
> E'er yield to Christ his dearest spouse to be.
> But sin has so by craft corrupted them
> And drawn them to its party, they contemn
> This glorious lover, and will not consent
> The Soul should yield him, or should repent,
> And so break off with other lovers who
> She yet doth love, and loth is to forgo.

Keach, *The Glorious Lover*, 172.

48 Keach, *The Glorious Lover*, 176.

49 Keach, *The Glorious Lover*, 264.

Conversion to Christ was crucial in Keach's understanding but it is, however, only the beginning of the Christian life. How to continue that life and live to the glory of God is the subject of Keach's two allegories, and so they form a natural sequel to the dialogues.

Maintaining godliness: the two allegories

The Travels of True Godliness was published in 1683, and its companion volume, *The Travels of Ungodliness*, in 1684. Keach described each of them as "an apt and pleasant allegory."[50] From the preface to the second volume, it is quite clear that Keach now had a reading public wider than his own Particular Baptist circle. Referring to the success of his first volume, he comments, "I hear [it] hath found a kind acceptance among all sorts of Protestants, whether Conformist or Nonconformists."[51]

These volumes sold well while Keach was alive. His bookseller at the time, John Dunton (1659–1733), remembering the popularity of Keach's publications, claimed that "*War with the Devil* and *Travels of True Godliness* (of which I printed ten thousand), will sell to the end of time."[52] Dunton clearly overestimated Keach's two volumes, yet many editions and reprintings of *The Travels* followed after his death, even until the middle of the nineteenth century. Though some sections in these writings were directed toward children and young people, they were intended for a wider readership covering all ages. Keach's aim was to equip them to face the hazards and opposition that they would inevitably meet with now that they had become Christians.

---

50 Keach, *The Travels of True Godliness* (London, 1817), title page.

51 Keach, *The Travels of Ungodliness* (Aberdeen, 1849), Preface.

52 John Dunton, *The Life and Errors of John Dunton* (London: John Nicholls, 1818), 177. John Dunton was a somewhat eccentric London printer responsible for printing a wide range of Anglican and dissenting authors, including some of Keach's works. He married one of the daughters of Dr. Samuel Annesley.

At the beginning of this allegory, Keach describes the kind of person whose life has been transformed by the supernatural power of God, and shows the "inward life and power of True Godliness."

> He that entertains True Godliness, is as much for the work of religion, as for the wages of religion. Some there be who serve God, that they may serve themselves upon God: But a true Christian desires grace, not only that God would glorify him in heaven, but that he may glorify God on earth: He cries, 'Lord, rather let me have a good heart than a great estate;' though he loves many things besides God, yet he loves nothing above God. The man fears sin more than suffering, and therefore he will suffer rather than sin: He is like a palm-tree, he will always flourish best when he is pressed down most.[53]

Keach was seeking to expose much of what passed for genuine religion in his day, and to ensure that his readers would become discerning, able to see the differences between genuine Christianity and that which he believed to be false. This explains, for example, why Keach's traveller, True Godliness, having knocked on the doors and been invited into the homes of such characters as Mr. Formalist and Mr. Legality, is eventually firmly rejected by them after considerable discussion and disagreement. These two men were clearly strangers to the experience of conversion. Keach wanted his readers to realize how easy, and yet how dangerous it was to be religious, without being converted to Christ.

The same aim lies behind Keach's sequel to *The Travels of True Godliness*. In *The Travels of Ungodliness*, the traveller is a very different character. Apollyon dispatches Tyrant Sin to earth with a

53 Keach, *The Travels of True Godliness*, 10.

specific mission to tempt and to deceive every kind of person. Keach traces Sin's journey in the world. He gives, for example, sketches of his effects on Cain, his evil influences in the days of Noah, his impact on the pharoahs who dealt so harshly with Israel, his influence on the Canaanite nations who were defeated by Israel and, in particular, his activities during the time of Christ and the apostles.

The greater part of the allegory focuses attention on the present travels of Tyrant Sin and his visits to Nonage, where he delights to keep young children in ignorance. This theme echoes Keach's concerns that led him to write his primers. Visits follow to Youthshire, to Sensuality, to Commerce and to the town of Religion. Keach sets out to expose Tyrant Sin by showing his readers the nature of sin and the multifarious ways in which sin affects ordinary people in all walks of life and at every age of life. It was meant to serve as a warning against the enemy who was seeking their destruction.

The aim of transforming the life of his readers and clearly pointing out the way to the city of God also lies behind the writing of this allegory. Keach creates a character called Neophitus who is battling with living in the world, but is helped on his way to the city of God by True Godliness, Theologue and Thoughtful. Keach wanted to encourage his readers by assuring them that ultimately Tyrant Sin would not triumph over Christ. The allegory ends with the defeat of Tyrant Sin: a judge and jury try him and many witnesses are brought against him. He is eventually found guilty of all the charges and shown no mercy, for the deserved sentence of eternal death is passed on him.

Having surveyed the contents of these primers, and of the four imaginative writings and drawn attention to their popularity while Keach was alive (and, in some cases, long after his death), it is natural to ask why these books were so popular. After all, these books were from the pen of a man who formed part of a religious minority in England, which was at the same time being harassed by the authorities. There are several reasons to be considered.

Keach's books were cheaply priced and therefore affordable to all but the poorest members of society. The cheapest of his works was probably available for 6d (sixpence), "the usual price for a book made up of a single sermon."[54] Books such as *The Travels of True Godliness* would have been available for a shilling, or at the most 1s. 6d. (1 shilling, sixpence). Keeble lists a wide variety of works including Bunyan's *Grace Abounding to the Chief of Sinners* and *The Pilgrim's Progress*, and Baxter's *A Call to the Unconverted*, which would have sold for a similar price.[55]

Then, Keach was easy to read. His style was clear, simple and plain. He was not laying out principles of doctrine in an erudite and sophisticated manner but drawing characters with his pen with whom his readers could readily identify. In *The Travels of True Godliness*, Riches, Poverty, Youth and Old Age were all depicted by Keach—and he made very clear in each case why they refused to have True Godliness lodging with them and why they finally drove him away. These characters, like all the others, were intended to be a mirror in which readers could see themselves.

This is well illustrated by what happened in the house of Mr. Legalist. When True Godliness went to his house, under the shadow of Mt. Sinai on the outskirts of the town of Religion, he quickly recognized how Mr. Legalist was like Morality. As the dialogue proceeds, it is quite clear that Mr. Legalist has false hopes of receiving forgiveness from Christ because he is relying on his own supposed holiness of life and outward conformity to the law. He does not understand that God forgives sin through believing on Jesus Christ and not by trying to live a holy life.

---

54 Keeble, *The Literary Culture of Nonconformity*, 134. This was the price of a printed sermon preached by Keach at the funeral of John Norcott, *A Summons to the Grave*, published in 1676, which I will consider in chapter 7.

55 Keeble, *The Literary Culture of Nonconformity*, 134.

True Godliness calls on him to turn his useless servants—Mr. Misbelief, Good-opinion and Self-righteous—out of the house, and he suggests that he move from Mt. Sinai. Mr. Legalist is now quite upset because he realizes that Moses will have to be put out as well. True Godliness assures him that he must do that, and also dismiss Blind-zeal, Ignorance and Legal-heart. In their place, he promises to send him True-zeal, Right faith, Broken-heart and Good-understanding. Such a challenge to his hopes draws out an angry response from Mr. Legalist, and he dismisses True Godliness, calling him a Libertine and an Antinomian because of his insistence that a man is justified by God's grace and not by his attempts to keep the law. So, by means of a well-sustained storyline, with lively dialogue, Keach communicates very effectively to his readers that salvation is not by works but by faith in Jesus Christ.

Keach also had a lively imagination, evident in both his allegories and poetic works. It is true that Keach did not have the gift of imaginative writing that characterized John Bunyan, nor could he compete with the poetic abilities of John Milton (1608–1674). This is perhaps one reason why *The Pilgrim's Progress* and *Paradise Lost* are still in print and read today, while Keach lies largely forgotten. James Barry Vaughn concluded that

> unlike Bunyan, Keach was unable to create excitement, tension, and interest in his dramatic situations because his characters never succeed in being real individuals, they are never more than abstract concepts, divine attributes, or aspects of human personality.[56]

In a similar vein, he says "most of his poetry is disastrously bad," apart from *The Glorious Lover*, where he says he "displays some

56 Vaughn, "Public Worship and Practical Theology in the Work of Benjamin Keach (1640–1704)," 304–305.

skill."[57] These seem somewhat harsh conclusions, and Vaughn appears to suggest that Keach's works were, to a large extent, a failure. While it is true that some of Keach's characters do not "come alive" in the same way as Bunyan's, that does not make him a failure. Keach's poem, *The Glorious Lover*, is certainly inferior to Milton's great epic, but it is not disastrously bad poetry as Vaughn suggests. Furthermore, there has been discussion over the sources that Keach used for his works, and there is no doubt that he borrowed extensively from a number of authors, including Bunyan and Milton.[58] However, genuine creative originality is a rare gift, and nearly all writers draw help and inspiration from others, consciously and unconsciously. What can be said is that Keach wrote with a desire to edify his readers and with a burning ambition to see them converted to Christ and established in godliness.[59] There will be differences of opinion about the value of his imaginative writings. What is beyond dispute is the fact that some of the books considered in this chapter were very popular. In some cases, they were even bestsellers in a competitive marketplace, well-received during his lifetime and for some generations afterward.

Keach was also down to earth and not afraid to express his human emotions. His writings exhibit an honest awareness that is born out of personal experience of the love of Christ, his own struggles with sin and his experience as a pastor. He was aware of the complexity of living in the real world and the difficulties and temptations facing Christians who truly seek to be godly. In his

57 Vaughn, "Public Worship and Practical Theology in the Work of Benjamin Keach (1640–1704)," 306.

58 Vaughn, "Public Worship and Practical Theology in the Work of Benjamin Keach (1640–1704)," 278–300, and David Aitken, "Benjamin Keach: 'The Glorious Lover', An Analogue of Paradise Lost?," *BQ*, 24 (1991): 132–135.

59 The same observation has been made about Bunyan's verse by Barry E. Horner. "The tinker was not interested in 'art for art's sake', but rather the poetic encapsulation of truth for the cause of effective evangelism and stimulating edification." Barry E. Horner, *Pilgrim's Progress: Themes and Issues* (Darlington: Evangelical Press, 2003), 312.

dialogue between fathers and children in the primers, Keach shows that he is well aware of the questions being turned over in the minds of children and young people. He is familiar with the sexual and other temptations that face young men and women and with the peculiar temptations of riches, on the one hand, and poverty, on the other. He also recognized the deceitful nature of sin and its ability to blind people to their need of salvation from sin. He was familiar with the attitudes that people adopted toward preachers like himself, belittling and scorning them because they continued to preach the gospel with passionate exhortations, urging people to repent of their sins and trust in Jesus Christ alone.

The godliness Keach advocated was not a killjoy religion, promoting a kind of sourness that restricts and eventually crushes human emotions. Nor was it a form of asceticism, urging a withdrawal from the world. On the contrary, he was attempting to equip young men and women and others and show them how to take their place in the world and live godly lives in the midst of dangers and difficulties.

Poetry was a natural way for Keach to express his emotions. There are often hymns of joy closing his books—expressing love toward Christ and a sense of wonder, together with praise and thanksgiving to God for his grace and goodness in salvation—demonstrating a delight in God and in Jesus Christ. *The Glorious Lover* is a love poem about the love of Christ for his people. Keach was clearly not ashamed of his humanity or of expressing his emotions. Keeble, having described what was often referred to in the seventeenth century as "heart religion," concludes thus:

> The emotional sterility so often attributed to Puritanism and the nonconformists developed not here [nonconformity] but in the work of court dramatists, and poets and of episcopalian divines. [60]

---

60 Keeble, *The Literary Culture of Nonconformity*, 214.

There was nothing "escapist" about Keach, although he believed fervently in the ultimate triumph of the kingdom of God. Consequently, he faced the real world with patience, perseverance and courage, and maintained personal godliness. He wrote to encourage others to follow his example, especially while the persecutions persisted during the 1670s and 1680s. Keach was no stranger to such experiences himself. It is no wonder, therefore, that Apollyon should threaten Thoughtful (in *The Travels of True Godliness*) "with great persecution, it being the portion of all who entertained True Godliness, insomuch as his very life might be in danger."[61] Godliness comforted Thoughtful with "many precious promises." This was how Keach saw himself in his role of a pastor, and it was how he equipped his readers to stand firm in their faith.

Finally, Keach was pre-eminently biblical. It is not simply that his doctrine was biblical, nor that he urged readers to be certain that they had experienced a real conversion to Jesus Christ. The Bible was his final authority, but it was also his source book. The Bible was about people who experienced similar dangers and struggles. It was full of metaphors and other figures of speech. It contained such literary forms as narrative, dialogue, poetry and parable. Keach appreciated this and was prepared to use the same methods to preach the gospel. If someone had asked Keach to justify his use of poetry and the use of his imagination, he would have almost certainly replied that he was only being biblical. The fact that much of Restoration drama, poetry and fiction promoted something other than godliness did not deter Keach or other Nonconformist writers. It is probably the case that his allegories were consciously intended to compete with the drama and fiction of his day with the express purpose of promoting godliness.[62]

---

61 Keach, *Travels of True Godliness*, 161.

62 Somerville, *The Discovery of Childhood*, 122.

Despite the fact that he was not the most gifted of poets or allegorists, these poems and allegories were among the most useful and popular works that he produced. Keach was not innovative in this regard but one of several Baptists who produced verse and allegory for children.[63] Attention has recently has been drawn to the fact that religious verse for children and young people "represents the flowering of a new genre."[64] If that is the case, then Keach may justly be seen as one of the pioneers. His *War with the Devil* and *The Glorious Lover*, first published in 1673 and 1679 respectively, predate the next book similar in purpose, *A Book for Boys and Girls* by John Bunyan, by almost a decade.

---

63 Somerville, *The Discovery of Childhood*, 25

64 Green, *Print and Protestantism*, 398.

CHAPTER 7

"A man of considerable parts and experience"

> So ought a minister, who is a pastor of a church of Christ, to have much spiritual treasure in his earthen vessel, i.e., he ought to have much spiritual wisdom, or a competent measure of knowledge, and of all the graces of the Spirit, and be a man of considerable parts and experience.[1]

Benjamin Keach came to London in 1668 and soon began serving as a pastor and preacher. His labours as a faithful and sensitive pastor, as the leader of a Protestant church, defending and protecting that church from the very real threats of popery, have been related. His attempts to promote godliness among children and young people in particular, seeking to establish the future of the church, have been described. His activities during the remaining years of persecution show that while he was still involved on a wider front in defending what he believed to be the truth, his principal

1 Keach, "The Scribe," *Parables One*, 264.

responsibilities involved him in preaching the Word of God to his growing congregation in Southwark. By continued study and expanding pastoral experience, he sharpened his abilities to handle "spiritual treasure," and emerged to become a capable, all-round, well-known and respected pastor and preacher of the gospel in London—not unlike the pastor whom he described as being "a man of considerable parts and experience."

In March 1676, Keach was asked to preach the funeral sermon for John Norcott, pastor of the oldest Particular Baptist church in London, now meeting in Wapping.[2] This is the earliest published sermon by Keach available to us.[3]

He was also involved in some controversies, principally with the Quakers, and to answer some of those arguments Keach composed yet another dialogue, *The Grand Imposter Discovered: Or, the Quakers doctrine weighed in the balance and found wanting*, which was published in 1675. In the same year he wrote a book to justify his practice of laying on of hands, called *Darkness Vanquished: Or, Truth in its Primitive Purity*.

He also engaged in his first clash with some of the views of Richard Baxter. On this occasion, it was a disagreement with him over the subjects of baptism, though what Keach actually wrote on that occasion has not survived. Then, along with Thomas Delaune, he undertook to write a massive work (running to almost 1,000 pages in the modern printing), originally entitled, *Tropologia, a Key to open Scripture Metaphors, together with Types of the Old Testament*.[4] This was published in 1681.

---

2 Norcott is sometimes spelled Norcot or Northcott.

3 The earliest extant writing of Keach is "To the Reader in Commendation of this Book," an introduction to Josias Bonham's *The churches Glory*. Keach's letter reads like many of his later sermons and, by endorsing Bonham's book, Keach reflects his own concerns to promote godliness. In the beginning of the letter he states, "Nothing makes a Wicked man so much like the Devil as Sin; nor nothing makes a Saint so much resemble Christ, as doth Grace and Holiness."

4 *Tropologia* has been published recently and undergone several reprints, but with

Principally the work of Keach, *Tropologia* was adapted from notes Keach had from sermons on various Scriptural metaphors that he had previously preached to his congregation.[5]

Keach also played an important pastoral role, along with several others, in the sad case of John Child. Keach had known Child from his Buckinghamshire days. Child had also been involved in Bunyan's church in Bedford, but he tragically committed suicide after living in London for some years.

The funeral sermon of John Norcott

Keach preached at Norcott's funeral on March 28, 1676. He had been in London less than a decade but was asked to preach at the funeral of one of the earliest leaders of the London Particular Baptists. He also composed an elegy in memory of Norcott, which was published alongside the sermon. Keach was living in Shadwell at the time, so Norcott—living in Wapping on the north bank of the Thames and downstream from London Bridge—had been his near neighbour.

The first appearance in London of Calvinistic Baptists who practiced believer's baptism is difficult to date. What is clear is that in 1638 six members left the so-called Jacob-Lathrop-Jessey church founded in 1616 in Southwark.[6] In the 1630s, during the ministry of one of their pastors, John Lathrop, some became convinced that baptism for infants was invalid. An amicable

---

a different title, *Preaching from the Types and Metaphors of the Bible* (Grand Rapids: Kregel, 1972). In this book, I refer to it as *Types and Metaphors*, using the 1972 pagination.

5 Keach, *Types and Metaphors*, Preface, x.

6 It is often referred to as the Jacob-Lathrop-Jessey congregation, named after its first three pastors. (Lathrop is sometimes called Lothrop or Lathorp. In this book, Lathrop has been used except where other writers have used another spelling). See Ernest F. Kevan, *London's Oldest Baptist Church* (London: The Kingsgate Press, 1933). Kevan was probably mistaken in recording the date as 1633 instead of 1638, although there is continued uncertainty about the precise dating. For a more detailed account, see Murray Tolmie, *The Triumph of the Saints: The Separate Churches of London 1616–1649* (Cambridge: Cambridge University Press, 1977), 7–27.

parting transpired and a distinct church was formed under the leadership of John Spilsbury (1593–c.1662/8).[7] It was this group that eventually became true Baptists and was the basis of the church that met in Wapping in some premises in Old Gravel Lane.

William Kiffin was one of those who left the church in Southwark and joined with the group under Spilsbury in 1638.[8] The Wapping church, still under Spilsbury's leadership, was one of seven in London that signed the 1644 *Confession of Faith*.[9] Spilsbury died in either 1662 or 1668 and was succeeded by John Norcott.[10] Very little is known of his ministry but, when Norcott died in 1676, Keach preached at his funeral.

Though the poem is not one of Keach's better compositions, he spoke well of Norcott in his "Mournful Elegy," indicating that his ministry was short: "This godly Preacher in a little space, / Much work did do, he swiftly ran his race."[11] His removal was seen as "God's most sore chastening hand" at a time of persecution, and Keach indicated that Norcott had not always been appreciated while he was alive. He lamented the loss of a powerful, arousing preacher, who spared nothing to win sinners to Christ:

---

7 James M. Renihan, "John Spilsbury (1593–c.1662/1668)." In Haykin, ed., *The British Particular Baptists 1638–1910*, 1:21–38.

8 The Kiffin Manuscript can be found in Barrie R. White, "Baptist Beginnings and the Kiffin Manuscript," *Baptist History and Heritage*, 2 (January 1967): 29–34, Champlin Burrage, *Early English Dissenters in the Light of Recent Research (1550–1641)* (New York: Russell & Russell, 1967 reprint), 2:292–305, and "Records of the Jacob-Lathrop-Jessey Church 1616–1641," *TBHS*, 1 (1908–1909): 203–245.

9 See Lumpkin, *Baptist Confessions of Faith*, 153–171.

10 Geoffrey Nuttall, "Another Baptist ejection (1662): the case of John Norcott," ed. William H. Brackney and Paul S. Fiddes with John H.Y. Briggs, *Pilgrim Pathways: Essays in Baptist History in Honour of B.R. White* (Macon: Mercer University Press, 1999), 185–188.

11 Keach, *A Summons to the Grave, or the Necessity of a Timely Preparation for Death* (London, 1676), Elegy.

Beloved John is gone, dear Norcot's dead;
That Man of God, who hath so often fed
Our precious Souls with Manna from above:
Whose powerful preaching did ingage our love
To Jesus Christ. O! he had care and skill
To feed poor souls and do his Master's will....
Poor sinners too like cause have to complain.
There's few like him surviving to arouse
Their sluggish souls out of their sinful drouse.
They now may sleep secure and not awake....
This Golden Trumpet's stopt, 'twill sound no more,
To warn them of what danger's at their door.
To win sinners to Christ he did not spare
His strength nor time, thought nothing was too dear
To part with all, if any ways he might,
Their Souls turn from false ways unto the right.[12]

Keach's sermon was from Psalm 89:48: "What man is he that liveth and shall not see death? Shall he deliver his soul from the hand of the grave." His doctrine was stated simply: "That all men must die."[13] He briefly confirmed this as a fact and then gave reasons why it was true: (1) all have sinned; (2) God has decreed all may die; and, (3) God will magnify his glorious attributes in the death and glory of the saints. The bulk of the sermon was taken up with the application of his text. Before he came to console the church and Norcott's family, Keach used the occasion to preach to the living, seeking to arouse their consciences, as it were, from sleep:

> Have not many of you refused His grace, his Son, and divers sweet and precious calls and offers of love...nay

12 Keach, *A Summons to the Grave*, Elegy.

13 Keach, *A Summons to the Grave*, 11.

> how many warnings have you had of the near approach of death? Nay, awakening summons to prepare for the grave...?[14]

> Do not think the whole work of your lives can be done upon a dying bed. Oh consider old age is unfit for labour...delays prove the ruin of many thousands; the night cometh, says Christ, when no man can work.[15]

> ...an accusing conscience will be a bad death-bed companion.... Sincerity of heart and a good conscience will be a good sanctuary at the hour of death.[16]

But Keach was not only a conscience-rousing preacher. He also developed the skill to minister comfort to those who grieve. He reminded the assembled believers that "death may hiss but it cannot hurt,"[17] and, as he came to comfort the church and the family, he drew his hearers to Jesus Christ, the great Shepherd of the sheep. He urged them to derive their support from him who "never dies, he lives for ever, and sure he that died for the sheep, whose own sheep they are, will take care of them; he will feed them and preserve them from danger."[18]

There is much in this sermon that is typical of Keach, and reflects some of the main features of Puritan preaching. In this funeral sermon, we see the two elements that are found in all of Keach's preaching: his intention to awaken the conscience of the unconverted so that they will see their danger and turn to Christ for salvation; and, his ability to bring comfort in times of grief by pointing them to the power and care of Christ. Keach

14 Keach, *A Summons to the Grave*, 25.
15 Keach, *A Summons to the Grave*, 37.
16 Keach, *A Summons to the Grave*, 44–45.
17 Keach, *A Summons to the Grave*, 59.
18 Keach, *A Summons to the Grave*, 73.

was a searching and yet comforting preacher, and the Lord Jesus Christ was the centre of all his preaching.

There is one further observation from this sermon that reads very much like parts of his *Tropologia*, published six years later. As he laments the loss of Norcott, a godly preacher, he reminds his readers of the work of the minister and uses a number of similes: comparing them to pilots (and the church to a ship), to shepherds who keep the flocks, to captains who encourage us in warfare and to trees that yield sap to give life. In *Tropologia*, he likens ministers to angels, stars, labourers, watchmen, trumpeters, spokesmen, clouds, fathers, stewards, planters, builders, pillars, shepherds, ambassadors and rulers.[19] While only shepherds appear in both lists, it nevertheless shows us how Keach, by incorporating such figures of speech into his sermon, was already developing his framework of thought in the mid-1670s before he published his encyclopedic tome in 1681.

Controversies over baptism, the Quakers and the laying on of hands

Throughout his life Keach was involved in controversies and conflicts. This does not necessarily mean that he was, by character, an argumentative man. Though keen to argue particular issues, he was not concerned to enter into personal attacks on individuals. Three of the issues that arose in the 1670s and 1680s are considered below.

Under Keach's polemical works, Thomas Crosby lists a sheet called *Mr. Baxter's Arguments for Believers Baptism*, dated 1674.[20] This appears to be the first time Keach published anything on the subject of baptism. He set out to show that Baxter had contradicted himself, and he used Baxter's own arguments to disprove infant baptism. The contradictory statement seized on by Keach reads as follows:

---

19 Keach, *Types and Metaphors*, 828–858.

20 Crosby, *History*, 4:311.

> That as personal faith, is the condition to God, of title to the priviledges of the adult; so, the profession of this faith, is the condition of his right to the church; and without this profession he is not to be taken in as an adult member, nor admitted to the privileges as such.[21]

Crosby records that Baxter argued his point so strongly that he left his reader with the impression that without a profession of faith no infant, let alone an adult, should be baptized and received into the church. By collecting these points together, Keach used them to show that Baxter, a paedobaptist, was in effect advocating the baptism of believers. Baxter was apparently upset by this treatment and refused to answer Keach.

Keach was not the first man to accuse Baxter of self-contradiction, but we do not know if Keach himself was aware of this. Thomas Crosby clearly was, as he knew of John Tombes' *Felo de Se: or Mr. Richard Baxters Self-destroying*, published fifteen years before, in 1659.[22] Keach's advantage over Tombes was that his answer was brief and therefore much cheaper to sell. It was "put into the hands of the hawkers" and spread all over London.[23] Baxter himself records that he could hear the hawkers selling Keach's sheet underneath his own window even as he wrote *More proofs of infants church membership, and right to baptism*—at the end of which he stated that he would not answer Keach![24]

It was, however, controversy with the Quakers that provided Keach with a much larger problem. Here he felt like he was

21 Crosby, *History*, 4:277.

22 Crosby, *History*, 4:279. The full title of Tombes' work is *Felo de Se: or Mr. Richard Baxters Self-destroying: Manifested in Twenty Arguments against Infant-Baptism, Gathered out of his own Writing, in his Second Disputation of Right to Sacraments* (London, 1659). For a full discussion of the contribution of John Tombes to the seventeenth-century baptismal debate. See Michael T. Renihan, *Antipaedobaptism in the Thought of John Tombes* (Auburn: B & R Press, 2001).

23 Crosby, *History*, 4:279.

24 Crosby, *History*, 4:279.

dealing with a heresy that threatened the life of the true church and coming from those who claimed to be real Christians. Furthermore, Hannah, his youngest daughter by his first wife, became a Quaker, which must have caused him a great deal of personal pain. At the time her father wrote his dialogue against the Quakers, she would have been only eight years old. Some years later, in 1696, she left her father's church and within a year had adopted the views of the Quakers. She was removed from the membership of Stennett's Seventh-Day Baptist congregation which she had joined.[25]

Hannah was one of many former Presbyterians, Independents and Baptists who identified themselves with the teachings of George Fox (1624–1691). The Quakers grew out of the religious controversies of the 1650s teaching that outward belief was powerless to save anyone and that the universal Inward Light, sometimes referred to as Divine Revelation or as the Christ within (based on John 1:9–18), was the only way to truth. This Inward Light was necessary to lead men and women into unity and continually revealed truth (teaching drawn from John 16:13). Quakers rejected the Bible's teaching on the Trinity, on human sinfulness and on justification by faith in Jesus Christ and denied the validity of baptism and the Lord's Supper. In particular, they denied the authority of the Bible.

Keach was quite clear in his own mind as to the danger presented by their beliefs. For him, denial of the existence of the God-Man, Jesus Christ, meant they should be regarded as heretics:

> Heretics, such as are Arians, Socinians, Eutichians, and Caffinites blaspheme him [Christ], ungod him, and take the crown off his head, rendering him no more than a mere creature. The Quakers utterly deny he hath any personal existence, or that he is an individual Person or

25 See Chapter 9.

> God-Man, now in heaven above, but strive to make people believe he is nothing but a mere inward or divine quality of light and power in all men.[26]

Keach produced a polemical dialogue called *The Grand Imposter Discovered*, in which he systematically described and criticized Quaker beliefs and practices. T.L. Underwood made extensive use of Keach's dialogue in his study of the conflict between Baptists and Quakers, using quotations from the dialogue at the head of each chapter in order to represent the attitudes of Quakers and Baptists toward one another.[27]

Keach does not appear to have been involved in the four public debates between the Quakers and the Baptists that took place in London between 1672 and 1674. It is possible that he was present for some of the debates. T.L. Underwood reports that on some occasions, 3,000 people attended them, but we have no direct proof of Keach's attendance.[28] His personal cir-

---

26 Keach, "The Pearl of Great Price," *Parables One*, 188. Keach placed Quakers alongside those who had led the early church astray in the third and fourth centuries, including men like Arius (*c.* 250–*c.* 336) and Eutyches (*c.* 378–454), and sixteenth-century Socinianism, named after Lelio Socinus (1525–1562) and his nephew Faustus (1539–1604), whose teachings still threatened the seventeenth-century churches, and a contemporary General Baptist, Matthew Caffyn (1628–1714), who in the 1670s was beginning to express doubts over the orthodox doctrine of the Trinity.

27 T. L. Underwood, *Primitivism, Radicalism, and the Lamb's War: The Baptist-Quaker Conflict in Seventeenth Century England* (Oxford: Oxford University Press, 1997), 122. See also A.S. Langley "Seventeenth Century Baptist Disputations, *THBS*, 6, (1918–1919): 216–243. Underwood's book is by far the most comprehensive book on the relationship between Baptists and Quakers. His thesis is that "primitivism," the desire to get back to the teaching and practice of the primitive New Testament church, was the driving force in both movements. There was, however, a clear distinction: the Baptists held firmly that the Scriptures were the final authority and that the Spirit would not contradict the Word; the Quakers, on the other hand, drove a wedge between the Word and the Spirit and effectively exalted human authority, though they believed that they were being led by the Spirit.

28 Underwood, *Primitivism, Radicalism, and the Lamb's War*, 20.

cumstances may have prevented him attending. In 1670, his wife died, leaving him with the sole care of a young family, before he remarried in 1672. In the London debates with the Quakers, Thomas Hicks played a leading role for the Baptists, among whom were Jeremiah Ives, Thomas Plant, William Kiffin and Hanserd Knollys. All of these men were Particular Baptists, with the exception of Jeremiah Ives. Knollys certainly knew Keach, as he had recently married him to Susannah Partridge in late April 1672. On the Quaker side were William Penn (1644–1718), George Whitehead, Isaac Penington, George Keith, Stephen Crisp and Thomas Elwood.

The Quakers had made heavy inroads among General Baptists in the Midlands and Buckinghamshire, so Keach would have already been familiar with them. Crosby reports that Ives, who had published *The Quakers Quaking* in 1656, had been involved in a debate with Quakers in High Wycombe prior to the London debates. This shows that there was already a considerable Quaker presence in Buckinghamshire.[29]

Keach's contemporary, Richard Barclay (1648–1690), provided some of the clearest presentations of Quaker theology and was writing prodigiously in the 1670s.[30] In 1676, in *An Apology for the True Christian Divinity* (one of thirteen books published by him in that period), Barclay made it very plain that the Inner Light within the individual—and not the Scriptures—was the final authority in matters of religion:

> Because the scriptures are only a declaration of the source, and not the source itself, they are not to be considered the principal foundation of truth and knowledge.... Yet because they give a true and faithful

29 Crosby, *History*, 2:231. Crosby also gives a detailed account of the first debate in which Hicks was cleared of having made false accusations against the Quakers.

30 *BDBR*, s.v. "Barclay, Richard."

> testimony of the source itself, they are and may be regarded as a secondary rule that is subordinate to the Spirit.... We truly know...only by the inward testimony of the Spirit or, as the Scriptures say, the Spirit is the guide by which the faithful are led by the Truth.[31]

This alone would have been sufficient for Keach and his Baptist friends to condemn Quaker teaching, for it opened the door to all kinds of errors. Keach did not believe they had the Spirit of God but rather that their claims were false and that they were not genuine Christians.

In 1675, Keach wrote *The Grand Imposter Discovered* to denounce their teachings, but it was never republished in his lifetime. Nevertheless, he continued to be critical of Quaker views, preaching strongly against them in later sermons and exposing them in *The Travels of Ungodliness*. David Copeland asserts that the strongest statement against Quakers is found here, but Keach's statement appears to have been edited out of later editions.[32] When the judge addressed Tyrant Sin at his trial, before he could plead guilty or not guilty, a "Friend" interrupted proceedings. He insisted on wearing his hat and showed contempt for the court and its authority. He refused to identify himself but Keach did, through the High Constable, Christianity:

> My Lord, he is a Criminal, and his Name is Imposter, alias, Erroneous; and we took the Prisoner in his House, in the Town of Heresie; and he endeavoured to hide under the Cloak of Light, Life, Power &c.[33]

---

31 Quoted by David A. Copeland, *Benjamin Keach and the Development of Baptist Traditions in Seventeenth Century England* (Lewiston: The Edwin Mellen Press, 2001), 64.

32 Copeland, *Benjamin Keach and the Development of Baptist Traditions*, 68.

33 Copeland, *Benjamin Keach and the Development of Baptist Traditions*, 68.

Then the Quaker, hat now removed, spoke for himself informing the judge that authority belonged to:

> The Light within all Men, or Divine Revelation, I care not which of them two; however I disown, Sir, Sacred Scripture to be the Judge; though People have in an Idolatrous manner so long adored him.... What is Sir Sacred Scripture but a lifeless Fellow, a pitiful Paper-Judge, a Dead Letter?[34]

From Keach's perspective, the Quakers presented a very real threat to the church because of their false doctrine.

No such threat existed in connection with the third area of controversy in which Keach was involved. This was of a different order altogether and concerned the laying on of hands. This was a practice that Keach had adopted and continued to advocate throughout his life. He had probably become familiar with this ordinance while a General Baptist in Buckinghamshire. When he came to London and adopted Calvinistic theology, his convictions about the laying on of hands were unaltered. William Rider, his predecessor in the church where he first became pastor, had also practiced the laying on of hands.[35] Keach was not alone among the Particular Baptists, and Hercules Collins—John Norcott's successor in Wapping—also advocated the practice. Keach published a reply to Mr. Henry Danvers' work against the practice of the laying on of hands, called *Darkness Vanquished: Or, Truth in its Primitive Purity*, in 1675. This was enlarged and

---

34 Copeland, *Benjamin Keach and the Development of Baptist Traditions*, 68.

35 Quoted in J.K. Parrett, "An Early Baptist on the Laying on of Hands," *BQ*, 15 (1953–1954): 325–327, 330. William Rider, *Laying on of Hands (or a plain discovery of the truth thereof, under those several considerations minded in the New Testament* (London, 1656). See also Ernest R. Payne, "Baptists and the Laying on of Hands," *BQ*, 15 (1953–1954): 203–215. Crosby traces the practice back to Anabaptists in Holland and to the 1660 General Baptist declaration of faith. Crosby, *History*, 4:291.

given a new title in the 1698 second edition, *Laying on of Hands upon Baptized Believers, as such, Proved an Ordinance of Christ.*

According to Keach, this issue was a matter of biblical church order. Laying on of hands was a church ordinance that should follow baptism and precede coming to the Lord's Supper. His argument was based on Hebrews 6:1–2 where six principles were laid out: (1) repentance from dead works; (2) faith toward God; (3) the doctrine of baptism; (4) laying on of hands; (5) resurrection from the dead; and (6) eternal judgement. Keach believed it was essential:

> It is a Foundation principle of God's House, or one of the great Pillars (next to Christ) on which it is built, it must needs remain; and very dangerous it is for any to take away a Foundation-stone.[36]

When hands were laid on a baptized believer, the minister would pray for an increase in the gifts and graces of the Holy Spirit so that they would hold fast to the faith professed in their baptism. Keach believed this to be consistent with New Testament practice. While Keach acknowledged that baptism and laying on of hands were not fundamentals of salvation, he claimed that they are fundamentals of a gospel church. One of his strongest statements is found in a sermon on the vineyard from Matthew 21:42. Here he shows that a minister, like a master-builder, must know how many foundations there are contained in "the constitution of a true regular gospel church, and also know how, and where to place them in order." He continued,

> ...for if a church want but one essential principle, it is defective, and no complete congregation, according to

---

36 Keach, *Laying on of Hands upon Baptized Believers, as such, Proved an Ordinance of Christ* (London, 1698), 75.

> the primitive constitution: if it hath six, as it appears it hath, and wants but one, it is imperfect.... These six principles therefore, as here laid down, are fundamentals of a gospel church: and some are such, so they all belong to babes in Christ, or are A B C of a Christian man, in order to his regular admittance into the church. True, a church may be a true church and formally true, too, (i.e., they may give themselves up to the Lord, and to one another, as a congregation, to walk together in the fellowship of the gospel) who may not be baptized, nor own laying on of hands; but then they must be considered, not a complete gospel church but in some things defective, in respect to its constitution and regular gospel form, or as wanting a pillar &c. A house may be a real house, though it may want a principal post it stands on; it may be pretty firm, and may stand though one be missing; however, it is not so safe, to want one principle of the doctrine of Christ.[37]

Unlike the conflict over Quaker teaching and practice, the laying on of hands was not a matter of life and death. Keach continued to hold strong views and no one was admitted to the Lord's Supper in the church at Horselydown unless they had been baptized and had hands laid on them. Most Particular Baptist churches rejected the teaching, and there is no reference to the subject in the 1689 *London Baptist Confession of Faith*, and no discussion of the matter in the General Assemblies of the Particular Baptists. Keach and Collins were key members of those London assemblies. It seems clear, therefore, that Keach and Collins were able to continue their practice without separating from their brethren.

---

37 Keach, "The Vineyard," *Parables Two*, 32.

Tropologia

Our attention now turns to the massive task that Keach undertook to put into print his studies of biblical metaphors and types. The work began as sermons and involved him in a prolonged and intensive study of the Scriptures. The resulting *Tropologia* was the closest Keach came to writing a systematic theology—though it would have been far from complete. He was not responsible for it in its entirety, but co-authored the book with his friend Thomas Delaune. Delaune is perhaps best known for his *A Plea for the Nonconformists*, published in 1684. There he argued "that we ought to believe *Nothing*, as an Article of Faith, but what God hath revealed, and the compleat revelation of God's will to us as contained in the Bible &c."[38] This was the essence of the Nonconformists argument of why they could not join in the rites and ceremonies of the Church of England. Although these ceremonies were not *forbidden* in Scripture, they had no direct *warrant* from Scripture and were therefore to be rejected. Delaune was a schoolmaster and was responsible for the first part of *Tropologia*.[39] This was the technical section explaining the various figures of speech in the Bible and the differences between types and parables. It was, in fact, partly translated and compiled from works of continental divines, particularly, Salomon Glassius's *Philologia Sacra*.[40]

---

38 Thomas Delaune, *A Plea for the Nonconformists, Giving the true State of the Dissenters Case* (London, 1684), 5. Delaune was replying to Dr. Benjamin Calamy's (1642–1686) invitation in a sermon about scrupulous consciences and putting the case clearly for Nonconformity. He found himself in Newgate Prison for his efforts and, despite protesting to Calamy about his unfair treatment, he died in prison.

39 *Tropologia* was originally published in four parts. The modern edition has reduced it to two parts.

40 Salomon Glassius, *Philologiae Sacrae, qua totius sacrosanctae Veteris et Novi Testamenti Scripturae* (Jena, 1623). Salomon Glassius (1593–1656) was professor of divinity at Jena and also superintended churches and schools in the duchy of Saxe Gotha. *Philologiae Sacrae* was his principal work. Four editions had been published by 1668, and it was last published in 1776. It was regarded as being very useful for the interpret-

The second part is Keach's work, and it deals with the metaphors of the Bible in a topical order, beginning with God, the Lord Jesus Christ and the Holy Spirit. The doctrine of the Trinity, the gospel and salvation from sin are dealt with under the heading of the Word of God. There are further sections on graces and ordinances, the church, men, sin and the devil, the means of grace, providence and affliction, the world, man's life and death, resurrection and heaven and hell, before he concludes with a section on the types of Christ from the Old Testament. It is encyclopedic, effectively covering some of the main heads of theology, but it is also intensely practical. His method was to take a metaphor and then analyze it from every possible angle and to give the parallel from the Scriptures. In this way, he provided the reader with his own exposition and interpretation of the metaphor. Spurgeon, with his keen sense of humour, drew attention to Keach's "laborious treatise" pointing out that it was "open to much criticism on the score of making metaphors run not only on all-fours, but on as many legs as a centipede."[41] Keach's work had its limitations, but it has yielded some very practical and warm expositions, as previous quotations demonstrate.

Written at a time of intense persecution, it is not surprising to find references to the papacy. For Keach, the image of the church as a bush on fire but not consumed (referring to Exodus 3:2) is a very apt metaphor of the church experiencing "hellish plots and contrivances" and fires that have been "kindled to consume the poor Church of God in England."[42] He picks up the imagery of the Christian as a soldier and as a runner, in order to explain the nature of the Christian life. William Gurnall (1617–1689) made

---

ation of the Bible, casting light on the language and phraseology of Scripture.

41 C.H. Spurgeon, *Lectures to my Students* (Pasadena: Pilgrim Publications, 1990), 109. Spurgeon is not dismissive of Keach's efforts and defends him against the condemnation of Adam Clarke, who stated that Keach's work debased the taste of both preachers and people more than any other work of its kind.

42 Keach, *Types and Metaphors*, 694.

use of the soldier imagery in *The Christian in Complete Armour* and Bunyan of the runner in *The Heavenly Footman*.

Tropologia is important for a number of different reasons. For modern readers who cannot easily gain access to Keach's long out-of-print writings, *Preaching from the Types and Metaphors of the Bible* (the twentieth-century version of *Tropologia*) makes Keach's thought accessible on a wide range of biblical subjects. Given the technical nature of the first section in particular, it was clearly intended as a means of help for young students and ministers in their preparation for preaching.[43] It is a book that examines how to interpret the Scriptures and provides insight into how the Bible was being interpreted and preached in the latter part of the seventeenth century. By using metaphors, Keach was employing image-based illustrations that made biblical teaching tangible, especially to those with limited literacy. He believed that such images were a great aid to effective preaching; they were "not intended to clear facts, but to explain doctrines, affect the heart, and convince the conscience."[44] Furthermore, some of the themes of his later sermons and books are found in embryonic form in *Tropologia*. For example, he deals with the biblical warrant for congregational support of ministers of the gospel, which served as a forerunner to *The Gospel Minister's Maintenance Vindicated*, which Keach wrote at the request of the 1689 Assembly in order that it could be circulated to all the churches.

In addition, *Tropologia* contains Keach's doctrine of the ordinances of the church. In particular, he expounds the significance

---

43 Keach, *Types and Metaphors*, "The Foreword," viii, quoted by Herbert Lockyer.

44 Keach, *Types and Metaphors*, "The Preface," xii. A thorough examination of Keach's use of metaphors in his sermons has been undertaken by Chris Holmes. Not only does he examine *Tropologia* but also Keach's sermons on the parables, together with his many other published sermons. See James Christopher Holmes, "The Role of Metaphor in the Sermons of Benjamin Keach" (Ph.D. dissertation, The Southern Baptist Theological Seminary, 2009).

of baptism and the Lord's Supper for the first time. Under "Baptism as a burial," he begins by showing the literal meaning of the verb, "to baptize," and how it means to cover all over with water as opposed to sprinkling. He then goes on to explain the significance of the burial metaphor. He concludes by working out some of the inferences of baptism, one of which states that if baptism is carried out by sprinkling, then it is "disorderly, and should be rectified." Another is that this baptism is "evangelical law," and the church ought "to practise it no otherwise than he [Christ] has prescribed, because it was once so delivered to the saints."[45]

With regard to the Lord's Supper, Keach vigorously opposes the Roman Catholic teaching of transubstantiation. It takes the words, "this is my body," literally, and Keach shows that it is actually figurative, a sign of Christ's body. As he explains the significance of the Lord's Supper, he explains why Christ instituted the ordinance, who ought to partake, what is required of those who do partake, how a Christian may receive the Lord's Supper with much comfort and, finally, what is the use of the Lord's Supper. It would appear, too, that Keach believed in the "real presence," that is, that the Lord's Supper is more than just a memorial feast. As Keach put it, "there is a mystical conveyance or communication of all Christ's blessed merits to our souls through faith held forth thereby, and in glorious manner received, in the right participation of it."[46]

Keach's massive study also contains materials that are not covered elsewhere in such detail in his writings. For example, some of the clearest statements he put into print on the Trinity are found here. It is also clear that he had a high view of the nature and the calling of the gospel minister and the need for order and discipline in the church. Throughout *Tropologia*, there are

---

45 Keach, *Types and Metaphors*, 629–632.

46 Keach, *Types and Metaphors*, 639. In this, Keach was following Calvin rather than Ulrich Zwingli in his understanding of the significance of the Lord's Supper.

many references to the Roman Church as well as to the persecution Dissenters were continuing to experience during the 1680s. The overall impression is that Keach is pre-eminently a man of the Bible. He believed it was the Word of God and aimed by his doctrine and teaching to establish his hearers in the truth of God's gospel. For Keach, such convictions were a matter of life and death. Exhorting his congregation to pray, he pressed home his message by saying:

> If the Gospel be so glorious, O! pray, whosoever thou art, that God would be pleased to open thine eyes, that thou mayest see it to be so, and cry mightily, that he would be pleased never to take it away from this poor nation, nor suffer its glory and brightness to be eclipsed by letting in Popish darkness again among us. If we once lose the Gospel, we may all cry Ichabod, the glory is departed from England; and with the church of old, say, "The crown is fallen from our heads, woe unto us that we have sinned."[47]

Finally, as in nearly all his works, Keach's skill as a pastor comes to the fore, showing that he was indeed "a man of considerable parts and experience." There is, for example, a section on "faith more precious than gold," where he concludes by answering four questions:

> 1. Will not a small or weak Faith save us, as well as a strong?
> 2. Why are some Christians are so weak in Faith?
> 3. How may I know a weak Faith from a strong?
> 4. How may a weak faith or hand be strengthened, and feeble knees confirmed?

---

47 Keach, *Types and Metaphors*, 566.

This is Keach at his best, providing instructive comfort for weak believers.[48]

I would suggest that *Tropologia* should be seen as a watershed in Keach's ministry. It was first published in 1681 at a point close to the middle of his life as a preacher—he was forty-two and in his prime, reaching a maturity of outlook and understanding. During these years, he continued to defy the authorities. Another twenty-two years of teaching and ministry lay ahead of him, fifteen of which would come after the Act of Toleration. *Tropologia* demonstrates how Keach interpreted the Bible and how he never lost sight of the central issue, namely, the saving knowledge of God and of Jesus Christ. Keach had formulated mature convictions across the whole spectrum of Christian doctrine, having worked his way out of his "Arminian errors" and imbibing the Calvinism characteristic of the Particular Baptists. Many of the matters that he was to write about later were but further developments or specific applications of his understanding of the Bible forged in these earlier years and expressed in *Tropologia*.

"*The English Spira*"—*the sad case of John Child*

There is one further matter to consider here. That is, Keach's pastoral role in—and understanding of—what happened to John Child. Keach did not play a primary role in this matter, but he did visit Child on several occasions when Child was in a severely depressed condition. Keach included an account of some of these events in *Some Passages of the Fearful Estate of John Child*.[49]

John Child was from Buckinghamshire. In the late 1650s, Child had become involved with John Bunyan's congregation in neighbouring Bedfordshire and was assigned visitation responsibilities

48 Keach, *Types and Metaphors*, 617.

49 Keach, "Some Passages of the Fearful Estate of John Child," *A Golden Mine Opened*, 48–52.

with Bunyan. By 1658, he had broken from the Bedford congregation and moved to London. When he was asked to give a written account to the Bedford congregation of his reasons for leaving, he acknowledged that he had been at fault in some things but the matter never seemed to be resolved.[50] He was actively engaged in preaching after 1658 in Buckinghamshire, Bedfordshire and Hertfordshire. Child came to London again later, on a more permanent basis, having been invited there by Thomas Plant. For a short while, in 1676, Child was a pastor in Gracechurch Street. He terminated his responsibilities there and then began to show signs of increasing instability, broadening his sympathies and beginning to wander between attending dissenting conventicles and the Church of England.

Publishing *For a More full and firm Union among all good Protestants*, Child argued that Dissenters should take the Lord's Supper in the Church of England. *A Second Argument* followed in 1683. By now, he was not only asserting that the state church had the essentials for salvation but he was attacking his former dissenting friends, telling them that they had espoused heretical opinions, that they were wrong to oppose bishops and accusing them of being covetous, ignoring the poor and leaving their ministers in penury.

James Jones, another Particular Baptist pastor in Southwark, replied to Child's accusations, castigating him and denouncing him as a hypocrite, a false brother and a liar. By July 1684, Child had plunged into despair and was inconsolable; his conscience was severely troubled, for the thought he had committed the unpardonable sin. He consulted with a number of pastors, many of

---

50 The most full and modern account of this unfolding tragedy is in Richard L. Greaves, *Glimpses of Glory: John Bunyan and English Dissent* (Stanford: Stanford University Press, 2002), 515–518. A contemporary account is supplied by Benjamin Dennis and Thomas Plant, *The English Spira: Being a Fearful Example of an Apostate* (London, 1693). It was explained in the preface that, had it not been for the troubled times, it would have been published much earlier.

whom he had criticized, including Keach and Bunyan, and all of them assured him that he had not committed the unpardonable sin. The evidence suggests they treated him sympathetically and also urged him to retract his accusations, which he did partially. But, this brought him no relief, and he found he was unable to repent of his sins, instead, regarding himself as a hopeless reprobate beyond help. His first attempt at suicide failed but, in October 1684, he succeeded in hanging himself with a leather strap while his wife slept at their home in Brick Lane, near Spitalfields. Child became known as "the English Spira" as his actions were similar to an Italian man named Spira who had apostatized from the faith during the sixteenth century. In the minds of those who tried to minister to John Child, his case had many parallels.

Keach's involvement shows a measured and careful assessment. He had known John Child for over thirty years, first in Buckinghamshire and then in London, when Child came to live near him in Shadwell. He observed that "he was a man of Considerable Natural Parts and Ability...yet seemed to be of a haughty Spirit, loving Applause and Popularity, which it may be feared was the cause of his Fall."[51] Keach had also seen him change his opinions and adopt Arminian views but says he first became alarmed when he heard Child say words to this effect: "I have seriously considered whether there be anything in Religion worth suffering for."[52] To a man like Keach, who had suffered for his own convictions, these words reflected a serious departure from the faith. After Child had conformed to the Church of England, he had attacked Dissenters and subsequently fell into a deep depression. Keach had been one of the first men the desperate Child sent to for help. Keach recorded many of the despairing words Child said about himself, and observed that when some came to visit him, Child resisted their attempts to pray for him.

51 Keach, *A Golden Mine Opened*, 48.

52 Keach, *A Golden Mine Opened*, 48.

Keach reserved his judgement on the poor man, "not knowing how God might deal with him, whose mercy is Infinite, for I do not believe Self-murther is an unpardonable sin."[53] Yet, at the same time, Keach himself had been shaken by the experience and said he was of the opinion that even if an atheist had met this man, he would have been convinced that there is a God, or a power above nature "who can touch, shake, and disorder, and turn into Confusion the strongest constitution of Body, by ministering and fastning terrible things upon the Soul."[54] For Keach, the sad case of John Child was a terrible warning to others of what might happen to someone who turns against God.

It would be easy to accuse Keach and others of being unsympathetic to John Child. The man was clearly unstable and Keach had already observed some of the outward signs of that instability in his character when he observed his haughty spirit some years before. James Jones had denounced him, and that may not have helped Child's condition. Toward the end of his life, it is evident that John Child was suffering acutely, in an advanced state of depression and despair, worsened by his religious defection. Keach showed John Child compassion and had urged him to seek medical advice (perhaps from Dr. John Roberts, who was a member of Keach's own congregation), but Child did not heed his advice. Keach also offered to bring two or three others with him and pray with Child, but again the offer was refused.[55] Keach constantly tried to persuade Child of God's mercy in Christ. He

> yet endeavoured with the utmost of his ability to comfort him, by shewing him the greatness of God's mercy to true penitent persons, together with the infinite value of Christ's Blood, telling him withal that he was glad to find

53 Keach, *A Golden Mine Opened*, 51.

54 Keach, *A Golden Mine Opened*, 52.

55 Dennis and Plant, *The English Spira*, 12–13.

John Owen (1616–1683) was considered by Keach to be the greatest gift of Christ to the late seventeenth-century church.

> he had the sense of his great Evil on his heart, or words to that effect and that he hoped this breaking was in order to healing: But Mr. Child said he doubted of that.[56]

Given Keach's sensitive pastoral heart, there can be little doubt that Keach would have experienced a great heaviness of spirit as a result of his dealings with this sad case.

Keach's varied activities as a pastor, sometimes being called on to defend the faith, and the substance of his early preaching in London, have been considered. It has been argued that the comprehensive and systematic study that led to the publication of *Tropologia*, provided a firm foundation for his future ministry. It is also clear, largely on the basis of his many references in his later sermons, that during these years Keach was also reading extensively the works of his Nonconformist contemporaries, men such as William Bates (1625–1699), Stephen Charnock (1628–1680), Thomas Goodwin, Thomas Manton and, in particular, John Owen, whom Keach regarded as the greatest gift of Christ to the late seventeenth-century church.[57] By this kind of interaction, he continued to strengthen and deepen his biblical and Calvinistic convictions. In this way, he was being prepared for the remaining fifteen faithful and fruitful years of his ministry, in the period of toleration following the ousting of James II and the accession of William of Orange and his wife Mary.

---

56 Dennis and Plant, *The English Spira*, 11.

57 Keach, *Parables One*, 58. In *Tropologia*, Keach acknowledges his use of John Owen in connection with the doctrine of the Trinity and, in particular, the person and work of the Holy Spirit (*Types and Metaphors*, 546). Later works of Keach on the covenant of grace were to show a similar familiarity with other Puritan writers.

CHAPTER 8

"The long'ed for presence"

> But ah! The *Winds* were cross, this made us fear
> We n're should have your long'ed for presence here.
> And when we heard you were upon the *Seas*,
> Our hearts rejoiced, yet had not perfect ease;
> We doubted still what dangers you might meet
> In that most *Glorious* and *Renowned Fleet*,
> Yet still our *Prayers* more fervent were and more
> To see your *Royal Person* safe on shore:
> And all the time in *England* you have been,
> What strange, amazing wonders have we seen?[1]

Benjamin Keach held strident anti-Catholic views, characteristic of Nonconformists, at the time he wrote *Sion in Distress*. Despite this, he did not appear to believe it was right to take up arms against a government that

1 Keach, *To their Most Excellent Majesties William and Mary, by the Grace of God, King and Queen of England, &c.* (1689). In *English Poetry Full-Text Database* published by Chadwyck-Healey Ltd.

endeavored to destroy the rights and religion of its subjects. At the same time, he deeply sympathized with those who had lost their lives in the aftermath of the Monmouth rebellion, a view that has been accurately expressed as "cautiously restrained, though with a clearly militant tone."[2] Keach would not take matters into his own hands and played no active part against the government in the Monmouth rebellion, or in events that led to the arrival of William and Mary. Keach was content to trust in the God's providence, pour out his heart in prayer and wait—sometimes with a fearful heart—for the "long'ed for presence" of the new Protestant king and queen to become a reality. This is reflected in his poem, written for "their most Excellent Majesties William and Mary," the new Protestant king and queen, whose coming he believed was the answer to his prayers, and that of many others.[3]

Keach believed firmly in God's providence in ordering all the affairs of nations for the benefit of his true church. The events of 1688 were, in his mind, the direct outworking of divine providence. Of the coming of William and Mary, he writes,

> For sure he's blind who can't discern most clear
> 'Twas by *Heavens Conduct* you were both brought here.
> Such a stupendious *Providence* before
> Was never known, and never may no more.[4]

With the departure of James II, Keach rejoiced at what he saw as the intervening hand of God and the beginning of the overthrow of Catholicism and the establishment of England as a Protestant nation. It was the dawn of a new day for Dissenters with new opportunities, as the heat of persecution abated.

---

2 Richard L. Greaves, *Glimpses of Glory: John Bunyan and English Dissent* (Stanford: Stanford University Press, 2002), 410.

3 Keach, *To their Most Excellent Majesties William and Mary.*

4 Keach, *To their Most Excellent Majesties William and Mary.*

The overthrow of the Papacy

While Keach believed that divine providence was responsible for bringing a new monarchy to England, he went a step further by claiming that the arrival of William and Mary actually signalled the drawing to a close of the 1260-day prophecy of Revelation 11:3.[5] We have already noted that many Dissenters shared his outlook with regard to Catholicism.[6] However, Keach was now affirming that the arrival of the new Protestant king was the first stage in God's overthrow of the Antichrist of New Testament prophecy and the unleashing of God's wrath on his enemies. Keach's understanding of the times was put into print in *Antichrist Stormed*, published in 1689, together with *Distressed Sion Relieved*.[7]

With the benefit of hindsight, it is not difficult to see that Keach was mistaken in his view and that he was not, at this point, accurately interpreting the Bible. His hope for the overthrow of God's enemies was biblical, but misunderstood and wrongly applied, because it was conditioned by current historical events. He wrote in order to instruct and comfort a people who had endured nearly thirty years of persecution, the most intense in recent memory. This is what he and many others believed at the time, and so it needs to be examined if one is to appreciate what William's arrival actually represented for Keach and his contemporaries.[8]

---

5 For a discussion of Keach's understanding of the book of Revelation and a brief consideration of a similar work by Hanserd Knollys on Revelation, see Kenneth G.C. Newport, "Benjamin Keach, William of Orange and Revelation," *BQ*, 36 (1995): 43–51.

6 See Chapter 5, n.37. Jonathan Arnold has criticized Newport's reading of Keach's eschatology (and my dependence on Newport) on two important details: the order and the date of eschatological events. Newport interpreted Keach to be saying that Christ would return after the end of the millennial kingdom, whereas, according to Arnold, Keach actually believed in the personal return of Christ prior to the thousand year reign. See Arnold, *The Reformed Theology of Benjamin Keach*, 202–245.

7 Keach, *Antichrist Stormed* and Keach, *Distressed Sion Relieved*.

8 While they may not have endorsed everything Keach stated in *Antichrist Stormed*, the book was advertised and commended by both the 1689 and 1691 national assemblies

Keach believed that the book of Revelation was a prophecy of the entire course of church history and that they were seeing the fulfillment of events, notably the downfall of the papacy and the Roman Catholic Church. He left his readers to draw their own conclusions from the evidence he presented, leaving it to them "to receive or reject according to your own conceptions and understandings."[9] He himself was convinced of his understanding of events, which would have led to an increased excitement of his faith and expectations.

For Keach, the blowing of the seventh trumpet in Revelation 11:15 marked the turning point in history. He believed the two witnesses in Revelation 11:1–14 represented God's faithful people who had recently withstood the onslaught of Antichrist. He also believed the killing of the witnesses referred to the hard times—"the ten Hot persecutions"—that the church had experienced during the reigns of Charles II and James II. Keach believed that during the latter part of this period (the hottest persecution being from 1681 to 1686), as James II sought to destroy the Protestant faith, Antichrist was making one final attempt to destroy the true church, "striking at the root and the whole constitution of English government, nothing being designed but the utter subversion of the Protestant religion."[10] "The street" of Revelation 11:8 was identified as England and the slaying of witnesses referred to the deaths of men and women like William Lord Russell, Alderman Cornish, the Earl of Essex, Elizabeth Gaunt and those who suffered in the storm of persecution after the Monmouth uprising. Now that the situation was dramatically reversed with the arrival of William of Orange, the two resurrected witnesses would begin to bear testimony once again. The seventh trumpet had sounded and the seven vials of God's wrath

---

of Particular Baptists. The 1689 Assembly also commended *Distressed Sion Relieved*.

9 Keach, *Antichrist Stormed*, 153.

10 Keach, *Antichrist Stormed*, 146.

would soon be poured out on God's enemies. Keach's optimistic expectations are expressed clearly:

> I am persuaded that His present majesty is raised up to do great things for Christ; and tho' some may strive to obstruct the work of God, and uphold and interest for the Beast, yet they shall be blasted in their designs, and come to shame and ruin in the end; for God is risen up, and His enemies shall be scattered.[11]

This does not mean that Keach expected the imminent return of Christ, for Keach believed this would take place only after the period of a thousand years during which the spiritual kingdom of Christ would advance. Nevertheless, he looked for the final ruin of Antichrist in 1697. These were not his own calculations but rather information he had gleaned from other writers about prophecy.[12] He wrote as one sincerely convinced of the truth of what he was writing, believing that the Bible was being fulfilled before his eyes. Keach's desire to show the nature and glory of the kingdom of Christ was to encourage the people, many of whom had lived through long years of hardship because of their Nonconformist convictions. Yet, the question remains: How much of Keach's optimism and excitement about the arrival of a new day would be tempered and eventually modified by the political realities facing the new Protestant king?

The Toleration Act of 1689

The overall attitude of the Church of England toward Nonconformists now changed. "The ice of Anglican intolerance had melted in the heat generated by the conflict with a Catholic

11 Keach, *Antichrist Stormed*, 188.

12 Keach, *Antichrist Stormed*, 136–137. Keach does not name his author but does mention Peter du Moulin once again.

king," and even the once-hostile Archbishop Sancroft was now urging his clergy to adopt a new attitude toward Protestant Dissenters.[13] Joseph Ivimey, the eighteenth-century Baptist historian, writing in 1811, referred enthusiastically to the Act of Toleration as "the Magna Charta [*sic*] of the Protestant Dissenters."[14] However, the Act passed in 1689 effectively left Dissenters as second-class citizens, providing them with a minimum of freedoms and leaving the distinct impression that any "toleration" was being granted begrudgingly. William III wanted a much broader policy of toleration but, despite Sancroft's pleadings, High Anglican churchmen remained very influential and managed to continue to marginalize Dissenters. Deep-seated and long-held attitudes of intolerance and prejudice could not be simply rooted out by parliamentary legislation.[15]

Nothing in parliamentary law assured Dissenters that they would now enjoy liberty of conscience. Freedom to worship publicly meant acquiring a licence to use a meeting-house—but the Act of Uniformity and the "Clarendon Code" still remained on the statute book. Instead, Dissenters were simply exempted from the penalties that had once been imposed on them—providing they took an oath of allegiance and supremacy to the crown and subscribed to the *Thirty-Nine Articles* of the Church of England (apart from the articles on church government and, for Baptists, infant baptism). The Test and Corporation Acts also remained in effect, meaning that Nonconformists remained barred from holding public office. Furthermore, there was no place for young Dissenters at the universities of Oxford or Cambridge.

---

13 John Coffey, *Persecution and Toleration in Protestant England 1558–1689* (Harlow: Pearson Education Limited, 2000), 198.

14 Ivimey, *History*, 1:477–478.

15 See Ivimey, *History*, 1:199–206, for details of the limitations and the continued intolerance and prejudice that followed the 1689 Act. For a modern and detailed analysis of the Revolution Settlement, see Harris, *Revolution: The Great Crisis of the British Monarchy*, 308–363.

Dissenters were "free," therefore, if they accepted that they were second-class citizens. The Act of Toleration effectively divided religious affiliation into two camps: those who accepted the Church of England and its bishops, and those who did not, the latter being excluded from politics and education. This was to be the lot of Dissenters for almost another 140 years—the Test and Corporation Acts was not repealed until 1828!

At some point in 1689, Keach was almost denied the opportunity to enjoy this new "freedom." Thomas Crosby records that he became so ill that his doctors, fellow ministers and family had given up all hope of his recovery. However, Hanserd Knollys came to see his friend and

> betook himself to prayer, and in an earnest and extraordinary manner, begged that God would spare him and add unto his days the time he granted to his servant Hezekiah. As soon as he had ended his prayer, he said, "Brother Keach, I shall be in heaven before you," and quickly left him.[16]

Crosby said that a number of people were skeptical about this remarkable event but assured his readers that he based it on living witnesses.[17] He had drawn attention previously to Knollys' unusual gift of prayer, recording that during the plague several sick persons were suddenly restored even while he was praying for them.[18] Keach recovered from his illness and lived for another fifteen years, dying in 1704. Knollys himself died shortly after this event in 1691, aged ninety-four.

---

16 Crosby, *History*, 4:307–308.

17 One of these may have been Susannah Keach who came to live with the Crosbys after her husband's death, although she died in 1727 before Crosby wrote his *History*. Or, perhaps Rebecca Keach, who became Crosby's wife, although she would have been only seven years old in 1689.

18 Crosby, *History*, 1:338.

When the Roman emperors ceased persecuting Christians, the new freedoms were a mixed blessing. The same was to be true in late seventeenth-century England, for now Anglicanism became a badge of respectability and there was no longer such a heavy price to be paid for maintaining a Nonconformist conscience. There was a real danger that mediocrity would become the norm and that churches would lose some of the distinctiveness that had marked them during the years of the Restoration. As he approached his fiftieth year, there is no evidence that the events of 1688 and 1689 led Keach to lose his edge. He remained undaunted in his labours, his convictions were as firm as ever and the thrust of his message remained unchanged.

This attitude characterized not only Keach himself, but also many of his fellow London Particular Baptist pastors. They drew up plans in July 1689 for the first national assembly of Particular Baptists, requesting that they meet in London later that year. For ten days, from September 3–12, 1689, "the Assembly of the Elders, Messengers, and Ministering Brethren, sent by, and concerned for, more than one hundred Baptized Congregations of the same Faith with themselves, from many parts of England and Wales" were able to meet in a way that had been impossible during the days of persecution.

Keach and the 1689 London Assembly of Particular Baptists

Benjamin Keach's name was included as one of the signatories responsible for sending out letters convening the assembly.[19] Joseph Ivimey recorded the mood of these leaders in a copy of the letter sent to the churches toward the end of July 1689. If Keach and others were excited at the prospect of the overthrow of the Antichrist, this was tempered not only by the political

---

19 Ivimey, *History*, 1:480. The others were William Kiffin, Hanserd Knollys, John Harris, George Barrett, Edward Man and Richard Adams. Kiffin and Knollys were appointed to receive replies to these letters.

realities facing the new king but also by the sober truth facing the churches emerging into a different environment after nearly thirty years of oppression. On the one hand, they recorded their thanksgiving to God for his wisdom and goodness in their recent deliverances and expressed new earnestness and expectations "for the accomplishing of those gracious promises and prophecies contained in the holy scripture relating to the latter days."[20] On the other hand, they lamented the present condition of the churches, "fearing that much of that former strength, life, and vigour, which attended is much gone."[21]

This same mood was reflected in "A General Epistle" sent out in the report of the Assembly's proceedings, containing a longer assessment of the real situation facing the churches.[22] This sober assessment was not the view of any one man, or of the seven London elders who had sent out the invitation in July. Thirty-two men, beginning with the names of Hanserd Knollys and William Kiffin, signed "A General Epistle." Keach's name is included, but the epistle is also "in the Name and behalf of the whole Assembly." Before the Assembly addressed any other issue, they considered the true state of the churches they represented.

Essentially, the epistle was a trumpet call to the churches to rouse them from their ease and call them to reformation. Deep concerns were expressed over the lack of zeal for God's house, that the churches, in general, were not living up to what they professed and that, in particular, the power of godliness had decayed, with only an outer shell remaining. This echoes one of the primary concerns that Keach first expressed in the 1670s

20 Ivimey, *History*, 1:478.

21 Ivimey, History, 1:480.

22 "A General Epistle." In *TA Narrative of the Proceedings of the Elders and Messengers of the Baptized Congregations, in their General Assembly, met in London on Septemb. 3 to 12, 1689, from divers parts of England and Wales: Owning the Doctrine of Personal Election, and Final Perseverance* (London, 1689), 3–8.

and 1680s.[23] *The Narrative of the Proceedings of the General Assembly* relates how the whole of the first day of the Assembly was spent "in humbling ourselves before the Lord, and to seek of him a right way to direct into the best Means and Method to repair our Breaches, and to recover our selves into our former Order, Beauty and Glory."[24]

These men concluded that the overall effect of almost thirty years of persecution had weakened the churches. Some ministers, like Abraham Cheare and the schoolmaster Thomas Delaune, had died as a result of imprisonment. In addition a number of ministers were old and approaching the end of their lives—men like Knollys, Kiffin and Henry Forty. Nehemiah Coxe (d.1688), another prominent London pastor, had only recently died. Furthermore, they concluded that urgent attention needed to be given to the question of financial provision by the churches for the ministry of the Word. The epistle drew attention to the neglect of this duty in many churches. As we will see, the Assembly was to address this issue very thoroughly.

Attention was also drawn to the failure of the churches to carefully observe the Lord's Day. The Assembly called on the churches to remember that God had done great things for them and that they ought to make a "suitable return of duty to God" and "act like people called, loved, and saved by him."[25] Finally, the epistle informed the churches that a solemn day of fasting and mourning had been appointed for October 10, 1689.

Calling the churches to pray and fast in this way indicates the seriousness of the Assembly. They were not carried away by the arrival of a Protestant king. Rather, they made a sober assessment of the situation and decided that it was requisite for the churches to confess their sins, to recognize not only the backslidings in the nation at large but their own sins also and, in

---

23 See Chapter 6.

24 "A General Epistle," *The Narrative*, 9.

25 "A General Epistle," *The Narrative*, 6.

particular, their decline in faith, love and zeal for the ways and worship of God. Attention was drawn to the evidences of God's judgements, seen in the death of the Lord's faithful witnesses (echoes of Revelation 11:3)—preachers of the gospel called home and few raised up to replace them—and to the smallness of success in the face of persecution. Finally, they were urged to pray for true, broken and penitent hearts, that God would pour out more of his Spirit, open up the Bible to them, bless them in their work so that many would be converted (including the Jews) and that love and unity would prevail in the churches.

This summary of the epistle shows us the kind of spirituality that marked men like Benjamin Keach. His godliness was characterized by a profound sense of dependence on God that was expressed in prayer. As he said,

> Prayer is a God-honouring duty, because it is part of holy worship; and not only so, but it ought to be mixed with other ordinances, all duties of sacred worship ought to be mixed with prayer; nay, we should not enter upon any civil or earthly business, without seeking first to God by prayer, but much more careful we should be to begin every part of God's worship with it. Before we preach we ought to pray, prayer ought to be joined with preaching, baptism ought to be administered with prayer; first we should look up to God. Laying on of hands must be with prayer. The Lord's supper must be with prayer. "Everything is sanctified by the word of God and prayer." Hearing, reading of God's word, meditation and watching must be with prayer. And as prayer should be used in every ordinance, so also in all trials, temptations, afflictions and troubles whatever; nay in eating and drinking, or what ever we do else, we should pray, and so we may expect a blessing from God, and all ordinances, mercies, and afflictions to be sanctified to

> us, and not otherways; therefore prayer must needs tend to the honour of God, and our good.[26]

Keach also believed that brokenheartedness was a mark of true godliness and expressed by a healthy form of self-examination leading to confession of sin and sincere repentance. Furthermore, this was not only done privately but it should have a public face, both in the Assembly and in the day of fasting appointed for the churches.

Keach, together with other the pastors, recognized that little success in the preaching of the Word and little evidence of divine blessing was an indication of God's chastening and judgement. This conclusion did not drive them to despair but rather made them more earnest in their repentance and prayers for his blessing. Finally, he believed that real godliness is expressed by a strong faith in God, a fervent love for the Lord Jesus Christ, zeal for the honour of God, for the worship of God and the keeping of the Lord's Day.

The July 1689 letter from the seven London elders also highlighted their fears about "the general unconcernedness...of giving fit and proper encouragement for the raising up an able and honourable ministry for the time to come."[27] Consequently, one of the main reasons for calling an assembly of the churches was to address this urgent matter.

Keach was appointed as the spokesman on the matter of the ministry and compiled *The Gospel Minister's Maintenance Vindicated*.[28] As a measure of how vital this matter was to them, in July 1689, prior to the Assembly, a copy was sent to each

26 Keach, "The Persistent Widow," *Parables One*, 438.

27 Ivimey, *History*, 1:478–479.

28 Keach, *The Gospel Minister's Maintenance Vindicated* (London, 1689). I am indebted to James M. Renihan at the Institute of Reformed Baptist Studies, Westminster Theological Seminary, for an edited version of this treatise. Subsequent quotations are from his repaginated version.

church, together with a commendatory letter signed by eleven of the London ministers. Then, at the conclusion of the account of the Assembly, there is the following note:

> This Assembly do declare their Approbation of a certain little book, lately recommended by divers Elders dwelling in and about the city of London, Intituled, *The Minister's Maintenance Vindicated*. And it is their Request that the said Treatise be dispersed amongst all the respective Congregations and it is desired that some Brethren of each Church take care to dispose of the same accordingly.[29]

On September 5, the Assembly discussed the matter fully and decided that a public collection was to be made through free-will offerings and voluntary subscriptions from the churches, to be administered by nine of the London ministers. The purpose of this fund was threefold: (1) to help those churches who were unable to provide for a minister to devote himself wholly to the work of the preaching of the gospel; (2) to send ordained men to preach as evangelists where the gospel had not been preached, and to visit the churches; and (3) to provide the means for men who were disposed to study and displayed some measure of teaching gift. According to Crosby, Keach himself and Benjamin Dennis, from the nearby church in Mile End Green, went "on an itinerant excursion to visit the churches," probably to further the second part of this plan.[30] This may not have been the only occasion that he was delegated to carry out Assembly business in this way, but precise recorded details of this kind of activity are rare.[31]

---

29 *The Narrative*, 18.

30 Ivimey, *History*, 3:434.

31 Murdina MacDonald records that Keach's name can be linked to several places

The Assembly was also careful to explain the spirit and intention of any decision made at the Assembly and communicated to the churches. They affirmed that the Assembly had no authority "to prescribe or impose any thing upon the Faith or Practice of any of the Churches of Christ." Rather, they sought to "be helpers of one another, by way of Counsel and Advice, in the right understanding of that perfect Rule which our Lord Jesus... has already prescribed, and given to his Churches in his Word."[32] The matter of ministerial maintenance needed to be established from that "perfect Rule."

Keach might not have been appointed as spokesman for the Assembly on this matter had it not been for the death of Nehemiah Coxe, a pastor of the Petty France congregation, earlier in 1689. The treatise that Keach produced was not breaking new ground. In *Tropologia*, when dealing with "Ministers compared to labourers," Keach had quoted at some length part of a sermon by Coxe, preached at the ordination of an elder in the city of London in 1681. In it, Coxe had argued very strongly for the maintenance of ministers by the church.[33] Coxe had demonstrated that this principle was established by the law of nature, that it was biblical—being established by the express command and appointment of

in Essex following the 1690 Assembly and also, in February 1691, to churches in the Hampshire Association but says, despite invitations, he probably did not go. MacDonald, "London Calvinistic Baptists 1689–1727," 44, 46.

32 *The Narrative*, 10.

33 Nehemiah Coxe, "A sermon preached at the Ordination of an elder and deacons in a baptized congregation in London," *Reformed Baptist Theological Review*, 1 (January 2004): 133–156. Nehemiah Coxe was, along with William Collins, pastor at the church in Petty France. In June 1689, shortly before the Assembly was convened, Coxe died. Otherwise, he would have been involved in the organizing of the Assembly. Because of this, the mantle of responsibility for producing the treatise probably fell on Keach. For Coxe, see Ivimey, *History*, 2:405–407, 3:330–334. Coxe was not breaking new ground either when he stressed the importance of ministerial maintenance, for the same principle had been expressed in the *First London Confession of Faith*, produced by the Particular Baptists in 1644 (see Article xxxviii). See Lumpkin, *Baptist Confessions of Faith*, 166. As we will see, Keach was ignorant of the 1644 *Confession* at the time he compiled his treatise.

Christ—and also that it was practical, because the neglect of such provision would lead to all kinds of evils, not least the discouragement of study and the laying up "of those stores of solid learning, which are so needful to a Minister."[34] Keach used Coxe's ordination sermon extensively, copying and paraphrasing large sections of it, rearranging other parts, as well as adding his own material in order to produce the finished treatise.[35]

The regular ministry of preaching as normative for the church was the burden of the treatise, and Keach presented the biblical rationale for this assertion. He showed his appreciation of the issues that were at stake in this matter:

> how much the honour of Christ, the reputation of His Glorious Gospel in the World; as likewise, the Good and Well-being of the Churches, depends upon a regular and Orderly Ministry, and the Continuation thereof; and so the churches to be under the supine neglect herein is very sad.[36]

This work, "commissioned" by the conveners of the Assembly, was very much a tract for the times. It pressed upon the consciences of church members their urgent duty to ensure that their preachers were: (1) properly chosen, meeting the qualifications laid down in 1 Timothy 3:1–7 and Titus 1:5–9; (2) solemnly ordained by prayer and the laying on of hands; and (3) properly provided for by the church. It argued that any restrictions imposed by persecution were in the past. As a result of toleration, there were new opportunities for evangelism that must be seized by the churches:

---

34 Keach, *Types and Metaphors*, 831–833, and Coxe, "A sermon preached at the Ordination of an elder and deacons."

35 Keach, *The Gospel Minister's Maintenance*. Renihan has identified those parts that are taken directly from Coxe.

36 Keach, *The Gospel Minister's Maintenance*, 6.

> When the late *Storms of Persecution* were upon us, many of *Christ's Spiritual Harvest-men* were much hindered and taken off their Work, and did many imploy themselves otherwise, in their other Affairs...but now the Providence of God has opened a great Door for the Gospel, and sent us Blessed Harvest Weather, and the Labourers alas! Being also very few, though the Harvest is great: How ought we to stick to our business?[37]

Keach provided a thorough treatment of the subject. He laid out the biblical principles and duties, along with thirteen arguments to prove the duty, and four motives to press home the duty. He then dealt with questions and objections, before concluding with the nature of the work of a true gospel minister. Because Keach and his fellow London elders believed that they were dealing with sin in the churches, the issues were argued robustly:

> Our main Business at this time, is not only to Assert the Minister's Maintenance to be an Institution of Christ; but also to prove it so to be, and that to with-hold it from them by a Church, who is able comfortably to provide for them, is a great and crying Sin and will be attended (we fear unless prevented by an unfeigned Repentance and Reformation) with severe Judgment from the holy God, who will not always bear with the Ignorant, much less the willful neglect of his own Holy Law.[38]

The report that followed the 1691 Assembly expressed hearty thanks for the public collection, and the churches were urged to continue their contributions. Some of the money had already been used for the purposes designated by the first Assembly of

---

37 Keach, *The Gospel Minister's Maintenance*, 33.

38 Keach, *The Gospel Minister's Maintenance*, 10.

churches.[39] Keach was still involved in the work of the Assembly but he was not one of those appointed to receive and disperse the funds.

The last national Assembly met in 1692. It was afterward decided to divide the one meeting into two, one part meeting in Bristol (at the time, the second largest city in England) at Easter, and one part in London at Whitsuntide.[40] By now, local associations of churches had been established, and it was considered an easier arrangement to meet in this way. The 1693 London Assembly proved to be the last for several years and was sadly marked by division over the issue of hymn singing, in which Keach himself was heavily involved.[41] In April 1704, the London Association met again, with thirteen churches attending. This was the last such meeting that Keach attended before his death in July of that same year.

The zeal with which Keach and his fellow London elders carried out what they believed was their duty to God, as reflected in *The Minister's Maintenance Vindicated* and the decisions of the 1689 Assembly, provide us with a perspective on another aspect of their godliness. Believing that a regular and settled ministry was instituted by Christ himself, these men were zealous for the well-being of Christ's church, and hence for the glory of God. Preaching the Word of God was central in Keach's own understanding of his work as a minister of Christ.

Did Keach's own congregation practice what their pastor preached? In this connection the question is sometimes raised about the financial arrangements made between Keach and his own congregation.[42] Suggestions have been made that he ran a

---

39 *The Narrative of the Proceedings of the General Assembly of the Elders and Messengers of the Baptized Churches, sent from divers parts of England and Wales, which began in London the 2d of June, and ended the 8th of the same, 1691* (London, 1691).

40 Seven weeks after Easter.

41 See Chapter 10.

42 James Barry Vaughn, "Benjamin Keach's *The Gospel Minister's Maintenance Vin-*

bookshop in order to supplement his income because his church failed to provide adequate support.[43] On the evidence available, no clear picture emerges. Back in Buckinghamshire, Keach had been a tailor, but there is no indication that he took up this trade once he came to London. Two additional sources of income appear to have been available to Keach. His will mentions "profits from selling (Dr) Roberts tincture elixir sugar plums and snuff," but gives no indication of whether Keach and his family used this to supplement their income.[44] When Keach came to live in Freemans Lane, Southwark, he certainly sold books from his home. The final page of *A Golden Mine Opened* contains a list of books by Keach. The following note is placed at the top of the page: "Books written and published by this Author, some of which the Impressions all being sold-off, are not to be had, which are thus marked *, to prevent trouble and charge of Letters." However, there is no indication anywhere that he needed to do this in order to provide for himself and his family.

The Second London Baptist Confession of Faith and Keach's Catechism

Benjamin Keach played no part in the drawing up of *The Second London Baptist Confession of Faith*. It was published by the 1689 Assembly but had already been in existence for twelve years. Persecution may have been part of the reason for the delay in printing and now there was an eagerness among Calvinistic Baptists to publish more fully their own confession of faith. Other Calvinistic Dissenters, the Presbyterians and the Independents had, some years earlier, produced the *Westminster*

---

dicated and the Status of Ministers among Seventeenth-century Baptists," *Baptist Review of Theology*, 3 (Spring 1993): 53–60.

43 Theo. F. Valentine, *Concern for the Ministry: The Story of the Particular Baptist Fund 1717–1967* (Teddington: Particular Baptist Fund, 1967), 15.

44 "The Will of Benjamin Keach," *Surrey Will Abstracts*, Vol. 26, 2001. Archdeaconry Court of Surrey 1700–1708, No. 820. See Appendix 1. Dr. John Roberts and his wife Prudence were members at Horselydown.

Confession of Faith in 1646 and the *Savoy Declaration* in 1658. When the 1677 *Confession* was first published it was pointed out that there was need for a new confession because copies of the *First London Confession of Faith* (1644) were now rare and "also that many others have since embraced the same truth which is owned therein."[45]

Keach was one of those who had "since embraced the same truth," and yet he had never seen a copy of the 1644 *Confession*, nor does he seem to have known of its contents or existence before 1691. This fact comes to light in Keach's short document, *To All the Baptized Churches and faithful Brethren in England and Wales, Christian Salutations*.[46] This is an apology for misrepresenting the first baptized churches about minister's maintenance and states, "I knew nothing of that Confession [1644] till I was informed of it by the offended Brethren, which was about a Fortnight before the last Assembly met together."[47] Keach's ignorance was understandable, especially when it is recalled that he was only four years old when it was first published! Furthermore, Keach had been converted and ministered among the General Baptists for over a decade and had embraced Particular Baptist theology only after coming to London in 1668.

The *Confession* of 1677 almost certainly originated with the church in Petty France where William Collins and Nehemiah Coxe were co-pastors. This was certainly the opinion of Ivimey,

---

45 "To the Judicious and Impartial Reader." In *A Confession of Faith put forth by the Elders and Brethren of Many Congregations of Christians (baptized upon Profession of their Faith) in London and the Country* (London, 1677), unnumbered second page. See also the Facsimile Edition, 2000 (Auburn: B & R Press, 2000).

46 Keach, *To All the Baptized Churches and faithful Brethren in England and Wales, Christian Salutations* (London, 1692). I am again indebted to James Renihan for an edited version of this document. See also James M. Renihan, *Edification and Beauty: The Practical Ecclesiology of the English Particular Baptists 1675–1705*. Studies in Baptist History and Thought, vol. 17 (Milton Keynes: Paternoster, 2008), 17–18.

47 *To All the Baptized Churches*, 2, in Renihan's repaginated version.

who describes these two men as "distinguished scholars and divines" and refers to a minute in the records of the Petty France church about the publishing of a confession of faith.[48] The confession found a wider acceptance among the churches in London before being published again for the 1689 Assembly. In 1681, both Hanserd Knollys and Nehemiah Coxe quoted from chapter 26, on "The Church," and in 1682 the Broadmead church in Bristol used the confession as a means of testing the beliefs of Thomas Whinnell, formerly a General Baptist, who was now attempting to join their assembly. He professed to believe the principles contained in the Baptist *Confession of Faith* and joined the church.[49]

When the 1689 National Assembly met, it "owned" this confession as "containing the doctrine of our faith and practice." Thirty-three ministers and messengers, in the name and behalf of some 108 different churches, signed it. The full statement reads:

> We the Ministers and Messengers of, and concerned for, upwards of one hundred Baptized Congregations in *England* and *Wales* (denying *Arminianism*) being met together in London, from the third of the seventh month, to the eleventh of the same 1689, to consider of some things that might be for the glory of God, and the good of these congregations; have thought meet (for the satisfaction of all other Christians that differ from us in the point of Baptism) to recommend to their perusal the confession of our faith, which confession we own, as containing the doctrine of our faith and practice, and do

48 Ivimey, *History*, 3:332. In "The Practical Ecclesiology," Renihan adds weight to Ivimey's opinion by presenting further evidence of their theological abilities.

49 For this evidence, I am dependent for my information on Renihan, *Edification and Beauty*, 27. It is interesting to note that Thomas Whinnell's name appears among the 33 names who signed the confession in 1689, by which time he was a pastor in Taunton.

desire that the members of our churches respectively do furnish themselves therewith.[50]

"Benjamin Keach, Pastor, Horse-lie-down, Southwark" was one of the thirty-three names included in the list. A few years later, he referred to the *Confession of Faith* while engaged in a debate with Gyles Shute of Limehouse over the validity of infant baptism:

> we steadfastly believe and readily grant it as an Article of our Faith, That all infants are under the Guilt and stain of original Sin as they come into the World, and that no Infant can be saved but through the Blood and Imputation of Christ's righteousness: And also we do believe, That all those dying Infants who are saved, God doth in some way or another (which is not known to us) sanctify them; for no unclean thing can enter into the Heavenly Jerusalem. See our confession of Faith.[51]

He appears to be referring to two separate chapters in the *Confession*, chapter 6, dealing with the fall of man into sin, and also chapter 10, on effectual calling. There are two further pieces of evidence that suggest Keach heartily endorsed the teaching of the *Confession of Faith*. The names of William Collins and Benjamin Keach appear in an "advertisement" prefaced to a reprint of the 1689 *Confession*, a fifth edition dated 1720. This indicates that Collins and Keach had sold the "property, right and title of the printing thereof, to John Marshall, Bookseller, at the Bible in Gracechurch Street."[52] They had therefore formerly

50 *The Narrative, 1689*, 18.

51 Keach, *A Counter-Antidote to Purge out the Malignant Effects of a Late Counterfeit, Prepared by Mr. Gyles Shute, an Unskilful Person in Polemical Cures: being An Answer to his Vindication of his Pretended Antidote, to prevent the Prevalency of Anabaptism* (London, 1694), 12.

52 See Renihan, *Edification and Beauty*, 22–23, for the full wording of the advertise-

owned the proprietary rights to the *Confession of Faith* and to the *Catechism*. Then, when the Maze Pond church of Southwark was first constituted in February 1694, it explicitly adopted the *Confession of Faith* in the first article of its church covenant.[53] The people who formed the Maze Pond church had separated from the nearby Goat Street church, where Keach was the pastor, over the issue of singing hymns in public worship, yet they seemed to have no hesitation in adopting the *Confession of Faith* as their own declaration of faith and practice. Their disagreement with Keach was not over any teaching in the confession, only over the propriety of singing hymns in public worship.

Keach's endorsement of the *Confession of Faith* meant that he belonged to mainstream historic biblical Christianity. We have traced his progress from his early days among the General Baptists and his disowning of "Arminian errors" to his adoption of views commonly called "Calvinistic" in the early 1670s. The *Confession of Faith* adopted by the 1689 National Assembly of Particular Baptists stands in the tradition of earlier Reformed confessions, drawing not only on the 1644 *London Confession*, but also the *Westminster Confession of Faith* and the *Savoy Declaration and Platform of Polity* of the Independents, published in 1658. In fact, the 1689 *Confession* almost invariably follows the changes made by the Independents.[54] The Particular Baptists had different convictions about the subjects and method of baptism, and they wished to make those clear, but at the same time they wished to declare that they were one in faith and practice with other Protestant believers. They explained their reasons for the *Confession* thus:

---

ment quoting E.B. Underhill, *Confessions of Faith and Other Public Documents Illustrative of the Baptist Churches of England in the 17th Century* (London: The Hanserd Knollys Society, 1854), 172.

53 For this information, I am dependent for my information on Renihan, *Edification and Beauty*, 29, n.103.

54 Samuel Waldron, *A Modern Exposition of the 1689 Baptist Confession of Faith* (Darlington: Evangelical Press, 1989), 428–429.

> to convince all, that we have no itch to clogge Religion with new words, but do readily acquiesce in that form of sound words, which hath been in consent with the holy Scriptures, used by others before us; hereby declaring before God, Angels, & Men, our hearty agreement with them in that wholesome Protestant doctrine, which with so clear evidence of Scriptures they have asserted: some things, indeed, are in some places added, some terms omitted, and some few changed; but these alterations are of such a nature, as that we need not doubt any charge of suspicion of unsoundness in the faith, from any of our brethren upon the account of them.[55]

Keach's name has been frequently linked with the catechism that is sometimes published with the *Confession of Faith*.[56] We know that Keach was not involved in the writing of the confession, and that William Collins was asked by the 1693 London Assembly to draw up a catechism.[57] Ivimey concluded that Collins was the author but clearly was puzzled as to how it came to be known as "Keach's Catechism."[58] We do not know the answer either, but the confusion might be traced back to the fact that both Collins and Keach owned the proprietary rights to these documents and Keach's name might have become associated with the catechism because of his well-known books for instructing children and young people.

Nonconformity was now operating in a new environment, and this explains how the Particular Baptists, among whom Benjamin Keach was now an acknowledged leader, faced the

55 "To the Judicious and Impartial Reader." In *A Confession of Faith*, unnumbered pages four and five.

56 For example, *The London Baptist Confession of Faith of 1689 and Keach's Catechism* (Choteau: Gospel Mission, n.d.).

57 Ivimey, *History*, 1:533.

58 Ivimey, *History*, 2:397.

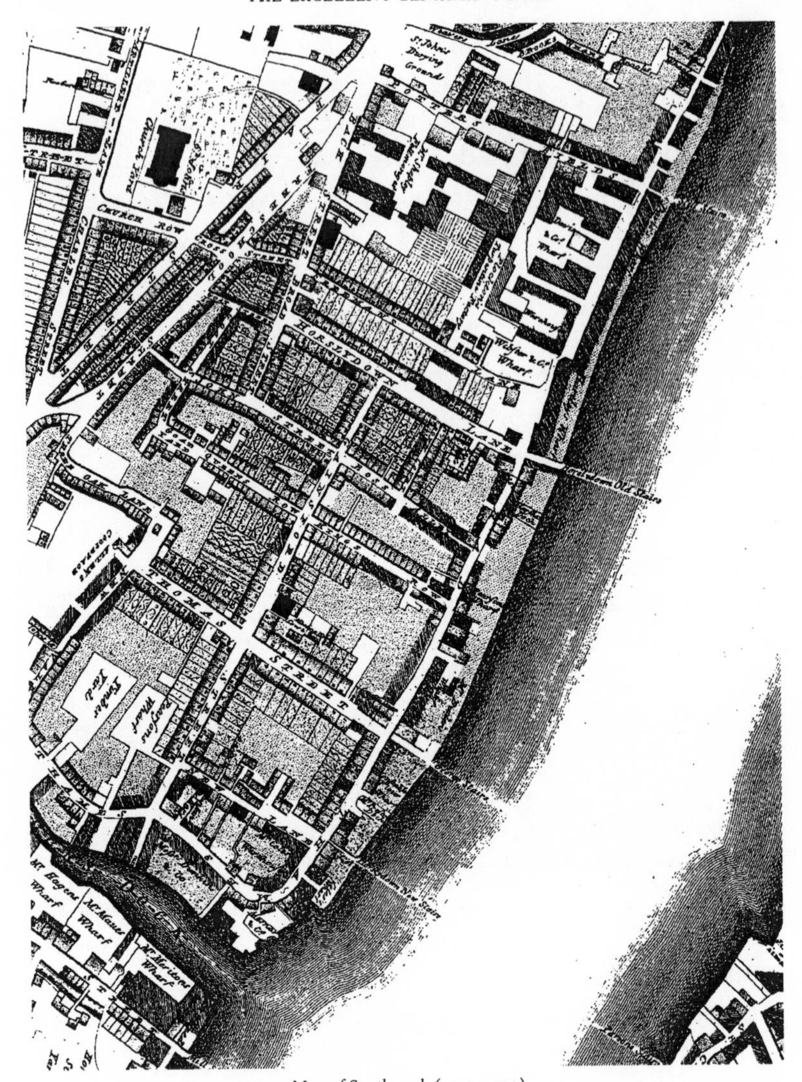

Map of Southwark (1792–1799)

Note: By the time this map was drawn, Tooley Street had become Back Street/Broad Street. Horselydown Lane runs southeast through Southwark toward the Thames.

situation confronting them. Many respected Nonconformist leaders had reached the end of their lives. Thomas Manton had died in 1677, John Owen in 1683, John Bunyan in 1688 and Richard Baxter was shortly to follow them in 1692. Among the Baptists, Nehemiah Coxe died in 1689 and was soon followed by the aged Hanserd Knollys in 1691. Keach, together with his ministerial colleagues, did their utmost to promote the cause of truth and godliness in the years immediately following the arrival of William of Orange. The advent of the "long'd for presence" did not lead to any complacency in Keach. Rather, with both hands, he seized the new opportunities created by the change in the monarchy. He did not get carried away on a wave of optimism about the fall of Antichrist. Instead, he continued to give himself to the pursuit of godliness, both personally and in the lives of the churches he had come to love.

This godliness was both intensely spiritual and practical. The same man that expressed his dependence on God in prayer also urged the churches to follow their God-given duty to pay their pastors a reasonable stipend. His zeal for the church of Christ, for the worship of God and the Lord's Day, was part of his zeal for "wholesome Protestant doctrine." What is remarkable is how much truth he and his contemporaries were willing to own in their *Confession of Faith*, in comparison with many in later centuries, including our day. It was surely a tragedy for Baptists that by 1832 and the re-establishing of the Baptist Union, Baptists were content with a doctrinal statement that limited union to those "who agree in the sentiments usually denominated evangelical."[59] In contrast, when Charles Spurgeon came to London he made it known that his convictions were unashamedly "Calvinistic." When the foundation stone of the Metropolitan Tabernacle was laid in August 1859 among the several articles

59 Ernest A. Payne, *The Baptist Union: A Short History* (London: The Baptist Union of Great Britain and Ireland, 1959), 61.

placed under the stone was a copy of the 1689 *Confession*. Spurgeon recorded:

> The articles placed under the stone are simply these: the Bible, the Word of God, we put that as the foundation of our church. Upon this rock doth Christ build the ministration of His truth. We know of nothing else as our standard. Together with this, we have put *The Baptist Confession of Faith*, which was signed in the olden times by Benjamin Keach, one of my eminent predecessors.[60]

This was not simply a piece of historical symbolism. Spurgeon believed and preached the doctrines that were summarized in that document; they were a summary of his own faith and practice.

Facets of Keach's godliness have been traced here but fundamental to them all was his commitment to the Bible as the Word of God and to "wholesome Protestant doctrine," as summarized in *The Second London Baptist Confession of Faith*. We now turn to Keach as pastor and preacher to consider the context and method of his preaching.

---

60 C.H. Spurgeon, *Autobiography, Vol.2 The Full Harvest, 1860–1892* (Edinburgh: Banner of Truth Trust, 1973), 10.

CHAPTER 9

"The ornament of my poor ministry"

What a great blessing faithful gospel-ministers are to a people, and to the church of God. Can a house be built without builders, or such who are skilled in that art and mystery? So how can souls believe without a preacher sent of God, or churches be built, unless God raise up some men, endowed with wisdom and skill in gospel mysteries, who well know both the matter and the form of a true church, and how to build it by the rule Christ hath left? And how should builders be encouraged and honoured for their work sake, they being labourers together with God, and stewards of the mysteries of Christ?[1]

The conviction that "faithful gospel-ministers" are one of God's great blessings to the church both informed the method and the manner in which Keach undertook all his work as a minister of the gospel. Faithfulness to

1 Keach, "The Vineyard," *Parables Two*, 33.

the Lord Jesus Christ was Keach's controlling principle as he constantly engaged in the task of being an overseer in the church of Christ. He understood this to mean that he was called to preach the Word of God so that people would be converted and to oversee the life of the church, building it by the rule that Christ had left in the Word. Preaching was his life's work, a calling he had received from God back in 1658, three years after he had been converted as a young man.[2] The commencement of persecution in 1664 had not dampened his conviction. Neither the jailor nor the sheriff was successful in silencing him when he was pilloried at Aylesbury—even when the sheriff, angry and frustrated, threatened to gag him.[3]

When he came to London in 1668 it was not long before he began to preach on a regular basis. Having embraced Particular Baptist doctrine, the congregation that was now under his leadership built a meeting-house at the end of Tooley Street, in Horselydown, as a result of the Indulgence issued by Charles II in 1672. He continued to preach wherever he had the opportunity, even if it meant suffering as a consequence, because preaching was God's "own ordinance."

Preaching was Keach's main task as a pastor. The context of his preaching and the oversight he exercised during the last fifteen years of his life, from 1689 until his death in 1704, form the background to the content of his preaching. First, however, it is necessary to examine the man himself, his understanding of the nature of the work he had undertaken, his conception of the church and its congregational life, together with what is known of the congregation that met in Horselydown, Southwark. Keach regarded these people as "the ornament of my poor ministry," many of them having been converted to Christ as a result of his

---

2 See Chapter 2.

3 Crosby, *History*, 2:204–208.

ministry.[4] Keach felt a special affection for them, and aware of his increasing age, told them that if they continued living in love

> you will cause my latter days to be most sweet and comfortable to me, after all those *Troubles*, *Sorrows*, and *Reproaches* I have met with, both from within and without.[5]

The church building and the congregation

When Keach first came to London he had found a home for himself and his family on the north bank of the Thames in Shadwell, but it appears that by the 1690s, with the threat of persecution now much diminished, he had moved to Freemans Lane, Horselydown.[6] Freemans Lane no longer exists, having been demolished in the late 1880s to make room for the southern approach road to the new Tower Bridge.[7] The street ran a short distance from the banks of the Thames, parallel to Horselydown Lane until it met the extension of Tooley Street. The meeting-house used by Keach's congregation was located in Goat-Yard Passage near St. John's church.[8] By the time Ivimey wrote his history in 1830, the building had been demolished, but he was able to give the following description:

---

4 Keach, "Epistle," *The Articles of the Faith of the Congregation of Horseley-down [Back Street]* (London, 1697), 1.

5 Keach, "Epistle," *The Articles of the Faith*, 2.

6 Sometimes on the title page or in the preface of his books published after 1689, Keach indicated that the book was available from his house in Freemans Lane, Southwark (i.e. in the preface to *A Golden Mine Opened*, dated September 13, 1694). During the years of persecution, he never gave any indication of his address.

7 Old Ordnance Survey Maps, *Bermondsey and Wapping 1872: London Sheet 77* (Newcastle-upon-Tyne: Alan Godfrey Maps, 1995). In 1676, John Ogilby and William Morgan published *A Large and Accurate Map of the City of London*. There were many other maps produced at this time, but few of them cover Southwark. Copies of Ogilby and Morgan's map may be viewed in Southwark Local Studies Library. For details of other printed maps of London at this time, see Ida Darlington and James Howego, *Printed Maps of London, circa 1553–1850* (London: George Philip, 1964).

8 *Regester*, unnumbered page.

> It was a wooden building, and stood at the north-west corner of Goat-yard-passage, now called Goat Street. The front door came into a short cross street, from Horselydown Back-street, to Free-school-street. A brick wall in front enclosed the meeting-house, with a court-yard, and lime trees on each side of the path leading to the principal door.[9]

Horselydown was part of the large borough of Southwark and is now squeezed into the area between the railway and the river, and runs down to the small inlet called Savory's Dock or St Saviour's Dock. In Keach's latter years, London had become the largest European city, developing as a major port along the river Thames. Southwark had grown up along the south bank of the Thames at the only bridging point, London Bridge. It became part of the bustling port of London with considerable commercial and industrial activity such as distilleries, rope works, tanneries and shipyards, with wharves and warehouses lining the river banks. By 1680, the population of Southwark had reached 32,000.[10] The Great Fire of London had not devastated Southwark in 1666, although fires had affected parts of the borough in 1676 and again in 1689. Where fire had never taken hold there was a close network of yards and alleys, and Goat-Yard Passage was one of these, lying back some 100 metres from the river.

There are no existing records that allow us to accurately reconstruct Keach's congregation, or even to give us a cross-section of their different occupations. Ivimey records that the meeting-

---

9 Ivimey, *History*, 3:409. Ivimey says he depended for his information on a friend, Mr. Benjamin Coxhead, a member of the Carter Lane congregation, a successor to Keach's own congregation, who could still remember the building. According to the introduction in the *Regester*, the church moved to Carter Lane, Tooley Street, in 1757, and then in 1833 to New Park Street. It was when they were meeting there that Spurgeon was called to be their pastor in 1854.

10 Richard Tames, *Southwark Past* (London: Historical Publications, 2001), 32.

house had to be enlarged several times and that it was capable of holding nearly a thousand people.[11] The surviving pages of the church register indicate that many in Keach's congregation lived within close proximity to the church building. The parish of St Olave's, Southwark, is mentioned several times. For example, it is evident that Benjamin Stinton (1676–1719) and his wife Susannah—Stinton was not only Keach's son-in-law but also his successor in the ministry at Horselydown—lived here. All their seven children are listed as being born "in the Parish of St Olive, Southwark," between 1700 and 1712.[12] Other families like Edward and Ann Sandford, also with seven children born between 1667 and 1681, came from adjacent Bermondsey. Moses Brown came from Kennington, while others came from parishes within the extensive borough of Southwark. One very notable exception was Isaac Marlow (1649–1719) and his wife Esther, who are listed as living in Richmond, which lay several miles to the west of London.[13] Marlow was a major figure in the controversy over hymn singing. Unlike his wife, though, he never appeared to be a member of the Horselydown church.[14] Keach's congregation seems to have numbered in the hundreds, but no precise numbers exist. Whitley could only give a broad indication and say that among the Baptists it was "the strongest [church] south of the river."[15]

Richard and Mary Stinton appear to have been members of the church for a considerable time. Their eldest daughter, Elizabeth, was born in 1663 and Benjamin, the sixth of seven

11 Ivimey, *History*, 3:410.

12 *Regester*, 11. Richard and Mary Stinton, Benjamin Stinton's parents and brothers and sisters are also included in the register but no place of birth is given for him. The Stintons senior, though, were members of Keach's congregation. Benjamin Stinton became pastor on Keach's death in 1704 but died at the relatively young age of 42 in 1719.

13 *Regester*, 7–8.

14 See Chapter 11.

15 W.T. Whitley, *The Baptists of London* (London: The Kingsgate Press, 1928), 116.

children, in 1676. It was this Benjamin who married Susannah Keach in 1699 when he was already functioning as a teacher in the church at Horselydown. The list of names that authorized Keach's *Articles* lists Benjamin Stinton as a "Teacher."[16] Another Stinton, Thomas, born in 1668, married Elizabeth Keach in May 1690, while Keach's youngest daughter, Rebecca, was to marry Thomas Crosby, who eventually became a deacon in the Goat Street congregation. Benjamin and his wife also had a fourth daughter, Rachel, but it is unclear whether she married.

Elias Keach, Keach's only son by his first marriage, was not a member of his father's church. He had left England and gone to America when he was nineteen. By 1692, he returned to London having been remarkably converted. He began to preach and formed a church in London. The joys of his father were soon turned to grief when Elias died in 1699, at the age of thirty-four.[17] (Later in this chapter, we will consider in more detail the relationship between father and son and the brief part Elias Keach played among the Particular Baptists in the 1690s.)

Of his daughters from his first marriage, Mary and Hannah, neither appears in the existing list of members of his congregation. Both had married. Mary Enby was the eldest and Hannah Green the youngest, and both of them were left £1 by Keach in his will.[18]

Keach was also to experience grief over Hannah. She was a member at Horselydown until 1696 when she joined Joseph's Stennett's Seventh-Day Baptist congregation. Their Church Book records that on March 14, 1696, "Hannah Green, daughter of Mr. Benj. Keach and a member of the church walking with him obtained a dismission from the sd. Church to walk with this

---

16 Keach, *The Articles of the Faith*, listed after the epistle dedicatory, unnumbered page 6.

17 Ivimey, *History*, 2:67–471.

18 *Surrey Will Abstracts*, Vol. 26, 2001. Archdeaconry Court of Surrey 1700-1708, no. 820. See Appendix 1.

congregation."[19] However, her sympathies were rapidly changing and, by the end of the year, Stennett reported to the church meeting: "Hannah Green and another had frequented Quaker meetings and seemed to be somewhat tainted with some of their principles."[20] By April of the following year, it was very clear that Hannah had embraced Quakerism. She had spoken of the Scriptures with contempt. She had denied the resurrection of the body. She had argued against the ordinances of baptism and the Lord's Supper and had opened her shop on the Sabbath day. Despite repeated attempts to "bring her off her errors," she remained intractable and was removed from the church because she had forsaken her profession of faith and was guilty of apostasy.[21] Keach had already expressed his convictions that Quaker teaching and practice was a serious departure from the teaching of the Scriptures, and therefore, the defection of his daughter Hannah would have been an occasion of great grief, even greater perhaps than the premature death of his son Elias.[22]

Keach's character and his calling as a minister

Near the end of his life, Benjamin Keach was unjustly accused by David Russen of immoral conduct in connection with the baptism of women.[23] Led by Joseph Stennett, his friends and acquaintances had very quickly risen to his defence and cleared his name. Throughout this book, Keach has been portrayed as a man of godliness, and this is nowhere more evident than in the way he conducted himself in his pastoral office. Crosby is probably the only person who has described his character in any

---

19 Church Book of the Francis Bampfield Congregation 1686–1843, Photograph Copy presented to Dr. Williams's Library by the Seventh-Day Baptist Congregation, Plainsfield, New Jersey, 1952, 46.

20 Church Book of the Francis Bampfield Congregation 1686–1843, 48.

21 Church Book of the Francis Bampfield Congregation 1686–1843, 52–53.

22 See Chapter 7.

23 See Introduction: "Another manner of character."

detail and the manner in which he undertook his work as a minister of the gospel:

> He, with unwearied diligence, did discharge the duties of his pastoral office, preaching both in season and out of season, visiting those under his charge, encouraging the serious, gently reproving the forward, defending the great truths of the Gospel, and setting them in the clearest light. How low would he stoop for the sake of peace! And, how would he bear the infirmities of his weak brethren! That such as would not be wrought upon by the strength of reason, might be melted by his condescension and good-nature. He was prudent as well as peaceable; would forgive and forget injuries, being charitable as well as courteous. He was not addicted to utter harsh censures of such as differed from him in lesser matters, but had a love for all saints, and constantly exercised himself in this, *To keep a conscience void of offence, towards God and towards men.*[24]

Keach would have conducted himself in this manner because he was persuaded that the Scriptures required this pattern of life of a man who was a minister of the gospel of Jesus Christ. During the 1670s, he had begun to produce notes from the figures of speech in the Bible that became *Tropologia*, and that work was to contain a significant section entitled, "Ministers and Churches."[25] Keach, as a minister of Christ, understood himself to be Christ's servant who was directly responsible to give an account of his stewardship to his Lord, for his was a position of trust. He was not, therefore, free to serve his own interests. Rather, he was required to be faithful in carrying out his Master's work, ensuring

---

24 Crosby, *History*, 4:304–305.

25 Keach, *Types and Metaphors*, Section 12, 828–858.

that the directions of his Master, given to him and to those who were members of the church, were obeyed. This faithfulness to Christ was a further expression of Keach's own godliness. Explaining this faithfulness in *Tropologia*, he writes:

> every Minister of Christ ought to be faithful in all things, wholly studying the profit, honour and interest of the Lord Jesus. They ought to be continually about his affairs, not leave the management of the Church, and concerns of the ministry, like some self-seeking priests of our days, to those, who are inexperienced, negligent, and worse; to follow their own concerns, and living in ease and pleasure, pursuing after the riches and vanities of this world, mattering not whether Christ be honoured or no, or whether his interest sink or swim, so that things go well with them, and they thrive in the world. There are too many such in this day, so that we may well say with the apostle, "All seek their own, and none the things that are Christ's."[26]

It was not a sense of self-importance that drove Keach to speak of the dignity of his office. On the contrary, Christ conferred that dignity and because ministers were Christ's ambassadors they should be received as such. He countered any suspicion that self-importance should motivate a true servant of Christ when he noted:

> what great dignity God hath conferred upon his faithful Ministers; and this title should procure an honourable esteem of them in the hearts of all persons to whom they are sent. And this is more necessary to the good success of their message, than is generally thought;

26 Keach, "Ministers compared to stewards," *Types and Metaphors*, 843.

> though it is evident, what Ministers speak upon this subject is misconstrued, as if they herein rather sought themselves, than to befriend the Gospel, or advance the honour of their Master. Men are ready to interpret it as a fruit of their pride, and an affectation they have of some outward grandeur, and worldly pomp, which they design to gain by such a magnificent title.[27]

In 1697, Keach published a book called, *The Glory of a True Church, and Its Discipline Display'd*, written for Baptist churches but "particularly to that under my care," that contained a summary of what he believed should be the work of a pastor.[28] He gives a fivefold function:

1. to feed the flock by preaching the Word of Christ, to administer all the Gospel ordinances and to be faithful and hard-working in carrying out these tasks, "studying to shew himself approved unto God,"
2. to visit the flock,
3. to pray for them at all times,
4. to be a good example in conduct, love, faith and purity of life, and,
5. to carry out the work with impartiality and humility.[29]

Keach stresses that preaching the Word is of first importance, but he also lays emphasis on pastoral care for the flock and the

---

27 Keach, "Ministers compared to ambassadors," *Types and Metaphors*, 854.

28 Keach, *The Glory of a True Church, and Its Discipline Display'd* (London, 1697), iii. A reformatted edition, with new pagination, was produced by M.T. Renihan (Spokane, Washington & Oxford, 1995). Page numbers refer to the original 1697 edition. Keach used the words "pastor," "bishop," "overseer" and "elder" interchangeably, reflecting scriptural usage. I am also indebted to Kenneth Dix for providing me with a privately edited version of Elias Keach's *The Glory and Ornament of a True Gospel Constituted Church* (London, 1697). This work of Keach's son is identical to that produced by his father.

29 Keach, *The Glory of a True Church*, 9.

importance of the character of the minister and his conduct. His conviction was that only pastors should administer baptism and the Lord's Supper, and he believed that a pastor's authority was limited to the church that had chosen and ordained him. This meant, in his view, there was no warrant for that pastor to administer the ordinances in another church, unless it were the case that the ordinances would be neglected altogether in that church.[30] These convictions further illustrate the high view Keach had of his own calling as a minister of the gospel and, in particular, as a pastor of the church at Horselydown.

Crosby not only described Keach's character but also depicted the manner in which he preached, indicating that there was a natural manliness about him and that, while he may not have been endowed with the greatest gifts of language, his sermons were marked by sound biblical teaching. His flock would have gone home satisfied, acknowledging that their preacher had not tried to entertain them with clever words and wit but rather had fed them with meat:

> He affected no unusual tones, nor indecent gestures in his preaching, his stile was strong and masculine. He generally used notes, especially in the latter part of his life; and if his sermons had not all the embellishments of language, which some boast of, they had this peculiar advantage, to be full of solid divinity; which is a much

30 Keach, *The Glory of a True Church*, 16–17. James Barry Vaughn suggests that Keach "differed sharply" from the 1689 General Assembly on this question. I cannot agree with him. The difference is slight, because although they said it was permissible, they too recognized that a pastor's sphere is limited and that necessity may require him to carry out this task on exceptional occasions. Vaughn, "Public Worship and Practical Theology in the Work of Benjamin Keach (1640–1704)," 328–329. The answer of the Assembly was: "That an Elder of one Church, may administer the Ordinance of the Lord's Supper to another of the same Faith, being called so to do by the said Church; tho not as pastor, but as a Minister, necessity being only considered in this Case" (*The Narrative of the Proceedings*, 18).

> better character for pulpit discourses, than to say, they are full of pompous eloquence and flights of wit.[31]

Thomas Crosby thus confirms that Keach was a man of personal integrity who aimed to live up to the calling that he had received from Christ as a minister of the gospel. In addition, Keach had an equally high view of the calling of the church, believing that the Bible also provided the paradigm for the life of the church.

Keach's conception of the church and congregational life

The Glory of a True Church, and Its Discipline Display'd was an important publication in the world of late seventeenth-century Baptists. While Keach drew heavily on similar works by the Independents, notably Isaac Chauncy (1632–1712), this was the first book on the doctrine and life of the church from the pen of a Particular Baptist.[32] His aim was "to write a Small and Plain tract concerning the Rules and the Discipline of a Gospel-Church that all men may not only know our Faith, but see our Order in this case also."[33] He wrote it principally in response to a request from the members of his church and another pastor, and by so doing he met one of the outstanding needs of the Particular Baptist churches at the time. These churches had recently emerged from a period of suffering and difficulty when at times their very existence had been threatened by persecution.

31 Crosby, *History*, 2:305.

32 Isaac Chauncy, *The Doctrine which is According to Godliness, Grounded upon the Holy Scriptures of Truth* (London, 1694). Dr. Chauncy was minister of Mark Lane Independent Church from 1687 to 1701. Isaac Watts (1674–1748) became his assistant in 1699, and his successor two years later. Chauncy wrote and preached extensively on church government, but apparently so wearied his congregation with endless discourses on the subject that they left him. Keach acknowledges the work of men like Chauncy. He stressed that his motive for writing was to provide something briefer and less expensive; see Keach, *The Glory of a True Church*, iv.

33 Keach, *The Glory of a True Church*, iv.

They were in need of some clear direction as to how to conduct their life together as gathered churches.

As has been noted, one of Keach's greatest pastoral concerns was the conversion to Christ of his hearers and readers, but this does not mean that he was concerned solely with conversion and with believers as individuals. He was also concerned for the corporate life of the church, that his members might understand the nature of the church itself, how it was to be governed and ordered and how each member was to fulfill his or her responsibilities. His church was not alone in this concern. Many of the questions that were asked at the national assemblies and association meetings requested advice about the detailed application of biblical teaching to the life and order of the church.

The title he used for his "Small and Plain tract" is revealing, because he spoke of *the glory* of the church. At the end of the tract, he explained that the glory and beauty of the church are derived from Jesus Christ, who is the foundation on which the church is built. This glory will be visibly demonstrated by such characteristics as the church's right ordering of all its affairs. Sincere love between the members, prayer for one another, and bearing with one another's weaknesses were also signs of the church's glory. The holiness of the member's lives, the evidence of God's presence among them, the administration of right discipline and the care and sympathy shown toward the poor and afflicted among them were also deemed essential characteristics by Keach.[34] He concludes this section by saying, "God has put a Glory and high Dignity upon the Church and in its Authority and Power."[35] It was not a new theme, but one that he had expressed before in his preaching:

> There is nothing that doth more beautify the Church of God, than good order.... Every member ought to know

34 Keach, *The Glory of a True Church*, 45–63. Keach lists some fourteen features.

35 Keach, *The Glory of a True Church*, 62.

> his place, and to strive to behave himself well.... All the saints should live in perfect peace, unity, and sweet concord together as children of the same Father, and heirs of the same crown and kingdom.[36]

These visible characteristics also come to expression in the church covenant that is printed at the end of the tract. In that covenant, the church undertook to fulfill "Gospel-Duties...in the Power, and Strength of the Blessed God, whose we are, and whom we desire to serve."[37] This church covenant shows the seriousness with which members took their responsibilities as they willingly placed themselves under the Word of God. They did not shrink back from undertaking to carry out what they regarded as their duty to God and to one another. This seriousness is expressed in the following way:

> Being fully satisfied in the way of Church-Communion, and the Truth of Grace in some good measure upon one another's Spirits, we do solemnly join ourselves together in Holy Union and Fellowship, humbly submitting to the Discipline of the Gospel, and all the Holy Duties required of a People in such a Spiritual Relation.[38]

Keach's view of the church as comprised of believers was in sharp distinction from the established Church of England and the nation of Israel in the Old Testament. He said that the latter

---

36 Keach, "The church compared to a family," *Types and Metaphors*, 713.

37 Keach, *The Glory of a True Church*, 71–74. For the full text of the church covenant, see Appendix 3. For a fuller treatment of church covenants and Keach's contribution, see Austin Walker, "Benjamin Keach: Cultivating corporate spirituality and church covenants." In G. Stephen Weaver Jr. and Ian Hugh Clary, eds., *The Pure Flame of Devotion: The History of Christian Spirituality. Essays in Honour of Michael A.G. Haykin* (Kitchener: Joshua Press, 2013), 363–382.

38 Keach, *The Glory of a True Church*, 72.

had two features in common: they were both national churches and they included their children as members.[39] This sharp distinction is a recurring theme in his writings as he stressed the true nature of the church. For example, in a sermon based on the parable of the householder in Matthew 20:16, he stated that

> this [nation of the Jews] being a typical church, it ceased when the antitype came, and then God severed a people out of that national church of the Jews, and out of the Gentile nations, to be his gospel-church, which consisted of holy and regenerated persons, though not taking any one particular nation, as a nation, into such a church-state...and from hence it appears, that the gospel-church, or churches, are not national, but congregational, all not consisting of the carnal seed of believers, but of the true spiritual seed.[40]

Three statements are significant in this quotation, indicating precisely whom Keach regarded as belonging to the true church: "holy and regenerated persons," "congregational" as opposed to "national" and "true spiritual seed" as opposed to the "carnal seed of believers." In his tract, he further identifies the beauty and glory of the church by identifying its members as "lively stones, i.e. converted persons," alluding to 1 Peter 2:5.[41]

The church, as Keach understood it, is fundamentally a congregation of gathered saints, of believers. It has been rightly said

---

39 Keach believed that, although there were true Christians in the national church, the Church of England was not an orderly church. "[T]ho we believe there are many Holy and Gracious Christians of the Communion of the Church of England, and that they are Members of the Invisible Universal Church, yet we do not believe the Church of England, nor any National Church, is an orderly true Constituted Visible Church of Jesus Christ, and therefore we separated from them" [Keach, *Light broke forth in Wales*, 250].

40 Keach, "The Householder," *Parables Two*, 61.

41 Keach, *The Glory of a True Church*, 6.

that "the essence of English nonconformity was the creation of non-parochial protestant congregations, or 'separate churches' as contemporaries described them."[42] Keach stood firmly in this separatist tradition, a dominant feature of Nonconformity, although he and his fellow Baptists went further than the Presbyterians and Independents, because they insisted that baptism was only for believers. Thus Keach's own definition of the church differed from them as well:

> A Church of Christ, according to the Gospel-Institution, is a Congregation of Godly Christians, who as a Stated Assembly (being first baptized upon Profession of Faith) do by mutual agreement and consent give themselves up to the Lord, and to one another, according to the Will of God; and do ordinarily meet together in one Place, for the Publick Service and Worship of God; among whom the Word of God and Sacraments are duly administered, according to Christ's Institution.[43]

This meant that once they had been baptized and hands had been laid on them, members entered into a covenant whereby they undertook to walk together in the fellowship of that particular congregation, to submit themselves to the care and discipline of the church and to worship God together.

Keach also drew attention to the offices of elder (already considered) and deacon. While chapter 26 of the *Confession of Faith*, "Of the Church," mentions deacons, it does not set out the nature of their work. Keach does this briefly and neatly, describing their particular work as "to serve tables, *viz*. to see to provide for the Lord's Table, the Minister's table and the poor's table."[44]

---

42 Murray Tolmie, *The Triumph of the Saints: The Separate Churches of London 1616–1649* (Cambridge: Cambridge University Press, 1977), 1.

43 Keach, *The Glory of a True Church*, 5–6.

44 Keach, *The Glory of a True Church*, 10.

The remaining sections of the tract are the most extensive. Here, Keach summarizes the duties of church members to their pastors and, by providing a series of biblical motives, urges them to fulfill those duties. Referring his readers to texts of Scripture as was his usual custom, Keach unfolded those duties, including praying for the pastor and teachers in the church, honouring and esteeming them, submitting to them in their exhortations and reproofs and defending them if they were unjustly reproached. He expected members to seek counsel from them when they faced troubles, to provide for their maintenance and not to be ashamed of their pastors if they suffered persecution. Keach clearly believed that there should be a close relationship between the pastors and teachers of the church and the people.

Then, following a brief statement about how members should be received, Keach described how the church was to use the power of the keys in the exercise of church discipline. He elucidated the steps that should be undertaken with those who fail to walk in an orderly way, either because of scandalous conduct or because they adopt heretical teaching. Keach believed that there were three kinds of church censures to be used by a gospel church: suspension from membership, withdrawing from a member who walks disorderly and, as a final step, excommunication. Nevertheless, whatever steps were taken, at each stage every effort was to be made to reclaim the erring church member.

The final two sections show Keach's concern to maintain peace and unity in the church. He draws attention to those who "dismember themselves" by separating from the church and trying to join another congregation. Such a practice he believed to be disorderly, and ought to be discouraged. Someone leaving one church should obtain an orderly dismissal. Keach was well aware of the shortcomings of pastors and members of the church and dealt in some detail with disorder and discord in the life of the church, showing how it could be prevented, corrected and removed—covering no less than twenty-three disorderly practices!

Among the things he mentioned as promoting disorder were a failure of members to follow the rule of Matthew 18:15–18 in the case of a private offence, a church or pastors turning a blind eye to sin, members deciding to go and listen to another preacher and take in "unsound notions," some dissatisfied members meeting behind the pastor's back to talk about church matters and accusations brought against elders but without two or three witnesses and therefore contrary to the rule of Scripture.

In *The Glory of a True Church*, Keach accomplished several things. First, he gave his church and others a more detailed exposition of chapter 26 of *The Second London Baptist Confession of Faith*, "Of the Church." That chapter was already the longest of the thirty-two chapters, and it would have been impractical for the *Confession* to go into detail at every point. Nevertheless, as the questions being asked at the assemblies and the association meetings indicate, there was a pressing need for some kind of document that dealt with these issues. Keach's tract attempted to deal with matters relating to the corporate life of the church. He wanted to strengthen the life of the local church and set out to accomplish this by stressing the need for a high level of commitment by each member. This came to expression supremely in the church covenant.

Then, his tract showed that he believed the Scriptures were sufficient not only for doctrine but also for every aspect of the life of the church. He believed passionately in an "orderly" church, by which he meant a church that was governed by the Word of Christ. On another occasion he illustrated it this way:

> In every kingdom there is a statute book…wherein all the fundamental laws, statutes and ordinances of that kingdom are written: so the word of God, or blessed gospel, is the great statute book of the church or of Christ's spiritual kingdom, in which all his laws and ordinances are recorded. A king appoints officers in his

> kingdom under him, to govern and order and manage all the affairs thereof, and to do all things by his authority, and in his name; even so hath Jesus Christ set officers in his church to order and govern his spiritual kingdom under him, by his authority, and in his name, and according to his blessed word, and they that submit not to his government, despise the king's authority; the officers are elders and deacons, whose work is expressly laid down in the gospel: nor do we read of any other office or officers he hath left in his church (and to abide) but only these two.[45]

In addition, Keach explained the various dimensions of the work of pastoral oversight that ought to be undertaken by a faithful minister of the gospel. He recognized that an overseer was only beginning his work when people were converted and baptized. If the church was a building made up of living stones, then each one had to take their place in the building. It was the testimony of his son-in-law that

> it was none of the least of his excellent qualifications for the ministerial work, that he knew how to behave himself in the church of God, in regard to the exercise of that discipline, which is so necessary to Christian society. With patience and meekness, with gravity and prudence, with impartiality and faithfulness, did he demean himself in his congregation; and with prudence and conduct, did he manage all their affairs upon all occasions; and was not only serviceable to them, but useful to many others.[46]

---

45 Keach, "The Wise and Foolish Virgins," *Parables Two*, 201.
46 Crosby, *History*, 4:305–306.

Finally, in this tract, Keach has bequeathed to succeeding ages of the church, materials that are essentially biblical in their nature. The modern church has paid a heavy price for neglecting to practice what the Scripture teaches about pastoral oversight. Surely one of the purposes of studying church history is to learn from the past and to weigh what others have said and practiced in the balances of the Word of God. Many of the disorders and causes of discord in the church today are precisely those that Keach addressed 300 years ago. Were he able to survey the pattern of life in the professing church of Christ today, he would have sadly concluded that much of the glory and beauty of the church had gone.

Elias Keach and the Articles of Faith

In 1697, Elias Keach published, *The Glory and ornament of a True, Gospel-Constituted Church, being a brief display of the discipline of the church at Tallow-Chandlers Hall.* He says that it was "composed by an experienced and worthy Minister of the Gospel, a great lover of your Peace and Well-being," which is without doubt an anonymous reference to his father.[47] In the same year, father and son also printed separate *Articles of Faith*, which formed a condensed version of the *Confession of Faith*. This version was in no way an attempt to undermine or to change any of the doctrines of the faith as set out more fully in the 1689 *Confession of Faith*. It is certain that they acted together because the two statements of faith are identical. The only difference is seen in the separate letters that each of them wrote for the particular congregations where they ministered. It was in these letters that they gave some specific reasons for the publishing of the *Articles*.

47 Elias Keach, *The Glory and ornament of a True, Gospel-Constituted Church, being a brief display of the discipline of the church at Tallow-Chandlers Hall* (London, 1697), iv.

Elias Keach (1665–1699), eldest son of Benajmin Keach, was also a minister of the gospel.

In his "Epistle" to his congregation, Benjamin Keach, aware of the shortness of his life, expressed his desire to leave behind "an account of holy doctrine and order and discipline."[48] Further on, he states that he also wanted to make a clear statement about the issues of the laying on of hands and the singing of hymns.[49] At the same time, he was a sensitive man, indicating that these issues should not lead to the congregation distancing themselves from those who held other convictions. He wrote:

> Yet my desire is you would nevertheless shew all Tenderness, Charity and Moderation to such as differ from you in those Cases, and not refuse Communion with them; and indeed your late sweet Temper appears to be such, that I need not press you to this.[50]

Both father and son were in agreement over the need for something brief and cheap because the original *Confession of Faith* was bulky and expensive, so that few in their congregations could afford it. Furthermore, both of them said it was also now "exceeding scarce."[51] Given that they were living in London and that it was less than ten years since the Assembly of 1689 adopted the *Confession*, their comment is very surprising. Did the fact that the Assembly had divided its meetings mean that the continued availability of the *Confession* had been overlooked?

Elias also agreed with his father about the laying on of hands and the singing of God's praises with hymns. However, his

---

48 Keach, "Epistle," *The Articles of the Faith*, 3.

49 The controversy over hymn singing will be considered in Chapter 11. For the statements about the laying on of hands and the singing of psalms, see Appendix 4.

50 Keach, "Epistle," *The Articles of the Faith*, 4.

51 Elias Keach, "To the Reader," *The Articles of the Faith of the Church of Christ or Congregation Meeting at Tallow Chandlers Hall* (London, 1697), unnumbered pages 3–4. The price of the *Confession of Faith* was 12d (12 pence or 1 shilling). See Keach, "Epistle," *The Articles of the Faith*, 3–4, for his father's statement.

principal reason for publishing this book was the vulnerability of some in his congregation to unbiblical teaching. Some of them seemed too easily drawn away by doctrinal error and showed a lack of understanding and discernment. He wanted to minimize this by placing in their hands something "in so narrow a compass, and at so small a Price...for their clearer Information and Confirmation in the Doctrine of God our Saviour."[52]

At this point, we need to ask how Elias Keach came to be writing in this vein. Earlier on we saw that at the age of nineteen, in 1684, he had left home and gone to America. No record exists that explains his motives for leaving, but when he first arrived he showed no real interest in religious matters, arriving there as "a very wild spark."[53] This suggests that perhaps he left England in order to remove himself from the influence of his father, his home and the church that met in Horselydown.

When Elias first arrived in America he attempted to pass himself off as a minister by preaching a sermon. As he was preaching, he stopped abruptly, overcome by a deep sense of shame. Realizing that he was an imposter, he acknowledged he had only been able to act the part because he was the son of Benjamin Keach. He found help from a Baptist minister in Pennsylvania, Thomas Dungan (d. 1688). Having been converted to Christ, Elias Keach was baptized and shortly thereafter ordained as a gospel preacher by the Cold Spring Baptist Church where Dungan was pastor.[54]

By 1689, Elias Keach had gathered a small body of believers together in Philadelphia County, Pennsylvania. This church

52 Elias Keach, "To the Reader," *The Articles of the Faith of the Church of Christ or Congregation Meeting at Tallow Chandlers Hall*, unnumbered, page 3.

53 Quoted by Ivimey, *History*, 2:468.

54 Ivimey, *History*, 2:467–471, and W.T. Whitley, "Baptists in the Colonies till 1750," *TBHS* 7 (1920–1921): 43–44. Thomas Dungan was from Ireland and had come to Rhode Island in the days of the Restoration. In 1684, Pastor Dungan and a small group of members from the church in Newport came south to Bucks County, Pennsylvania, and established themselves as a Baptist church.

became known as the Lower Dublin Baptist Church—although at its founding there was only one Irishman, the other members being Welsh and English! They were Particular Baptists, just as Elias had been taught in his youth back in England. This congregation also was known as the Pennepek Church, named after the local creek,[55] and from this church sprang the Philadelphia Baptist Association.

Elias travelled throughout Pennsylvania and New Jersey. As a result of his preaching, people were converted, baptized and became members of the Lower Dublin Baptist Church. Because they were scattered over a wide geographical area, they had a number of meeting places—Philadelphia, Chester, Burlington, Middletown, Cohansey and Salem—but they were all considered general members of the Pennepek Church.[56]

While in Pennsylvania, Elias Keach married Mary Moore, daughter of the Lord Chief Justice of Philadelphia. Despite Elias' successful labours, he decided to return to England in 1692 and soon began to preach in London.[57] In a letter sent to his successor in Pennepek, Elias states that he had come to London and preached with great success, baptizing some 130 persons in the space of six months. He also writes that when the church was constituted, his father and Hercules Collins, from the church at Wapping, had laid hands on him, ordaining him to the ministry of that church.[58]

Apart from the books already mentioned, Elias Keach also produced a book of hymns, two sermons on the grace of patience, and four sermons on justification. He died in the prime of life in

---

55 William Cathcart, *The Baptist Encyclopaedia* (Philadelphia: Louis H. Everts, 1881), 1:638–639. Pennepek is variously spelled Pemmepecka, Pennypack, Pennepeck or Pennepack.

56 Horatio Gates Jones, *Historical Sketch of the Lower Dublin (or Pennepek) Baptist Church* (Morrisania, 1869), 5–7.

57 Cathcart, *The Baptist Encyclopaedia*, 1:639.

58 Ivimey, *History*, 2:469–470.

1699, leaving behind his wife, Mary, and their son Benjamin.[59] When Benjamin Keach drew up his will, it was his grandson, also named Benjamin, who was one of the main beneficiaries: "to my grandson Benjamin Keach £5 to apprentice him and £5 more in books."[60]

Elias Keach's influence was important to the formation of the Philadelphia Baptist Association in 1707 and, through him, his father's influence was also felt in America. The laying on of hands after baptism and congregational hymn-singing became established principles. They were formally incorporated as two additional chapters in the new edition of *The Second London Baptist Confession of Faith* that the Philadelphia Association approved in 1742—probably a direct result of the *Articles of Faith* that father and son produced in 1697.[61] The *Articles of Faith* was the first generally used Baptist confession in America and, in 1712, appeal was made to Elias Keach's confession of faith and church covenant in an effort to resolve a dispute, suggesting that these works were still in use as well.[62] It is also probable that Elias Keach promoted the use of his father's catechisms and *Instructions for Youth*.

Elias Keach would likely have produced more works but he died in his thirties, after a brief illness, and was soon followed by his father. As it was, Elias was responsible for extending his father's influence across the Atlantic and into America.

---

59 There is some dispute over the date of his death. His funeral sermon dates his death as October 27, 1699, yet most modern records date it 1701. Further details of Elias Keach may be found in Ivimey, *History*, 3:533–540.

60 *Surrey Will Abstracts*, 820.

61 Lumpkin, *Baptist Confessions of Faith*, 348–349.

62 Lumpkin, *Baptist Confessions of Faith*, 349.

CHAPTER 10

"Entrusted with the Word"

> They are entrusted with the Word, the faithful Word and doctrine of God is committed to them; they must see they preach nothing for doctrine, but what is the direct and undeniable truth and mind of God; they must not corrupt the Word, not intermix it with the traditions of men.[1]

The sermons of Benjamin Keach constitute the greater part of his writings and the majority of them were published in the last decade of his life. The sermon he preached at John Norcott's funeral in 1676 is the earliest sample we have of his preaching.[2] *Tropologia*, published in 1681, was clearly developed from some of his sermon notes. But it was not until after 1689, when freedom of the press became a reality, that Keach was able to publish his sermons more widely.

---

1 Keach, "Ministers compared to watchmen," *Types and Metaphors*, 834.

2 See Chapter 7.

The works he published in the decade or so before his death varied in length. For example, a single sermon on Proverbs 3:6, *God Acknowledged: Or, the True Interest of the Nation*, was preached on December 11, 1695—the day William III had appointed as a day for public prayer and humiliation. It was printed shortly afterward in 1696. A much larger work, *The Display of Glorious Grace: Or, the Covenant of Peace Opened*, followed in 1698, consisting of fourteen sermons based on Isaiah 54:10. Then the massive *Gospel Mysteries Unveil'd: Or, Exposition of all the Parables*, also based almost entirely on sermons, was published in 1701.[3]

John Dunton, who was one of Keach's publishers and had expressed the opinion that Keach's *War with the Devil* and *The Travels of True Godliness* would sell to the end of time, was perhaps more accurate in his assessment of Keach's preaching by referring to him as "a popular preacher."

> This War-Like Author is much admir'd among the Anabaptists, and to do him right, his Thoughts are easy, just and pertinent. He's a popular Preacher, and (as appears by his awakening Sermons) understands the Humour and Necessity of his Audience.[4]

---

3 Keach, *Gospel Mysteries Unveil'd* has been reprinted as *Expositions of the Parables, Series One and Two* (Grand Rapids: Kregel, 1991). It is the modern edition that is referred to in this book as *Parables One* or *Parables Two*. There were also three sets of sermons by Keach that will be considered in chapter 13, namely, *The Marrow of True Justification*, published in 1692, *The Everlasting Covenant*, a sermon preached at the funeral of his friend Henry Forty in 1693 and *A Medium Betwixt Two Extremes*, published in 1698. This is because they are polemical in purpose and directed against the "Baxterians," and so a whole chapter will be devoted to the Antinomian controversy and the doctrine of justification by faith. There are some overlapping points and so a consideration of *A Display of Glorious Grace* will be included both in this chapter and Chapter 13.

4 Dunton, *The Life and Errors of John Dunton*, 177. See Chapter 7, n.47. Dunton uses the word "humour" here in its older meaning, the disposition and state of mind of his hearers. By "popular" he was saying that in his opinion, Keach was a man who was well received by ordinary people.

Among seventeenth-century Particular Baptists, Keach published the largest number of sermons, supporting Dunton's assessment that Keach was popular among "the Anabaptists" (a term that was still sticking burr-like to Particular Baptists despite their attempts to remove it). Hanserd Knollys and William Kiffin were other respected leaders among London Baptists, but neither of them came near to competing with Keach's output of published sermons. The latter numbered over 200, and this single fact makes a consideration of his sermons necessary. Keach's concerns for the conversion of his hearers and for their growth in godliness forms the backdrop for considering Keach as a preacher of God's free grace. He saw himself and other preachers as Christ's spiritual watchmen who had been given a great responsibility to preach God's Word, administer Christ's ordinances and care for the flock of God.[5]

It was God's free grace that came to supreme expression in the outworking of the covenant of grace that constituted "the great salvation" that Keach loved to proclaim.

> This salvation...was contrived and found out by the wisdom of God before the world began. Hence Christ is said to "be a Lamb slain from the foundation of the world" (Rev. 13:8); that is, in the decree, counsel and purpose of God: Christ was set up from everlasting as the great and glorious Mediator and Saviour of all that would believe in him, or that were given unto him by the Father...God thought of us poor sinners, and found out this way of salvation before we had a being, yea even from eternity, foreseeing us fallen in the first Adam, brought into deplorable condition of wrath and misery.[6]

---

5 Keach, *Types and Metaphors*, 834–836.

6 Keach, "The Great Salvation," *A Golden Mine Opened*, 370–371.

Keach regarded the subject of the covenant of grace as being fundamental to a right understanding of what the Bible said about salvation and the work of each person of the Trinity in the work of salvation. This appears to be the principal reason, for example, as to why Keach decided in 1699 to reprint a sermon he preached in 1693, at Henry Forty's funeral, *The Everlasting Covenant*, and to add further material in order to develop his theme.

Preaching peace with God

The details of this covenant of grace were worked out most fully in a series of fourteen sermons called *The Display of Glorious Grace*, which was published in 1698.[7] His concern was to open up Isaiah 54:10: "'For the mountains shall depart and the hills be removed, but My kindness shall not depart from you, nor shall My covenant of peace be removed,' says the Lord, who has mercy on you." Preaching at a time when peace in Europe was uppermost in the mind of the nation, Keach told his hearers he was pessimistic about how long it would last. Rather, he preferred to draw their attention to "a Peace which being made shall be lasting, and never be removed," a peace that God had promised in the gospel.[8]

These sermons reflect Keach's adherence to Reformed orthodoxy as expressed in *The Westminster Confession of Faith*, *The Savoy Declaration* and *The Second London Baptist Confession*, which he had approved by signing in 1689. Judging by the margin notes

---

7 Keach, *The Display of Glorious Grace: Or, the Covenant of Peace Opened* (London, 1698). The title page quotes Psalm 89:34, but the fourteen sermons are in fact an exposition of Isaiah 54:10.

8 Keach, *The Display of Glorious Grace*, 4–5. Keach is probably referring to the Treaty of Ryswick signed by France, United Provinces, England and Spain and the Emperor in 1697. It is also interesting to note that he is still awaiting the seven last plagues of Revelation and the fall of Babylon but is content to wait and see what is produced by divine providence as 1700 approaches.

in his sermons and the quotations he used, Keach had also read and interacted with a wide range of contemporary Puritan authors in preparing his sermon materials. These included William Bates, Stephen Charnock, Isaac Chauncy, David Clarkson, John Cotton, Thomas Goodwin, Thomas Manton, John Owen, Samuel Petto (c.1624–1711) and Matthew Poole (1624–1679), as well as the *Westminster Catechisms*.[9] Along with these men, Keach believed that the Bible clearly taught the doctrines of original sin, including the imputation of Adam's sin and the covenant of works, and that salvation found its source in God's eternal electing love. In his sermons, Keach particularly emphasized the biblical teaching about justification by faith, including the imputation of Christ's righteousness to sinners, and stressed the necessity of the Spirit's work in regeneration and sanctification. He was likewise orthodox in his convictions about the person, work and offices of Jesus Christ, on the hypostatic union—that

> two whole, perfect, and distinct natures were inseperably joined together in one person, without conversion, composition or confusion: which person is very God and very man, yet one Christ, the only mediator between God and man

—and on the qualifications of Christ to be the Redeemer of his people and the offices he fulfilled as prophet, priest and king.[10]

These doctrines were not set out in isolation from one another, but presented in one coherent plan of salvation. In eight explanatory propositions that he laid down by way of a premise in *The Display of Glorious Grace*, Keach showed that he understood the free grace of God to be one comprehensive plan of salvation.

9 Keach, *The Display of Glorious Grace*, 216–217, where he refers to the *Westminster Larger Catechism* to argue against Richard Baxter's notion of two separate covenants.

10 *Second London Confession of Faith* (London, 1689), chapter 8, paragraph 2.

The plan entailed the fulfillment of God's sovereign will that was planned in eternity, executed in history and consummated in glory. God foreknew from eternity that a breach would arise between God and his creatures and, in order to show his glory and his grace, God the Father entered into a covenant with his Son, and through the obedience of Jesus Christ, God determined to save many of his fallen creatures. Keach was emphatic that God did not minimize the breach that he foresaw. Rather, he recognized that it was great, both on man's part, due to his guilt, disobedience, rebellion, enmity against God and hardness of heart and, on God's part, because of his enmity against sinners, his hatred of sin and the curse of the broken law of God.

The actual breach between God and man took place in history when Adam, as the public head and representative of all humanity, broke the covenant of works. This covenant required perfect righteousness on the part of Adam. He failed to obey, though, and brought ruin upon himself and the whole human race. So it was that no man or angel could possibly repair the breach between God and man that resulted from Adam's sinful disobedience. Man was consequently left as both a debtor and a criminal. Unless God had chosen beforehand to intervene in grace, salvation would have been impossible. But, said Keach, God was not only *just* but also *gracious*. By his special electing love, God showed his sovereign mercy and grace in his willingness to save sinners. This love came to expression in the covenant of grace, whereby God the Father provided a Saviour, the second Adam, his own Son, to undertake to die in the place of sinners and make peace between God and man.

The obedience and death of Jesus Christ was central in this "great salvation" and also in Keach's preaching of the covenant of grace, for Christ not only confirmed but also ratified the covenant by acting as a "surety." By this term, Keach viewed Christ as the one who was going to succeed through his *obedience* where Adam had failed by his *disobedience*, thus becoming a surety of a better covenant (see Hebrews 7:22). Keach taught that a surety is a sponsor, or someone "who undertakes for one or more Persons whose Credit is gone or is not good."[11] As he explained:

> [Christ] engaged as the Surety of the Covenant, to restore to Man, or to all God's elect, that Righteousness which Man lost, that as we were made Sinners by Adam's Disobedience, so by his Obedience we should all be made righteous; that as the Sin of the First Adam was imputed to our condemnation, so his Righteousness, as our Covenanting Head, might be imputed to all his Seed, and all this according to the Contrivance of God's Infinite Wisdom, and to answer the Design, Purpose and Proposal of God the Father, in the Council of Peace.[12]

Keach further affirmed that not only was the blood that Christ shed in his death the price for the sinner's redemption, but he also paid the price for all the grace shown to sinners.

> For tho we have all Covenant Grants, and Blessings freely given to us, or merely of God's Free Grace, yet Faith, a New Heart, Regeneration, Repentance, Pardon, and Peace, and all other Grace, and Blessings here, and Glory hereafter were all purchased for us by the Death of Christ; for as you heard Christ did more than pay our debts.[13]

This comprehensive plan of salvation not only formed the foundation for Keach's own understanding of God's work of salvation, but it also provided a unified structure for him as a preacher of God's free grace. In preaching this salvation, Keach

---

11 Keach, *The Display of Glorious Grace*, 86.

12 Keach, *The Display of Glorious Grace*, 93.

13 Keach, *The Display of Glorious Grace*, 115.

expected hearers to see the greatness of their salvation and recognize that it was the work of God from beginning to end—therefore, they could rely on God entirely. He explained to them that as result of the covenant of peace, their sins were forgiven and they were justified by faith in Christ. All the accusations of sin, the law, Satan and their own consciences, were silenced by Christ's intercession. All their needs would be supplied, their graces strengthened, their enemies subdued, their afflictions would work for their good and—above all—they had been brought to God, who was now at peace with them though Jesus Christ. He told them: "You stand firmer, and more sure in this Covenant, than Adam stood in Paradise before he fell."[14]

It is no surprise to find that the covenant of peace was a recurring theme in his preaching for over thirty years. Tom Nettles is surely right when he states that an understanding of the covenant of peace is the key to appreciating Keach's theology. It "is the driving force in and gives coherence to Keach's entire theological system."[15] Keach's understanding of the covenant of peace was essentially biblical and representative of those who embraced Calvinistic theology in that day.

Keach's Calvinism was a firm rejection of any supposed freedom of the human will to enter into this covenant with God and expressed a measure of righteous indignation against the idea of free will, being persuaded that such a notion robbed Christ of his glory as the Mediator. Firm Calvinist though he was, Keach did not lean toward hyper-Calvinism, nor did he by his doctrine contribute toward the development of hyper-Calvinism in the succeeding generation, as has sometimes been suggested.[16] Keach

---

14 Keach, *The Display of Glorious Grace*, 303.

15 Tom J. Nettles, "Benjamin Keach, 1640–1704." In Haykin, ed., *The British Particular Baptists 1638–1910*, 2:102. In this article, Nettles provides a useful and brief summary of what Keach taught under some of the main heads of systematic theology.

16 Nettles, "Benjamin Keach," *The British Particular Baptists*, 2:120–126. Nettles firmly refutes the suggestion made by James Barry Vaughn, "Benjamin Keach." In Timothy George and David Dockery, eds., *Baptist Theologians* (Nashville: Broadman Press, 1990),

clearly believed in what is called the "free offer of the gospel." Preachers had a biblical warrant to urge unbelievers to come to Christ, pointing out their responsibility to repent of their sins and believe on Christ, something that is foreign to hyper-Calvinism. Picking up on the imagery of a preacher as an ambassador of Christ, Keach affirmed that this picture informs us not only of the high value that we should place on the gospel but also of the "great and absolute necessity of Preaching the Gospel."[17] Such preaching included a "free offer of the gospel," which is very evident in the following exhortation to the unconverted:

> Sinners be ye exhorted, and fully persuaded to hearken to Christ's Ambassadors, and carefully to receive their Message.... To accept of Terms of Peace by closing with Christ, by believing in him.... What do you say Sinners? Will you strive to take hold of Jesus Christ? Believe in him, cry to him for Faith, resolve to lay down your Arms: What answer shall I return to my Great Master? Do not make a Pause, but speedily come to a Resolution, your lives are uncertain.[18]

The free offer of the gospel was characteristic of all of Keach's preaching. In *The Great Salvation*, a series of fifteen sermons on Hebrews 2:3, he urges his readers:

> O haste to Jesus Christ, come to him, for that is the way, and the only way, as you have heard, to be delivered from Wrath. You know not how near you are to fall under the

---

60. Vaughn suggests that Keach was close to hyper-Calvinism because of his attitude toward foreign missions. Nettles also quotes Ivimey's persuasion that if some of Keach's Baptist successors had preached in the same manner as Keach and others, then the churches would not have experienced decline as a result of their hyper-Calvinism.

17 Keach, *The Display of Glorious Grace*, 146.

18 Keach, *The Display of Glorious Grace*, 149–150.

> Wrath of God, and then it will be too late: God gives you space to repent, and to take hold of his Salvation; you will, Sinners, have no Excuse, no Plea in the great Day if you neglect the Day of your Visitation, and slight the Offers of God's Infinite Grace and Favour![19]

Again, in expounding the parable of the pearl of great price, Keach asserts that it is "an indispensable duty" that sinners actively seek Jesus Christ:

> Will any say it is in vain to seek Jesus Christ, they may as well say it is in vain for ministers to preach to sinners, and in vain for them to read, hear and pray; hearing and living are joined together; for as "faith comes by hearing," so life comes by hearing also: "Hear and your soul shall live," Is. 55.3. This finding, this hearing, and this believing is all one and the same thing: when seeking of Christ is of no use, preaching will be of no use also. But know, O ye sinners, that seeking of Christ, and finding him are joined together. Therefore it is an indispensable duty for sinners to seek Jesus Christ.[20]

This urging of sinners to turn to Christ was one of the joys of preaching for Keach. He regarded it as nothing less than his calling, "to proclaim that Peace which is already made, and endeavour to persuade Sinners to accept of it on those Terms offered to them, that they may be reconciled to God."[21]

Furthermore, he believed that this gospel of peace was to be proclaimed universally to all kinds of sinners. On the other hand, he did not believe in universal redemption, which teaches

---

19 Keach, "The Great Salvation," *A Golden Mine Opened*, 483.

20 Keach, "The Pearl of Great Price," *Parables One*, 200.

21 Keach, *The Display of Glorious Grace*, 145.

that Jesus Christ died for all men, and is one of the main tenets of Arminian theology. To Keach, that idea was now unthinkable and unbiblical. If universal redemption were true, it would mean that Christ's purpose had actually been frustrated and that he was not the Saviour he claimed to be, for it was very evident that not everyone was saved:

> If Christ laid down his Life to Redeem every Man and Woman in the World, hath he his whole Purchase? A Man would think himself cheated, or strangely deceived, that laid down a Thousand Pounds to redeem Ten Men, when he finds there are not above Three or Four indeed actually Redeemed; this renders Christ's Blood spilt in vain for the greatest part for whom it was shed, or who he intended to Redeem thereby, and so he is deceived, or disappointed.[22]

Spurgeon, who shared Keach's biblical convictions to the full, said of his predecessor, "Very sweetly did Mr. Keach preach the great fundamental truths of the gospel, and glorify the name and work of Jesus." He found his sermons to be "rich in savour" and preached by "one who loved the whole truth in Jesus, and felt its power."[23]

This last comment by Spurgeon concerning the power of the truth is also evident in *The Display of Glorious Grace*. Christ had made peace by his death on the cross, a peace with God that is experienced and enjoyed by those who have believed on Christ. They come to enjoy free trade with heaven, having access to the Father by the Spirit, and enjoy "the best things of heaven and God." They now trade in things of inestimable worth, "things [that] are only given to his own People, to his Beloved ones, as a

22 Keach, *The Display of Glorious Grace*, 158–159.

23 Spurgeon, *The Metropolitan Tabernacle: Its History and Work*, 31.

Pledge of his Eternal and Special Favour in Christ," riches that are "soul-satisfying and soul-fattening."[24] Keach speaks out of his own experience of those "Choice and Blessed Experiences" that had enriched his soul, and declares: "He is so Good, yea so Precious, so Sweet in his Love and Favour, that I am not able to express it.... Therefore, pray, taste yourselves, and then by experience you will find it to be as I say."[25]

Keach was a faithful watchman. Spurgeon also says of Keach's preaching that

> he was very solid in his preaching, and his whole conduct and behaviour betokened a man deeply in earnest for the cause of God. In addressing the ungodly, he was intensely direct, solemn and impressive, not flinching to declare the terrors of the Lord, nor veiling the freeness of divine grace.[26]

When Keach preached fifteen sermons on Hebrews 2:3 ("How shall we escape if we neglect so great a salvation?"), he divided up his text into two doctrines. First, there were "the ways in which salvation is great and glorious" (the first seven sermons) and second, there were the means how this salvation may be neglected (the remaining eight sermons). In this second section, Keach warned his hearers not only of the danger of neglecting God's salvation but also of the sin and evil of doing so.[27] He explained what it meant to neglect God's salvation, and he identified the kind of people he had in mind. Those, for example, who never trouble to think about it or refuse to hear the gospel preached, those who refuse the offer of mercy, those who prefer

24 Keach, *The Display of Glorious Grace*, 268–270.

25 Keach, *The Display of Glorious Grace*, 265.

26 Spurgeon, *The Metropolitan Tabernacle: Its History and Work*, 31

27 Keach, "The Great Salvation," *A Golden Mine Opened*, 367–500. These sermons are little more than detailed sermon outlines.

sinful pleasures and those who postpone thinking about it until old age, sickness and death come. At the root of all of these reactions, Keach identified unbelief: "It is through unbelief this Salvation is neglected, Men believe not: The grand neglect centres here, this is the killing Evil, the Sin of all Sins, the Plague of all Plagues."[28]

As Spurgeon observed, Keach was unflinching in declaring the terrors of the Lord, yet he was also urgent in pleading with those who had neglected salvation to flee to Christ.[29] Keach was well aware that there would be those who would object to this kind of preaching and might regard threatenings of divine wrath and vengeance as legal doctrine and an attempt to frighten men out of their sins and produce in them the kind of horror that overtook poor John Child.[30] Keach distances himself from such preaching in the final sermon in this series on Hebrews 2:3, when he notes various kinds of legal doctrine. For example, there are those who frighten men and fill them with servile fear but do not call them to repentance out of love for God; or those, like the Quakers, who said that all who are eternally saved must attain to their own sinless righteousness; or those who preach obedience to the law or the gospel as the way to acquire eternal life.[31] Keach, on the contrary, believed that preaching the wrath of God was part of his calling as a preacher, and he drew attention to the fact that God's justice was never seen so fully as in the suffering and death of his Son, Jesus Christ, and that repentance was "pure gospel" on account of Christ having satisfied divine justice. Repentance was not a harsh doctrine but "it is sweet and blessed Tidings to hear that there is Repentance vouchsafed to poor Sinners, yea, for the worst of sinners."[32]

---

28 Keach, "The Great Salvation," *A Golden Mine Opened*, 449.

29 See n.18 and n.19 above.

30 See Chapter 7.

31 Keach, "The Great Salvation," *A Golden Mine Opened*, 490–495.

32 Keach, "The Great Salvation," *A Golden Mine Opened*, 491–492.

As Keach preached peace with God through faith in Jesus, it is evident that he was a man characterized by earnestness. He was earnest in his concern to be a faithful watchman and an ambassador of Jesus Christ by preaching this gospel. And, he was in deadly earnest for his Christian hearers that they would enter into a fuller appreciation of God's great salvation purchased by the death of Jesus Christ and, as his people, would enjoy the God who was now *their* God as a result of the covenant of peace. He was also earnest with those who were still unbelieving—reasoning, persuading, exhorting and pleading with them to repent of their sins and turn in faith to Jesus Christ so that they too might enjoy God's great salvation.

Preaching perseverance

The largest part of *A Golden Mine Opened* comprises sixteen sermons entitled, "The Blessedness of Christ's Sheep," and deals with the final perseverance of the saints.[33] Keach based these sermons on Christ's words in John 10:27–28, "My sheep hear My voice, and I know them and they follow Me. And I give them eternal life, and they shall never perish, neither shall any pluck them out of my hand." Here Keach took a zoom lens and focused closer attention on one specific part of the covenant of grace (or peace), namely, the perseverance of the saints.

Keach presents the biblical case for this doctrine by providing ing eleven arguments that we will consider briefly. In doing this, we will also be able to observe how the covenant of grace provides coherence to his sermons.

Keach begins by expounding the character of Christ's sheep and the character of the Shepherd, Jesus Christ, but this is preliminary to the burden of this series of sermons. He makes it clear that though believers can never finally fall way, they can backslide and "break their bones and wound their consciences"

33 Keach, "The Blessedness of Christ's Sheep," *A Golden Mine Opened*, 73–317.

because of sin and Satan's wiles. Here we see the sensitive pastor, well aware of human weakness and the effects of remaining sin:

> Our chief enemies are those of our own house; the devil could do little hurt from without, had he not such a strong party for him and siding with him in our bowels, or within us. This inbred enemy always lies in wait to betray us; and if we take not the more care, will prevail against us, and at one time or another trip up our heels, especially that sin which doth chiefly beset us, most Christians having their constitution-sin, though no godly man hath a beloved sin: yea the seed of all sin still remains in our base hearts, and hence it is our danger is great, which appears may not be so clearly, till the providence of God brings us into such a state, occasion or company, whereby Satan hath an opportunity to excite and stir up, or draw forth that sin or evil seed into act that lies hid within us.[34]

In their weakness, Keach directed his readers to God's grace, reminding them that "we stand not by virtue of that grace which is in our cisterns, but by the grace that is in God's fountain."[35]

Having covered these matters by way of an extended introduction, Keach comes to his eleven arguments for why none of the saints of God will ultimately fall away. At each point, he expounds passages of the Bible to establish the doctrine, so that his hearers are grounded in God's truth (in what follows, there are simply summaries of his teaching without his extensive biblical references).

The first and second arguments rest on God's eternal election and the absolute sovereignty of God the Father. This section on

34 Keach, "The Blessedness of Christ's Sheep," *A Golden Mine Opened*, 165.

35 Keach, "The Blessedness of Christ's Sheep," *A Golden Mine Opened*, 167.

God's decree of election reflects the teaching of chapter three of *The Second London Baptist Confession of Faith*. Keach stresses that this election is absolute and that God cannot go back on his purpose to save. Election is moreover personal, and that God's decree embraced not only the end in view but also the means of salvation.[36] The elect were chosen in Christ and the union between Christ and his sheep, while decreed in eternity, was only effected in time. His third argument is also related to the decree of election. God's love is infinite and everlasting, and thus it secures believers from perishing.[37]

Fourth, the love of Jesus Christ for his sheep is an infinite and everlasting love, and a love that is demonstrated in Christ's humiliation and his bearing the wrath of God and curse of the law in his death. Christ will not allow his sheep to perish, because that would deny his love. He showed his love by calling them, renewing them, justifying them and putting his Holy Spirit in them, so that they will persevere and finally be saved. Then, the certainty of salvation is secured by the covenant of grace, because it is an absolute covenant that can never be broken, for it is confirmed and ratified by the blood of the testator.[38]

Keach's sixth argument was that "a child may as easily beget itself in the womb before itself was, as a man can form Christ in his own soul, or regenerate himself; tis God that doth it, the Holy Spirit that begets us."[39] The elect, he affirmed, are begotten of God, and born of the Spirit. Once they are born of God they cannot cease to be the children of God. Even Peter and David,

---

36 Keach, "The Blessedness of Christ's Sheep," *A Golden Mine Opened*, 172. Keach also believed in preterition, or the passing by of others, on the basis of Romans 9:11–13.

37 Keach records his third argument as his second, but he appears to have miscalculated. Hence my numbering is always one ahead of Keach.

38 Keach, "The Blessedness of Christ's Sheep," *A Golden Mine Opened*, 202–211. This section contains a brief and useful summary of Keach's view of the covenant of grace.

39 Keach, "The Blessedness of Christ's Sheep," *A Golden Mine Opened*, 212.

who fell into grievous sin, were restored, because they were born of God and therefore could never finally fall away.

In the seventh place, Keach maintained that believers are united to Christ by faith. This took the form of a marriage union between Christ and his church, with Ephesians 5:31–32 providing a vivid metaphor. Stressing the strength of Christ's love, Keach asked:

> Will any of you that have a spouse, a wife that you dearly love, suffer her to be torn to pieces, and basely murdered before your eyes, if you could prevent it? And do any think that Christ, who hath all power in heaven and earth, power over sin, the world, the devil, yea over hell and death; will He I say, ever suffer His spouse to be destroyed and murdered by sin, the world, the devil? Strange! Did He die for her, and has He married her, and made her one Spirit with Himself; and will He leave her to conflict, to fight and war with an enemy that He knows is too strong and mighty for her, and not come in, rush into her assistance, to save and rescue her from such bloody, cruel and barbarous enemies? No doubt He will rise up with indignation and jealousy, to save every soul that is so related and united to Him.[40]

Eighth, Keach then considered the nature of the death of Christ and reasoned that this too secured the final salvation of the saints. His line of argument was based on Romans 8:33–34. If Christ died in the place of the elect and they are justified, then no one can successfully bring a charge against them, because the sins of the elect have been imputed to Christ and his righteousness and obedience have been imputed to them. Keach emphasized that the atonement has the salvation of particular

---

40 Keach, "The Blessedness of Christ's Sheep," *A Golden Mine Opened*, 223–224.

persons in view and is not universal, and therefore all for whom Christ died shall be saved.[41]

Keach took his ninth argument from the effects of the death and resurrection of Jesus Christ. He said that when Christ was discharged from death, all his elect were discharged from eternal death. All God's people receive the gift of the Holy Spirit and Keach appears to make "the earnest," "the witness" and "the sealing" of the Spirit the common experience of every Christian, aligning it very firmly with assurance of salvation:

> The Holy Spirit is also the earnest of the saint's inheritance (Eph 1.13). 'Tis given to them as an earnest of that glory they shall one day absolutely be possessed of: 'Tis given to assure them, that as certainly as they have received the Holy Spirit here, and he is in them, so certain it is that they shall be saved, or have the eternal inheritance... it is no small matter that God gives us, when he gives the Holy Spirit to us; for as he is that principle of life in us, so he gives us a full assurance of eternal life hereafter: and it is upon this earnest money a saint may be said to live, whilst in this world; nay, and it will defray all his charge, and supply all his need and manifold wants, as long as he lives upon the earth, even until he comes to the full possession of his inheritance above.[42]

Keach returned to his original text, John 10:28–29, for the tenth argument. Saints cannot fall away because they are in the hand of the Father, which was nothing less than a metaphor for God's almighty power. They were also in Christ's hand, which

---

41 Keach, "The Blessedness of Christ's Sheep," *A Golden Mine Opened*, 253–255, Keach quotes Isaac Chauncy on particular redemption at length. Isaac Chauncy, *Treatise on the Doctrine of Godliness* (London, 1694), 203–204.

42 Keach, "The Blessedness of Christ's Sheep," *A Golden Mine Opened*, 260–261.

included not only his saving power but also his love expressed in his resolve to keep them, and in his priestly heavenly intercession for them.

Finally, Keach eleventh assertion was that the very nature of true and saving faith argued for the final perseverance of the saints. Keach encouraged his hearers and assured them:

> Grace shall prevail over corruption, though there seems more smoke than fire, more sin than grace, more weakness than strength, more darkness than light, more fear than faith, yet grace shall be victorious; grace is that principle of life in the soul, the law of God written in the heart, which shall never finally be obliterated any more, or God's image, that shall not utterly be defaced.[43]

What is impressive in these eleven arguments is the breadth of biblical vision and teaching that Keach brings to his sermons. Although he takes the covenant of grace as one of the arguments why saints will persevere, it is evident that aspects of this covenant are included in his other arguments. This series of sermons is not simply an exposition of the biblical text but an examination of all that underlies the words of Christ, and so it becomes more of a topical series of sermons on the theme of the perseverance of the saints. Whether he is considering the work of the Father, the work of the Son or the work of the Spirit, Keach perceives each engaged in the salvation of the saint—therefore, there can be no failing of the supernatural power of the grace of God.

Despite this emphasis on the absolute sovereignty of God, Keach did not believe that a Christian could be indifferent toward godliness. In the final sermon of this series, Keach deals with this matter, together with other similar questions and objections. To combat indifference on the part of a Christian, he asks

---

43 Keach, "The Blessedness of Christ's Sheep," *A Golden Mine Opened*, 286.

his readers whether the hope of obtaining victory in war tended to make a soldier careless. Did it not rather animate him to fight more courageously? He then turned to a biblical example, pointing out that although Paul in Acts 27 assured everyone with him on the ship that there would be no loss of life as a result of the storm, he nevertheless demanded care on the part of the sailors if they were to be saved from drowning.[44] Keach insisted that God ordained both the means and the end. To anyone who says, "I am elect and therefore I can live as I please," Keach replies, this "is the Language rather of a Devil than of a Man, much less of a saint."[45]

As in *The Display of Glorious Grace* (1698), Keach is the ambassador of God's free grace in "The Blessedness of Christ's Sheep" (1694). He believed in the absolute sovereignty of God, and as he came toward the conclusion of these sermons, he publicly repudiated those "Arminian errors which when I was Young, I had from some Men of corrupt Principles sucked in."[46] Keach preached what he had experienced, "the Riches of God's Love and Goodness to me," and was now preaching with the aim that all his hearers might enjoy the same divine love and goodness. He reminded and exhorted them,

> In the Gospel-Days Christ chose a few poor Fisher-Men and refused the Learned and the Wise Men after the flesh: nay and hid the Mysteries of the Kingdom of Heaven from the Wise and Prudent; and all this as an Act alone of his Sovereignty… O do not forget, that the Design of God in contriving our Salvation in his Eternal Wisdom by Jesus Christ, was wholly to advance his own

44 Acts 27:13–38.

45 Keach, "The Blessedness of Christ's Sheep," *A Golden Mine Opened*, 300.

46 Keach is referring to the first book he wrote, *The Child's Instructor*, when he was in his early twenties. See Chapter 4.

> Glory, and the Freeness and Riches of His Grace and to abase and humble Man unto the Dust.[47]

Preaching the parables

Keach was always seeking to be an effective communicator of the truth of the gospel and, not surprisingly, saw the advantage of using the ready-made illustrations in the parables. He published what was the fruit of twelve years of study, three years before his death, in 1701.[48] To the best of his knowledge, no one else among his contemporaries had undertaken to study and preach on the parables as extensively as Keach did. What was it about the parables that caught his interest and led Keach to preach through many of them for a number of years at seven o'clock on a Lord's Day morning?[49]

Keach considered that there were four advantages in preaching the parables over other parts of the Scripture: (1) they were a great aid to the memory; (2) they helped the mind to study the meaning of what has been heard; (3) they stirred up the affections and awakened the conscience, so that "when hell in a parable is set out by a furnace of fire, and conscience by a gnawing worm" it has a marked impact on the hearer; and (4) they informed the judgement of the weak, so that the deep things of God are understood.[50] This suggests that Keach's motives for preaching in this way were *pastoral*. By using the parables, he could be more effective in reaching both the minds and the hearts of his congregation. Keach did not believe that the parables were just moral stories. They opened up the important

---

47 Keach, "The Blessedness of Christ's Sheep," *A Golden Mine Opened*, 314–315.

48 Keach, *Gospel Mysteries Unveil'd*.

49 "To the Reader." In Keach, *The Counterfeit Christian: Or, the Danger of Hypocrisy* (London, 1691). Here Keach explains the origins of this series of sermons on the parables as "a Morning Exercise on the Lord's-Day at Seven a clock," begun more than a year ago. He mentions plans to print the whole series by subscription.

50 Keach, *Parables One*, 3.

doctrines of the gospel and especially highlighted the necessity of faith in Christ. The rules of a godly life, Keach maintained, were known before Christ came. What people needed to hear were the mysteries of salvation by the Lord Jesus Christ. At the same time, Keach was very aware that those who heard the parables might remain in darkness, just as Christ had indicated in Matthew 13:10–13. Keach said that there were two kinds of knowledge: one was merely notional and factual that had no lasting impact on a person's life while the other was effective and experimental, leading to faith in Christ. He concluded: "as nothing is more difficult and hard to understand as a parable, until it is opened and explained, so nothing is more clear, when it is fully understood."[51]

The parables, then, provided Keach with the opportunity to preach on a wide range of subjects. Here he could deal with such things as hypocrisy, the devil's ploys when the gospel is preached, the marks of the real Christian, prayer, the church, marriage, the judgement of God, the coming of Christ and heaven and hell. The breadth of Keach's preaching is impressive, and he took pains to play what he called "right gospel music." He believed a preacher that

> would make sweet music, must not harp too much on one string, or have only one distinct note. So a preacher that would make right gospel-music, must not always preach on one particular gospel truth, but he must touch melodiously upon every string; not preach justification always, as if there were nothing else to instruct the people in, but must insist on sanctification also; the first as our title to heaven, and the other as our meetness for heaven; nor must a minister, who would make true gospel music, preach only on the promises, but also on the

51 Keach, *Parables One*, 4.

> precepts; not of what Christ hath done for us, but also what he wrought in us, and must also be done by us, etc.[52]

At times he is polemical, especially in contending against "Baxterianism," but Keach was invariably evangelistic in his thrust, aiming at the conversion of his hearers. In the parable of the Good Samaritan, for instance, he identifies different kinds of hearers. There were those who were very ignorant, those mortally wounded, those partially healed, those who know and cast off Christ, those who delay and those who are healed. These categories give us some insight into the pastoral heart of Keach and the different spiritual states of the people he was trying to instruct in the mysteries of the kingdom. Keach's way of preaching the parables further illustrates what John Dunton meant when he described Keach as a "popular preacher" who "understood the Humour and Necesssity of his Audience."[53]

Keach also published a few sermons on the Old Testament, notably on Jacob's dream of seeing a ladder reaching from the earth into heaven. It was based on Genesis 28:12 and was called *Christ Alone the Way to Heaven* (1698).[54] These are sermons with some quaint exegesis. The ladder is Christ and his human nature is the foot of the ladder and his divine nature is the top. Keach displays some ingenuity in setting out the person and work of Christ as prophet, priest and king from this exposition. These sermons were dedicated to six Particular Baptist churches in Hampshire, some of which Keach knew personally, probably when he had been sent with Benjamin Dennis on national assembly business. He probably preached other Old Testament texts to his congregation in Horselydown, but these were never

---

52 Keach, "Children in the Market Place," *Parables One*, 280.

53 See note 3.

54 This book also contains a sermon on Romans 8:1 and a critique of Samuel Clarke's *Scripture Justification*. I will consider this critique in Chapter 13.

published. Keach seems to have concentrated on publishing sermons largely from the New Testament. *Tropologia*, however, includes metaphors and types from the Old Testament, and his sermons on the covenant of grace in *The Display of Glorious Grace* were based on Isaiah 54:10.

The searching and discriminating preacher

When Keach preached on the parable of the sower from Matthew 13:3–23, he drew attention to the fact that Christ deals with different kinds of hearers. He observes that one weakness on the part of preachers is their failure to take note of this. Keach did not fall into that trap by assuming that everyone to whom he preached was a true Christian. He inferred from his exposition of this parable that

> it is no certain sign a man is a child of God, and shall be saved, because he hears the Word of God preached, or loves to hear sermons, or makes a visible profession of religion, and becomes a church member, and does many things that are commendable, or praiseworthy, for all these things are common to reprobate or unsound professors as with elect ones; nay, though a man holds out in religious practices for many years unsuspected, yet afterwards he may decay and wither.[55]

Keach also preached a sermon from Matthew 12:43–45 entitled, *The Counterfeit Christian, or the Danger of Hypocrisy*. He preached it first in August 1690 and published it a year later. This was shortly after the political and ecclesiastical climate in England had changed and persecution had ceased, at least in the form it had taken from 1660 to 1689. Was there a temptation at

---

55 Keach, "The Sower," *Parables One*, 149.

this time to lower the biblical standards? If so, Keach was alive to the dangers and recognized in this the devious hand of Satan:

> Let men think what they please, certainly there is no Devil like this Devil: If he can persuade a Man that he is whole and not sick at all, and so needs no Physician; and that when the Gospel is preached to Sinners, and the Danger of Unbelief is opened, yet it doth not affect him, nor concern him, he being become a righteous Person; what hopes can there be for such a one? Alas, the Ministers of Christ have received no Commission to offer Christ to any but Sinners.[56]

According to Keach, the counterfeit Christian is the man in his text, now indwelt by seven other spirits more wicked than the original unclean spirit. The point of the parable is to show that unless men repent radically, they go from bad to worse. Keach was persuaded this had an important application to the present dangers facing the church. The man in the parable was, in Keach's estimation, a hypocrite, possessing only the common gifts and graces of the Spirit but with a religion comprised mainly of negatives. Keach provides a character sketch of the man he has in view. He has escaped some terrible evils and sins, but the habits of sin are ingrained, and his unclean nature remains unchanged. This man does not feel the purity of the law of God and thinks that sin is limited to the outward acts of sin. He has never seen the spirituality of the law, as Paul did in Romans 7:9. Thus, while he may have undergone some changes in his life, they are not the changes associated with regeneration. Yet, this is a man who does some good, who prays and hears sermons, has a kind of faith, has been baptized, has become a church member, perhaps even a preacher and, in the eyes of men, lives a blameless

56 Keach, *The Counterfeit Christian*, 19–20.

life—yet he has never actually been regenerated and united to Christ. Keach observed that such a person may "fall away" because he was never effectively saved in the first place.

Keach is dealing here with very difficult and demanding aspects of pastoral work. While it was his joy to preach the gospel and freely to offer Christ to sinners, it was also his duty to deal with those who were mistaken in their judgement about themselves, men and women who—despite being "religious"—were building on mistaken and unsound principles.

Besides the individual who may have been deceived, Keach had a wider concern for the welfare of the whole church of Christ. He was concerned that the churches had not been faithful enough, "tho I know of none to charge, yet I am afraid we have generally failed herein."[57] He believed that there were "brazen foreheads" in many congregations who resisted God's faithful ministers, "many covetous, earthly and hard-hearted Professors and Members in churches."[58] He was also of the opinion that this was one of the principal reasons why there were so many backbiters and tattlers in their congregations.[59] It was his conviction that the presence of such people in the body of the church was a hindrance to the spread of the gospel and the conversion of sinners. They weakened the hands of the saints, brought grief to the hearts of the godly, because they were a source of trouble to the church and brought reproach on the name of Christ by their conduct. This may sound like a sweeping condemnation, but Keach was very conscious of the damaging and blinding effects of pride, self-confidence, vain-glory and formalism in religion and the existence of hypocrisy in the professing church.

---

57 Keach, *The Counterfeit Christian*, 53.

58 Keach, *The Counterfeit Christian*, 49.

59 Keach, *The Counterfeit Christian*, 50.

He drew up twelve tests "by which we may examine our own hearts."[60] It was not an exercise in morbid introspection and Keach was well aware that he ran the danger of shaking even a true Christian whose judgement was weak. These tests included such questions as:

- whether a person had ever been thoroughly convicted of their sinful and lost state.
- whether there were some secret sins in a person's life.
- whether Christ was precious to the individual.
- whether a person was more inclined to judge the faults of others before they judged themselves.
- whether a person obeyed Christ's commandments motivated by love for him.

This was searching, discriminating preaching intended to sift the false professing Christian from the true believer.

The sermon ends with a call to the self-righteous, the proud, the carnal and the formal to repent of their sins and for the genuine believer to rejoice:

> Mourn O England! What a Number of filthy, debauched, treacherous, proud, drunken, swearing and unclean Christians (as they are called) hast thou in the Bowels of thee? They shew their sin as Sodom, and hide it not, and yet glory as if they were the only People of God. Awake Sinners, before God's Judgements are poured out upon you, for certainly great Wrath is at the Door. God hath wrought Wonders for the Deliverance of this Nation, but ye slight and contemn them: Neither Mercies nor Judgements will humble you; what would you have, since nothing God doth, pleases you? Certainly the Almighty

---

60 Keach, *The Counterfeit Christian*, 54–55.

> will not bear with you much longer, if you repent not.... But you who are truly pious and sincere ones, rejoice, you who mourn for your own Sins and the Sins of the Land; you are secured from the hungry Lion, your Day is coming, the Kingdom of Jesus Christ is near, your Redemption is at hand; lift up your Heads, and praise God for ever.[61]

Such sermons did not make for easy preaching or for comfortable hearing and may give the impression that Keach was a somewhat harsh and legalistic preacher. But he would have seen this as a vital part of his work as a faithful watchman:

> Ministers, or Christ's spiritual Watchmen, must give warning, when they see danger approaching, and therefore had need be men of knowledge. They are called seers; if they have no eyes, they cannot be called seers.[62]

As we have seen in his allegorical writings and his poetic dialogues, *War with the Devil* and *The Glorious Lover*, Keach was at war. As a preacher, he saw himself as someone who was at war with sin, wherever iniquity showed its ugly head. Therefore, warning was part of his responsibility if he were to be a faithful watchman who had delivered his soul from the blood of his hearers.[63] In his calling as a preacher, Keach desired to be a faithful ambassador of Christ, bringing good news of peace with God. He had a burning desire to awaken any among his hearers who was still spiritually dead, including those who were outwardly religious. At the same time, he also desired to encourage those who were, by the grace of God, responding to the preacher's

61 Keach, *The Counterfeit Christian*, 56.

62 Keach, "Ministers compared to watchmen," *Types and Metaphors*, 834.

63 The use of the watchman is derived from Ezekiel 33:1–11.

message. Keach was a preacher of the covenant of grace, of God's great salvation, of God's free grace to undeserving sinners, and his Calvinism, far from inhibiting him, only made him more earnest in pleading with sinners to repent of their sins and put their faith in Jesus Christ.

CHAPTER 11

"The hardest Dispensation of late"

> I have, dear Brethren, passed under the hardest Dispensation of late, that ever I met withal since I have been in the World; but I hope I can say my Sorrow or Grief, is chiefly because the Name of God hereby suffers, and his People are exposed to Reproach. I desire to live no longer than to promote Peace and Union to my Power in all the Churches of the Saints; though I am represented as one that hath not indeavoured after it, because of my Writing in the Defence of Singing the Praises of God.[1]

For Keach to admit that what happened in the early 1690s was "the hardest Dispensation...that ever I met withal since I have been in the World," indicates the extent of pain and difficulty that he experienced as a

1 Keach, *To all the Baptized Churches and Faithful Brethren in England and Wales, Christian Salutations* (London, 1692), 1.

result of a controversy that arose among Particular Baptists.[2] Bearing in mind the reproach he bore in the pillory in Aylesbury and Winslow in 1664, the imprisonments he had suffered, together with the difficulties he and his congregation in London had endured during the years of oppression from 1668 to 1689, this was a remarkable admission. The controversy was over the question of whether there was biblical warrant for the practice of singing hymns in public worship.[3]

The pain would have been deep for at least two reasons. First, the controversy led to a split in his own congregation. Second,

---

2 Keach, *To all the Baptized Churches*. I am indebted to James Renihan for making available a copy of this document. It is effectively an acknowledgement of certain errors and offensive words that Keach had used in a book called, *A Sober Reply to Mr. Robert's Steed's Epistle Concerning Singing* (London, 1691). This book was published anonymously, but the acknowledgments in *To all the Baptized Churches* by Keach clearly identify him as the author. Keach, along with others involved in the disagreement, had been called to account by the 1692 General Assembly, and they also acted as if he were the author of *A Sober Reply*. See *A Narrative of the Proceedings of the General Assembly* (London, 1692), 9–10.

3 A variety of literature has been devoted to the place of Keach in the history of English hymnody and to the controversy surrounding Keach's introduction of hymn singing into the church at Horselydown. Among the most important are: Hugh Martin, *Benjamin Keach (1640–1704): Pioneer of Congregational Hymn Singing* (London: Independent Press, 1961); James Patrick Carnes, "The Famous Mr. Keach: Benjamin Keach and His Influence on Congregational Singing in Seventeenth-Century England" (M.A. thesis, North Texas State University, 1984); MacDonald, "London Calvinistic Baptists"; Vaughn, "Public Worship and Practical Theology in the Work of Benjamin Keach (1640–1704)"; Clifford, "Benjamin Keach and Nonconformist Hymnology," *Spiritual Worship*, 69–93; David W. Music, "The Hymns of Benjamin Keach: An Introductory Study," *The Hymn* (1983): 147–152; Donald C. Brown, "To Sing or Not to Sing: Seventeenth-Century English Baptists and Congregational Song," *Handbook to the Baptist Hymnal* (Nashville, Tennessee: Convention Press, 1992), 55–64; James C. Brooks, "Benjamin Keach and the Baptist Singing Controversy: Mediating Scripture, Confessional Heritage, and Christian Unity" (Ph.D. dissertation, Florida State University, College of Arts and Sciences, 2006); Michael A.G. Haykin and Jeffrey Robinson, "Particular Baptist Debates about Communion and Hymn-Singing." In Michael A.G. Haykin and Mark Jones, eds., *Drawn into Controversie: Reformed Theological Diversity and Debates Within Seventeenth-Century Puritanism*, Reformed Historical Theology, Vol. 17 (Göttingen: Vandenhoeck & Ruprecht, 2011), 284–308.

like the destructive fires that sometimes broke out in London, this controversy spread and quickly divided the elders and churches of London, separating men who had come through hard times of persecution together and who had become good friends. The disagreement sadly drew clear lines of division and "ultimately involved, on one level or another, virtually the entire leadership of the London Calvinistic Baptist community."[4] The elder statesmen among these Baptists were divided: Hanserd Knollys agreed with Benjamin Keach, while William Kiffin held the contrary view. Keach desired peace and unity in the churches, but 1691 and 1692 were years marked by division in his own congregation, among the elders of the London churches and in the national assemblies.

Controversy in Horselydown

It is clear that the question of whether a hymn should be sung in public worship had been an issue in the church almost since the time Keach had been called by the church as their pastor. Keach had introduced a hymn to be sung at the conclusion of the communion service in the early 1670s. A few had always been in disagreement, but the issue had always been contained—that is until those who held the contrary view to Keach found someone willing to champion their cause.

Edward Sandford was one of those in disagreement, and he had also been one of the messengers of the church who went with Keach to the 1689 Assembly.[5] Sandford and his wife Ann had married in 1666, and their son-in-law was Luke Leader, who had married Mary Sandford in 1689.[6] The names of Edward and Ann Sanford and Luke and Mary Leader are four of the more prominent ones in the group of nine men and seventeen women

---

4 MacDonald, "London Calvinistic Baptists," 62.

5 *Narrative of the Proceedings of the General Assembly* (1689), 24.

6 *Regester*, 3, 7.

who withdrew from the Horselydown church in 1691 over the issue of congregational hymn singing.[7]

The nine men who withdrew were also responsible in 1691 for publishing *Truth Cleared: Or, a brief Narrative of the Rise, Occasion, and Management of the present Controversy concerning Singing in the Worship of God.*[8] They felt they had been misunderstood and unfairly treated. This book contains their own version of proceedings in the church at Horselydown, contrary to that presented by their former pastor in his publications. Keach was blamed for having originally introduced hymn singing, and they claimed that those who disagreed with him endured the practice because they could not do anything to prevent it, thus suggesting it had been imposed on them. They objected to "their using a precomposed and prelimited form of Words, which they read to the People, and then in uniting their voices, directly contrary to the Rule of God's Word."[9] They objected to the way a crucial church meeting had been conducted at which the

7 Maze Pond Church Book 1691–1708. The nine men who withdrew were: Silvanus Heathcote, Edward Little, John Monticue, Abraham Faulkner, Edward Sandford, Isaac Twinn, William Prober (Probard), John Leader, Jr. and Luke Leader. The seventeen women were: Sarah Shrubb, Ann Sandford, Isabella Brent, Mary Robarts, Katherine Carpender, Ann Polferrey, Mary Monticue, Esther Marlow, Sarah Leader, Mary Leader, Elizabeth Twinn, Elizabeth Faulkner, Elizabeth Gillum, Sussanah Hill, Elizabeth Man, Margaret Little and Mary Careles.

8 Silvanus Heathcote, etc., *Truth Cleared: Or, a brief Narrative of the Rise, Occasion and Management of the present Controversy concerning Singing in the Worship of God. With an Account of several Letters that have passed between Mr. Benjamin Keach and Isaac Marlow, relating to an Appeal. As also of an Inspection made into both their books, by several worthy and honourable Elders, who have given their Judgment, subscribed with their own Hands, in Vindication of Isaac Marlow's Sheet of Observations on Mr Keach's Book. Whereunto is added a further Collection of Mr. Keach's Abuses, Falsehoods, and Misrepresentations, contained in his said Treatise, called The Breach in God's Worship, etc. As also some further evidence under the Hands of Several Brethren (that were late members of his Church) to detect several others of his Abuses therein* (London, 1691). The book is a valuable source, because it contains some of the correspondence that passed between Keach and Marlow, as well as Keach's *A Sober Appeal for Right and Justice*.

9 Heathcote, *Truth Cleared*, 41.

majority of the congregation had voted for singing as an essential part of the worship of God. They especially drew attention to the fact that the decision had been agreed "only through the Heat and Vigour of Mr. Keach and some few more," and later pointed out that some were afraid of speaking "by reason of Mr. Keach's hot Spirit, which he sufficiently showed in obstructing and curbing those that did speak."[10] A considerable part of their book was also given over to answering what they perceived to be a personal, and at times, bitter attack on Isaac Marlow by Keach and others.[11]

Controversy on wider scale

The handling of the controversy became more difficult for Keach because of the involvement of Isaac Marlow. Marlow was a wealthy London jeweller, and one of the men appointed by the 1689 Assembly for the collection of the Public Fund, a cause dear to Keach's heart. At the 1689 Assembly, Marlow had been a delegate from the Mile End Green Church, pastored by George Barrett.[12] It was Marlow, by his pen, who became the principal opponent of Keach's introduction of hymns into public worship, referring to Keach's practice as that "mischievous Error which you so vigorously promote, to the disturbance of your brethren."[13] In addition, Marlow had married Esther Leader in Amsterdam and, when he and his wife returned to London, they attended the church in Horselydown. His wife, father-in-law and others

10 Heathcote, *Truth Cleared*, 31, 35.

11 The version of events in *Truth Cleared* is similar in its bias against Keach to that found in the Maze Pond Church Book. See n. 14.

12 *Narrative of the Proceedings of the General Assembly* (1689), 22. George Barrett was one of the London pastors who shared Marlow's convictions about congregational singing, together with Edward Man, pastor of Houndsditch, Robert Steed, pastor at Broken-Wharf (with Hanserd Knollys) and Richard Halliwell (Holliwell), also from Houndsditch.

13 Isaac Marlow, *A Brief Discourse concerning Singing in the Public Worship of God in the Gospel-Church* (London, 1691), 14.

of his wife's family were members at Horselydown, although Marlow himself never appeared to have joined the church.[14] He was not one of the nine men that withdrew from the Horselydown congregation, but his wife was one of the seventeen women who did. This group eventually formed a new congregation at nearby Maze Pond in Southwark in February 1694.[15]

It is clear from the many references in the Maze Pond Church Book that Marlow not only wrote against Keach, but he was also one of the men who was constantly consulted by the disaffected group. Marlow was not the author of *Truth Cleared*, but the nine disaffected men were clearly intent on defending him from attack and provided a platform for him to defend himself and his views.

Due to the fact that Marlow was not a member of the Horselydown church, Keach found that he could not confine the issue within his own church. This fact helps to explain why Keach found the matter so hard to resolve, and why he sought the help of the 1691 Assembly by writing *A Sober Appeal for Right and Justice*, an action that attracted immediate criticism from Marlow.[16] In Marlow's eyes, the Assembly had no authority for debating the issue of the membership of those in Horselydown who were against singing. And the fact that it had been raised on the last day of the Assembly, after many messengers had already left, was provocative, rubbing salt into an existing wound.[17]

---

14 MacDonald, "London Calvinistic Baptists," 52. Although Isaac and Esther Marlow and three of their children are listed in the *Regester* (pages 7 and 10), there is no indication that Isaac Marlow was ever a member of Keach's congregation.

15 Maze Pond Church Book 1691–1708, MS Angus Library, Regent's Park College, Oxford.

16 Heathcote, *Truth Cleared*, 5–6.

17 MacDonald, "London Calvinistic Baptists," 56. MacDonald provides a detailed account of the controversy as it affected the London churches, using the Maze Pond Church Book as one of the major sources. However, she notes on page 83, that "one obvious prejudice which runs through the narrative of Maze Pond's earliest years is a fundamental bias against Benjamin Keach."

Keach interpreted the withdrawal from communion in March 1691 by the anti-singing lobby as disorderly conduct. He believed that the 1691 Assembly (which met on June 2–8) had agreed with him by saying that those who had left were wrong in their conduct and ought to have remained in the church. This shows that this controversy was about more than just hymn singing. It was also a matter of church authority and church discipline. The nine who left accused Keach and the church of bringing in corporate hymn singing "rashly without any Debate, and contrary to Promise."[18] Thomas Dawson, an elder in the church, allegedly likened the conduct of the anti-singers to that of Korah, Dathan and Abiram, who had rebelled against Moses.[19] On the other hand, the anti-singers believed that Keach was depriving them of a fair hearing in the church. They were convinced that they were being misrepresented to the world. The anti-singers had also aggravated the matter and incurred the displeasure of Keach by distributing some of Marlow's anti-singing literature among his congregation. They also circulated statements from other London pastors disputing Keach's interpretation of what the June Assembly had said. By the end of October, the nine men had been excommunicated from the church, though the matter was to rumble on for another ten months before the women finally left. Both groups (the men and women) then joined the Cripplegate church for two years, before leaving it without that church's consent and returning to Southwark to form the Maze Pond Church.[20]

Given this evidence, it is not surprising that Keach referred to this as "the hardest dispensation" he had experienced in his life. It was painful to see men and women who had long been part of the church now in such strong disagreement with him

18 Heathcote, *Truth Cleared*, 30.

19 Maze Pond Church Book, 32. See Numbers 16:1–2.

20 Maze Pond Church Book, 56–59, 61–62.

that they withdrew from communion, disrupting the unity of the church. Some of them had shared in the responsibilities of leadership, others had been converted to Christ as a result of his preaching. Prior to 1689, they had stood together during persecution. Keach had married a number of them and buried some of their young children who died in infancy. Yet, in Keach's eyes their decision to withdraw was schismatic, something he regarded as a great evil. He told each one of those who withdrew, "you have dismembered yourselfe in refusing to have communion with this church."[21] It was also frustrating for him to deal with Isaac Marlow, whose actions appeared to be constantly undermining the unity of the church. As Murdina MacDonald notes, he was faced,

> by a group of strong-willed articulate men who appear to have been coached by Isaac Marlow in their confrontation with him. He seems to have responded by seeking to crush rather than negotiate with them, demanding that they either return to communion or seek membership with some other church.[22]

Keach's conduct

Before considering whether he was guilty of trying to crush those who were opposed to his practice, and bearing in mind the prejudice against Keach in the Maze Pond Church Book and to some extent in *Truth Cleared*, it is right to consider Keach's motives and fundamental concerns. His letter, written after the 1692 Assembly, is revealing, because it reveals that Keach's grief was not occasioned by an attack on his personal reputation. Rather, he says: "I hope I can say my Sorrow or Grief is chiefly because the Name of God hereby suffers, and his People are

---

21 Maze Pond Church Book, 47.

22 MacDonald, "London Calvinistic Baptists," 58.

exposed to Reproach."[23] As a Christian man, as a leader in the London churches and as a pastor and a preacher, he was grieved over the harm caused to the name of God and to the church of Christ. A deep note of sorrow sounded in the opening sentence of the letter that he sent out to the churches represented in the 1692 Assembly:

> *Behold how good and how pleasant it is* (saith the Psalmist) *for Brethren to dwell together in Unity*, Psal. 133.1. But O how grievous a thing is the contrary, *viz.* to see Brethren live in Discord, in Strife and Contention. Our Saviour saith, *By this shall all Men know ye are my Disciples, if ye love one another*, John 13.35.[24]

Later he adds another sad note, reflecting on how Satan has obtained a foothold among them and their need for repentance:

> O that we would consider what Spirit we have been led by, or some of us, and repent in Dust and Ashes: Is not the Evil of making Discord among Brethren, one of the six things that God hates, yea that thing which is Abomination to him? *Prov.* 6.[25]

In his letter, Keach makes a public apology for his own conduct. His aim was to "make my Acknowledgments as publickly as the Offences were given."[26] Keach's retraction included an apology for his error in misrepresenting the first baptized churches (those who had subscribed to the 1644 *Confession of Faith*) over the matter of the maintenance of ministers. He then

23 Keach, *To all the Baptized Churches*, 1.

24 Keach, *To all the Baptized Churches*, 1.

25 Keach, *To all the Baptized Churches*, 2. See Proverbs 6:16–19.

26 Keach, *To all the Baptized Churches*, 2.

apologizes for some harsh expressions, uncharitable and unsavory censures, reflections and reproaches. These were all related to what he had put in print during the exchanges of arguments for and against congregational singing, principally with Marlow. This letter containing Keach's apologies and retractions was dated June 27, 1692, which would have been just over a month after the conclusion of the 1692 National Assembly in London (May 3–24) and some eight months after the events in the church at Horselydown that had led to the withdrawal of the anti-singing lobby. By the time the assembly met, the furor caused by the controversy over corporate hymn singing had been referred to a group of seven men whose brief was to attempt to restore a measure of order and peace.[27]

Those who had been involved in the war of words were all asked:

> Whether you are willing to be determined by the said brethren, and resolve to do what they shall determine, in order to the removing of all those reflections that are written in all the books printed on both sides about the controversy of singing. &c. The matters to be debated and determined are only respecting *reflections* and matters of *fact*.[28]

William Kiffin, Edward Mann, George Barrett, Hercules Collins, Benjamin Keach, Robert Steed and Richard Halliwell all agreed to abide by the decision of the seven arbitors. Isaac Marlow's name is conspicuous by its absence, for he refused to abide by their decision. Soon afterward, contrary to their request, Marlow published again, this time *Some Brief Remarks*, which not only

27 The seven men appointed were all from outside London: Andrew Gifford of Bristol; Edward White of Eversholt, Bedfordshire; Henry Austin of Norwich; Robert Keate of Wantage, Berkshire; John Wills of Allestrey, Derbyshire; Samuel Buttall of Plymouth and John Scott. See Ivimey, *History*, 1:520.

28 Ivimey, *History*, 1:520.

showed his strong independent streak but also alienated him from the sympathy of many in the Assembly.[29]

The seven men concluded that all sides in the controversy had erred. They rebuked them graciously for their lack of love and Christ-like conduct, pointing out "that the ways you have taken to discover the nakedness of your brethren have been irregular, and tended rather to beget greater offences and stumblings, than convincing, healing and recovering."[30] All were then exhorted to acknowledge their faults and to cease from writing further in the same vein. They were warned that anyone who continued to "sow offences, discords and devisions, among the churches, should be marked."[31] Finally, they requested that all the books containing the harsh words that had been responsible for fuelling this controversy should no longer be sold or circulated in any way but deposited with an appointed person who would dispose of them as they saw fit. The man appointed by the assembly for this task was Richard Adams, co-pastor with William Kiffin at the Devonshire Square church in London.[32]

That Keach submitted himself to the decisions of his brethren at the 1692 Assembly shows us the measure of the man. He demonstrated by his letter that he was not by disposition a proud and arrogant man, but one able to take rebuke and counsel and to submit himself to other men. However, that is not to say that Keach was without fault, for he appears to have been quick-tempered and, at times, inclined to impatience. In 1691, there were at least two church meetings held at Horselydown where the subject of hymn singing was considered. These appear to have been occasions when Keach's impatience was

---

29 MacDonald, "London Calvinistic Baptists," 65.

30 Ivimey, *History*, 1:521.

31 Ivimey, *History*, 1:522.

32 Keach, *To all the Baptized Churches*, 5. Keach requested that anyone who had a copy of *A Sober Reply* that it be sent to Richard Adams, thus complying with the Assembly's request.

unhappily displayed. Mention has already been made of "the Heat and Vigour of Mr. Keach and some few more" that allegedly resulted in the church adopting the practice of corporate hymn singing. The first-hand records of these meetings are in the Maze Pond Church Book, and they contain bias against Keach. Those records indicate that at one meeting, when Samuel Bagwell showed some sympathy toward the anti-singing lobby, suggesting that the church could bear with their scruples of conscience, Keach became passionate and reproved Bagwell, "brother doe you know what you doe, you had as good take a knife and stab me in the heart."[33] At a second meeting, on October 2, 1691, the anti-singing lobby were called to account by the Horselydown church and asked why they had concluded that they could no longer be part of the church. The account says that Keach lost his temper when Mary Leader explained why she could not accept corporate hymn singing, in that

> he replyed quick upon her, and looking earnestly at her, saying you have learnt a fine piece of Relidgion ha'nt you, I confess I am troubled to see you that are but a Babe should pretend to such knowlidg above others or to that effect, and then turning to her husband Bro: Luke Leader he said you have finely dragg'd her up. To which he replyed that God was his witness and she also whether he had perswaded her to that minde or to that effect, and further said to Mr Keach he thought he did verry ill to reflect after that manner on the Sisters and overaw them. And Bro: Sandford spake to the same effect at which Mr Keach broak out into a wonderful passion, and in that strange unbecomming Sperit break out into Prayer without any

33 Maze Pond Church Book, 1691–1708, 32. On page 40, it was recorded that Samuel Bagwell was one of three men later sent by the church at Horselydown to the anti-singing lobby in an attempt to win them back.

> notis thereof to the People, they being many of them confusidly talking together, and in his Prayer called upon God to judge these men, and went on after that manner.[34]

The record relates that at that point, Leader and Sandford, unable to join in that prayer, put on their hats and—together with the rest of the group—left the meeting. Without the records of the Horselydown church, and knowing neither all that had led up to these meetings, nor how men like Luke Leader and Edward Sandford had conducted themselves in the meeting, it is not possible to give an entirely fair assessment of Keach's conduct. It would appear, though, that on this occasion Keach was guilty of a measure of frustration, anger and impatience by his words and actions. Crosby, in his assessment of Keach, drew attention to his quick-temperedness:

> The vivacity of his temper sometimes exposed him, to sharp and sudden fits of anger, which occasioned no small uneasiness to himself, as well as those who had given him any provocation; but those fits were but of short continuance, and so the trouble occasioned by them was soon over: And the goodness and tenderness of his nature was such, as afterwards made sufficient amends to those who had fallen under his resentment. Besides, if his natural passion, at any time, so far transported him, as to cause him to speak any rash or offensive words, he was presently recovered, and would with the greatest humility and frankness retract what he had said; and thereby did discover, that not the least degree of prejudice, remained in his breast.[35]

---

34 Maze Pond Church Book, 1691–1708, 65.

35 Crosby, *History*, 4:307.

Crosby provides no specific examples either of his anger or his humility in retracting statements (such as Keach had demonstrated in the 1692 letter), and there is no record of reconciliation to Luke Leader, Edward Sandford or Isaac Marlow. Others involved in the controversy may have published letters similar to that of Keach. If so, they have not survived, but the letter Keach wrote commends his Christian character and is consistent with what Crosby said of him.

Sadly, the same cannot be said of Isaac Marlow. He had not agreed to the proposal of the Assembly but followed up *Some Brief Remarks* with a second volume in 1694, entitled, *The Purity of Gospel Communion*, seeking to justify the decision to separate from a church "on grounds of corrupt manners, erroneous doctrine, false worship, or the corrupt ministry of gospel ordinances," which would have included corporate singing.[36] Even when, three years later, he was censured by a group of London elders, Marlow continued to fight. He eventually left London around 1700, retiring to Leominster where he died in 1719.[37]

In contrast to Marlow, Keach added no more coals to the fires of controversy. Instead, he produced the letter of apology addressed to all the churches among the Particular Baptists. Did Keach retract, though, any of his angry words spoken against the anti-singers in the Horselydown church meetings? It is evident that he did not relish controversy for it cut him to the bone. He also recognized that it exposed him to his own weaknesses and constitutional sins. He rather desired peace and unity. That desire was not fulfilled in his own congregation, and he felt the separation that took place there very keenly. He showed his human frailties by letting his sense of frustration and anger get the better of him on occasion. Furthermore, he regretted the division the controversy had caused on a wider scale and expressed this in his letter to the churches:

36 Quoted in MacDonald, "London Calvinistic Baptists," 70.

37 Clifford, "Benjamin Keach and Nonconformist Hymnology," *Spiritual Worship*, 77.

> But I would have you all know and bear me Witness, I am grieved in my very Soul that this Ordinance should be deemed to have such a Tendency, for I for my own part can as freely have Communion with my Brethren who do not own Singing, I mean proper Singing of God's Praises, as with such who are of my Judgment in that matter: every Truth is not an Essential of Communion, some Precepts are appointed for the Being of a visible Church, and others for the more comfortable Being thereof.[38]

Having considered Keach's role in the controversy, and the way that he conducted himself in it, it is natural to ask why—if it caused such division in his own church and also among the London churches—Keach introduced corporate hymn singing in the first place. There must have been compelling reasons for him to do so. It is not surprising to discover that for a man who accepted the final authority of the Scriptures, it was the study of those Scriptures that led him to introduce this practice into the life of the church at Horselydown.

The significance of Keach's practice

The significance of Keach's practice has been simply stated by Hugh Martin: he was "the first to introduce the regular singing of hymns into the normal worship of an English congregation."[39] This was also a view shared by Crosby.[40] This practice was not introduced overnight but had been a slow process, carried on over many years. Early in his ministry in Southwark, Keach had introduced the singing of a hymn, as opposed to a psalm, at the conclusion of the Lord's Supper. This was in 1673, some

38 Keach, *To all the Baptized Churches*, 1–2.

39 Hugh Martin, "The Baptist Contribution to Early English Hymnody," *BQ* 19, (1962): 199.

40 Crosby, *History*, 4:299.

eighteen years before he published *The Breach Repaired in God's Worship*. Keach then took a further step by introducing corporate hymn singing into services of thanksgiving and fasting and perhaps baptismal services.[41] It is also the case that Keach used hymns on other occasions, for example at funerals, as both his hymn books, *Spiritual Melody* and *Spiritual Songs* contain funeral hymns.[42] It would also appear that a hymn was sung at the Morning Exercise that he began around 1689, when Keach began preaching on the parables. This was a lecture that began at seven o'clock in the morning, an addition to the normal meetings on the Lord's Day. By the time the church at Horselydown had introduced hymn singing as a regular feature of their worship in March 1691, it would appear that this was the climax to a practice Keach had been making increasing use of for many years. By publishing *Spiritual Melody*, Keach was taking a necessary practical step. If his congregation were going to sing hymns, they needed a collected body of suitable material—and this is what Keach aimed to provide. Alan Clifford is persuaded that this 1691 hymn book, *Spiritual Melody*, was the first English hymn book ever to be used in congregational worship.[43]

Keach's Horselydown congregation does not appear to have been the only congregation singing hymns before 1691. Keach wrote:

---

41 Keach, *The Breach Repaired in God's Worship: Or, Singing of Psalms, Hymns and Spiritual Songs proved to be an Holy Ordinance of Jesus Christ* (London, 1691), viii.

42 Keach, *Spiritual Melody, containing near three hundred Sacred Hymns* (London, 1691) and *Spiritual Songs, being the Marrow of the Scriptures, in songs of Praise to Almighty God, from the Old and New Testament* (London, 1700). Keach also published a collection of 100 hymns in 1696, called *A Feast of Fat Things*, which became the second part of *Spiritual Songs* in 1700.

43 Clifford, "Benjamin Keach and Nonconformist Hymnology," *Spiritual Worship*, 76. He points out in the footnote that Hugh Martin disputes this fact but says Martin provides no hard evidence for priority to be given to Barton's *A Century of Select Hymns* (1659) or John Mason's *Songs of Praise* (1674).

> many Christians had rather have those *Hymns* we sing in our publick Assemblies printed, that so they might the better know them, and examine the matter therein contained, to see whether they do agree with the Word of Christ, and likewise the better sing them with understanding. And 'tis not unknown what a multitude of godly Friends have desired to have me write them out several of those *Hymns* that have upon divers occasions been sung in some particular Congregations. Now to prevent that trouble and to satisfie them, I promis'd to Print the most of those *Hymns*, and so have done, as they will find them in the latter part of this Tract.[44]

This introduction of corporate singing by Keach eventually proved too much for a minority in Keach's congregation. Marlow, alarmed by this new trend, published *A Brief Discourse concerning Singing* in 1690. In the following year, soon after the March church meeting that formally approved congregational singing, Keach responded by publishing *The Breach Repaired in God's Worship*.

Keach had inherited the practice of the laying on of hands from the General Baptists and never departed from this practice. "Songless services" also appear to have been characteristic of General Baptist worship for most of the seventeenth century. Yet, Keach began to change his view and abandoned this practice soon after becoming a pastor in London. Thomas Grantham had reinforced the General Baptist practice in a book called *Christianismus Primitivus*, published in 1678, and so did the General Baptist Assembly of 1689, regarding such activities as "carnal formalities."[45] Given Keach's background among the

---

44 "To the Reader." In Keach, *Spiritual Melody*, unnumbered pages 7–8.

45 Clifford, "Benjamin Keach and Nonconformist Hymnology," *Spiritual Worship*, 75–76.

General Baptists, it might seem surprising that he became convinced about the place of congregational hymn singing.

Among the Particular Baptists, though, there were clearly signs of change. At least three men and one church came to believe that corporate singing was an ordinance of divine worship: Vavasor Powell (1617–1670), the Welsh Baptist; Hanserd Knollys, though he at first believed it was solo singing that was warranted; and Hercules Collins, who by 1680 was supporting the practice of congregational singing. The church meeting at Broadmead in Bristol was also in the habit of singing psalms, a practice that was also found among Anglicans, Presbyterians and Independents.[46] However, Keach was doing more than singing psalms. He was composing hymns. His rationale for this is found in the introduction "To the Reader" in *Spiritual Melody*:

> We are exhorted to *sing Psalms, Hymns and Spiritual Songs*, and since we have none left in the Form in the Scripture, it follows, that those who God has gifted that way, ought to compose them; for a Hymn or Song cannot be without its Form. Certainly God doth not enjoyn a Duty on us, that he hath not left sufficient Rule how to come at it, nor have we any ground to expect the extraordinary Gift anymore.[47]

Keach probably changed his views fairly soon after arriving in London. So began the process that was to end in 1691 with the decision by the Horselydown church to adopt congregational singing, following the precedent that Christ established in Matthew 26:30. By 1681, Keach was arguing in print for singing hymns in his *Tropologia*. His argument at that point is quaint,

---

46 Clifford, "Benjamin Keach and Nonconformist Hymnology," *Spiritual Worship*, 76, and Haykin, *Kiffin, Knollys and Keach*, 92.

47 "To the Reader." In Keach, *Spiritual Melody*, unnumbered pages 8–9.

for by following the Bible annotator Henry Ainsworth, Keach identifies the singing of the birds in Canticles 2:12 to be the saints who,

> feeling the comforts of God's Word and Spirit, do sing the praises of God, with psalms, and hymns, and spiritual songs.... In our judgment the godly are compared to birds principally upon this consideration, i.e., in respect to their singing, which is laid down in several places of scripture as an undoubted duty; I wish that Christians, who are not in the practice thereof, would consider of it.[48]

When he came to writing *The Breach Repaired*, Keach produced a much fuller and more carefully argued case from the Bible to establish that singing was a gospel ordinance. However, the link with *Tropologia* is very important. *Tropologia* was a very large volume and, priced at 20 shillings, was far too expensive for most people to purchase. In any case, it was now very scarce. Keach wanted his readers to recognize the direct link between his study of the Scriptures and the hymns that he had composed and was now publishing. He assured his readers that

> in this small Tract...is contained great part of the principal things under divers Metaphors opened in that Book, though they are there more largely insisted on I do not judge all those *Hymns* I have taken from Metaphorical Scriptures, proper to be sung...yet I doubt not but they may be all of use to the Reader, all being congruous with God's Word and according to the analogy of Faith.[49]

Vaughn has drawn attention to the parallel between Keach's hymn book and *Tropologia*, showing that there is a hymn for

48 Keach, *Types and Metaphors*, 694.

49 "To the Reader." In Keach, *Spiritual Melody*, unnumbered pages 2–3.

nearly every section of Keach's study of biblical metaphors. Did Keach compose a hymn for congregational use at the end of each sermon based on a biblical metaphor? The similarity between the table of contents of "the Folio" and "this small Tract" is such that this seems to be the only conclusion. Vaughn is certain that Keach's "hymns are a metrical summary of his *magnum opus*."[50]

It is clear that although congregational singing was becoming increasingly a part of worship among Baptist churches, Keach was a trailblazer, being the first to introduce the regular singing of hymns into public worship. He may also have been the first to produce a hymn book for congregational use. But why did Keach come to change the view that he probably inherited from General Baptist practice? Taking into account the controversy that surrounded him, we must also judge whether or not his arguments carry weight.

Keach's theology of hymn singing

Keach and Marlow approached the subject of hymn singing with diametrically opposed views. For Keach, the introduction of congregational hymn singing was a "going forward in the glorious work of reformation," but for Marlow such singing was a sign of a falling away from the truth.[51] In his introduction to *The Breach Repaired*, Keach had referred to the neglected ordinance of singing, and noted that reformation in the church was a hard and difficult work. He was surely speaking from experience. He had been working on introducing hymns into the worship of the church in Horselydown for nearly twenty years—and only a few months before he wrote this book, he had experienced the bitter

---

50 Vaughn, "Public Worship and Practical Theology," 133–134, 152–153. On the basis of this similarity, Vaughn says he finds it "difficult to accept that regular congregational hymn singing did not begin at Horselydown until 1691" ("Public Worship and Practical Theology," 134).

51 Keach, *The Breach Repaired*, 112.

split in his congregation. Furthermore, he was concerned to halt the spiritual declension that was evident in the churches, a concern previously expressed by Keach and the other conveners of the 1689 Assembly, and a concern also expressed by Marlow. But Keach reached an entirely different conclusion than Marlow. He believed that the "want of God's presence" in the churches was in part due to "the neglect of this great duty" of corporate singing.[52] As had been evident throughout Keach's life, the Bible, as the Word of God, was his authority. When faced with the question of whether to sing the praises of God, he naturally went back to his Bible in order to discover if there was a warrant for corporate singing by the church of Jesus Christ.

The crucial biblical texts for Keach were Colossians 3:16 and Ephesians 5:19–20 which spoke of "psalms, hymns and spiritual songs" and urged "singing and making melody in your heart to the Lord." His main point was that the singing of psalms, hymns and spiritual songs was a holy ordinance of God, a part of gospel worship, and that it was a permanent ordinance in the church of Christ. Singing was "a musical melodious modulation or tuning of the voice, expressing our spiritual Joy, for edifying one another, and for glorifying God," and was therefore to be distinguished from praying.[53] To sing together with a melodious voice was the biblical rule for singing. This was in stark contrast to the view of Marlow who said that singing was inward, inaudible and spiritual, and not verbal and vocal. If there was to be any singing, Marlow argued, it was to be by those specially gifted to edify the church in this way, and never an activity to be undertaken by the whole congregation. Given Marlow's insistence that singing was only an inward exercise of the soul and the mind, it is easy to see why Keach suggested that this was akin to Quakerism.[54]

---

52 Keach, *The Breach Repaired*, 176.

53 Keach, *The Breach Repaired*, 15.

54 Keach, *The Breach Repaired*, 122.

Keach argued from Job 38:7 that if the angels sang at creation then it was the duty of men to sing, because singing was an act of divine worship and an expression of joy. Furthermore, he demonstrated that singing was characteristic of the saints before the law was given. Moreover, in both the law and the gospel, there can be found clear Scriptural precepts that established singing as an ordinance of Jesus Christ for his church. And, it was instituted and required of the New Testament churches by the Holy Spirit. Finally, he cited a number of early church fathers to show that congregational singing was the practice of the early church and also of more recent Christian groups like the Waldensians in Italy and various Presbyterian and Independent contemporaries.[55]

Keach believed that if the church was to obey the exhortation to "let the Word of Christ dwell in you richly in all wisdom," as Colossians 3:16 said, then the church must preach that Word, hear it, meditate on it and understand it before they could sing it. This gives us insight into the way that Keach's mind was working and confirms the link he drew between the sermons in *Tropologia* and the hymns he wrote for congregational praise. To a large extent, the hymns that Keach wrote were a summary of his sermons.

Keach was also careful to underline the necessity of grace in the heart when engaged in singing: "the tongue is the instrument, but it must be tuned with grace, or the music will not be sweet in Christ's ears."[56] Furthermore, he was well aware that some believed that "psalms, hymns and spiritual songs" were three titles for different kinds of psalms, and answered that

---

55 The Waldensians were based in northern Italy and were evangelical in their theology. They had been persecuted by the Roman Catholic Church before the Reformation and afterward, but survived. There had been a massacre in Keach's own lifetime (1655) that had evoked intervention on the part of Cromwell, and sympathy from Milton, expressed in a sonnet.

56 Keach, *The Breach Repaired*, 92.

objection by asking on what grounds the songs of Moses, Deborah, Isaiah, Habakkuk, Simeon, Zechariah and Mary should be excluded.[57] If others objected that unbelievers could not offer real praise to God, Keach pointed out that there were unbelievers in the worshipping congregation in Corinth. Singing, moreover, was a moral duty. Although only the saints are able to sing spiritually, yet it is the duty of every person to praise God.

A significant part of *The Breach Repaired* is taken up with refuting Isaac Marlow and dealing with other objections. Marlow comes in for heavy criticism, Keach accusing him of erecting a "mighty man of straw" and "missing the mark."[58] One of Marlow's main objections focused on the issue of using human compositions in the worship of God and on imposing those forms on the church, thus quenching the Spirit and corrupting the worship of God. "You are against all outward and external ordinances," complained Keach.[59] Keach was determined to be fully understood, and also rejected Marlow's accusation of formality in worship:

> We are not pleading for formal Prayer, not formal Singing, nor formal Preaching either...but for spiritual Prayer, spiritual Singing and spiritual Preaching, and only for spiritual and Gospel Ordinances.[60]

Keach found Marlow's approach sour to his taste and wanted to end his book on a positive and sweet note. Drawing all his threads together, he concluded by saying that singing was a universal ordinance to be carried out by a variety of persons, in all places, in almost all conditions, by both men and women and by all creatures in heaven and earth. And, that it was something

57 Keach, *The Breach Repaired*, 96.
58 Keach, *The Breach Repaired*, 122.
59 Keach, *The Breach Repaired*, 158.
60 Keach, *The Breach Repaired*, 159.

God honoured with his presence and gracious acceptance. Keach concluded with an exhortation to the saints, showing them how to sing:

> with Grace in your hearts, labour after holy and heavenly frames, we must sing with the affections; let your joyful noises be from the sense of God's Love in a dear Redeemer to your own souls. Let it be exciting your graces; let Faith be in exercise in the duty, as well as in prayer and under the Word. Let it be with inward joy; remember it is your duty to rejoice evermore, and what then can hinder your singing God's Praises at any time? Let it be for spiritual Mercies and Blessings; chiefly more for deliverance from your sin, than for your suffering.[61]

The practice of joyful, corporate praise of God invigorating the spiritual life of the church was Keach's principal concern in the whole issue. This predominant theme should not be clouded by the controversy that surrounded Keach's innovation. Keach had the better argument and was more consistently Scriptural than Marlow, who at times was not only erecting a "mighty man of straw," but even clutching at straws in a desperate bid to win an argument.[62] Keach entered into the debate because he felt he had to do so out of his concern to establish biblical practices. *The Breach Repaired* sets out very clearly what he believed was the biblical warrant for corporate hymn singing. He wanted to promote the praise of God by using psalms, hymns and spiritual songs, and to help arrest the decline in spirituality in the churches by reviving this aspect of her corporate life.

---

61 Keach, *The Breach Repaired*, 191–192.

62 Clifford, "Benjamin Keach and Nonconformist Hymnology," *Spiritual Worship*, 82, shows Marlow abandoning sound reasoning when he argued, "since women are forbidden to speak in church, and singing is a form of speaking, therefore not all must sing together."

The hymns Keach wrote

The similarity between *Troplogia* and the hymns in *Spiritual Melody* is not just a happy coincidence. It indicates something that was crucial to Keach, and what he regarded as the appropriate content of hymns. He did not believe that singing was to be restricted to psalms any more than a preacher was restricted to simply reading or quoting the Bible. The preacher "may use other words to edify the Church, provided they agree with, or are congruous to the Word of Christ."[63] The same rule that applied to preaching was to be applied to singing: "our sermons are no more made for us in God's word than our hymns are."[64] Keach's criterion for singing a human composition was plainly stated. It must be in agreement with the Word of God. This provides an explanation for the distinctive doctrinal content of nearly all of Keach's compositions.

However, Keach's hymns are not merely a paraphrase of Scripture or a sung commentary on the sermon. They are to have their own identity as a hymn, complete in itself, a feature that was also to be characteristic of the hymns of Isaac Watts. Earlier, when considering Keach's poetic dialogues, it was pointed out that Keach did not have the poetic gifts of John Milton or the imagination of John Bunyan. A similar observation may be made with respect to his hymns, for Keach did not have the same measure of gift in writing hymns as, for example, Watts, Charles Wesley (1707–1788) or John Newton (1725–1807). However, Keach did pave the way for them.

Keach's verse has often been dismissed as doggerel at worst or as "too uncouth to gain wide acceptance in the Augustan age."[65] Very few, if any, of his hymns appeared in subsequent eighteenth-

---

63 Keach, *The Breach Repaired*, 93–94.

64 Keach, *The Breach Repaired*, 137.

65 Watts, *The Dissenters*, 311.

century hymn books.[66] It is true Keach was capable of writing incredibly poor verse, as the following lines demonstrate:

> 1. This World's a Sea, our Soul's a Ship
> With raging Tempest tost;
> And if she should her Anchor slip,
> She doubtless will be lost....
>
> 4. Repentance like a Bucket is
> To pump the water out;
> For leaky is our Ship, alas,
> Which makes us look about.[67]

Despite these lines, other efforts reflected more poetical skill, even if they were not in the same class as Watts and Wesley. It is true his compositions are not of a high quality and soon after his death others wrote much better hymns. This probably explains why Keach's hymns did not enjoy widespread use.[68] However, Keach was not primarily interested in writing good poetry. His hymns are what have been called "metrical sermons."[69] They are written so that the truths that have been preached remain in the memory and can be sung as part of the corporate worship of God.

In his preface, "To the Reader," Keach underlined what he believed was the value of having God's truth in the form of verse. He thought that the book of hymns would prove to be of great advantage to children who have a natural inclination to learn rhyming verse, and thus be an antidote to "such Songs and Ballads which generally tend to corrupt Youth" (provided, of course, their parents were willing to teach their children).[70]

66 Vaughn, "Public Worship and Practical Theology," 150–151.

67 Keach, *Spiritual Melody*, Hymn 104.

68 Music, "The Hymns of Benjamin Keach," 152.

69 Vaughn, "Public Worship and Practical Theology," 162.

70 "To the Reader." In Keach, *Spiritual Melody*, unnumbered page 4.

Keach wanted children to learn to sing and be affected by the truth. He seemed to appreciate that singing had a greater potential for stirring up the heart than mere recitation of verse. However, his main motive was to provide the church with hymns that would be suitable for family and congregational worship so that they could fulfill their "indispensable duty so sing Psalms and Hymns, &c."[71] Keach believed he had some measure of gift to accomplish this and so produced his two hymn books.

Many of Keach's hymns are songs of praise to God, clearly intended as hymns of adoration. This was an expression of his desire to reintroduce singing into the church and thus to reform and revive her spiritual life. For Keach, that meant centring on God and his salvation in the Lord Jesus Christ and, therefore, being doctrinal in his themes. So, in *Spiritual Melody*, the first thirteen hymns each focus on an attribute of God—for example, his eternity or his immensity.[72] Another hymn, reflecting how important the covenant of grace was in his thinking, is entitled "The Covenant & Faithfulness of God":

> 2. We with our mouths will, Lord, make known,
> *thy Faithfulness* always;
> O help us for to trust in it,
> And that too all our Days!
>
> 3. Thy Covenant thou wilt hold fast,
> as thou hast Sworn of Old;
> Thy Promises from first to last,
> fulfilled shall we behold.
>
> 4. The *Heavens* they shall Praise the Lord,
> for *Wonders* thou hast done;

---

71 Keach, *Spiritual Melody*, unnumbered page 6.

72 Keach, *Spiritual Songs*, Hymns 5–17.

And all thy *Saints*, with one accord,
Shall Praise thy Name alone.

5. Thy *Loving Kindness* shall not fail;
nor shall thy *Faithfulness*:
O sing unto the Lord, ye *Saints*,
And him for ever Bless.[73]

A second theme characteristic of Keach was justification by faith in Christ and the gift of Christ's righteousness. Keach expressed the truth he so passionately believed and preached, in the following lines:

4. Your *wedding Robes*, they are, I know,
richly embroidered;
No *Princess* was e'er *cloathed* so,
that King did ever wed.

5. It shines *bespangled* with *Gold*
and such who have it on
The *King* with joy doth them withhold,
and loves to look upon.

6. How may we then continually
in Jesus *Christ* rejoice,
and sing to him *melodiously*,
with Heart and cheerful Voice?

These two samples are fairly typical of Keach's doctrinal hymns. A great number of his hymns were clearly inspired by his study of the Scriptures, and specifically by the metaphors of Scripture.

David W. Music has considered some of the sources Keach

73 Keach, *Spiritual Songs*, Hymns 8, 12–13.

used for the composition of his hymns. He provides evidence that Keach was not always original in his compositions but borrowed extensively from other composers, three of whom were his contemporaries, John Mason (c.1646–1694), William Kethe (d. c.1594), John Patrick (1632–1695) and William Barton (c.1603–1678).[74] Keach appeared to act as an editor of existing hymns, yet he gives no indication that he was doing so, thus leaving himself open to the charge of plagiarism. If it was his aim to collect together materials that he deemed suitable for a congregational hymn book, it is reasonable to assume that besides writing his own hymns he would borrow from other sources and adapt them. Transferring material without acknowledging sources was a fairly common practice in the seventeenth century. Furthermore, Music has defended Keach from the charge of plagiarism, reasoning that "it is difficult to believe that he was trying to pass off these borrowings as his own work, for many of them came from the most popular hymnic works of his day."[75]

Benjamin Keach wrote some 500 hymns, published two hymn books and was largely responsible for removing "songless worship" and introducing corporate hymn singing into Particular Baptist churches. He provided a biblical rationale for the practice, believing that singing in melodious unison was one of the chief expressions of spiritual joy. This contrasted to "songless worship" that deprived Christians of one of the principal ways they could express their enjoyment of God, edify one another and glorify God. Keach had been one of those Particular Baptists who, in 1689, had written a letter inviting the churches to a General Assembly, expressing their concern about the loss of spiritual strength and vigour and decline in the churches.[76] The congregational singing of God's praises was one way of restoring that spiritual vigour.

74 Music, "The Hymns of Benjamin Keach," 148–149.

75 Music, "The Hymns of Benjamin Keach," 148.

76 See Chapter 8.

It is sobering to note, though, that a righteous and biblical cause can often become stained and harmed by human failings. According to Proverbs 12:18, words spoken rashly can be like the piercings of a sword. Judging by the response of the national assembly to the controversy, this was true of both parties involved in the dispute. Keach would have wanted to reform the church without the division that it caused in his own church and between his friends and fellow elders in London. He believed that those who opposed the singing of God's praises had portrayed him as a man who had disturbed the peace and unity of the church, and that in so doing they had misrepresented him. He was not without fault in the way he handled the matter in his own church, or in the way that he sometimes expressed himself in his writing. But the evidence shows that he conducted himself more honourably and with greater integrity than Isaac Marlow. The fact that he was misrepresented brought great pain to Keach because it meant that his real motives and desires were concealed. In addition, Marlow appeared to be a man who tended to be "a law unto himself," stirring up members of Keach's own congregation and refusing to listen to the counsel of others who were seeking to resolve the controversy. In contrast, Keach listened to his fellow pastors, submitted himself to them and publicly withdrew the offending remarks he had made in a letter to the churches.

The two things that he longed for were the reformation and reviving of the churches, and their peace and unity. Sadly, instead of unity there was strife and division that proved very difficult to heal. This caused Keach intense grief. The London Particular Baptists, so united in days of persecution, were now seriously divided over this issue. The effects, however, were not confined to London. In estimating the damaging effects of this controversy, Murdina McDonald concluded:

> If to the elements of schism, serious ideas, numbers of persons involved, the threat of division along singing

> and non-singing lines, the proliferation of pamphlets and the extension of the debate to country churches is added the threat to the reputation of Keach and Collins, and by extension, to the London elders themselves, the damaging and potentially damaging effects of this controversy were considerable.[77]

Keach had to pay a high price for pressing forward with what he believed was of first importance, namely, the reformation of the church and her conformity to the New Testament pattern of worship. He was a man who loved peace and unity, but he was also a man of determination who would not let even a painful controversy stand in the way of establishing the gospel ordinance of corporate singing.

77 MacDonald, "London Calvinistic Baptists," 64.

CHAPTER 12

"An orderly true constituted visible church of Jesus Christ"

> Now in the old Will or old Testament, Infants were admitted to this Privilege of Church-Membership in that Legal or National Church of the Jews; and, their Names not being mentioned, as having right to any Gospel Ordinance, as Baptism, or the Lord's Supper.[1]

Since the time of his youth among the General Baptists in Winslow, when he had first professed his faith in Jesus Christ and been baptized, Benjamin Keach had been convinced that believer's baptism was the teaching of the New Testament. He had been baptized in 1640 as an infant in the Church of England in his native village of Stoke Hammond. Despite becoming a Christian through the instrumentality of Matthew Mead, Keach did not retain Mead's views concerning

1 Keach, *Light broke forth in Wales*, 66–67.

infant baptism. Rather he adopted views that—after 1660—were regarded as heretical and schismatic. One of the indictments against Keach at his trial in Aylesbury in 1664 was his rejection of the validity of infant baptism. However, Keach was firmly persuaded of two principles: (1) one had to believe first and then be baptized in order to become a disciple of Christ and a member of the church of Christ; and, (2) immersion was the biblical mode and sprinkling was an improper method. He held these two convictions about baptism until his death in 1704. They brought him into conflict not only with Anglicans, but also with other Nonconformists, with whom he otherwise had much in common.[2]

The Baptist church model

Keach and his fellow Baptists, both General and Particular, were firmly in the Separatist tradition. This tradition was unacceptable, both politically and ecclesiastically, during the Restoration period, since it was seen as a form of subversive radicalism.[3] Keach did not subscribe to the notion of a national church that the Anglicans and men like the Presbyterian Richard Baxter wanted, for he believed in the separation of church and state.[4] In addition, like other Puritan-Separatists who also became Baptists, Keach was strongly wedded to the conviction that entrance into church fellowship was through a profession of faith and baptism by immersion (with, in his church, the laying on of hands). This was reinforced by a church covenant agreed to by

---

2 See Chapter 2 where Keach's view on infant baptism was first considered.

3 For a detailed study of the links between Particular Baptist and Puritan-Separatism ecclesiology, see Howson, *Erroneous and Schismatical Opinions*, 317–334.

4 Baxter rejected the notion of liberty of conscience as a basis for social and religious stability. He did not believe in freedom for any religion but freedom for the true, namely, the Protestant religion that was to be maintained by the power of the civil magistrate. See Carl R. Trueman, "Richard Baxter on Christian Unity: A Chapter in the Enlightening of English Reformed Orthodoxy," *Westminster Theological Journal* 61 (1999): 57–58.

all the members, together with the ongoing disciplined life of the entire church. By defending the Baptist interpretation, with what he believed was the biblical practice of baptism and the implications for a gathered church of baptized believers, his convictions became an inevitable indictment against the Church of England. Keach did not argue that there were no Christians in the national church. He did, however, assert that it was not an orderly gospel church and could never be one so long as it continued to practice infant baptism. As he declared:

> ...tho we believe there are many Holy and Gracious Christians of the Communion of the Church of England, and that they are Members of the Invisible Universal Church, yet we do not believe the Church of England, nor any National Church, is an orderly true Constituted Visible Church of Jesus Christ and therefore we separated from them.[5]

Particular Baptists repeatedly disassociated themselves from Anabaptists in their confessions of faith and other writings. However, the prejudice associated with the name "Anabaptist" was very hard to shake off, and the effects of Daniel Featley's *The Dippers Dipt: Or, The Anabaptists duck'd and plung'd over head and ears, at a disputation in Southwark*, published in 1645, with Thomas Edwards' *Gangraena* in the following year, strengthened that prejudice.[6] Featley, in particular, did not go

---

5 Keach, *Light broke forth in Wales*, 250. See also Chapter 8, n.35.

6 Daniel Featley, *Katabaptistai Kataptustoi. The Dippers Dipt. Or, The Anabaptists duck'd and plung'd over head and ears, at a disputation in Southwark. Together with a large and full discourse of their 1. Original. 2. Severall Sorts. 3. Peculiar errours. 4. High attempts against the state. 5. Capitall punishments; with an application of these times* (London, 1645), and Thomas Edwards, *Gangraena: or a Catalogue and Discovery of many of the Errors, Heresies, Blasphemies and pernicious Practices of the Sectaries of this time, vented and acted in England in these four last years: as also a Particular Narration of divers Stories, Remarkable*

unanswered.[7] Those who drew up the *First London Baptist Confession of Faith* in 1644 spoke of themselves as "those churches which are commonly (though falsly) called Anabaptists."[8] Featley was critical of aspects of this confession of faith, and when it was revised in 1646, some parts were modified to address the accusations of Featley.[9] The men at the 1646 Assembly did not change their views, but were sensitive about the way their views were being received. They made concessions in the way that they stated them in order to counter the accusations against them and to clear their name. Hostile propaganda against Baptists was still being produced sixty years later. For instance, David Russen, who falsely accused Keach of immorality in connection with baptizing women, also cast a slur on all who practiced believer's baptism. It was left to Keach's friend, Joseph Stennett, to answer David Russen and also to clear Keach's name.[10]

Keach's writings on baptism

Keach's pen had been busy, especially during the 1690s, the controversy over hymn singing notwithstanding. He had produced no less than six books arguing against infant baptism, promoting what he believed was biblical teaching about baptism and the nature of a true gospel church. Six years after he came to London,

---

Passages, Letters, and Extract of many Letters, all concerning the present Sects; together with some observations upon and Corrolaries from all the forenamed Premisses (London, 1646).

7 Samuel Richardson, *Some brief Considerations on Doctor Featley his Book intituled, The Dippers Dipt, Wherein in some measure is discovered his many great and false accusations of divers persons, commonly called Anabaptists, with an Answer to them, and some brief reasons of their Practice* (London, 1645).

8 Lumpkin, *Baptist Confessions of Faith*, 153.

9 For the details and significance of the changes, see Richard P. Belcher and Anthony Mattia, *A Discussion of the Seventeenth Century Particular Baptist Confessions of Faith* (Southbridge: Crowne Publications, 1990), 5–10.

10 Joseph Stennett, *An Answer to Mr David Russen's Book entituled Fundamentals without a foundation or a true picture of Anabaptists etc.* (London, 1704).

Joseph Stennett (1663–1713) was pastor of the Sabbatarian Baptist (Seventh-Day Baptist) congregation meeting at Pinners' Hall, London. He was Particular Baptist and often supplied the pulpit for churches that met on Sundays as well. A friend of Benjamin Keach, Stennett vigorously defended him against the accusations of David Russen.

Keach was assaulting Richard Baxter's views in *Mr. Baxter's Arguments for Believer's Baptism*, but this was small in comparison with his output in the 1690s.[11]

Keach began with *Gold Refin'd: Or, Baptism in its Primitive Purity* in 1689, which set out his understanding of the practice and purpose of believer's baptism, repeating much of what he had said earlier in *Tropologia*. The book also contained the arguments he used to refute Richard Baxter, but was principally against the views of William Smythies of Cripplegate.[12]

Pedo-baptism Disproved followed in 1691, aimed at some men representing the Athenian Society, who had published answers to queries about infant baptism in a paper called the *Athenian Mercury*. Keach answered them and also included in his response "twenty Sylogistical Arguments to disprove Infant Baptism."[13]

The Rector Rectified and Corrected, published in 1692, was a substantial book of over 200 pages answering William Burkitt (1650–1703), the rector of Milden in Suffolk. In this book, Keach was coming to the aid of John Tredwell and the Baptist church in Lavenham, whom Burkitt had assailed, unjustly accusing them of making proselytes by baptizing them in a dirty horse pond.[14]

The Ax Laid to the Root was an exposition and application of Matthew 3:10, in which Keach aimed one further blow at the foundation of infant baptism and the view of church

11 Keach's pamphlet published in 1674 has not survived. Richard Baxter also found Keach's views on the church unacceptable and was unwilling to give liberty of conscience to those who held such convictions. He favoured the monarchy, a national church with bishops and church liturgy. Somewhat reluctantly he became a Nonconformist after the 1662 Act of Uniformity.

12 Keach, *Gold Refin'd: Or, Baptism in its Primitive Purity* (London, 1689).

13 Keach, *Pedo-Baptism Disproved: being an answer to two printed papers called the Athenian Mercury* (London, 1691).

14 Keach, *The Rector Rectified and Corrected: Or, Infant-Baptism Unlawful* (London, 1692). Crosby, *History*, 4:282–286, gives a full account of the circumstances that led to Keach's book. Burkitt had preached a sermon against the Baptists in 1691, repeated the substance of it in the barn when the Baptists met there, and then printed the sermon, *An Argumentative and Practical Discourse on Infant Baptism*, in 1692.

Richard Baxter (1615–1691) was an influential Presbyterian Nonconformist leader who endured a great deal of persecution—both fines and imprisonment—for the views he held. He was a pastor in London at the same time as Benjamin Keach but they held very different views regarding baptism, the separation of church and state, the nature of the church and justification by faith.

membership it implied. It was published in 1692 and included Keach's answers to the views of John Flavel (1627–1691), Joshua Excell and Mr. Rothwell.[15]

A Counter-Antidote followed in 1693, arguing strongly against the views of Mr. Gyles Shute of Limehouse, a member of the Stepney Independent church where Matthew Mead was then minister.[16] Among Shute's accusations was the notion that Anabaptists were counterfeit.

Finally, Keach turned his attention to Wales and Mr. James Owen's *Children's Baptism from Heaven*. Even though this was written in Welsh, Keach found a translator, Robert Morgan of Swansea, and wrote his reply *Light broke forth in Wales*, published in 1696.[17] This was reprinted in 1705, after Keach's death, under the title of *Believer's Baptism*, together with a Welsh edition. These writings established Keach as the foremost defender of Baptist views in the latter decades of the seventeenth century.

Keach was not particularly innovative in his views of baptism. He was expressing and applying what other seventeenth-century Baptists had said before him. He took up his pen to defend himself and other Baptists against his contemporaries who were attacking Baptist convictions. John Spilsbury had written as early as 1643, and had been followed by both William Kiffin and Hanserd Knollys. John Norcott, at whose funeral Keach had preached, published a book on baptism in 1672, and Hercules Collins, his successor in Wapping, also produced works on baptism, as did Thomas Delaune, Nehemiah Coxe and Philip Cary.[18]

---

15 Keach, *The Ax Laid to the Root: or, One more blow at the Foundation of Infant Baptism, and Church-membership* (London, 1692).

16 Keach, *A Counter-Antidote to Purge out the Malignant Effects of a Late Counterfeit, Prepared by Mr. Gyles Shute, an Unskilful Person in Polemical Cures: being An Answer to his Vindication of his Pretended Antidote, to prevent the Prevalency of Anabaptism* (London, 1694).

17 Keach, *Light broke forth in Wales*.

18 See Bibliography: 4. Other seventeenth-century Particular Baptist works on believer's baptism.

These men were often engaged in controversy and were strenuous in defending and propagating their convictions. These works were in addition to the relevant chapters of *The Second London Baptist Confession of Faith*, drawn up in 1677 and republished by the 1689 Particular Baptist National Assembly, which summarized the common understanding of what they believed the Bible taught about the church, baptism and the Lord's Supper. It should be kept in mind that this was not the confession of just a few churches, but the testimony of over 100 churches from London and other parts of England and Wales.[19]

Keach, therefore, was not alone in entering into the controversy over baptism. In doing so, moreover, he did not aim to attack *personally* those who held views contrary to his own. Rather, he wished to bring to bear on the subject careful, biblical reasoning. Dealing with the objections of Gyles Shute to believer's baptism, Keach wrote that

> if I or my reverent brother [Hercules] Collins have in any Writing of Ours used hard Words, we have cause to be troubled, for the Truth never gained anything that way: 'Tis not hard Words, but hard Arguments that must do the business; a soft Answer (as Solomon saith) turneth away Wrath.[20]

Writing to James Owen and paedobaptists in Wales, Keach assured them that "tho I am an Enemy to your Opinion and Practice…yet [I am] a dear Lover of your Persons and precious Souls."[21] Keach argued in this manner because he loved his fellow Christians and was convinced that infant baptism was not true baptism:

19 *The First London Confession of Faith* had been signed in 1644 by seven London churches.

20 Keach, *A Counter-Antidote*, 3.

21 "Preface" to Keach, *Light broke forth in Wales*, iii.

> The Baptism of the Adult, or that of Believers, is that one or only Baptism of Christ's Visible Church; for those Members of the visible Church in the Primitive times, that were washed in Baptismal Water, professed themselves washed in Christ's Blood, and they that were sincere had the thing signified, as well as the Sign when they were baptized, but Infants never made any such profession, therefore Infant Baptism was not the first and one Baptism that Christ left in his Church.[22]

Keach's theology of baptism

Because there is a considerable amount of repetition in Keach's six works on baptism, it will be easier to trace out the common themes rather than deal with each volume individually, and thereby continually restate Keach's principal arguments for the practice of believer's baptism. In some of those volumes, when Keach is interacting with, and arguing against, the opinions of individual paedobaptist writers, it must be admitted that his reasoning and writing is hard to follow. The simplest statement rejecting infant baptism is found in *The Articles of Faith*:

> That the Infants of Believers ought not to be baptized, because there is neither Precept, or Example, or any certain Consequence in the Holy Scripture for any such practice: And we ought not to be wise above what is written. And that a human Tradition or Custom ought not to be regarded, but that it is sinful, and abominable.[23]

Keach regarded infant baptism as a human tradition introduced into the church in the early centuries after Christ and the apostles, and was adamant that it was not a practice warranted

22 Keach, *Light broke forth in Wales*, 251.

23 Keach, *The Articles of the Faith*, Article XXI: Baptism, 20–21.

by the teaching of the Bible.[24] However, *The Articles of Faith* contain none of his detailed reasons for the rejection of infant baptism and the assertion of believer's baptism. These reasons are found in his other writings on baptism, his sermons on the parables and in *Tropologia*—and are closely tied to Keach's understanding of the covenant of grace.

Attention has already been drawn to the importance of the covenant of grace in Keach's theology.[25] His understanding of this covenant lies at the heart of his rejection of infant baptism. He believed that there were two covenants, the covenant of works and the covenant of grace, and that these two were radically different:

> The Covenant of Works, as to the Tenure of it runs thus, i.e. Do this and live; but the covenant of Grace runs thus in the Tenure of it, i.e. Believe and be saved.... The One puts men upon working, or doing for Life; the other puts them upon believing, and working from Life.[26]

The covenant of works was made with Adam, as the common head of all humankind. The covenant of grace was made with Christ and all his elect. The essence of the covenant of works

---

24 In rejecting infant baptism, Keach is of one mind with John Spilsbury, the earliest Particular Baptist writer on baptism. Spilsbury wrote: "For sure I am, that there is neither command, nor example in all the New Testament, for any such practice as I know, and whatsoever is done in the worship of God, or obedience to Christ, without his command, or apparent example approved of by Christ, is of man, as a voluntary will-worship, after the commandments and doctrines of men, Col.2:20,21,22; the which Christ testifies against as a vain thing" ["Epistle to the Reader" in John Spilsbury, *A Treatise concerning the lawful subject of Baptism* (London, 1643)]. Hercules Collins uses similar language, asserting: "Infant-Baptism neither hath Precept nor Example in God's Word" [Hercules Collins, *Believers-Baptism from heaven, and of divine institution, infants-baptism from earth, and human invention* (London, 1691), 31].

25 See Chapter 4.

26 Keach, *The Display of Glorious Grace*, 180.

was that life was promised to Adam on condition of his obedience, and death was threatened to him on his disobedience. Keach believed that the covenant made with the nation of Israel at Sinai was another edition of the covenant of works. It issued a command—"Do this and live"—but it was not given in order to justify Israel, because they had already lost the ability to obey God. God, however, still enforced this covenant because he had the authority to command obedience. The covenant of grace was established on a different basis, not of works but of grace, and was made by Christ on behalf of his elect with the promise "Believe and be saved." This distinction between the two covenants is vital in understanding Keach's defence of believer's baptism, for he believed that what he termed "the covenant of circumcision" with Abraham was part of the covenant of works and not of grace.

The paedobaptist argument put forward by William Burkitt, James Owen, Gyles Shute and others, laid great stress on the importance of the covenant that God made with Abraham in Genesis 17:7–14, in particular the parallel between circumcision in the old covenant and baptism in the new. They argued that if the infants of Jewish parents were circumcised then the infants of Christian parents ought to be baptized, a parallel Keach consistently rejected as unbiblical and therefore unwarranted.[27] He believed that the covenant with Abraham had two aspects, and that it was effectively two covenants: one made with Abraham's natural seed—the covenant of circumcision—and the other with his spiritual seed—the covenant of grace. The covenant of circumcision included all Abraham's natural seed—Ishmael and Isaac and, of the next generation, Isaac's sons Esau and Jacob. Furthermore, this covenant of circumcision was made to

27 In answering Burkitt and Owen, Keach made considerable use of the "Anglican Antipaedobaptist" John Tombes. For example in Keach, *The Rector Rectified and Corrected*, 13, 16, 41, 107 and 115. For a summary of Tombes' teaching on the covenant with Abraham, see John Tombes, *A Short Catechism about Baptism* (London, 1659), Questions 15–38.

distinguish Abraham and his descendents from other nations and was concerned only with national and civil promises, such as the land of Canaan given to those who obeyed the commandment to be circumcised. As such, this covenant of circumcision was an external and legal covenant that God made with Abraham and his fleshly seed. Keach regarded it as part of the covenant of works, because it promised life on the condition of obedience. Keach affirmed in his sermons on Matthew 3:10 that God had now taken his axe to this legal and external covenant, and had brought in a new, gospel covenant.[28]

Men and women who became believers, whether they were Jews or Gentiles, were included in the covenant of grace, with its foundation in divine election. In the Old Testament, the covenant of grace was made with Isaac and then with Jacob, rather than with Ishmael and Esau. Keach argued from Romans 9:6–13 that Scripture taught that the children of the promise were counted as the seed, and not the children of the flesh. From Galatians 3 and 4, he further argued that it was only those who were of faith that were blessed with believing Abraham, and that they alone were the sons of Sarah, the freewoman, and born according to the promise of God. By contrast, the fleshly seed were sons of Hagar, the bondwoman.

Keach repeatedly emphasized the importance of believing for those who were to be baptized. Describing the royal charter of the gospel, or the spiritual corporation of the covenant and gospel church-state, he said:

> You must be a believer, you must be born again, be a new creature, and so must your children, before you or they can either be free-men and women of this corporation or be fellow citizens with the saints and household of God.[29]

---

28 Keach, *The Ax laid to the Root.*

29 Keach, *The Rector Rectified and Corrected*, 31.

And again:

> the Covenant of Grace made with Abraham and his Seed, doth not intend his Carnal Seed, according to the Flesh; but his Spiritual Seed, or such as had the Faith of Abraham...[it] extends to none but the Holy and Elect Seed, to none but the Spiritual Seed, to such who are Christ's, or true believers in Christ only.[30]

Circumcision was not a sign and seal of the covenant of grace, "but only a seal of Abraham's faith, or a confirmation of the faith he had before he was circumcised."[31] The true parallel to circumcision in the flesh, Keach asserted, was circumcision of the heart by the work of the Holy Spirit: "putting away the body of sin, etc., is a sign of the truth of grace, and of an interest in the righteousness of Christ Jesus."[32] Therefore, for Keach and his fellow Baptists, baptism could not be regarded as the New Testament equivalent of circumcision.

On the basis of this, Keach believed there was no place for the baptism of infants. Baptists, like Keach, therefore adopted a different form of church membership, not only from the nation of Israel in the old covenant, but also from the Church of England and from fellow Presbyterian and Independent Dissenters. They argued for a church composed only of regenerate and baptized believers. They regarded the nation of Israel as a typical church, made externally holy by ceremonial and typical holiness. In the old covenant situation, infants were admitted to the privileges of membership in a legal or national church of the Jews, but now the axe had been laid to that root. The turning point in history was the coming of the Lord Jesus Christ and the pulling down of "that old barn":

30 Keach, *Gold Refin'd*, 100–101.

31 Keach, *Gold Refin'd*, 104.

32 Keach, "Circumcision, what it was a type of," *Types and Metaphors*, 993.

> But now the Lord Jesus Christ was come, with his fan in his hand, to separate the wheat from the chaff, and not let them lie any longer together on that floor in that old barn, i.e., in the legal Jewish church-state, according to the external covenant of peculiarity God made with Abraham, and his natural seed as such: which had stood near its full period of time prefixed by the Almighty, but now must be pulled down, Jesus Christ being come, and just going to build a new spiritual garner, or Gospel-church, to put all his choice grain or wheat into; *viz.*, all believing and true penitent persons…for the Jewish church was not to abide or continue any longer than till the death and resurrection of Jesus Christ; it being a typical church. When the Antitype was come, that must needs vanish away.[33]

Keach made the same point in his arguments against James Owen:

> Now in the old Will or old Testament, Infants were admitted to this Privilege of Church-Membership in that Legal or National Church of the Jews; and National Church-Privileges are now made null and void by the Gospel-Covenant which is Christ's last Will and Testament, in which infant Church-Membership is quite left out, their Names not being mentioned, as having right to any Gospel Ordinance, as Baptism, the Lord's Supper, etc.[34]

Keach defended his practice and that of Baptist churches on several fronts, the argument relating to the covenant being the

33 Keach, "The Fan in His Hand," *Parables One*, 41.

34 Keach, *Light broke forth in Wales*, 66–67.

principal one. In a second and very closely related argument, Keach denied that being a child of elect and believing parents and being baptized as an infant guaranteed eternal life. This was a major pastoral concern for Keach. His strident language betrays his fears for the purity of the church of Christ if this presumption about eternal life prevailed in the minds of those "who tell the people they were made 'the children of God, members of Christ, and inheritors of the kingdom of heaven' in their baptism, or rather rantism":[35]

> O the danger of this pernicious doctrine! How many flatter themselves with the hopes of heaven from this false foundation, thinking they sucked in the true faith, and true religion, with their mother's milk, and were made Christians by a priest's scattering a little water on their faces when babes, though they live in a manner of horrid sins, and are enemies to the life and power of godliness? This is a way of making Christians which Christ and his apostles never taught; and it is a healing of the hurt of the people slightly, taking them off from seeking after grace and true regeneration; for if they were made true Christians then, regenerated then, doubtless their state is good; and so it is to be feared, thousands of them conclude, and never doubt of their salvation.[36]

Keach's fears were well founded, for William Burkitt, the Anglican incumbent of Milden, claimed that by baptism infants were regenerated. Keach was equally strong in refuting Burkitt's claim:

---

35 Keach, "The Unclean Spirit," *Parables Two*, 330. "Rantism" is another term for sprinkling as opposed to immersion.

36 Keach, "The Unclean Spirit," *Parables Two*, 330.

> We do affirm you have as much ground of faith as any promise of God, to pray that God would illumine a stone or a tree as you have to pray that by baptism he would regenerate an infant. If you pray not in faith you sin, and if you have no promise of God to ground your faith upon, when you pray God by baptism to regenerate an infant, then you cannot pray in faith.[37]

Keach was fearful that if such a doctrine were held, then the baptism of infants would tend to put "profane wretches into the church," resulting in a church full of "false professors" and the purity of the church compromised.[38] Keach regarded this teaching by some proponents of infant baptism as erroneous, because it not only compromised the purity of divine worship but also gave people a false assurance that they were Christians. Thus, a barrier was created to true reformation and revival in the church:

> the inhabitants of the Earth are cheated, and deluded with a Shadow and empty Name that signifies nothing; and certain I am, until Christendom...is Unchristianed of this pretended Rite...there will never be a thorough Reformation.[39]

As with the controversy over hymn singing, so in the matter of baptism: Keach's greatest concern was for the continuing reformation of the church. He was not only contending for purity of worship in each true gospel church, but also for sound doctrine

---

37 Keach, *The Rector Rectified and Corrected*, 82–83.

38 Keach, *Light broke forth in Wales*, 98.

39 Keach, *Light broke forth in Wales*, 234. Philip Cary shared this conviction in *A Solemn Call*, 242, when he claimed that infants being baptized, instead of professed repenting believers, and sprinkling practiced, instead of dipping, made void the commands of Christ. He regarded such practices as great abuses of divinely instituted worship and called for a thorough reformation of the church.

and godly conduct among the members of that church. The practice of infant baptism undermined the work of reformation because it allowed unconverted infants to become members of the church and if, on becoming adults, they never professed faith, but remained in the church, this could only destroy the holiness of the church and sap her vitality.

If some paedobaptists presumed that infant baptism was the means of regeneration—leading to a compromising of the purity of the church—Keach did not fall into a similar trap because of his belief in election. He believed that God's electing grace was the ultimate cause of an individual's salvation. Yet, he also believed that God made use of means in the conversion of children and that believing parents were, by their instruction, prayers and example, the principal means God uses. Thus, his counsel to parents was unmistakable:

> Train up your Children in the fear of God and set them a good example, and pray for them, and over them and give them good Instruction and godly Counsel and Admonition: And see that you neglect not to Catechise them daily, that so they may understand early, the main Grounds and Principles of Religion; but dread to Baptize them in Infancy, or before they have the inward and Spiritual Grace signified in true Baptism.[40]

As a pastor, Keach faced a high infant mortality rate and the consequences are seen in the family records in the *Regester*. When asked the difficult question about the salvation of infants who died in infancy, he referred his readers to *The Second London Baptist Confession of Faith*: "Infants dying in infancy are regenerated and saved by Christ through the Spirit: who worketh when,

40 Keach, *Light broke forth in Wales*, 95.

and where, and how he pleaseth."[41] He insisted that if such children were saved, it was only because God was gracious. He believed that God was able to regenerate and sanctify infants by his free and sovereign grace. He explained the teaching of the confession by stating, "all those dying Infants who are saved, God doth in some way or another (which is not known to us) sanctify them; for no unclean thing can enter into the heavenly Jerusalem."[42] He believed that children were saved on the same basis as adults. They were not innocent nor was there some point at which children reached the age of discretion.[43]

A third line of argument was drawn from a consideration of the meaning of *baptizõ*. Keach asserted that the biblical mode of baptism was clearly immersion, and not sprinkling or pouring. In *Tropologia*, he gives us the "judgment of the learned," that the "primary, proper and literal signification" of the word is "to drown, immerge, plunge under, overwhelm, as also to dip, which is done by plunging."[44] Gyles Shute, in one of his publications answered by Keach, had been adamant that immersion was not the only possible mode and suggested that sprinkling and immersion were alternative modes of baptism. Keach was equally insistent that the very meaning of *baptizõ* did not leave the church with alternatives modes, that such reasoning as Shute's was absurd, and that immersion was the plain meaning and therefore "an essential, not an accident of Baptism."

---

41 Chapter 10, Effectual Calling.

42 Keach, *A Counter-Antidote*, 12.

43 For a contemporary treatment of this subject by Reformed Baptists, see David Kingdon, *Children of Abraham: A Reformed Baptist View of Baptism, the Covenant, and Children* (Worthing: Henry E. Walter and Haywards Heath: Carey Publications, 1973), 92–100; Waldron, *A Modern Exposition of the 1689 Baptist Confession of Faith*, 149–151; and, Fred A. Malone, *The Baptism of Disciples Alone: A Covenantal Argument for Credobaptism versus Paedobaptism* (Cape Coral: Founders Press, 2003).

44 Keach, "Baptism a Burial," *Preaching from the Types*, 629.

> If there were more modes of Baptism than one, then there were different significations of the same ordinance, and all of them could not be held forth in the Baptism of each person; for such that were Dipped, tho' it was but the Head only, were taught the proper Mysteries represented thereby, and those that were sprinkled only with Water, or had Water poured upon them, were taught the proper Symbols or signification of that mode: but how absur'd that would be I leave to all impartial men to consider.... If dipping was one mode and Sprinkling another, then would Baptism and Rantism be both ordinances of Christ.... But we deny Sprinkling is Baptism for Dipping of the whole Body[;] is an essential, not an accident of Baptism.[45]

Romans 6:3–5 provided Keach with a fourth line of reasoning to prove that immersion was the proper mode of baptism for those who professed their faith in Christ. Keach was fond of quoting a whole group of witnesses to show that baptism represents the death, burial and resurrection of Christ, including several of the church fathers, Daniel Tilenus (1563–1633), whom he described as "a great Protestant writer" and several contemporary paedobaptists.[46] This truth, he repeatedly assured his readers, could never be symbolized either by sprinkling or by pouring, but could be accurately symbolized only by immersion. Referring to Tilenus' comments on Romans 6:3–5, Keach approved of his conclusion:

---

45 Keach, *A Counter-Antidote*, 7.

46 Keach, *A Counter-Antidote*, 9–10. These included Ambrose, Ignatius, Basil the Great, Tilenus in his *Disputations*, Matthew Poole's *Annotations*, the Westminster Assembly's *Annotations*, William Perkins and four contemporary Anglican clergymen: Dr. Sharp, Archbishop of York; Dr. Fowler, Bishop of Gloucester; Dr. Sherlock, Dean of St. Paul's Cathedral and Dr. Tillotson, Archbishop of Canterbury. The fact that he could call as witnesses the last four would have added weight to Keach's argument.

> Baptism is the first Sacrament of the New Testament instituted by Christ, in which there is an exact Analogy between the Sign, and the thing signified. The outward Rite in Baptism is threefold[:]
>
> 1. Immersion into the Water
> 2. Abiding under the Water
> 3. A Resurrection out of the Water.[47]

Keach was anxious to point out to any advocate of infant baptism that this symbolism could not be true of an infant, but only of a believer in Christ. To the converted person, being baptized was an outward sign of having been united to Jesus Christ by faith. Baptism was

> a sign of his Fellowship with Christ in his Death, Burial, and Resurrection, and of his being grafted into him, and of Remission of Sins, and of his giving himself up to God, through Jesus Christ, to walk in Newness of Life.[48]

Keach was equally clear that baptism by immersion had no saving power in and of itself, but was an outward sign of the inward reality of the saving grace of God. However, immersion was the only possible mode because only immersion provided the appropriate analogy.

This also explains Keach's use of Matthew 28:18–20, often referred to as "the Great Commission" of the risen Lord Jesus

---

47 Keach, *A Counter-Antidote*, 9, quoting Tilenus' *Disputations*. Daniel Tilenus was born in Silesia and came to France in 1590 and joined the French Reformed church. He came into conflict with this body of believers when he adopted Arminian views. He wrote to James I in support of the Episcopalian form of church government in Scotland (over against Presbyterianism) and paid a short visit to England at the king's invitation. Keach was prepared to use Tilenus' arguments to buttress his doctrine and understanding of baptism.

48 Keach, *The Articles of the Faith*, Article XXI: Baptism, 20.

Christ, as another line of argument. James Owen was one of several who believed that infants were included in the command to baptize, but Keach was quick to point out that this was a mistake. Not only did this passage enforce the mode of baptism as immersion by the use of the word *baptizō*, but it also showed that infants were not the proper *subjects* for the baptism authorized by Christ.

Keach made a number of observations from this passage. It was a commission of Christ, he said, of One who had recently been raised from the dead and had been given authority by the Father to permanently establish how God was to be served during the gospel age. Keach drew attention to the fact that making disciples necessarily involved teaching, for being a disciple required a profession of repentance toward God and faith in the Lord Jesus Christ. As the repentance and faith required must *precede* baptism, infants were not the proper subjects of baptism. Keach also observed that the apostles of Christ were to go to *all* the nations, into cold countries as well as hot ones, and make disciples before baptizing them—not dipping them in hot climates and sprinkling them in cold as some were accustomed to argue!

Finally, Keach explained, because baptism was to be administered in the name of the triune God, it was high-handed for anyone to baptize an infant who was incapable of being taught and discipled.[49] Therefore, according to Keach, only professing believers were to be baptized. Or, as he described them in other biblical terms, those who knew the Lord in the way described in Jeremiah 31:32–34 and Hebrews 8:8–12. He maintained that these verses relating to the knowledge of God under the new covenant were consistent with the Great Commission, indicating that all those from among the nations taken into the covenant of grace should be discipled and taught this knowledge.[50]

---

49 Keach, *Gold Refin'd*, 64–65.

50 Keach, *Light broke forth in Wales*, 53.

There was nothing new or original in the teaching of Keach about believer's baptism. The debate was intense at times, from the 1640s onward. Keach himself was at pains to point out that he drew from a wide range of writers (both Baptist and paedo-baptist) in order to set out his own convictions.

The importance of Keach's writings on baptism

Keach was the leading apologist for believer's baptism in the fifteen years after 1689. There are at least four reasons why these sermons and writings were important.

In the first place, baptism was not an incidental practice in Baptist church polity. While Keach said baptism by immersion was not necessary to salvation, he did believe that it was still important. Believer's baptism and the Lord's Supper were the two sacraments commanded by Christ to be observed perpetually by his church, and baptism was an integral part of the Great Commission given to the church by Christ. Keach stressed its importance in the following balanced statement:

> We lay no more stress upon it than we ought; we say it is a Duty incumbent upon all believers—a holy Ordinance of Christ, one of the great Sacraments of the New Testament, and they that reject it, do reject part of the Counsel of God. Yet we do not lay such stress upon it, as some do upon Infant Baptism. We do not say, Men cannot be saved, unless they be baptized.[51]

By stressing believer's baptism, Keach was also setting down what he considered to be one of the marks of the New Testament church, distinguishing believers in Christ from the world. He believed that those who practiced infant baptism were guilty of serious error, especially Anglicans like William Burkitt, who

---

51 Keach, *Gold Refin'd*, 160–161.

confounded the church and the world by trying to make the new covenant gospel church a national church. Keach insisted that the church "ought to be Congregational, a holy and separate people, like a *Garden inclosed*."[52] In Article xxii ("Of a true Church") in the Horselydown *Articles of the Faith*, the church is identified as those

> among whom the Word of God is duly and truly preach'd; and Holy Baptism, the Lord's Supper, and all other Ordinances are duly administered, according to the Word of God, and the Institution of Christ in the Primitive Church.[53]

Keach's congregation continued to practice the laying on of hands, which they regarded as an ordinance of Christ, and confined the observance of the Lord's Supper to baptized members of the church. Membership of a gathered church was restricted to those who gave evidence of their election by their faith, repentance and godly life. Outwardly, baptism served as an identifying mark of a professing believer. The normal pattern following a man or woman's profession of repentance and faith in the Lord Jesus Christ was baptism by immersion. This was followed by the laying on of hands, after which that person was admitted to the Lord's Supper. All baptized believers coming to the Lord's Supper would have covenanted together, not only to care for one another but also to live holy lives in keeping with their calling as the church of Christ, and to be present whenever the church was assembled for the worship of God.[54] There was, therefore, a very strong sense of belonging, with each baptized individual undertaking to fulfill their responsibilities as members of the corporate

52 Keach, *The Rector Rectified and Corrected*, 155.

53 Keach, *The Articles of the Faith*, Article XXII: Of a true Church, 22–23.

54 Keach, *The Articles of the Faith*, Article XXII: Of a true Church, 22–23.

body. Baptism was an integral element in church membership as practiced by the Particular Baptists. This was the view advocated not only by Keach but also by William Kiffin, who, in 1681, had published *A sober discourse of the right to church communion, wherein is proved by scripture that no unbaptized person may be regularly admitted to the Lord's Supper.*[55]

Keach's emphasis on baptism underlined the conviction held by Baptists that not only were the church and the state separate institutions, but also that they were continuing the work of the Reformation begun by Martin Luther and John Calvin nearly 200 years before. For Baptists, the Reformation was the beginning of the removal of anti-Christian darkness embedded in the Roman Catholic Church. As much as Keach and his fellow Particular Baptists appreciated the contribution of earlier Independents like William Ames, Henry Ainsworth and more latterly John Owen, because of their views on the gathered church, these men were still paedobaptists. Keach and his fellow Particular Baptists went further than dissenting Presbyterians and Independents, largely because of their distinctive view of the covenant with Abraham and the new covenant in Christ. Particular Baptists were persuaded that only the true spiritual seed of Abraham—those who had repented of their sins and believed on Christ—should be baptized and be members of the church. It was this that Keach was restating again and again in the controversies with paedobaptists. In doing so, he was repeating what earlier generations of Baptists in the Separatist tradition had been saying.

---

55 William Kiffin, *A sober discourse of the right to church communion, wherein is proved by scripture that no unbaptized person may be regularly admitted to the Lord's Supper* (London, 1681). Not all Baptists agreed with Keach and Kiffin and the churches that assembled in 1689 for the first National Assembly. John Bunyan, while he agreed with Keach on all the principal points of Calvinistic theology, disagreed over the importance of baptism. He believed in immersion but would not insist on it as a qualification for partaking of the Lord's Supper.

In the final decades of the seventeenth century, Baptists were still coming under attack from a number of different directions, some of the fire being particularly vicious. After 1689, it was still important for Baptists to establish, explain and defend their own identity, and Keach was not slow to take up the challenge with his pen. He was the kind of man who possessed a keen sense of duty to defend what he believed to be true. He had done so in the years prior to 1689 when he was being openly persecuted, and he continued to do so after 1689, when persecution continued but took less threatening forms. Therefore, whenever those who wrote in defence of infant baptism assailed the Baptists for their convictions, Keach invariably answered them.

This not only involved the theological arguments that have already been considered, but a rebuttal of some of the false accusations that were made against them. For example, William Burkitt of Milden had attempted to discredit John Tredwell of Lavenham and accused him of baptizing proselytes

> in a nasty horsepond, into which the filth of the adjacent stable occasionally flows...that they rather resembled creatures arising out of the bottomless pit, than candidates of *holy baptism*.[56]

By the time Keach had replied to Burkitt, a certificate was printed in *The Rector Rectified and Corrected*, signed by five Baptists and six non-Baptists, declaring that Burkitt had "very unjustly reproached the People called Anabaptists," and testified that his reports and assertions were "utterly and notoriously false."[57] Keach concluded his book with the following gracious rebuke to William Burkitt:

---

56 Crosby, *History*, 4:285.

57 Keach, "A Certificate under the Hands of several sober and impartial Persons," in *The Rector Rectified and Corrected*.

> And now, *Sir*, by this time I hope you will see more cause of blushing (than [Tredwell] hath) at your Attempt, and rash *Censuring and Condemning*, and in a bad manner *reproaching of Christ's Holy Ordinance*, and Sacred Institution, and his poor and Despised People, who wish you and all Men well, and did not, nor do intend any Evil against you, nor had troubled our selves with you, had you not begun with us. The Lord give you Repentance to the acknowledgment of the Truth, and grant more Love and Charity one to another: *for who art thou that judgest another Man's Servant.*[58]

On other occasions, both Gyles Shute and James Owen suggested that Baptists were guilty of indecency and immorality, supposing that people were baptized naked. This was not a new accusation. In previous years, Daniel Featley and Richard Baxter had made the same suggestions.[59] Keach protested to James Owen in an indignant tone:

> We provide comely Cloathes for the Administerer, both from Head to Foot; and our Men also that are baptized have Cloathes provided for them; and for the Women, Gowns and Petty-Coats are made on purpose, and they go into the water dressed more decently perhaps, than many Women came into Christian assemblies.[60]

His reply to Shute is in similar vein:

> We know [Baxter and Featley] as well as you, were too much guilty of backbiting, vilifying, and reproaching of

---

58 Keach, *The Rector Rectified and Corrected*, 212.

59 Keach, *A Counter-Antidote*, 7–8.

60 Keach, *Light broke forth in Wales*, 261.

> us; yet they had no ground in the least to cast this odium upon us; we challenge all Men of any person living to produce one instance that ever Man or Woman by any of our perswasion was Baptized naked.[61]

James Owen leveled one further accusation against Keach and others who shared his views, namely, that they were guilty of breaking the sixth commandment by endangering the lives of those they baptized. Keach gave this accusation a curt reply, dismissing it as "an abominable and false accusation."[62] Keach continued by testifying that he had baptized hundreds of men and women, at all times of the year, in times of bitter frost and snow, when the ice had to be broken first. He said he had baptized persons of weak and sickly constitution, heavily pregnant women, others seventy and sometimes eighty years old, and had never found anyone whose life had been endangered. He concluded by saying that in his own experience, going back some forty years, he had heard of many thousands being baptized at all seasons of the year, and he was certain that no one's health had been put at risk and that no one had lost their life as a result.[63] The reference that Keach makes to baptizing "hundreds" is one of the very few references that exists in his writings to the effectiveness of his ministry as a preacher of the gospel, first during his early years in Buckinghamshire and then subsequently in London. It was a mark of the man that he never referred directly to such things and only mentions the fact here in order to defend his own practice.

Despite his vigorous defence against the charges of immorality brought against the Baptists, it did not prevent David Russen from charging the elderly Benjamin Keach with immorality. In all his

61 Keach, *A Counter-Antidote*, 8.

62 Keach, *Light broke forth in Wales*, 257.

63 Keach, *Light broke forth in Wales*, 257.

dealings with others who defended the practice of infant baptism and who occasionally indulged in personal attacks, Keach appeared to be fair and avoided personal retaliation. Crosby may have been a little biased, because he too was a Baptist and Keach's son-in-law, but his final assessment of Keach's conduct in dealing with the defenders of infant baptism was that

> in his several answers...it appears that he had made himself master of this controversy, and kept close to the rules of disputation, and avoided all indecent expressions, and personal calumnies, and generally got the better of his antagonists.[64]

Keach in perspective

Benjamin Keach was a second-generation Particular Baptist[65] who, in the providence of God, lived for fifteen years after the Act of Toleration. He was an heir of the Separatist tradition and a man who vigorously maintained his views on baptism and the nature of the church after he and his fellow Dissenters had emerged from the furnace of persecution in 1689. It would be very easy to dismiss Keach as being a man who was argumentative, constantly fighting with antagonists. Spurgeon was surely right when he pointed out that men like Keach were fighting not only for their identity but also for their very existence. Spurgeon observed that in his own day:

> Baptists are received into the family of Christian denominations without needing to defend their existence... but in those days our brethren were despised and sneered at, and had to fight for existence.[66]

---

64 Crosby, *History*, 4:286–287.

65 Ed. note: meaning there had been Particular Baptists in England for a generation previous to his.

66 Spurgeon, *The Metropolitan Tabernacle: Its History and Work*, 26.

As Spurgeon went on to say:

> Mr. Keach had his hands full of disputes with [John] Flavel and men of less note, but he deplored rather than delighted in them, and often lamented the unchristian spirit of those who denied that the Baptist churches were churches at all, and otherwise opprobriously assailed brethren with whom they were agreed in all other matters.[67]

This reluctance to be involved in disputes over baptism is confirmed by Keach's own pen. Expressing his own desire to promote peace, and lamenting the dishonour brought to God's name by those who sometimes assailed him, he defended his response by saying,

> we have been provoked...to vindicate our selves, and therefore none who are unprejudiced can blame us. Should we suffer our selves to be loaded with Reproach and Infamy, and not endeavour (in a just way) to clear our selves and that Truth of Christ we are so well established in, from the certain Testimony of the sacred Scripture?[68]

Baptism was a very significant issue in the latter part of the seventeenth century, and Keach was a major player in the controversy. The idea of a gathered church comprised only of baptized believers was well established among Baptists, as Keach observed. It gained acceptance among others quite slowly, though strong prejudices against Baptists remained. In the eyes of some, it remained subversive, and the memory of

---

67 Spurgeon, *The Metropolitan Tabernacle: Its History and Work*, 27.
68 "Epistle to the Reader." In Keach, *The Rector Rectified and Corrected.*

sixteenth-century Anabaptist excesses still coloured attitudes toward Particular Baptists. However, after 1689, Particular Baptists became a permanent part of the ecclesiastical fabric of society, and it was Benjamin Keach who played a key role, particularly in the 1690s, in giving them biblical credibility and helping to establish and maintain their distinctive practice and identity without a sense of shame.

After Keach's death in 1704, his son-in-law, Benjamin Stinton, succeeded him as a pastor in the church in Horselydown. Stinton began to collect documents for the writing of the history of Baptists, but his premature death in 1718 prevented him from doing so.[69] That task eventually fell to another son-in-law of Keach, Thomas Crosby. Crosby was frustrated by Daniel Neal's "ill use" of the Baptist materials that had been given to him for inclusion in his *History of the Puritans*. A meagre five pages were devoted to "their [Baptists] rise and progress...their confession of faith, their character, and their sufferings...and that too with great partiality."[70] In order to do justice to the English Baptists, Crosby wrote four volumes, the first of which was a lengthy historical defence of Baptist practice and principles. That Crosby felt compelled to do so is further confirmation that Keach's own strenuous labours were necessary if Baptist principles and practice were to be maintained. It would be several more generations before Spurgeon could say that Baptists no longer needed to defend their existence.

---

69 Benjamin Stinton, *A Repository of Divers Historical Matters Relating to the English Antipaedobaptists, Collected from Original Papers of Faithful Extracts* (Angus Library, Oxford, 1712).

70 "The Preface." In Crosby, *History*, 1:ii

CHAPTER 13

"Law and Work-mongers"

I am afraid many good Christians are not sensible of the sad danger they are in. I cannot see but that the Doctrine some Men strive to promote, is little better that Popery in a new Dress. Nay one of the worst branches of it too, shall any who pretend to be true Preachers of the Gospel, go about to mix their own Works of their sincere Obedience with Christ's Righteousness; nay, to put their Obedience in the room and place of Christ's Obedience, as that in which they trust and desire to be found?[1]

During the last fifteen years of his life, Keach was "seemingly indefatigable," producing nearly thirty works covering a wide range of subjects.[2] Attention has already been drawn to the fact that Keach never appeared to avoid theological and practical issues if he became

1 Keach, *The Marrow of True Justification*, 17.

2 MacDonald, "London Calvinistic Baptists," 77.

persuaded that some truth of the Bible was at stake. The hymn singing controversy had involved him in controversy within his own denomination, the Particular Baptists, sadly creating divisions among them and causing great pain to Keach himself. The controversy over baptism affected a much wider audience and would have brought him much more into the public eye, in London particularly, but also in other parts of England and Wales. This controversy was not merely about who should be baptized and the mode to be used, but it had wider implications. Keach was questioning fundamental assumptions that Roman Catholics, Anglicans and paedobaptist Dissenters were making about who were to be regarded as members of the church.

A third controversy also thrust Keach into the public eye and, once again, brought him into conflict with the views of the renowned Puritan Richard Baxter, twenty-five years his senior. This controversy was focused on justification by faith and, in particular, on the nature of a believer's righteousness. It became known as the Neonomian (or "new law") controversy, and arose out of Baxter's teaching that obedience to a new law brought in by Christ—an obedience that took the form of saving faith and holy living—was the basis of one's personal saving righteousness. Although Baxter died in 1691, this controversy did not die with him.

Keach consistently opposed this Neonomian teaching as a fundamental error. Toward the end of a sermon based on Matthew 3:12, preached at some time in the 1690s to his regular London congregation in Horselydown, Southwark, Keach affectionately but plainly warned:

> And to you, sinners, if you would be found wheat in the day of Christ, then receive Christ's true doctrine, labour to distinguish between truth and error; beware of that strange and new scheme that darkens the free-grace of God, and tends to destroy the covenant of grace; remember to exalt Christ alone in your salvation. How do

> some turn the gospel of God's free grace into a law, by the performance of which, as the conditions of life and justification, tell thee, thy salvation doth depend. See what subtle opposers (of the clearest gospel) are risen up amongst us, and labour to avoid them; though their tongues should seem to be tipped with silver, yet their doctrine is copper.[3]

The preacher had in mind the views promoted first in the writings of Richard Baxter, and then subsequently by Daniel Williams (c.1643–1712) and Samuel Clarke (1626–1701). The issues he identified and the way he spoke, indicate the seriousness of the matter to Keach. He believed that the teachings of these men undermined the covenant of grace and turned the free grace of God into a law of human obedience, obscuring the righteousness of Christ imputed to the believing sinner. He was persuaded that this was no mere quirk in their theology. Therefore, the true biblical teaching on justification by faith must be expounded and their error must be exposed. It is not surprising that Keach referred to them as "Law and Work-mongers"[4] who "strive to mix the King's wine with their muddy water."[5] He believed that these men were adulterating the biblical gospel by their particular teaching.

Throughout the 1690s, the "Neonomian controversy" was a major issue for the London churches in particular. The immediate occasion that produced the controversy, appears to have been the reprinting of the sermons of Tobias Crisp (1600–1643), *Christ Alone Exalted*, in 1690.[6] Keach was not in complete agreement

3 Keach, "The Fan in His Hand," *Parables One*, 52.

4 Keach, *The Display of Glorious Grace* (London, 1698), 77.

5 Keach, "The Marriage Supper," *Parables Two*, 151.

6 Tobias Crisp's son, Samuel Crisp, republished *Christ Alone Exalted* in 1690. These sermons had first been printed in 1643 and provoked Richard Baxter and Samuel Rutherford (1600–1661) to oppose them as antinomian. When they were published

with Crisp, but said that he would rather "erre on their side, who strive to exalt wholly the Free Grace of God, than on theirs, who seek to darken it and magnifie the Power of the Creature."[7]

In 1690, when Crisp's sermons were reprinted, Richard Baxter was lecturer at Pinners' Hall. He died in 1691, but in his last days he described these sermons as antinomian, just as he had when they were first published in 1643. This sparked off a round of publications in the years after his death, and "Neonomian," "antinomian," "free-grace" and "Baxterian" became part of the theological jargon of the day. Keach played a large part in the controversy and was with others who upheld the "Old Doctrine of Justification...branded with the black Name of Antinomians."[8] The four principal works he produced that focused on this issue are: *The Marrow of True Justification* (1692); *The Everlasting Covenant, A Sweet Cordial for a drooping Soul* (1693); *The Display of Glorious Grace* (1698); and *A Medium Betwixt Two Extremes* (1698). He also made frequent references to the controversy in other published sermons, such as *A Golden Mine Opened*, and in his extended series of sermons on the parables that he began preaching as Sunday morning lectures in 1689 (published in 1701).[9]

Keach was a clear-minded thinker and preacher, and in *The Display of Glorious Grace*, a series of sermons on Isaiah 54:10, he explained the principal difference to his congregation in the following way:

> We say, that Justification of a Sinner, is the acceptance of his Person, or the pronouncing him Just and Righteous in God's sight, through the Imputation of the Righteousness

again in 1690, Baxter replied with *The Scripture Gospel Defended...against the Libertines* in 1690, followed by Daniel Williams's *Gospel-Truth Stated and Vindicated* in 1692. For more details of Crisp see *BDBR*, s.v. "Crisp, Tobias."

7 "Epistle to the Reader." In Keach, *The Marrow of True Justification*.

8 "Epistle to the Reader." In Keach, *The Marrow of True Justification*.

9 Keach, *Parables One* and *Parables Two*.

Daniel Williams (c. 1643–1716)

> of Christ, whereby he hath a full Right and Title to Eternal Life. They say, That Justification is nothing else but the pardon of sin, i.e. the not executing the Punishment of Sin due by the Law of Works, and an acceptance of a Man so long as he performeth the New Condition of Sincere Obedience.[10]

Those who muddied the waters

Keach's own understanding of justification was settled early on in his life. Writing in 1692, he said, "When I was a Lad, I was greatly taken with a Book called, *The flowing of Christ's Blood freely to Sinners, as Sinners.*"[11] This was the book, already referred to, by John Saltmarsh, *Free Grace: or the flowings of Christ's blood freely to sinners*, first published in 1645. It had been popular in the 1640s, and a sixth edition was published in 1649. As with the work of Tobias Crisp, it was published again in 1700 as part of the Neonomian controversy.[12]

This was significant because Richard Baxter had long regarded John Saltmarsh as being an Antinomian, together with both Paul Hobson and John Bunyan.[13] Saltmarsh had been an army chaplain in Cromwell's army and when, in 1645, Baxter became an army chaplain, to his horror, he discovered a prevailing spiritual laxity, typified, he believed, by writings like those of Saltmarsh. The blame for this laxity he laid at the door of the Antinomians—those who taught free grace, a once-for-all justification on the grounds of a divine righteousness imputed to them. He was convinced that this view was responsible for the laxity that he had discovered, because it undermined the need for personal holiness. Baxter began to rethink his position, and

---

10 Keach, *Display of Glorious Grace*, 83.

11 Keach, *The Marrow of True Justification*, 8. Keach's "endorsement" of Saltmarsh may be similar to his "endorsement" of Crisp.

12 A tenth edition, published in 1700.

13 Richard Baxter, *The Scripture Gospel Defended* (London, 1692), preface.

Samuel Clarke (1626–1701) was an annotator of the Bible and a pastor in Wycombe, Buckinghamshire. Keach opposed Clarke's "new law" teaching.

by 1649 he had reached his conclusions. He rejected the doctrine of justification in the recently published *Westminster Confession of Faith*, and held firmly to his own convictions until his death in 1691.[14] Baxter's views have been summarized in the following way:

> Baxter's gospel presents Christ's death as an act of universal redemption, penal and vicarious though not strictly substitutionary, in virtue of which God has made a new law offering amnesty to penitent breakers of the old law. As obedience to the new law, repentance and faith are one's personal saving righteousness, which effectual calling induces and preserving grace sustains. Called "Neonomianism," this scheme is substantially Amyraldian, with Arminian "new law" teaching added.[15]

It was these views, first promoted by Baxter, that were adopted by Daniel Williams and Samuel Clarke. Williams was a Welshman and a Presbyterian who came to London in 1687, after twenty years in Dublin. In London, he became very friendly

---

14 Iain Murray, "Richard Baxter—The Reluctant Puritan?" In *Advancing in Adversity*, Westminster Conference Papers, 1991, 1–24. Murray states that Baxter consciously rejected the *Westminster Confession*'s teaching on justification (*viz.* that God justifies sinners by imputing to them the righteousness of Christ) and that he regarded the consequences of teaching this as pernicious. He also states that Baxter wrote hundreds of pages on this subject, from his first book in 1649 until his last in 1691, so there can be no mistaking his meaning (see pages 8–9).

15 J.I. Packer, "Baxter, Richard." In *New Dictionary of Theology*, ed. Sinclair B. Ferguson and David E. Wright (InterVarsity Press: Leicester, 1988), 82–83. For a fuller explanation of the background to Baxter's view, see J.I. Packer, *A Quest for Godliness: The Puritan Vision of the Christian Life* (Crossway: Wheaton, 1990), 156–160; Hans Boersema, *A Hot Peppercorn: Richard Baxter's Doctrine of Justification in its Seventeenth-Century Context of Controversy* (Zoetermeer: Boekencentrum, 1993); Thomas Eugene Hicks, Jr., "An analysis of the doctrine of justification in the theologies of Richard Baxter and Benjamin Keach" (Ph.D. dissertation, The Southern Baptist Theological Seminary, 2009).

with Baxter and preached for him when the old man was indisposed. On his death, he succeeded Baxter as lecturer at Pinners' Hall and pastored a church in New Broad Street, Petty France. He was already preaching against "Antinomian errors" before he began to write. He wrote four books from 1692 to 1699: *Gospel-Truth Stated and Vindicated* (1692); *A Defence of Gospel Truth* (1693); *Man Made Righteous by Christ's Obedience* (1694); and, finally, *An End to Discord* (1699).

Samuel Clarke was an annotator of the Bible and a pastor in Wycombe in Buckinghamshire. He had been responsible, together with Edward Veale, for amending the fourth edition of Matthew Poole's commentary. In 1698, he published his views in *Scripture Justification*. Keach was very quick to pick up his pen and provide a critical review of Clarke's contribution, publishing it twice in 1698, first in *A Medium Betwixt Two Extremes*, and then again in *Christ Alone the Way to Heaven*.

Keach preferred to use the term "Baxterian" to describe the views not only of Baxter but also Williams and Clarke. His colourful phrase for them as "Law and Work-mongers" shows his distaste for their teaching, which represented a serious departure from the biblical view of justification that had been rediscovered by Martin Luther in the sixteenth century and fully expressed in the three major seventeenth-century confessions of faith of the English Puritans.[16]

Keach's critique of Baxterianism

Keach had been alert to the error in Baxter's teaching several years before the controversy erupted with the republication of Crisp's sermons, but he did not begin to write extensively against

---

16 In each of *The Westminster Confession of Faith* of the Presbyterians (1646), *The Savoy Declaration* of the Independents (1658) and *The Second London Baptist Confession of Faith* of the Particular Baptists (1689), chapter 11 provides the orthodox statement of the doctrine of justification by faith.

Baxter's teaching until the early 1690s. In the 1700 edition of his best-selling allegory, *The Travels of True Godliness*, first published in 1683, Keach made a significant addition. In a letter to his readers, he told them he was now taking into account particular errors current in his day, especially Baxterian and Antinomian errors. Keach wished to keep up to date and instill a discerning spirit into his readers by portraying different kinds of false—but often attractive—"alternatives" to biblical godliness.[17] Thus, in his journey, Keach's young traveller met a man of "strange countenance," a "Baxterian."[18] On being questioned by Godliness, the Baxterian explained what he meant by evangelical righteousness:

> Faith and sincere obedience to the gospel, by which, through Christ's merits, I expect to be justified, so far as I am enabled to walk up to the rule of the promise, God having received a full recompense by his Son's obedience, fore the breach of the severe law of perfect obedience; he has removed that law, and our dear Saviour has merited a mild law of faith and sincere obedience; and now if we obey this new law, and sincerely serve the Lord, we shall be justified in his sight, and eternally be saved.[19]

Refuting this teaching, Keach pointed out that such teaching established human righteousness as the basis of justification rather than the perfect righteousness of the perfectly obedient Christ. Keach argued that what the Scriptures called true righteousness was the righteousness of God, because Christ is God, thus reinforcing the fact that the righteousness by which sinners are justified is not a human righteousness. He further asserted

---

17 For the identification of this important change made by Keach in the 1700 edition of *The Travels of True Godliness*, I am indebted to Jonathan W. Arnold (Arnold, *The Reformed Theology of Benjamin Keach*, 166).

18 Keach, *The Travels of True Godliness* (London, 1817), 103.

19 Keach, *The Travels of True Godliness*, 104.

that only this righteousness of God answers the rectitude of God's holy nature and holy law. Finally, he affirmed that the Scriptures taught that God had graciously provided this righteousness and would not accept a mere human righteousness in order to justify the sinner. Keach had made an accurate assessment of Baxter's teaching. He had already familiarized himself with Baxter's views and the consequences of his reasoning, and exposed what he was persuaded were the fundamental errors in Baxter's teaching. Thus, Keach was already well equipped to deal with the Neonomian controversy and weave it into *The Travels of True Godliness*.

Once Crisp's *Christ Alone Exalted* had been republished in 1690, and Baxter and Williams had begun to make their replies, Keach began to preach and write extensively against their teaching. He used much stronger language to describe the teaching than he used in the controversies over baptism and hymn singing. He came to regard Baxterianism as a "partial apostacy,"[20] a "poisonous notion,"[21] "a bold and bare-faced attack against this grand fundamental of Christianity"[22] and that preachers of such views were not "true Gospel-Ministers."[23] This was because he was persuaded that a mistake in the doctrine of justification was a fundamental and subversive error, striking at the heart of the biblical gospel and the free grace of God in salvation. In Keach's view, Baxter and Williams were essentially Arminian in their theology, attributing too much power to human ability. Once Baxter had attacked Crisp as antinomian in his Pinners' Hall lectures and published *The Scripture Gospel Defended* in 1691, Keach was persuaded that it was now necessary to expose the errors he recognized in Baxter and in Williams. Entering the dispute in 1692, Keach explained in the epistle dedicatory of

20 Keach, "The Sower," *Parables One*, 145.

21 Keach, "Every Valley Shall be Filled," *Parables One*, 11.

22 Keach, *A Medium Betwixt Two Extremes* (London, 1698), 32.

23 Keach, *A Medium Betwixt Two Extremes*, 34.

The Marrow of Justification why he felt compelled to preach and write as he did:

> that all may see that we are in this, and in all other great Fundamentals of Religion, established in the same Faith with our Brethren, and all Sound and Orthodox Christians in the World: and cannot but look upon ourselves greatly concerned, to see how Men by Craft and Subtilty endeavour, through Satan's Temptations (though I hope some do it not wittingly) strive to subvert the Gospel of Christ, and corrupt the Minds of weak Christians. An Error at a Fundamental point, is dangerous and destructive, but should we mistake some Men we have to do with, we should be glad: The Lord help you to stand fast in the Truth, as it is in Jesus (in which through Grace you are well established:) Our Days are perilous; Satan seems to be let loose upon us, and is in great rage, his time being but short.[24]

Keach was reluctant to enter into this controversy, longing for truth, peace and unity to prevail among Christians.[25] He seems to have no doubt that Baxter was a sincere man, but he was also convinced that he was very mistaken in his doctrine of justification. He also felt keenly the division that this controversy was already causing among London's dissenting churches in particular.

The Marrow of True Justification contained two sermons on Romans 4:5, "But to him who does not work but believes on Him who justifies the ungodly, his faith is counted for righteousness," in which Keach expounded key aspects of the orthodox doctrine of justification, arguing that all good works done by a sinner are

---

24 "Epistle Dedicatory." In Keach, *The Marrow of True Justification.*

25 "Epistle Dedicatory." In Keach, *The Marrow of True Justification.*

totally excluded in the justification of a sinner in the sight of God. Justification is wholly due to the free grace of God through the imputation of the perfect righteousness of Jesus Christ by faith. In the process, he briefly exposed other errors, like those of Roman Catholicism and Socinianism, before turning his attention more fully to Baxter and Williams. Keach identified several key points where Baxterianism was found wanting.

With regard to the death of Christ, Keach maintained that Baxterians did not properly represent Christ as the Head, Representative and Surety who died as a substitute in place of his elect. Rather, they said that by his death Christ acted as a mediator and abolished the law that required perfect obedience, providing God with a satisfying recompense. In *The Display of Glorious Grace*, Keach explained more fully:

> In the Covenant of Redemption, say they, Christ made God amends for our breach of the Law of perfect obedience, by himself alone, and for himself only, that he might be a fit Mediator, and Merit a new Law of faith and sincere Obedience; (for their Covenant of Grace is a Law of Obedience) which Law or Covenant he Confirmed by his Death.[26]

Thus, Keach identified what he thought was the root of this error in the new law teaching. It taught that there were two distinct covenants, the covenant of redemption and the covenant of grace. Keach, however, regarded these as different parts of one covenant.

The crux of Keach's objection to Baxter and Williams was their insistence that a *subjective* righteousness—an individual's own faith, sincere obedience and personal holiness—provided the righteousness that justifies the sinner in God's sight. Christ, they claimed, had merited this "new law" in the covenant of

---

26 Keach, *The Display of Glorious Grace*, 212–213.

grace. Keach constantly resisted this subjective righteousness as a basis for justification, saying,

> we do not tell you, you must be holy and then believe in Jesus Christ; but you must believe in him, that you may be holy. You must first have Union with him, before you can bring forth fruit to God; you must act from Life, and not for Life.[27]

According to Keach, Baxterianism conceded too much to the Arminian doctrine of sin and, in contrast, he stressed that no one had the ability to remove the enmity in their hearts against God. Keach was convinced that the Bible taught that all the faculties of the soul, including the will, were fallen, and that

> till a Man comes to see his own wretched and woful condition, and understands the Nature of God, and the Nature and Tenure of the Holy Law of God, he cannot discern that absolute necessity there is of a perfect and compleat righteousness to Justifie him in God's sight.[28]

By making sincere obedience the basis of justification, Keach believed that Baxter and Williams became legal preachers ("law mongers") and not preachers of God's free grace. Williams, in particular, comes in for heavy criticism for holding forth "the Gospel to be a Law, or Command of Duty, as a Condition with the Sanction of *Threats* upon Non-performance, and *Promises of Rewards* upon Perfomance of *sincere Obedience*."[29] This insistence on sincere obedience, says Keach, is nothing less than salvation by works, or "little more than Popery in a new dress."[30]

27 Keach, *The Marrow of True Justification*, 37.
28 Keach, *The Marrow of True Justification*, 3–4.
29 Keach, *The Marrow of True Justification*, 36.
30 Keach, *The Marrow of True Justification*, 17.

Keach also insisted that making faith, sincere obedience, and personal holiness the righteousness that justifies not only rebuilds salvation by works but also does away with the need for the perfect righteousness of Christ, in both his active and passive obedience. According to Baxterianism, nothing of Christ's righteousness was imputed to those who believe on Christ. Those who believed did not need it, for they were justified by their own righteousness. In this way, Baxter and Williams denied that the righteousness of Christ was the only basis for the justification of the sinner and undermined the grace of God at the heart of the gospel.[31] In contrast to this, Keach asserted that Christ was the appointed Head, Representative and Surety of his people and that he made full compensation to God's justice by his death on behalf of his elect. Christ's active and passive obedience are the grounds of the sinner's righteousness and are imputed to the sinner by faith. As Keach said:

> Nothing renders a Man righteous to Justification in God's Sight, but the Imputation of the perfect, Personal Righteousness of Christ, received only by the faith of the Operations of God.[32]

Furthermore, according to Keach, the Scriptures taught that faith is "the hand to take hold of, receive, and apply Christ and his righteousness."[33] Strictly speaking, it was not faith that justified the ungodly. Faith was only the instrument that laid hold of

---

31 Jonathan Arnold has pointed out that this statement is an oversimplification and that I and others have unintentionally misrepresented Baxter. Such misunderstanding is largely due to Baxter's ability to give different (or nuanced) meanings to commonly used terms. Baxterians, Arnold suggests, did believe that Christ's passive obedience could be imputed to the believer. Furthermore, he says that Baxter changed his mind later in his life and allowed for some kind of imputation of the active obedience of Christ. For a discussion of these issues, see Arnold, *The Reformed Theology of Benjamin Keach*, 172.

32 Keach, *The Marrow of True Justification*, 8.

33 Keach, *The Marrow of True Justification*, 6.

Christ and his righteousness. Therefore, it was Christ who justified the sinner. In contrast, Baxter said that justifying faith was essentially a belief that God accepted the holiness of the individual and their sincere obedience to the gospel.

Finally, Keach was also critical of Baxterianism because he said, this "new Doctrine is but a piece of old Judaism," bringing a person back under the condemnation of the law: "let our obedience be never so sincere, if it is not perfect, we are still Debtors to the Law and are accursed by it, unless we believe in Jesus Christ."[34] Such teaching undermined the comfort and assurance of the person who had put their faith in Christ and his perfect righteousness. By placing confidence for acceptance with God in an imperfect yet sincere obedience, an individual could lose their justification, something quite unthinkable for Keach:

> If our Faith and Obedience be interrupted or utterly lost, Justification is interrupted and utterly lost likewise…'tis impossible, if we are Justified and accepted as just Persons, and graciously acquitted by the Righteousness of Christ, there should be the least stain, imperfection, or spot, in our Justification.[35]

In 1698, six years after he published *The Marrow of True Justification*, Keach published *A Medium Betwixt Two Extremes*. It was an exposition of Romans 8:1 but contained an important addition, "A Postscript, containing a few Reflections upon some passages in Mr (Samuel) Clarke's new book, intituled *Scripture Justification*." Clarke had adopted the views of Baxter and Williams, and there is little new in Keach's criticism of "new law" teaching. Clarke, too, rejects the righteousness of Christ, "The righteousness he contends for is not the Righteousness of one, but the

34 Keach, *The Marrow of True Justification*, 22.

35 Keach, *The Marrow of True Justification*, 12.

Righteousness of many, i.e. every Man's own Faith and sincere Obedience, contrary to what Paul affirms, Rom. 5:17,18,19."[36] Keach accused him of diluting the moral law of God:

> This Man contends for a mild Law; certainly the Moral Law remains a perpetual Rule of perfect Obedience: let this Man shew us where and how he can prove that God in the Gospel only commands sincere imperfect Obedience to the Moral Law: the Law surely loses no part of its sanction by the Gospel; that it as holy, just and good as ever.[37]

In dealing with the consequences of this "new law" teaching of Samuel Clarke, Keach underlined what he had said about Baxter and Williams. Their doctrine left the individual still under condemnation, imperfectly justified and with no assurance possible in this life. Keach added, "besides it confounds Justification with Sanctification, nay it makes them but one and the same thing: Nay more, that by a Law Righteousness is to be obtained, and so Christ is dead in vain."[38]

Here, Keach identifies two further implications of new law teaching, touching on crucial areas of New Testament teaching. The first concerned the confusion of justification and sanctification, which was yet another feature of Roman Catholic doctrine. Keach had already pointed out to his congregation the necessity to distinguish between these "two garments":

> But, pray brethren, see, I beseech you, to take care rightly to distinguish between the garment of justification, and that of sanctification; many confound these two together,

36 Keach, *A Medium Betwixt Two Extremes*, 41.

37 Keach, *A Medium Betwixt Two Extremes*, 60.

38 Keach, *A Medium Betwixt Two Extremes*, 38.

> and strive to mix our inherent righteousness in our justification, with the righteousness of Christ: this was the error that Mr Baxter led the people into (though I hope he was a good man, God might open his eyes before he died). It is, sirs, a dangerous thing to adhere to such a notion; this is to make our justification to be partly by works, and partly by grace. I tell you once again, all works of righteousness, either done by us, or wrought in us, are utterly excluded in our free justification. O! how do I long to see you all well established in this great fundamental truth of the gospel![39]

The second area of concern for Keach was a key point in the controversy over justification, and is found in the final phrase, "and so Christ is dead in vain." As has been evident throughout his life, Keach aimed to be biblical in both his principles and his reasoning. His argument, in this instance, was the same in principle as that in Galatians 2:21: "for if righteousness comes through the law, then Christ died in vain." If a new milder law of God was now in place, that meant personal human righteousness could secure justification, then Christ had died for no real purpose, and the imputed righteousness of Jesus Christ—his life of perfect obedience and his death in the place of sinners—was thereby nullified.

The teaching of the "new law" men left Keach lamenting the state of affairs in the church. Yet he refused to be downcast because he believed that the truth was God's truth, and that it would triumph in the end.

> Ah poor England, poor church of God, where are thy brave old Heroes, that stood up to maintain the Truths of Christ? What Apostasy is here from the Orthodox

39 Keach, "The Marriage Supper," *Parables Two*, 156.

> Faith? What decay of doctrinal and practical Christianity? What dark clouds spread over our heavens? How many are fallen from the faith? But I must leave Mr Clarke to an abler pen.... Now that the Lord would scatter this Cloud, and all other dangerous Errors, let it be all our Prayers both Day and Night. Yet I doubt not but the present opposition against this Fundamental Point of Faith will cause the Truth in the end to shine more clear and bright, which the Lord grant in his Infinite Mercy, to the praise of his own Glory. Amen.[40]

Keach was not a lone voice in exposing the errors of Baxterianism. One of the other important voices was that of the Independent, Isaac Chauncy, pastor of the church that met in Mark Lane, predecessor to Isaac Watts.[41] Another was John Flavel who wrote *The Occasions, Causes, Nature, Rise, Growth and Remedies of Mental Errors*, in which he chiefly considered the writings of Tobias Crisp and dealt with some twenty causes of error against the background of this controversy.[42] Thomas Goodwin (the younger) also produced a volume in 1695 to defend the biblical doctrine of justification, called *A Discourse of the True Nature of the Gospel*.[43] Perhaps the most judicious contribution came from the pen of the Scottish Presbyterian, Robert Traill (1642–1716). It is called *A Vindication of the Protestant Doctrine of Justification from the Unjust Charge of Antinomians*, and

40 Keach, *A Medium Betwixt Two Extremes*, 52.

41 Isaac Chauncy wrote several anti-Neonomian books and tracts including, *Neonomianism Unmasked: or the Ancient Gospel Pleaded Against the Other Called a New Law* (London, 1692); *The Doctrine Which is According to Godliness* (London, 1694); *Alexipharmacon, or a Fresh Antidote against Neonomian Bane, and Poison to Protestant Religion* (London, 1700).

42 John Flavel, *The Occasions, Causes, Nature, Rise, Growth and Remedies of Mental Errors*. In *The Works of John Flavel*, 6 vols. (London: Banner of Truth Trust, 1968), 3:413–492.

43 To be distinguished from the elder Thomas Goodwin (1600–1680).

had originated as a letter from London sent to a friend in September 1692. Traill also published six sermons on Galatians 2:21 dealing with these issues.[44]

The significant contribution of Benjamin Keach in this controversy has often gone unmentioned. Keach appears to have been one of the few Particular Baptists to take up the issues at stake in this controversy.[45] He reveals himself as an astute judge of theological trends, having identified "Baxterianism" in the early years of the 1680s, several years before the Neonomian controversy broke out in London in the 1690s. One of Keach's principal concerns was the protection of his congregation in Horselydown from the poisonous effects of this false teaching. In the case of *The Marrow of True Justification*, others apparently prevailed on him first to preach these sermons and then to publish them.[46] *The Display of Glorious Grace* began as a series of fourteen sermons preached to his congregation, in which his aim was to open up the biblical doctrine of the covenant of grace and deal with the errors of Baxterianism where it was relevant to his congregation. His sermon on Romans 8:1, *A Medium Betwixt Two Extremes*, was preached to answer a specific question asked by one of his members and provided him with the opportunity of publishing his own assessment of Samuel Clarke's recently released *Scripture Justification*.

Benjamin Keach, together with some of his dissenting contemporaries, was jealous to defend the biblical doctrine of

---

44 Robert Traill, *A Vindication of the Protestant Doctrine of Justification from the Unjust Charge of Antinomians*. In *The Works of Robert Traill*, 4 vols. (Edinburgh: Banner of Truth Trust, 1975), 1:252–296; *Righteousness in Christ* in *The Works of Robert Traill*, 4:156–234.

45 Arnold's 2013 study of Keach corrected my original assertion that Keach was the *only* Particular Baptist to take up this issue. In the first edition, I omitted to mention the contribution made by Thomas Edwards, also a Particular Baptist, to the Neonomian controversy. Edwards wrote *A plain and impartial enquiry* (1693), *A short review* (1693) and *The parasalene dismantled* (1699). See Arnold, *The Reformed Theology of Benjamin Keach*, 169.

46 "Epistle Dedicatory." In Keach, *The Marrow of True Justification*.

justification—that is what led him to write as he did. In this regard, he was a faithful watchman crying from Sion's walls; above all, he wanted to defend the truth of the gospel and maintain the honour of God's name.

The significance of justification and Keach's preaching

Attention has already been drawn to the fact that Keach was involved in a number of theological controversies in the 1690s, including congregational hymn singing, baptism and justification. Two other controversies were to follow. The first concerned Mr. Zachary Housel and Mr. Coward who denied the existence of heaven and the immortality of the soul, provoking Keach to write against them and set out the biblical teaching shortly before his death in 1702.[47]

The second controversy arose in 1699 and concerned which day should be kept as the Christian Sabbath. For Keach, this was potentially more serious, because it was personal and also threatened yet another division in his own congregation. Joseph Stennett, a close friend of Keach and who he asked to take his funeral, belonged to a small group of Particular Baptist churches, known as Seventh-Day Baptists. They were convinced that Saturday was still to be observed as the Sabbath day of rest, rather than Sunday. Keach's youngest daughter by his first marriage, Hannah Green, had joined Stennett's church in 1696 (only to be removed the following year because she had adopted Quakerism); ten others followed her in 1699.[48] A crisis similar to that provoked by the hymn-singing controversy was avoided when Keach preached on the matter and then published *The Jewish*

47 Keach, *The French and English impostours detected: Or, Zach. Housel and D. Coward tried by the word of God, and cast. Wherein also the errors...[the latter] are laid open; shewing what cause he had to think again. And the immortality of the soul fully convinced, in the form of a tryal* (London, 1702).

48 The reference to Hannah Green's orderly recommendation from Horselydown is found in the *Bampfield Church Book, 1686–1843*, under the entry for March 14, 1696.

Sabbath Abrogated, in 1700.[49] Keach believed that the seventh-day Sabbath was erroneous, because it tended to re-establish the covenant of works and justification by the law, and because it promoted schism in the church. He was persuaded that the Lord's Day was the day of Christ's resurrection, the first day of the week, and it replaced the seventh day that represented the old covenant.

> The Lord made and created the Seventh-day, and afterwards made it the Sabbath to answer the end and design of the Old Creation and the Old Covenant. So the Lord created the first day; and when the new Creation was brought in, he made it for a day of sacred Rest, and for his solemn Worship, answering the end and design of the new Creation.[50]

On the other hand, Keach believed that many Seventh-Day Sabbatarians were "very good and pious Christians."[51] This would have undoubtedly included Joseph Stennett, who, despite finding his convictions attacked in the book, bore Keach no grudge, and was very quick to rise to Keach's defence when David Russen accused him of immorality. Keach added that it was a harmless error in many cases, because some kept both the seventh and the first day out of conscience before God; and, furthermore, it enabled men like Stennett to preach in other churches on the Lord's Day![52]

---

49 Keach, *The Jewish Sabbath Abrogated: or, The Saturday Sabbatarians confuted* (London, 1700). In this fairly substantial book, Keach set out to prove that the seventh-day Sabbath had been abrogated and that the Lord's Day was a divine appointment. His argument was substantially that of John Owen in his treatment of the Sabbath rest of Hebrews 4:9, except Keach did not believe that the Sabbath was a creation ordinance and that Adam and the patriarchs observed that day. Rather, he thought that it began under Moses.

50 Keach, *The Jewish Sabbath Abrogated*, 213.

51 Keach, *The Jewish Sabbath Abrogated*, 170.

52 Keach, *The Jewish Sabbath Abrogated*, 172–173.

In assessing each of the controversies, it is clear that the one relating to justification by faith is by far the most important, because as Keach himself recognized, it had to do with the fundamentals of the faith. Benjamin Keach contended earnestly for the biblical doctrine of justification by faith as the sixteenth-century Reformers had recovered it, and as it had been expressed in the seventeenth-century confessions of faith. Keach had signed *The Second London Baptist Confession of Faith* just prior to the outbreak of the Neonomian controversy. He regarded Martin Luther and John Owen as two of the greatest lights in the church in the past 200 years. The principal reason for this was their solid grasp of the importance of justification by faith alone.

The threat of the Roman Catholic Church was something Keach had felt throughout his life as a dissenting preacher of the gospel. Before 1689, the threat was expressed largely by persecution, something Keach frequently pointed out in his books, particularly in his poetry. After 1689, the threat came from a different direction: from false doctrine that struck at the very heart of what Keach believed was the biblical gospel. On more than one occasion, Keach pointed out that "new law" doctrine, making faith and sincere obedience our justifying righteousness, was "much like Bellarmine," that is, Robert Bellarmine (1542–1621) who was the leading proponent of Roman Catholic theology against Protestantism after the Council of Trent.[53]

Keach did not live long enough to see the full effects of the "new law" teaching of Baxter, Williams and Clarke, but there is no doubt that he and others were right to oppose it. Keach was happy to clearly identify himself with orthodox, biblical Christianity, subscribing to *The Second London Baptist Confession*

53 Keach, *A Medium Betwixt Two Extremes*, 38. Robert Bellarmine was a Jesuit theologian who devoted himself to answering Protestantism. His greatest work was a three-volume *Disputations on Controversies about the Christian Faith against the Heretics of this Time* (1586–1593). It was regarded as one of the best expositions of Roman Catholic dogma expressed by the Council of Trent.

of Faith—something Baxter would never have done—and subsequently drawing up *The Articles of the Faith* for his church at Horselydown. It is significant to note that Baxter was "averse to almost all creeds." While Baxter had a high personal regard for the Westminster divines, he thought that to impose their views on others was dangerous, divisive and destructive.[54] The tragedy of Baxter was that in reacting to some of the excesses and abuses of the doctrines of grace he first observed in the New Model Army in the 1640s, he veered in the opposite direction and ended up opposing the biblical gospel—injuring the cause of truth and unity that was closest to his heart. There is no doubt that the views of Baxter, and those whom he influenced, contributed to a weakening of doctrinal convictions among Presbyterians. The reaction against Calvinism was largely begun and led by Baxter, and continued by Williams and Clark into successive generations. The astute observation has been made that

> by denouncing what he regarded as the irrationality of Antinomianism, Baxter had modified Calvinism in a way which opened him to the charge of Arminianism, and among the next generation of Presbyterian ministers were those who insisted on free will as well as free grace to an extent that made nonsense of the Calvinist scheme.[55]

Iain Murray has also observed that Baxter's notions of justification against imputed righteousness were, in part, republished by John Wesley (1703–1791) and had a considerable influence on Methodism on both sides of the Atlantic.[56] Among critiques of Baxter, that of J.I. Packer is devastating. He concludes that

---

54 Murray, "Richard Baxter—The Reluctant Puritan?" In *Advancing in Adversity*, 9.

55 Watts, *The Dissenters*, 376–377. Watts is quoting Roger Thomas, "The Break-up of Nonconformity" in Geoffrey Nuttall, et al, *The Beginnings of Nonconformity* (London: J. Clarke, 1964), 49–50.

56 Murray, "Richard Baxter—The Reluctant Puritan?" In *Advancing in Adversity*, 19.

Baxter's views led not only to a decline in the doctrine of justification but eventually to the loss of biblical Christianity. Baxter

> actually sowed the seeds of moralism with regard to sin, Arianism with regard to Christ, legalism with regard to faith and salvation, and liberalism with regards to God.[57]

The damage done to successive generations is sufficient evidence to conclude that men like Keach were absolutely right in opposing the teachings of Baxter. Keach was persuaded of the divine authority of the Word of God and held an orthodox and biblical doctrine of justification by faith. He was determined to root the faith of his congregation, not in the vagaries of human opinion, but in the truth of the Bible. A careful study of Keach's sermons on justification confirms that this was both a principle and a practice for him.

If we examine Keach's own preaching, we find that he maintains all the strands of the biblical teaching. This is clear from his *Marrow* sermons on Romans 4:5, and from many statements throughout his sermons from the 1690s onward. One of the fullest statements he made about justification is found in a sermon on the scribe, from Matthew 13:52, preached on November 4, 1693. It is typical of Keach that he should bring justification and preaching together, effectively expounding what he had come to regard, for the last thirty years or so, as his life's work. He maintained that scribes should be rich in spiritual things, of

> the necessity and excellency of Christ, in his person and offices, and to understand the purpose and nature of his incarnation, birth, life, death, resurrection, ascension and intercession. They should understand or have a true and saving knowledge of the doctrine of justification by

57 Packer, *A Quest for Godliness*, 160.

Jesus Christ; the grace of God being the original and efficient cause or spirit of it; the death of Jesus Christ being the meritorious cause, and the righteousness of Christ, in his perfect active obedience and suffering, the meritorial cause thereof; not that his merits and righteousness purchased or procured such favour and grace, that our inherent righteousness, and sincere faith and obedience, should with his merits, justify us; but that all our own righteousness, faith and obedience is utterly excluded in point of justification before God, or at the bar of his justice; and that it is Christ's obedience to the preceptory and penal part of the law, which is the matter or material cause of our justification only: for "as by one man's disobedience many were made sinners: so by the obedience of one shall many be made righteous," Rom. 5:19. Christ's active obedience or righteousness being our only title to heaven, and his bearing the pangs of hell for us, and in our stead, that only which delivers us from hell and eternal wrath; also that imputation of the righteousness is the formal cause of our justification; and the glory of God, in all his holy attributes, and our eternal happiness the final cause thereof.

They ought to know, that every man by nature is alike miserable, even the elect themselves, being all dead in sin, and are by nature the children of wrath as well as others, Eph. 2:3. They being not actually justified, but contrariwise condemned, until they do believe in Christ, or are transplanted by the Spirit of God out of the first Adam into the second Adam: though all that shall be saved were decretively justified from everlasting and virtually when Christ rose again from the dead, yet they were no more actually justified from eternity, than they were actually glorified from eternity, which was only decretively, or according to God's decree and purpose;

> nor no more actually justified when Christ rose from the dead, than they actually ascended unto heaven, when Jesus Christ, as our head, representative, and forerunner, ascended to heaven.[58]

Keach's understanding of justification by faith has all the hallmarks of biblical orthodoxy and can be briefly summarized in the following way:

> (1) *The need for justification:* this he believed was the consequence of human sinfulness. He believed that in God's eyes all have sinned in Adam, are therefore sinners by nature and by practice, and are therefore liable to God's holy wrath and condemnation in hell because they are all guilty of breaking God's holy law.
> (2) *The nature of justification*: justification is God's judicial act, pardoning guilty sinners and declaring them righteous in his sight. He denied that God regarded sinners as actually justified from eternity. They remained in a state of condemnation until the moment they believed in Jesus Christ.
> (3) *The source of justification*: solely, the free grace of God is the original and efficient cause of it, and in no way by human effort or initiative.
> (4) *The grounds of justification*: Christ's vicarious righteousness and his substitutionary death on the cross. Keach was particularly keen to stress the imputation of both the active and the passive obedience of Christ as the grounds of our justification, as Romans 5:19 taught, and that Christ died for the elect.
> (5) *The means of justification*: by faith in Jesus Christ alone.
> (6) *The fruits of justification*: holiness of life is inseparable from justification. There must be an evident repentance

58 Keach, "The Scribe," *Parables One*, 267–268.

and a changed life of obedience to God, together with good works.
(7) *The final end of justification*: the glory of God and the eternal blessedness of those whose title to heaven is the imputed righteousness of Christ.

It was not merely Keach's orthodox beliefs that moulded Keach into a preacher of justification by faith. Keach felt far more sympathy for Tobias Crisp than for Richard Baxter, because Crisp exalted the free grace of God, even though he did not agree with him in every respect. It was the fullness, freeness and suitableness of the grace of God in Jesus Christ that Keach loved to preach. Above all, it was Christ in his glory and excellence who he proclaimed in order to draw sinners to him and to transform their hearts by filling them with wonder, praise and thankfulness to God. This was in strong contrast to Richard Baxter who seemed to lack this kind of emphasis.[59] Keach put it simply:

> Christ is the Way; it is by his Righteousness alone, we are justified in the sight of God, his perfect Obedience to the Law, is our Title to eternal Life, and by his death (who bore hell pangs for us) we are delivered from Everlasting Wrath and Condemnation.[60]

In another sermon on the marriage supper, from Matthew 22:4, he spoke with considerable feeling of Christ's willingness and sufficiency to save:

> Jesus Christ stands ready waiting, having all his glorious wedding robes on, being every way decked as a bridegroom

---

59 Murray, "Richard Baxter—The Reluctant Puritan?" In *Advancing in Adversity*, 18. See also Austin Walker, "Benjamin Keach and the 'Baxterian' Controversy of the 1690s," *Reformed Baptist Theological Review*, III:1 (January 2006).

60 Keach, *Christ Alone the Way to Heaven*, 12.

> for the bride; and says, "Come unto me all ye that labour, and are heavy-laden, and I will give you rest," Matt. 11:28. They, and they only that believe in Christ, that come to Christ, do enter into rest. Christ is the only rest for the soul; there is rest from the labour and sore bondage of the law; in him is rest, also, from the guilt of sin, and from the fear of wrath, and divine vengeance, the punishment of sin; and Jesus Christ is ready to give this rest to all that believe in him, or that come to this wedding supper; "All that the Father giveth me, shall come to me; and he that comes to me, I will in no wise cast out," John 6:37.[61]

It does not seem that Particular Baptists were as badly infected as Presbyterians by Baxterianism, although without further study it is difficult to assess what contribution Keach made in this regard. His sermons demonstrate that he maintained a biblical balance, avoiding not only the Neonomian error but also Antinomianism and hyper-Calvinism. In the generation that followed Keach, some Particular Baptists went in the latter direction. The question of eternal justification was already being raised in Keach's day, and he dealt with the issue in his sermon on Romans 8:1, *A Medium Betwixt Two Extremes*. Although God sees the elect as justified and glorified from eternity, this does not mean they are *actually* justified in eternity, Keach argued, "we say that righteousness is not imputed to the actual and personal justification of any man till he has actual union with Christ."[62] Hyper-Calvinism cramps the freeness of God's grace and, sadly, became a feature of men like John Brine (1702–1765) and, to a somewhat lesser extent, one of Keach's successors, John Gill. Gill, unlike Keach, was hesitant to exhort the unconverted and would not urge them to turn from their sin in repentance and cast themselves on Christ.

---

61 Keach, "The Marriage Supper," *Parables Two*, 156.

62 Keach, *A Medium Betwixt Two Extremes*, 24.

Instead, he denied the free offer of the gospel and also taught the doctrine of eternal justification.[63]

From his earliest days as a preacher, Benjamin Keach preached the biblical doctrine of justification by faith in Jesus Christ within the context of the covenant of grace. In his generation, he followed the exhortation "to contend earnestly for the faith which was once for all delivered to the saints" (Jude 3). He was not a lover of controversy, fighting over words. He was, first and foremost, a man who, because of the freeness of God's grace, had tasted the love of Christ for himself and had come to love Christ as his Redeemer. As an ambassador of Christ, and out of that treasure store of grace, he preached to others that they too could taste that same grace and love of Christ.

Justification by faith today

Benjamin Keach strove to maintain the biblical doctrine of justification by faith. He regarded it not only as one of the fundamentals of the Christian faith but also as lying at the heart of the gospel entrusted to him as an ambassador of the Lord Jesus Christ. As a preacher, he recognized that Richard Baxter's subjective righteousness, consisting in a person's faith, repentance and new obedience, radically changed the message of the gospel, making human righteousness (rather than Christ's righteousness) the basis on which God accepts a person. As a pastor, he recognized that this same subjective righteousness effectively destroyed the assurance of salvation that belongs to all those who are trusting in Christ alone for their salvation.

In the present day, there is an ongoing controversy very similar to that of the 1690s.[64] The Reformation doctrine of justification by

---

63 For an assessment of Gill's ministry, and his hyper-Calvinism in particular, see Robert W. Oliver, "John Gill (1697–1771)." In Haykin, ed., *The British Particular Baptists, 1638-1910*, 1:160–162.

64 See Fred A. Malone, "Justification by Faith Alone in Contemporary Theological Perspective: A Critique of 'New Covenant Nomism'," *Reformed Baptist Theological Review*,

faith alone is being called into question. There are suggestions that faith must be accompanied by obedience and that good works are an element in faith itself. Do faith and works together justify us? Is justification becoming confused with sanctification? In the light of the Neonomian controversy of the 1690s, this sounds like very familiar language. Surely there is a salutary lesson to be learned from what happened in the eighteenth century following the Neonomian controversy. Would it not be a tragedy to see history being repeated in this generation and the next? Benjamin Keach stands as an example of faithfulness in what it means to preach and defend the heart of the gospel of the Lord Jesus Christ.

1:1 (January 2004): 105–132. This article provides a broad picture of some of the key issues in the modern debate about justification by faith.

EPILOGUE

"The excellent Benjamin Keach"

Benjamin Keach was a preacher of the gospel for forty-six years. He spent thirty-six of those years in London where he became a leader among the Particular Baptists. Soon after his arrival in London in 1668, he was appointed pastor of a church in Horselydown, Southwark, on the south bank of the Thames. He remained there until his death in 1704. This church grew in numbers and, by the end of the century, was the most important Particular Baptist congregation south of the Thames.

Keach died on the morning of July 18, 1704, following a short illness. In his will, he described himself as "infirm and weak."[1] His friend, Joseph Stennett, visited him before he died and Keach asked him to preach the funeral sermon from the second half of 2 Timothy 1:12: "for I know whom I have believed and am persuaded that He is able to keep what I have committed to Him

1 "The Will of Benjamin Keach," *Surrey Will Abstracts*, Vol. 26, 2001, Archdeaconry Court of Surrey 1700–1708, No. 820. See Appendix 1.

until that Day."[2] Keach's request suggests that although he was weak in body, he was still strong in faith in his Saviour and Lord, Jesus Christ. His son-in-law Thomas Crosby spoke of his last hours in which he

> told his wife he recommended her to a better husband, the Lord Jesus Christ; and exhorted his children to love, peace and unity, and a steadfast adherence to Christ and his ways. A little before expiring his daughter *Hannah*, who was among the people called *Quakers*, came in to see him; whom, when he saw, he endeavoured to talk with, and shewed a great eagerness and desire to do so, but his speech failing, prevented him.[3]

Benjamin Keach was buried in The Park, a Baptist burial ground in Southwark, but Stennett was ill and could not preach his funeral sermon. And, although he did preach it at a later date, he could not be persuaded to publish it.[4]

It was Stennett, a few months prior to Keach's death, who had come to the defence of his older friend, when a false accusation of immorality was made against him in connection with the practice of believer's baptism. The slur on Keach's character had been successfully removed by Stennett's actions. Stennett had not only denied the charge against Keach, but had also strongly affirmed that Keach had "another manner of Character."[5] The eccentric John Dunton (one of Keach's publishers) provided a verbal caricature of the author, but he also suggested that Keach

2 Crosby, *History*, 4:309.

3 Crosby, *History*, 4:308–309.

4 Unlike many Dissenters, Keach was not buried in Bunhill Fields, a plot that lay outside the northern walls of the City of London. The Park burial ground no longer exists, having been built over as the borough of Southwark grew.

5 See Prologue.

was a popular awakening preacher, held in high esteem among his contemporaries:

> Here comes Mr Keach, mounted upon some Apocalyptical Beast or other, with Babylon before him, and Sion behind him and a hundred thousand Bulls and Bears and Furious Beasts of Prey roaring, ramping and bellowing at him, so hideously, that unless some kind angel drops from the clouds, and hacks and hews very plentifully among them, he must certainly be torn as small as a love-letter. This War-Like Author is much admir'd among the Anabaptists.[6]

By his faithful preaching and his consistent example throughout his life, Keach earned a reputation that was to outlive him. Joseph Ivimey, the early nineteenth-century Baptist historian, described Keach as one of those "useful and distinguished ministers" that characterized the Particular Baptists after 1689, saying, he hoped "that the principles and zeal of a Keach...will live again in the ministers of all our churches."[7] Ivimey held Keach in high esteem, often referring to him as "the excellent Benjamin Keach."[8] Spurgeon, too, described Keach "as one of the most useful preachers of his time," and believed he was "as a pillar and a brazen wall among the Baptist churches of his day, and was in consequence deservedly held in honour."[9] In the twentieth century, Keach was described as the "single most important apologist for Calvinistic Baptist views," particularly during the last decade of the seventeenth century when his literary output was prolific.[10]

---

6 Dunton, *Life and Errors of John Dunton*, 177.

7 Ivimey, *History*, 3:x–xi.

8 For example, Ivimey, *History*, 1:338; 2:129, 157, 3:113, 541.

9 Spurgeon, *The Metropolitan Tabernacle: Its History and Work*, 25, 33.

10 MacDonald, "London Calvinistic Baptists," 77.

The assessment of contemporaries, and those who have subsequently considered the life and writings of Keach, suggest that during his life he excelled in a number of different ways and was worthy of esteem. Benjamin Keach was not a great man, as many would judge greatness, but he was a good man. He was consistent in his godliness, patient in his sufferings, conscientious and energetic as a preacher, pastor, writer and apologist. He was a faithful and a useful man, one who was pre-eminent among his Particular Baptist brethren, and who, during the last fifteen years of his life in particular, was highly respected in wider ecclesiastical circles.

To say that he excelled in many ways is not to turn a blind eye to his faults and limitations. He possessed a fiery spirit, and that temper appeared to get the better of him at certain points as, for example, during the hymn-singing controversy. Yet, as other aspects of that controversy demonstrated, Keach was also a humble man who was willing to listen to the counsel of others, seek forgiveness from those he offended and write a letter to the churches withdrawing his remarks that had caused offence.

He was not as talented as John Bunyan in his imaginative gifts, or as capable as John Milton in his poetic abilities, and some of those limitations may be seen among the hymns that he composed. Nor was he endowed with the intellect and theological acumen of a man like John Owen. Nevertheless, he was a competent and well-read theologian who, at the same time, was aware of his limitations and dependence on others. He did not try to pretend that he was a learned scholar of Owen's calibre. In one of his works on baptism, he drew attention to the use he had made of biblical Hebrew and Greek, Latin, German and Dutch authors but then immediately added that

> I would not have you think, I understand all those languages; but I have had the Assistance of a Learned

> Person...who is my Friend and Acquaintance, that so the work might the more fully and effectively be done.[11]

Keach was also typical of his age in that he shared the common dissenting view that the papacy was the Antichrist. He, together with the majority of his contemporaries, fell foul of trying to read too much into the book of Revelation, identifying particular passages in the book with contemporary events. Most Dissenters saw the book as a prophecy of key events unfolding throughout the whole history of the church. He wrongly anticipated the imminent overthrow of the Roman Catholic Church on the basis of calculations of some of the numbers in Revelation and the arrival of the future Protestant king, William of Orange. This engendered a false optimism but, in Keach, it was tempered by a firm faith in the providence of God. This was one of the reasons why he did not support taking up arms, as some Dissenters did, during the Monmouth rebellion. However, given the great political and ecclesiastical upheavals of the previous two centuries and the immediate threat to Protestantism from perceived tyranny and arbitrary rule of James II, it is understandable why Keach and many other Dissenters believed they could identify events in England in the late 1680s with events described in parts of the book of Revelation.

Keach was, first and foremost, a Christian man and a Protestant Dissenter. Protestant blood flowed in his veins as *Sion in Distress: Or, the Groans of the Protestant Church* clearly display. After coming to London, he became a convinced Calvinist in his theology as he came to understand the Bible's teaching on the covenant of grace. He was a Baptist from his teenage years, despite the fact that he was baptized as an infant in the Church of England and subsequently converted to the Lord Jesus Christ through the ministry of Matthew Mead, a convinced paedobaptist. From his early days as a preacher among the General Baptists in the

11 "Epistle to the Reader." In Keach, *The Rector Rectified and Corrected.*

northern part of Buckinghamshire, he was firmly in the Separatist tradition and, as his thinking matured, Keach became a "full-blooded" Baptist Dissenter because of his convictions regarding the constitution and discipline of the gathered church. This came to expression in his views concerning the worship of God, baptism, the laying on of hands and church membership, the church covenant and church discipline, as well as his spirited defence of proper maintenance for pastors. Yet, it did not lead him to ignore his duty of promoting love and peace among Christians with whom he differed:

> Speak well of all your brethren who hold the head, or are sound in the faith, in respect of all fundamental principles, though not in every thing of your opinion in some points of religion: for peace among ourselves ought not to be restrained only to members of that church we belong unto, but to all the saints, let them be Presbyterians, Independents, or Baptists. I do not mean that it is your duty to hold church-communion with all; no, that cannot be, unless all were of one judgment in all the essentials of church-constitution: for mutual love is not to be the rule of our church-communion and fellowship, but the word of Christ.[12]

Keach was characterized by a great concern for the church of Christ and, in particular, he displayed a love for her peace and unity. After 1689, Keach was involved in a number of debates. It would be easy—and wrong—to portray Keach simply as a tough-minded controversialist who was principally engaged in promoting his own interests. One needs to appreciate his constant efforts to promote love, peace and unity in the churches. It was this desire for peace that led him to address the churches,

---

12 Keach, "Fire, Salt and Peace," *Parables One*, 300.

after his heated dispute with Isaac Marlow and others, over whether it was right for a congregation to sing hymns or not. The division caused Keach a great deal of personal pain and did great damage among the Particular Baptist churches. In an effort to repair the damage, Keach wrote to the churches, explaining to them that

> I desire to live no longer than to promote Peace and Union to my Power in all the Churches of the Saints; though I am represented as one that hath not indeavoured after it, because of my Writing in the Defence of Singing the Praises of God.[13]

Keach was not narrow-minded, interested only in promoting love and peace among those who shared his own particular convictions. More broadly, he expressed regrets over the way Gyles Shute, a paedobaptist, had attacked him and Hercules Collins of Wapping over their views on believer's baptism. He affirmed to Shute that he was not interested in using hard words to criticize another *man*, but rather bringing hard arguments to bear on the *matter* being considered. In his view, the apparent lack of love among Christians was a serious sin of omission:

> For my part I hope I can say I love them in whom I see the Image of God, that differ from me, in the like degree as those of my own opinion. I am persuaded the want of Love to one another is one of the greatest Sins of this Age and that which is a high Provocation to God.[14]

Even in the Neonomian controversy, which Keach regarded as a very serious attack on the biblical doctrine of justification

---

13 Keach, *To all the Baptized Churches.*

14 Keach, *A Counter-Antidote*, 3.

by faith—the very heart of the gospel—Keach expressed his longings for peace and unity, but not at the expense of truth. He feared that "the Design is to wound the Truth and us," but continued, "O when shall we see that Truth, Peace, and Union longed for!"[15] The truth of God and his gospel was paramount for Benjamin Keach, but that did not prevent him from strenuous efforts to maintain truth, peace and unity, even when he was embroiled in controversy.

There was at least one notable occasion when Keach was able to maintain truth and peace. In his controversy with those who maintained that Saturday was the Sabbath day, Keach, in his usual manner, firmly and vigorously defended his understanding that the Sabbath day was now the first day of the week by preaching a series of sermons and then publishing them. Keach had been distressed over the loss of some of the members of the Horselydown church to the Seventh-Day Baptists. However, it does not appear that Keach's book undermined his friendship with Joseph Stennett, the most prominent Seventh-Day Baptist in London, whom Keach asked to preach his funeral sermon four years later.

No estimate of Keach will ever be accurate, unless his convictions regarding the Bible are fully understood. He was a man of integrity, who made it his aim to live by biblical principles and biblical convictions. The Bible, as the Word of God, was his supreme authority and guide. His religion was one of sincere obedience to that Word. His first concerns were not his own interests and advantage but the honour and the glory of the God whom he served. Keach possessed a deep sense of gratitude to and love for God, who he fervently believed had graciously set his love on him and had saved him from his sins. Keach was impatient and intolerant of an insincere mercenary religion. He preached against such a spirit, saying that

---

15 "Epistle Dedicatory." In Keach, *The Marrow of Justification*. The "Happy Union" between Presbyterians and Independents was effectively wrecked by the Neonomian controversy. See Watts, *The Dissenters*, 296–297.

> many men care not to do anything for the honour of God, further than it makes, as they conceive, directly for their own interest and advantage. Tell some men of this or that ordinance and command of Christ, they presently object, may I not be saved without it? Is it necessary to salvation? These men only make religion as a bridge to carry them to heaven; mere mercenary souls! Alas! A true Christian obeys and serves Christ sincerely, that he may glorify and honour his holy name, knowing he deserves more at his hands, than he is ever able to perform, not doubting his labour shall ever be in vain in the Lord; the very work is wages to him.[16]

This kind of spirit characterized him from his early days, becoming more marked as he advanced in years.

He made it his aim to have a conscience that was without offence toward either God or men. This made him God's free man and engendered in him a bold spirit. For example, in the 1660s when but a young man, he did not allow himself to be intimidated by those in authority. Though he suffered imprisonment and the indignity of the pillory, he would not compromise his convictions, but stood his ground firmly and bore his sufferings patiently. Persecution, far from crushing his spirit, only tended to reveal greater qualities of faith and an unswerving determination to serve God, rather than yield his conscience to human authorities. Keach believed that

> persecution never does godly Christians any harm; they grow the more, not only in number but in goodness. It refines and purifies them, it purges and makes them white, they grow in faith, in patience.[17]

16 Keach, "Saints compared to soldiers," *Types and Metaphors*, 730.

17 Keach, "Saints compared to Palm trees," *Types and Metaphors*, 755.

It was in such a spirit that he endured opposition until William of Orange arrived in England.

Furthermore, Keach was a man of prayer who had learned to depend on God in every circumstance in his life. He could never have maintained his integrity throughout his life as a Christian and a preacher of the gospel unless he had learned to draw his strength and wisdom from God. He wrote:

> By prayer we confess we are poor depending creatures, and cannot help ourselves, save ourselves, nor direct our paths, nor deliver ourselves from dangers feared, and that all our wisdom, strength and succour, is from God, and hereby we give glory to God.[18]

Keach was marked not only by integrity but also by a spirit of faithfulness, diligence and earnestness, especially in his labours as a Christian pastor. Crosby portrayed his active life as "one continued scene of labour and toil," and preaching the gospel of the Lord Jesus Christ as his greatest pleasure.[19] Keach did not have a strong constitution and his diligence in the study and in preaching exhausted him. He was not ashamed of his Christian faith, or of his Calvinism, or his Baptist convictions. He was not the kind of man who would hold back any truth that he believed, even when it might bring him into conflict with a close friend like Joseph Stennett.

It was these characteristics of faithfulness, diligence and earnestness that made Keach a useful and popular preacher. He preached the Lord Jesus Christ, and the grace of God, not only as one who had discovered and understood the truth of the grace of God in the teachings of the Bible, but also as one who had experienced the power of that grace in his own life. He asked the question

---

18 Keach, "The Persistent Widow," *Parables One*, 440.

19 Crosby, *History*, 4:304.

> who can admire sovereign and undeserved mercy more than they that have been in the depths of sorrow and misery, and are forever delivered and raised to glory and eternal happiness?[20]

Indeed, he regarded this experience of God's grace through Jesus Christ as one of the essential elements in faithful and effective preaching:

> He that ministers the Word, ought principally to experience the grace of God in his own heart, and the power of it, in that grand and evangelical work of regeneration; as also to understand those blessed mysteries of the sacred Scriptures, that he may unfold them to others, and have a lawful call, which altogether constitutes, though he never saw a university.[21]

This explains why his preaching was marked by fervency and zeal. For Keach, this too was an essential element in preaching: preachers should deliver their sermons hot, "cold meat is not so refreshing and sweet as that which is hot; a minister must preach with life, and holy fervency of spirit; cold and lifeless preaching, makes cold hearing."[22] He preached to the mind and heart and conscience of his hearers. He was earnest with them, not only urging them to repent of their sins and flee from the wrath of God, but also pleading with them to turn to the Lord Jesus Christ.

Keach was a Calvinist. He believed that God saves sinners, and his understanding of the Bible's teaching on regeneration and conversion clearly showed his clear grasp of those doctrines. These doctrines never prevented him from urging his hearers to

---

20 Keach, "The Pharisee and the Publican," *Parables Two*, 430.

21 Keach, *Types and Metaphors*, xi.

22 Keach, "The Scribe," *Parables One*, 271.

> receive this Saviour, believe in him, and you shall be saved whosoever you are: It is not the greatness of your Sins that can hinder or obstruct him from saving your Souls; though your Sins be as red as scarlet, or as red as Crimson, he will wash them all away, and shall make you as white as Wool, as white as Snow.[23]

Benjamin Keach excelled in one particular characteristic, namely, Christian manliness and courage. Preaching from the metaphor that the righteous are as bold as a lion (Proverbs 28:1 and Micah 5:8), Keach described the godly man as one who was valiant and courageous for truth.[24] Such men, he said, were characterized by: (1) speaking for the truth when others speak against it; (2) endeavoring to clear the truth from reproach and infamy; (3) contending earnestly for the truth; (4) visibly professing and publicly owning the truth; (5) suffering for the truth when called to do so; (6) standing for the truth when others turn their backs on it; and (7) maintaining every truth, but more especially that truth which was most opposed in the day in which they lived. All of these characteristics are clearly exemplified in the life of Benjamin Keach.[25]

Keach was as bold as a lion. Persuaded of the truth and supreme authority of God's Word, Keach believed he was engaged in a righteous cause. He endeavored to maintain a good conscience, convinced that God was with him. He was a man who believed that by serving Christ faithfully, he was certain of victory and assured of a great reward. Gripped by these convictions, he was valiant and courageous for truth. As we have unravelled the various events in the life of this servant of God, the motives

23 Keach, "The Great Salvation," *A Golden Mine Opened*, 385.

24 Keach, "Saints compared to lions," *Types and Metaphors*, 766–767.

25 This theme has been further developed in Austin Walker, "'Bold as a lion': The spirituality of Benjamin Keach," *Eusebeia: The Bulletin of the Jonathan Edwards Centre for Reformed Spirituality* 4 (Spring 2005): 17–46.

underlying Keach's manliness and courage have become increasingly apparent.

We have discovered the fundamental reasons why Benjamin Keach was an excellent man. He not only aimed to live by biblical principles and biblical convictions but he was driven by biblical motives. He was a sincere man who had resolved before God to live a godly life. He displayed a determination and courage to maintain that godliness throughout his Christian life.

The motives that spurred Keach to be bold as a lion and preach the same things to his contemporaries are the same motives that ought to arouse Christians in every generation to greater earnestness in their service to God. Benjamin Keach serves as a faithful mentor in these things, and his exhortation is as valid 300 years after his death as it was in his own day:

> Let Saints show themselves bold and courageous in the cause and interest of God, and their souls. A fearful timorous spirit becomes not a Christian. Have you a good cause? Have you a good call? Have you a good conscience? Have you a good captain? What then do you fear? In the strength of the Lord, be as bold as a Lion; and in order thereunto, get the truth into your affections, see that you have received the truth in the love of it: and be sure you approve yourselves to be sincere; for it is sincerity that emboldens a Christian, and makes him valiant.[26]

26 Keach, "Saints compared to lions," *Types and Metaphors*, 766–767.

Benjamin Keach (1640–1704)

APPENDIX 1

The will of Benjamin Keach

Benjamin Keach of St. Olave, Southwark,
gentleman, infirm and weak 18 July 1704

to my grandson Benjamin Keach £5 to apprentice him and £5 more in books, the profits from selling (Dr) Roberts tincture elixir sugar plums and snuff over the cost of keeping the Dr and his wife Prudence Roberts and part assigned to my son in law Benjamin Stinton to my wife Susanna[h] Keach for life and then two fifths to my daughter Rebecca and the rest to my daughters Elizabeth, Susan[nah] and Rachel for seven years for copartnership with son in law Stinton expired; to my daughters Mary Enby and Hannah Green £1 each; residue and lease of my house to my wife, exec.

Witnesses
Francis Cotts,
John Allen, notary public on Rotherhithe Wall
Proved 7 Feb 1705/06 to exec.[1]

---

1 "The Will of Benjamin Keach," *Surrey Will Abstracts*, Vol. 26, 2001. Archdeaconry Court of Surrey 1700–1708, No. 820. In Surrey History Centre, Woking.

APPENDIX 2

The twenty-eight witnesses to Keach's character

COLLECTED BY JOSEPH STENNETT, 1703

We whose Names are underwritten (being Neighbours and Acquaintance of Mr Benjamin Keach, and divers of us Paedobaptists, some of us in the Communion of the Church of England) having for many Years known his good Conversation as a Christian and as a Minister, do solemnly declare and testify that we are entirely satisfied, that Mr David Russen's Assertion in his Book, entituled [*Fundamentals without a Foundation* page 31] that the said Mr Keach has been lately accus'd of Uncleaness, is false, groundless and malicious; for we never before heard of any such Accusation made against him by any Person whatsoever, or that he was ever charged with the least Immodesty; and we believe Mr Russen might with as much Justice have accus'd any other pious and modest Man in the World. This we think ourselves in Justice bound to declare, to prevent Mr Keach's Labours and Books (several of which in Mr Russen's Opinion deserve due Commendation) from being slighted or rendered useless to any. And we doubt not, that Mr Keach might have the Testimony of a Multitude of Hands besides ours to what is abovesaid.

In witness of which we set our Hands, September 6,1703.

Richard Wilkinson
Joseph Collett
John Hollis
Charles Cox
Joseph Worley
Benjamin Wyatt
Thomas Foster
John Standard
Joshua Farrow
John Roberts
William Willmott
Robert Cabbel
John Valley
Richard Newnham
Valentine Glover
Richard Richardson
Edward Hinchclive
John Cholmley
Joseph Chitty
Tho. Hollis
Thomas Mayo
William Leader
George Ongley
John Moore
Edward Fleming
John Gough

Anthony Quarles
John Webb[1]

About the witnesses

Stennett enlisted the help of a range of men to act as witnesses. For example, he used three deacons from Keach's own church, Joshua Farrow, John Roberts and John Valley.[2] Then, he turned to two prominent Baptist members at Pinners' Hall, Broad Street. The brothers John and Thomas Hollis were from a family of wealthy drapers. John Hollis (d.1736) was a manager of the Particular Baptist Fund and his brother, Thomas Hollis III (1659–1731), was the first major trustee of the Particular Baptist Fund.[3] From the church meeting in Lorimers' Hall in Basinghill Street, he enlisted Richard Wilkinson, a messenger at the 1704 London Assembly.[4] From outside London, he sought the help of John Moore (1662–1726) a pastor in Northampton and John Webb, a pastor from the Taunton area of Somerset.[5]

1 Extracted from Stennett, *An Answer to Mr David Russen's Book*, 250–251.
2 Ivimey, *History*, 3:48, 411.
3 Valentine, *Concern for the Ministry*, 2.
4 Ivimey, *History*, 2:415; 3:48.
5 Ivimey, *History*, 3:370; 1:539.

APPENDIX 3

"Keach's Covenant"

THE SOLEMN COVENANT OF THE CHURCH OF CHRIST

Meeting in White-street,
at it's Constitution; June 5, 1696

We who desire to walk together in the Fear of the Lord, do, through the Assistance of his Holy Spirit, profess our deep and serious Humiliation for all our Transgressions. And we do also solemnly, in the Presence of God, of each other, in the Sense of our own Unworthiness, give up ourselves to the Lord, in Church state according to the Apostolical Constitution that he may be our God, and we may be his People, through the Everlasting Covenant of his Free grace, in which alone we hope to be accepted by him, through his blessed Son Jesus Christ, whom we take to be our High Priest, to justify and

Ezek. 16:6,8
2 Cor. 8:5
Hos. 2:23
2 Cor. 6:16

Church Communion Proved

sanctify us, and our Prophet to teach us; and to [be] subject to him as our Law-giver, and the King of Saints; and to conform to all his Holy Laws and Ordinances, for our growth, Establishment and Consolation; that we may be as a Holy Spouse unto him and serve him in our Generation, and wait for his second Appearance, as our glorious Bridegroom.

Exod. 26:3,4,6
Isa. 62:5
Psa. 122:3
Eph. 1:23; 4:16
1 Peter 2:5

Being fully satisfied in the way of Church-Communion, and the Truth of Grace in some good measure upon one anothers Spirits, we do solemnly join our selves together in a holy Union and fellowship, humbly submitting to the Discipline of the Gospel, and all Holy Duties required of a People in such a Spiritual Relation.

Psa. 93:5
Isa. 55:8
Luke 1:74–75

1. We do promise and ingage to walk in Holiness, Godliness, Humility, and Brotherly Love, as much as in us lieth to render our Communion delightful to God, comfortable to ourselves, and lovely to the rest of the Lord's People.

2 Cor. 7:1
1 Tim. 6:11
2 Peter 1:6–7
Acts 20:19
Phil. 2:3
John 13:34;15:12

2. We do promise to watch over each others Conversations, and not to suffer Sin upon one another, so far as God shall discover it to us, or any of us; and to stir up one another to Love and good Works; to warn, rebuke, and admonish one another with Meekness according to the rules left to us of Christ in that Behalf.

1 Peter 1:22
Lev. 19:17
Heb. 10:24–25
1 Thess. 5:14–15
Rom. 15

3. We do promise in an especial manner to pray for one another, and for the Glory and Increase of this Church, and for the Presence of God in it,

Eph. 6:18
James 5:16

and the pouring forth of his Spirit on it, and his Protection over it to his Glory.

Col. 4:12

4. We do promise to bear one anothers Burdens, to cleave to one another, and to have a Fellow-feeling with one another, in all Conditions both outward and inward, as God in his Providence shall cast any of us into.

Gal. 6:2
Heb. 12:2; 13:3
Rom. 12:15
2 Cor. 11:29

5. We do promise to bear with one anothers Weakness, Failings and Infirmities, with much Tenderness, not discovering to any without the Church, nor any within, unless according to Christ's rule, and the Order of the Gospel provided in that case.

1 John 3:17–18
Gal. 6:1
1 Thess. 5:14
Rom. 15:2
Eph. 4:31–32

6. We do promise to strive together for the Truths of the Gospel and Purity of God's Ways and Ordinances, to avoid Causes, and Causers of Division, endeavouring to keep the Unity of the Spirit in the Bond of Peace; Eph. 4:3.

Jude 3
Gal. 5:1
Titus 3:9–10
2 John 10

7. We do promise to meet together on Lord's Days, and at other times, as the Lord shall give us Opportunities, to serve and glorify God in the way of his Worship, to edify one another, and to contrive the good of his Church.

Heb. 3:10; 10:25
Mal. 3:16
Rom. 14:18; 15:16
Eph. 4:16

8. We do promise according to our Ability (or as God shall bless us with the good things of the World) to Communicate to our Pastor, or Minister, God having ordained that they that Preach the Gospel should live of the Gospel. (And now can anything lay a greater obligation

2 Cor. 9:7
2 Cor. 8:9–12:13
Gal. 6:6

upon the Conscience, than this Covenant, what then is the Sin of such who violate it?)

These and all other Gospel-Duties we humbly submit unto, promising and purposing to perform, not in our own Strength, being conscious of our own Weakness, but in the Power, and Strength of the Blessed God, whose we are, and whom we desire to serve: To whom be Glory now and evermore. Amen.[1]

1 Extracted from Keach, *The Glory of a True Church*, 71–74.

APPENDIX 4

Of Laying on of Hands & Of Singing of Psalms

Of Laying on of Hands

XXIII. We believe that laying on of Hands (with Prayer) upon baptized Believers, as such is an Ordinance of Christ and ought to be submitted unto by all such Persons that are admitted to partake of the Lord's Supper; and that the end of the Ordinance is not for the extraordinary Gifts of the Spirit, but for a farther reception of the Holy Spirit of Promise, or for the Addition of the Graces of the Spirit, and the Influences thereof; to confirm, strengthen, and comfort them in Christ Jesus; it being ratified and established by the extraordinary Gifts of the Spirit in the Primitive Times, to abide in the Church, as meeting together on the first Day of the Week was, Acts 2:1. that being the Day of Worship, or Christian Sabbath, under the Gospel; and as Preaching the Word was, Acts 10:44. and as

Heb. 5:12; 6:1–2
Acts 8 & 19:6
Eph. 1:13–14
Acts 8 & 19:6

Baptism was, Matt. 3:16 and Prayer was, Acts 4:31 and singing Psalms &c was, Acts 16:25–26 so this of laying on of hands was, Acts 8 and 19. For as the whole Gospel was confirmed by Signs and Wonders, and divers Miracles and Gifts of the Holy Ghost in general, so was every Ordinance in like manner confirmed in particular.

Heb. 2:3–4

Of Singing of Psalms

XXVII. We believe that singing the praise of God, is a holy Ordinance of Christ, and not a part of Natural Religion, or a moral Duty only; but that it is brought under Divine Institution, it being injoined on the Churches to sing Psalms, Hymns, and spiritual Songs; and that the whole Church in their Publick Assemblies (as well as private Christians) ought to sing God's Praises, according to the best Light they have received. Moreover, it was practiced in the great Representative Church, by our Lord Jesus Christ with his Disciples, after he had instituted and celebrated the Sacred Ordinance of his Holy Supper, as a commemorative Token of Redeeming Love.[1]

Eph. 5:19
Col. 3:16
Acts 16:25
Heb. 2:12
James 5:13
Matt. 26:30
Mark 14:26

1 Extracts from Keach, *The Articles of the Faith*, and Elias Keach, *The Articles of the Faith of the Church of Christ or Congregation Meeting at Tallow Chandlers Hall* (London, 1697). These are two statements that were included in the articles of faith of the two churches, reflecting areas of distinctive practice common to the congregations pastored respectively by father and son. These articles were later incorporated into *The Philadelphia Confession* of 1742, the confession of faith of the Philadelphia Baptist Association, demonstrating the influence of both Benjamin and Elias Keach on the early Baptists of America. Lumpkin, *Baptist Confessions of Faith*, 348–353.

BIBLIOGRAPHY

1. *Benjamin Keach: An annotated bibliography*

The principal sources for compiling a bibliography of Benjamin Keach's works are found in Thomas Crosby (1738), Walter Wilson (1814), W.T. Whitley (1916), Edward C. Starr (1952–1976) and the *Short Title Catalogue* 2 (Wing). For details of these, see the Bibliography 2. More recently, Jonathan W. Arnold, David A. Copeland and D.B. Riker have produced detailed bibliographies for the works of Keach (see Bibliography 3).

In addition, when Keach published *A Golden Mine Opened* in 1694, he provided on the last page a list of "Books written and published by this Author, some of which the Impressions all being sold-off, are not to be had, which are marked*, to prevent trouble and charge of Letters." This was not intended to be a bibliography, and Keach does not always gives the details of dates, but it is important because it confirms, for example, the 1666 edition of *Sion in Distress*, and lists one or two other works not found in any other bibliography.

Wherever it has been possible, I have checked existing bibliographies by tracking down actual editions of Keach's works. No one existing bibliography appears to list all of Keach's works. Furthermore the recent publication of Keach's poetical works by Chadwyck-Healey attributes to Keach a number of poems none of which are listed in any other bibliography. It has not been possible for me to confirm Keach's authorship of these and they are not included in the following Keach bibliography. Further research is needed in order to confirm authorship and to date and list them in the manner I have adopted below.

This bibliography lists his works in chronological order in order to demonstrate the development of his thought and the prolific nature of his output especially in the last fifteen years of his life. Where I have considered it helpful I have provided explanatory notes. For full details of Keach's works that were reprinted during and after his life, the reader is referred to Edward C. Starr's bibliography. I do not claim that I have compiled a complete bibliography; rather I have attempted to take it a step further than previous bibliographers.

In each case, London is the place of publication.

1664

A New and Easy Primmer

No copies are known to be in existence. Most were destroyed as a result of his appearance at the Aylesbury Assizes in 1664. Keach refers to this primer in a list on the last page of *A Golden Mine Opened*, 1694. He refers to the book "for which I suffered in the Reign of Charles II; for asserting Believers Baptism in opposition to Infants etc. in the Year 1664." It is thought that he rewrote this primer from memory and published it as *The Child's Instructor*. This is also listed in *A Golden Mine Opened*, but no date of publication is given. Starr's bibliography refers to a 5th edition in 1679 and a Boston edition in 1685. The latter was called *The Protestant Tutor for Children*.

Keach also published *Instructions for Children: or, the Child's and Youth's delight. Teaching an easy way to Spell and Read true English. Containing the Father's Godly Advice, directing parents in a Right and Spiritual manner to educate their children.* It contains a preface by Hanserd Knollys. No date is given for the first edition, but a 2nd edition was published in 1693 and a 3rd edition in 1702 under the title *Instructions for Youth*. Ian Green lists fifteen editions up to 1723. Starr lists a 30th edition for 1763. This shows that is was a steady selling book in the late seventeenth and early eighteenth centuries.

1666

Sion in Distress: Or, the Groans of the Protestant Church. Or, The Sad and Lamentable Complaint of Sion and her Children

No copies of this first edition have survived. Keach mentions the 1666 edition in the introductory "To the Reader" in *Distressed Sion Relieved*, and also in *A Golden Mine Opened*.

1668

(The Glory of a True Church, and its Discipline Display'd. Wherein a true Gospel-Church is described: Together with the Power of the Keys, and who are to be let in, and who to be shut out)

Despite one edition of this work in the Angus Library dated 1668, all others appear as 1697. Keach does not list this in *A Golden Mine Opened*, and given the development of his thought at this time it is highly unlikely that he produced this in 1668. Furthermore, it was in 1668 that he moved from Buckinghamshire to London. It would appear that the date 1668 is therefore wrong. This is confirmed by the fact that the pagination in the 1668 is quite different from the 1697 editions and that it also contains advertisements for works published in the eighteenth century. It is fairly clear therefore that the date of the edition in the Angus Library is a printer's error and that MDCLXVIII (1668) should read MDCCLXVIII (1768)—sixty-four years after Keach's death. I am indebted to Susan Mills for her help in this important correction.

1670

A Pillar set up, to the memory of his first dear and beloved wife

No copies known to be in existence. Mentioned and summarized by Crosby, *History*, 4:273–274.

1673

War with the Devil: or, The Young Man's Conflict with the Powers of Darkness: in a Dialogue discovering the Corruption and Vanity of Youth, the horrible Nature of Sin, and Deplorable Condition of Fallen Man. With an appendix containing a Dialogue between an Old Apostate and a Young Professor

This was one of Keach's "best-sellers." Ian Green lists nineteen editions from 1673 to 1728. Starr records a 22nd edition in 1776 and a new edition in 1795.

1674

Light from the Son of Righteousness

Listed only by Keach in *A Golden Mine Opened*, but he indicated it was no longer available. He provided no date. From his list it would seem reasonable to suggest it was published in the mid-1670s.

Mr. Baxter's Arguments for Believers Baptism

Also listed in *A Golden Mine Opened*, but no longer available.

"To the Reader in Commendation of this Book." In Josias Bonham, *The churches Glory: Or, the Becoming Ornament, being a Seasonable Word, tending to the Provoking, Encouraging and Perfecting of Holiness in Believers*

1675

Darkness Vanquished: Or, Truth in its Primitive Purity, being An answer to a late Book of Mr Henry Danvers, Intituled A treatise of laying on of Hands. Wherein His mistakes and cloudy apprehensions about it are in a faithful and friendly manner rectified, his grand objections answered, and imposition of hands upon baptized Believers, as such with Prayer for the Spirit of Promise is proved, to be a holy and divine Institution of Jesus Christ, and accordingly practiced by the Apostles and primitive Saints. Together with the testimony of many famous Writers, both Ancient, and of later times concerning it

This was enlarged and republished under a different title in 1698.

The Grand Imposter Discovered: Or, The Quakers doctrine weighed in the Balance, and found wanting. A Poem, by way of Dialogue: wherein their chief and most concerning Principles are laid down, and by the Authority of God's holy Word clearly refuted

1676

A Summons to the Grave: Or, the Necessity of a Timely Preparation for Death. Demonstrated in a sermon preached at the funeral of that most eminent and faithful servant of Jesus Christ Mr John Norcot. Who departed this life March 24, 1675/76

An elegy on the Death of that most Labourious and Painful Minister of God Mr John Norcot

1678

"Introduction" to W. Balmford, *The Sea-mans Spiritual Companion*

1679

The Glorious Lover: A Divine Poem, Upon the Adorable Mystery of Sinners Redemption

Starr lists a 2nd edition in 1685 and a 4th edition in 1696.

1681

Sion in Distress: Or, the Groans of the Protestant Church

A further development of the theme first published in 1666. Starr mentions 2nd and 3rd editions published in London and Boston during Keach's lifetime. Ian Green lists at least five editions from 1681 to 1692.

Tropologia, a Key to open Scripture Metaphors, together with Types of the Old Testament

Thomas Delaune was responsible for Book I on sacred philology. This section was partly translated and partly compiled from Solomon Glassius, *Philologiae Sacrae, qua totius sacrosanctae Veteris et Novi Testamenti Scripturae*, Jena, 1623. The remaining Books were Keach's own work on the metaphors, allegories and similitudes of the Old and New Testaments.

1683

The Travels of True Godliness, from the Beginning of the World to this Present Day, in an apt and pleasant Allegory: shewing the Trouble, Oppositions, Reproaches and Persecutions he hath met with in every age; together with the Danger he seems to be in at present, by Vice, Papists and other grand Enemies; also where he make his final Abode

This allegory was a "best-seller" and went through many editions in Keach's lifetime and was reprinted in both America and Britain throughout the eighteenth and the first half of the nineteenth centuries. The original place of publication, however, was London.

1684

The Progress of Sin: Or, the Travels of Ungodliness: Wherein, the Pedigree, Rise (or Original) Antiquity, Subtilty, Evil Nature, and Prevailing Power of Sin is fully Discovered: In an apt and Pleasant Allegory: Together with The great Victories he hath obtained, and abominable Evils he hath done to Mankind, by the help of the Devil, in all his Travels from the beginning of the World, to this very Day, as also, the Manner of his Apprehension, Arraignment, Tryal, Condemnation and Execution

A 2nd and 3rd edition of this allegory were published during Keach's lifetime in 1684 and 1700. It did not sell as well as *The Travels of True Godliness* but still proved to be popular. It continued to be printed throughout the eighteenth century and into the middle of the nineteenth century,

1685

The victorious Christian: Or, the triumph of faith. Being prison meditations

No copies are known to be in existence; mentioned by Crosby, *History*, 4:313.

1689

Antichrist Stormed: Or, Mystery Babylon, the Great Whore, and Great City, proved to be the present Church of Rome.

Distressed Sion Relieved: Or, the Garment of Praise for the Spirit of Heaviness, wherein are discovered the grand causes of the churches trouble and misery under the late dismal dispensation. With a compleat history of and lamentation for those renowned worthies that fell in England by Popish rage and cruelty from the year 1680 to 1688. Together with an account of the late admirable and stupendous providence which hath wrought such a sudden and wonderful deliverance for this nation and God's Sion therein. Dedicated to William and Mary

A sequel to *Sion in Distress*, 1666 and 1681

Gold Refin'd: Or, Baptism in its Primitive Purity. Likewise Mr. Smythie's arguments for Infant-baptism in his late book entituled, The Non-communicant, fully answered

The Gospel Minister's Maintenance Vindicated. Wherein, A regular Ministry in the Churches is first asserted, and the objections against a Gospel maintenance for ministers answered

To their Most Excellent Majesties William and Mary, by the Grace of God, King and Queen of England, &c.
Poem written on the accession to the throne of William III and Mary II and attributed to Keach in *English Poetry Full-Text Database* published by Chadwyck-Healey.

1690

"Introduction." In Philip Cary, *A Solemn Call unto all that would be owned as Christ's Faithful Witnesses, speedily and seriously, to attend unto the Primitive Purity of the Gospel Doctrine and Worship: Or, a Discourse Concerning Baptism*
It is possible that Keach was the principal author. His name follows those of William Kiffin, John Harris, Richard Adams and Richard Steed at the conclusion to this "Introduction." Given that Keach was the principal apologist among the Particular Baptists in this period for believer's baptism, it is reasonable to conclude that he was responsible for the "Introduction" to Cary's book.

1691

The Counterfeit Christian: Or, the Danger of Hypocrisy: Opened in Two sermons:

An Answer to the Athenian Mercury, Vol. 4 Numb 14 concerning infant baptism with an account of divers queries sent by the author (and some others) to the Athenian society, which they have not yet answered

Pedo-Baptism Disproved: being an Answer to two printed Papers (put forth by some Gentlemen called the Athenian Society, who pretend to answer all questions sent to them of what Nature soever) called the Athenian Mercury, one put forth November 14,

and the other November 28, 1691. In which Papers they pretend to answer eight queries about the lawfulness of Infant-Baptism
A second edition published the same year adds "twenty syllogistic arguments to disprove infant-baptism."

The Breach Repaired in God's Worship: Or, Singing of Psalms, Hymns and Spiritual Songs proved to be an Holy Ordinance of Jesus Christ. With an Answer to all Objections. As also An Examination of Mr Isaac Marlow's two papers, one called, "A Discourse against Singing &C." and the other "An Appendix." Wherein his Arguments and Cavils are detected and refuted
A further enlarged edition under the same title was issued in 1699. This contained an answer to DuVeil and an Appendix by Thomas Winnell. A second edition followed in 1700.

A Sober Reply to Mr Robert's Steed's Epistle concerning Singing. Wherein All his Objections against that Way he calls the Common and Popular Way of Singing Psalms. &c. are Impartially Examined, and in the Spirit of Meekness, fully Answered

An Answer to Mr Marlow's Appendix. Wherein his Arguments to prove that Singing of Psalms, Hymns and Spiritual Songs, was performed in the Primitive Church by a Special or an Extraordinary Gift, and therefore not to be practiced in these Days, are Examined, and clearly Detected. Also some Reflections on what he speaks on the word Hymnos: And on his undue Quotations of divers Learned Men. By a Learned Hand

"A Sober Appeal for Right and Justice," together with some correspondence between Keach and Marlow. These are found in Heathcote, Silvanus etc. *Truth Cleared: Or, a brief Narrative of the Rise, Occasion and Management of the present Controversy concerning Singing in the Worship of God. With an Account of several Letters that have passed between Mr. Benjamin Keach and Isaac Marlow, relating to an Appeal. As also of an Inspection made into both their books, by several worthy and honourable Elders, who have given their Judgment, subscribed with their own Hands, in Vindication of Isaac Marlow's Sheet of Observations on Mr Keach's Book. Whereunto is added a further Collection of Mr. Keach's Abuses, Falshoods, and Misrepresentations, contained in his said Treatise, called The Breach in God's Worship, etc. As also some further evidence under the Hands of Several Brethren (that were late members of his Church) to detect several others of his Abuses therein*

Spiritual Melody, Containing near Three Hundred Sacred Hymns

1692

The Banquetting-House: Or, A Feast of Fat Things: A Divine Poem, opening many Sacred Scripture Mysteries; profitable for all who would attain the saving Knowledge of God, and of Jesus Christ; and sufficient to fill the soul with joy, and to ravish the hearts of all true Christians

The Marrow of True Justification: Or, Justification without Works: (opened in two sermons at Horselydown) now published with some additions

To all the Baptized Churches and faithful Brethren in England and Wales, Christian Salutations

An appendix to an answer unto two Athenian Mercuries concerning paedo-baptism containing 27 syllogistic arguments, proving infant baptism a mere humane tradition. The gentlemen called the Athenian Society in the last of the said Mercuries to have syllogisms

Confidence corrected, error detected, and truth defended: Or, some farther reflections upon the two Athenian Mercuries, lately published about infant baptism, by Philalethes Pasiphilus

The Rector Rectified and Corrected: Or, Infant-Baptism unlawful

1693

The Ax Laid to the Root: or, One more blow at the foundation of infant baptism, and church membership. With an answer to Mr John Flavel's Vindiciarum Vindex. *Also to Mr Rothwell's Paedo-baptismus vindicatur. Part I. Part II Against Flavel's "Vindiciarum Vindex", Rothwell's "Paedo-baptismus vindicatur"; and also against Joshua Exell's "A serious inquiry into, and certain producing of plain and express proofs, that John Baptist, did as certainly baptize infants as the adult"*

The Everlasting Covenant, A Sweet Cordial for a drooping Soul: Or, The Excellent Nature of the Covenant of Grace Opened. In a Sermon Preached January the 29th. at the Funeral of Mr. Henry Forty, Late Pastor of a Church of Christ, at Abingdon, in the County of Berks. Who Departed this Life Jan. 25th 1693 and was Interr'd at Southwark

1694

A Counter-Antidote to purge out the Malignant Effects of a Late Counterfeit, prepared by Mr. Gyles Shute, an Unskilful Person in Polemical Cures: being An Answer to his Vindication of his Pretended Antidote, to prevent the Prevalency of Anabaptism

A Golden Mine Opened: or, The Glory of God's Rich Grace Displayed in the Mediator to Believers: and His Direful Wrath against Impenitent Sinners. Containing the Substance of near Forty Sermons upon several Subjects

Containing:

A Trumpet Blown in Sion: Or, an Allarm in God's Holy Mountain: Containing An Exposition of that Metaphorical Scripture Matth. iii. 12. Lately delivered in Two Sermons, and now Published to awaken the Drowsie and Formal Professors of this Age. Wherein the Nature of God's Wrath both Internal and Eternal is discovered, as seizing upon the Chaff, and Burning of

it up with Unquenchable Fire. Together with an Account how Professors may know whether they are Wheat or Chaff
Two sermons.

The Blessedness of Christ's Sheep: Or, No final Falling from a State of true Grace. Demonstrated in Several Sermons, lately Preached, and now for general Good Published. Wherein all the grand Objections usually brought against the Saints final Perseverance, are fully answered
Sixteen sermons on John 10:27–28.

The Trial of the False Professor: Or, the Danger of Final Apostacy
Three sermons on Hebrews 6:4–6.

The Great Salvation: Or, the Salvation of the Gospel Great and Glorious
Fifteen sermons on Hebrews 2:3.

A Trumpet Blown in Sion: Or, an Allarm in God's Holy Mountain: Containing An Exposition of that Metaphorical Scripture Matth. iii. 12. Lately delivered in Two Sermons, and now Published to awaken the Drowsie and Formal Professors of this Age. Wherein the Nature of God's Wrath both Internal and Eternal is discovered, as seizing upon the Chaff, and Burning of it up with Unquenchable Fire. Together with an Account how Professors may know whether they are Wheat or Chaff
This was also published separately from *A Golden Mine Opened*.

1696

A Feast of Fat Things Full of Marrow
This was a reissue of *The Banquetting House*, 1692. In addition, it contained other songs and a hundred hymns.

God acknowledged: Or, the True Interest of the Nation, opened in a sermon preached Dec. 11, 1695, a Day of Public Prayer and Humiliation
A sermon on Proverbs 3:6.

"The Introduction: Proving, There is no Actual Justification, or Actual Union with Christ before Faith." In *Actual Justification Rightly Stated containing a True Narrative of a Sad Schism made in a Church of Christ at Kilby in Leicester-Shire. Proving that none of the Elect are Actually Justified before Faith.*

This item is not listed in any modern bibliography as the author did not conclude his introduction in the usual manner by giving his name. It is attributed to Keach by Crosby, *History*, 4:314 and followed by Ivimey, *History*, 2:385, but no date is given by them. There is no internal evidence that Keach is the author either in the twelve-page "Introduction" or in the remaining fourteen pages. However, the author's discussion of the issues certainly reflects Keach's convictions expressed in his other writings, namely that actual justification takes place only when a person believes in Christ and not in eternity or when Christ died and rose again.

These were also the convictions of Henry Coleman. In 1696, Coleman had answered critics who had accused him of "dangerous errors." He was the pastor of the church at Kilby. There had been a schism in the church as a result of a disagreement over the question of when a person was actually justified. At the 1689 National Assembly, Coleman and Benjmain Winkles had been the only representatives present from Leicestershire. It appears they were from the same congregation and that subsequently Winkles together with others were responsible for the schism.

Given that Keach was on the committee that addressed this same issue at the 1689 Assembly and was also involved in the Antinomian controversy of the 1690s, it would have been very understandable if he had been asked to write an introduction to this slim publication. That Keach was the author of "The Introduction" was certainly the conviction of Thomas Crosby, his son-in-law.

Light broke forth in Wales, expelling darkness: Or, the Englishman's Love to the Ancient Britains. Being an Answer to a Book, Intituled, Children's Baptism from Heaven; published in the Welsh Tongue, by Mr. James Owen

A further edition was published posthumously in 1705 called *Believers baptism: or, Love to the Antient Britains displayed. Wherein the chief arguments for infant baptism are collected, stated, and fully answered.* A Welsh edition was also published in 1696 and recast in 1705.

1697

"Advertisement." In *A Just Vindication of Mr William Collins, and of Several Other Elders and Ministers, from the Unjust Reflections of Mr Isaac Marlow*

In the hymn singing dispute with Marlow, Keach took the blame for a mistranslation by Collins that led to considerable misunderstanding. The tract is undated but the "Advertisement" is signed by Keach and dated March 27, 1697.

An Appendix to answers of two Athenian Mercuries, concerning Pedo-baptism. Containing twenty-seven syllogistical arguments, proving infant-Baptism a mere human tradition

The Articles of the Faith of the congregation of Horsely-down [Back Street], as asserted this 10th of the 6th month, 1697

The early seeker, and the love of a dying Saviour

Listed only by Crosby, *History*, 4:311.

The Glory of a True Church, and its Discipline Display'd. Wherein a true Gospel-Church is described. Together with the Power of the Keys, and who are to be let in, and who to be shut out

A short Confession of Faith, containing the Substance of all the Fundamental Articles in the larger Confession, put forth by the Elders of the Baptized churches, owning Personal Election and Final Perseverance

1698

Christ Alone the Way to Heaven: Or, Jacob's Ladder Improved. Containing four Sermons lately preached on Genesis xxvii: xii. Wherein the Doctrine of Free-Grace is display'd, through Jesus Christ. Also, discovering the Nature, Office, and Ministration of holy Angels. To which is added one sermon on Rom. 8.1. With some short reflections on Mr. Samuel Clarke's new book, intituled Scripture Justification

The Display of Glorious Grace: Or, the Covenant of Peace Opened. In Fourteen sermons lately preached in which the errors of the present day, about reconciliation and justification, are detected
Fourteen sermons on Isaiah 54:10.

Laying on of Hands upon Baptized Believers, as such, Proved an Ordinance of Christ. In Answer to Mr Danver's former book Intituled, A treatise of Laying on of Hands
This is a second edition of Keach's 1675 *Darkness Vanquished.*

A Medium Betwixt Two Extremes. Wherein it is proved that the whole First Adam was condemned, and the whole Second Adam justified

1699

An answer to Mr Marlow appendix...also some reflections on what he speaks on the word [in Greek] Hymnos...by a learned hand

A Call to Weeping: Or, A Warning touching approaching Miseries. In a sermon preached on the 20th of March 1699. At the funeral of Mrs Elizabeth Westen, late wife of Mr John Westen

"*An epistle in commendation of the treatise.*" In Robert Prudom, *Truth unveiled by Scripture light, in three parts. Written for the sake of those that desire to behold it in its native beauty, to which is added, an appendix, which the author desires to leave as a legacy to his children*

1700

Beams of Divine Light: Or, some brief hints of the Being and Attributes of God, and of the three Persons in the Godhead

The covenant and catechism of the church of Christ meeting at Horsely Down in Southwark

The Jewish Sabbath Abrogated: Or, the Saturday Sabbatarians confuted. In Two Parts. First, Proving the Abrogation of the Old Seventh-day Sabbath. Secondly, That the Lord's-Day is of Divine appointment. Containing Several Sermons newly preach'd upon a special Occasion, wherein are many arguments not found in former Authors

Spiritual Songs, being the Marrow of the Scriptures, in songs of Praise to Almighty God, from the Old and New Testament

This was a third and enlarged reissue of *Spiritual Melody* (1691) and *The Banqueting House* (1692 and 1696).

1701

Gospel Mysteries Unveil'd: Or, Exposition of all the Parables, and many express similitudes

1702

The French and English impostours detected: Or, Zach. Housel and D. Coward tried by the word of God, and cast. Wherein also the errors... [the latter] are laid open; shewing what cause he had to think again. And the immortality of the soul fully convinced, in the form of a tryal

A 2nd edition was published in 1702 and a 3rd enlarged edition was published in 1703.

1704

"An epistle to the Reader." In Robert Prudom, *A new world discover'd, in the prospect-glass of the holy Scripture: Being a brief essay to the opening scripture-prophecies, concerning the latter days*

2. *Other primary sources*

Baxter, Richard. *Aphorismes of Justification, with the Explication annexed. Wherein also is opened the Nature of the Covenants, Satisfaction, Righteousnesse, Faith, Works &c., Published especially for the use of the Church at Kederminster in Worcester*. London, 1649.

_______. *Of Justification: Four Disputations Clearing and amicably Defending the Truth, against the unnecessary Opposition of divers Learned and Reverend Brethren*. London, 1658.

_______. *The Scripture Gospel Defended and Christ, Grace and Free Justification vindicated against the Libertines*. London, 1690.

Bayne, Peter. *Documents Relating to the Settlement of the Church of England by the Act of Uniformity of 1662 with an historical introduction*. London, 1862.

Bonham, Josias. *The churches Glory: Or, the Becoming Ornament: being a Seasonable Word, tending to the Provoking, Encouraging and Perfecting of Holiness in Believers*. London, 1674.

Bunyan, John. *Differences in Judgment about Water Baptism no Bar to Communion* in *The Complete Works of John Bunyan*. 3 vols. Marshallton: The National Foundation for Christian Education, 1968, 1:436–464.

Burnet, Gilbert. *History of his own time: from the restoration of Charles II to the treaty of peace at Utrecht, in the reign of Queen Anne*. London, 1837.

Calendar of State Papers, Domestic Series 1663–1664, 116, SP29/98, Thomas Disney to Luke Wilkes.

_______. 1663–1664, 595.

_______. 1668, 232. Richard Bower of Yarmouth to Joseph Williamson, secretary to Lord Arlington, Secretary of State.

_______. 1680–1683, 613.

Cary, Philip. *A Solemn Call unto all that would be owned as Christ's Faithful Witnesses, speedily and seriously, to attend unto the Primitive Purity of the Gospel Doctrine and Worship: Or, a Discourse Concerning Baptism*. London, 1690.

Carlyle, Thomas. *Oliver Cromwell's Letters and Speeches*. 2 vols. New York: John B. Alden, 1885.

Chauncy, Isaac. *Neonomianism Unmasked: or the Ancient Gospel Pleaded Against the Other Called a New Law*. London, 1692.

_______. *The Doctrine which is According to Godliness, Grounded upon the Holy Scriptures of Truth*. London, 1694.

_______. *Alexipharmacon, or a Fresh Antidote against Neonomian Bane, and Poison to Protestant Religion*. London, 1700.

Church Book of the Francis Bampfield Congregation 1686–1843. Photograph Copy presented to Dr. Williams Library by the Seventh-Day Baptist Congregation, Plainsfield, New Jersey, 1952.

Clarke, Samuel. *Scripture Justification: or, a Discourse of Justification, According to the Evidence of Scripture-Light: wherein the Nature of Justification is fully open'd; the Great Point of Justification by Works, both of Law and Gospel, is clearly Stated*. London, 1698.

A Confession of Faith put forth by the Elders and Brethren of Many Congregations of Christians (baptized upon Profession of their Faith) in London and the Country. London, 1677. Facsimile Edition, 2000 (Auburn: B & R Press, 2000). Sometimes known as *The Second London Baptist Confession of Faith*.

Coxe, Nehemiah. "A sermon preached at the Ordination of an elder and deacons in a baptized congregation in London," *Reformed Baptist Theological Review* I (January 2004): 133–156.

Crosby, Thomas. *The History of the English Baptists*. 4 vols. London, 1738–1740. Facsimile copy, Arkansas: The Baptist Standard Bearer, n.d.

Delaune, Thomas. *Angliae Metropolis, or the Present State of London with Memorials*. London, 1681.

_______. *A Plea for the Nonconformists, Giving the true State of the Dissenters Case*. London, 1684.

Dennis, Benjamin and Thomas Plant. *The English Spira: Being a Fearful Example of an Apostate*. London, 1693.

Dunton, John. *The Life and Errors of John Dunton*. London: John Nicholls, 1818.

Edwards, Thomas. *Gangraena: or a Catalogue and Discovery of many of the Errrors, Heresies, Blasphemies and pernicious Practices of the Sectaries of this time, vented and acted in England in these four last years: as also a Particular Narration of divers Stories, Remarkable Passages, Letters, and Extract of many Letters, all concerning the present Sects; together with some observations upon and Corrolaries from all the forenamed Premisses*. London, 1646.

English Poetry Fulltext Database, Chadwyck-Healey Products, Cambridge: Electronic CD Rom., n.d.

Featley, Daniel. *Katabaptistai Kataptustoi. The Dippers Dipt: Or, The Anabaptists duck'd and plung'd over head and ears, at a disputation in Southwark. Together with a large and full discourse of their 1. Original. 2. Severall Sorts. 3. Peculiar errours. 4. High attempts against the state. 5. Capitall punishments; with an application of these times*. London, 1645.

The First London Confession of Faith, 1644. In William L. Lumpkin, *Baptist Confessions of Faith*. Valley Forge: Judson Press, 1959, 144–171.

Flavel, John. "Mount Pisgah: A Sermon preached at the Public Thanksgiving, February 14, 1668–9, for England's Deliverance from Popery, Etc." In *The Works of John Flavel*. 6 vols. London: Banner of Truth Trust, 1968, 4:307–335.

________. "The Occasions, Causes, Nature, Rise, Growth and Remedies of Mental Errors." In *The Works of John Flavel*. 6 vols. London: Banner of Truth Trust, 1968, 3:413–492.

Guildhall Library, London, Parish Register for St. Mary Woolnoth, Ms. 7635/2, 3 January 1654/5.

Heathcote, Silvanus etc. *Truth Cleared: Or, a brief Narrative of the Rise, Occasion and Management of the present Controversy concerning Singing in the Worship of God. With an Account of several Letters that have passed between Mr. Benjamin Keach and Isaac*

Marlow, relating to an Appeal. As also of an Inspection made into both their books, by several worthy and honourable Elders, who have given their Judgment, subscribed with their own Hands, in Vindication of Isaac Marlow's Sheet of Observations on Mr Keach's Book. Whereunto is added a further Collection of Mr. Keach's Abuses, Falsehoods, and Misrepresentations, contained in his said Treatise, called The Breach in God's Worship, etc. As also some further evidence under the Hands of Several Brethren (that were late members of his Church) to detect several others of his Abuses therein. London, 1691.

Howe, John. *The Works of John Howe*. 6 vols. London: Religious Tract Society, 1863. 6:339, 343.

Jessey, Henry. *The Lord's Loud Call to England*. London, 1660.

Jones, Horatio Gates. *Historical Sketch of the Lower Dublin (or Pennepek) Baptist Church*. Morrisania, 1869.

Keach, Benjamin. *The Marrow of True Justification: Or, Justification without Works*. Birmingham: Solid Ground Christian Books, 2007.

________. *The Travels of True Godliness, from the Beginning of the World to this Present Day, in an apt and pleasant Allegory*. Birmingham: Solid Ground Christian Books, 2005.

________. "The Will of Benjamin Keach." *Surrey Will Abstracts*, Vol. 26, 2001, Archdeaconry Court of Surrey, 1700–1708, No. 820.

Keach, Elias. *The Glory and ornament of a True, Gospel-Constituted Church, being a brief display of the discipline of the church at Tallow-Chandlers Hall*. London, 1697.

Kiffin, William. *A sober discourse of the right to church communion, wherein is proved by scripture that no unbaptized person may be regularly admitted to the Lord's Supper*. London, 1681.

________. *The Life and Death of That Old Disciple of Jesus Christ and Eminent Minister of the Gospel, Hanserd Knollys*. London, 1692.

L'Estrange, Sir Roger. *Toleration Discuss'd*. London, 1663.

The London Baptist Confession of Faith of 1689 and Keach's

Catechism. Choteau, Montana: Gospel Mission, n.d.

Manton, Thomas. *One Hundred and Ninety Sermons on the Hundred and Nineteenth Psalm*. 3 vols. London, 1680. Edinburgh: Banner of Truth Trust, 1990.

Marlow, Isaac. *A Brief Discourse concerning Singing in the Public Worship of God in the Gospel-Church*. London, 1691.

Maze Pond Church Book 1691–1708. MS Angus Library, Regent's Park College, Oxford.

Mead, Matthew. *The Almost Christian Discovered, or the False Professor Tried and Cast*. London, 1675. Reprint; Morgan: Soli Deo Gloria Publications, 1993.

A Narrative of the Proceedings of the Elders and Messengers of the Baptized Congregations, in their General Assembly, met in London on Septemb. 3 to 12, 1689, from divers parts of England and Wales: Owning the Doctrine of Personal Election, and Final Perseverance. London, 1689.

A Narrative of the Proceedings of the General Assembly of the Elders and Messengers of the Baptized Churches, sent from divers parts of England and Wales, which began in London the 9th of June, and ended the 16th of the same, 1690. London, 1690.

A Narrative of the Proceedings of the General Assembly of the Elders and Messengers of the Baptized Churches, sent from divers parts of England and Wales, which began in London the 2d of June, and ended the 8th of the same, 1691. London, 1691.

A Narrative of the Proceedings of the General Assembly, Consisting of the Elders, Ministers and Messengers, met together in London from several Parts of England and Wales, on the 17th day of the 3rd month, 1692, and continued unto the 24th of the same. London, 1692.

Ogilby, John and William Morgan. *A Large and Accurate Map of the City of London 1676*. A copy of this may be viewed in Southwark Local Studies Library, 211 Borough High Street, London SE1 1JA.

Owen, John. *The Works of John Owen*. 16 vols. London: Banner of

Truth Trust, 1965–1968. Vols. 8 and 14 contain sermons and articles related to the threat of popery.

Parish Registers 1537–1758. Stoke Hammond, Bucks Record Office, PR195.

PRO, RG4/4188. *A perfect and Compleat Regester of Marrages, Nativities and Burials belonging to the Congregation that Meeteth on Horselydown, over whom Benjamen Keach is Overseer.*

Puritan Sermons 1659–1689, Being the Morning Exercises at Cripplegate, St Giles in the Fields and in Southwark by seventy-five ministers of the Gospel in or near London. 6 vols. Reprint; Wheaton: Richard Owen Roberts, 1981. 5:547–727; 6:1–622.

Richardson, Samuel. *Some brief Considerations on Doctor Featley his Book intituled, The Dippers Dipt, Wherein in some measure is discovered his many great and false accusations of divers persons, commonly called Anabaptists, with an Answer to them, and some brief reasons of their Practice.* London, 1645.

Rider, William. *Laying on of Hands (or a plain discovery of the truth thereof, under those several considerations minded in the New Testament).* London, 1656.

Russen, David. *Fundamentals without Foundation: Or, a True Picture of the Anabaptists, in their Rise Progress and Practice. Written for the Use of such that take 'em for Saints, when they are not so much as Christians.* London, 1703.

Saltmarsh, John. *Free Grace: or the Flowings of Christ's blood freely to Sinners.* London, 1645.

The Savoy Declaration of Faith and Order, 1658 in *Evangelical and Congregational, 'The Principles of Congregational Independents.'* Evangelical Fellowship of Congregational Churches, 1995, 47–92.

Stennett, Joseph. *An Answer to Mr David Russen's Book entituled Fundamentals without a foundation or a true picture of Anabaptists etc.* London, 1704.

Stepney Meeting Church Book (1644–1894). Entries for April 13, 1684 and Feb. 17, 1683. These records are held by Tower

Hamlets Local History and Archive Library, 277 Bancroft Road, London E1 4DQ.

Stinton, Benjamin. "The Tryall of Mr Benja. Keach who was prosecuted for Wrighting against Infant Baptism with an Account of ye Punishment inflicted upon him for ye same: Anno 1664." In *A Repository of Divers Historical Matters Relating to the English Antipaedobaptists, Collected from Original Papers of Faithful Extracts*. Angus Library, Oxford, 1712, No. 21, 93–104.

Surrey Quarter Sessions QS2/4–6. In Surrey History Centre, Woking.

Tombes, John. *Felo de Se. or Mr. Richard Baxters Self-destroying: Manifested in Twenty Arguments against Infant-Baptism, Gathered out of his own Writing, in his Second Disputation of Right to Sacraments*. London, 1659.

______. *A Short Catechism about Baptism*. London, 1659.

Traill, Robert. "A Vindication of the Protestant Doctrine of Justification from the Unjust Charge of Antinomians." In *The Works of Robert Traill*. 4 vols. Edinburgh: Banner of Truth Trust, 1975, 1:252–296.

______. "Righteousness in Christ." In *The Works of Robert Traill*. 4 vols. Edinburgh: Banner of Truth Trust, 1975, 4:156–234.

Turner, G. Lyon. *The Original Records of Early Nonconformity under Persecution and Indulgence*, 3 vols. London: T. Fisher Unwin, 1911–1914.

Vincent, Thomas. *God's Terrible Voice in the City*. London, 1667. Reprint. Philadelphia: Soli Deo Gloria, 1997.

The Westminster Confession of Faith in Philip Schaff, *The Creeds of Christendom*, 3 vols. Grand Rapids: Baker Book House, 1966, 3:600–673.

Williams, Daniel. *Gospel-Truth Stated and Vindicated: Wherein some Of Dr Crisp's Opinions Are Considered and the Opposite Truths are Plainly Stated and Confirmed*. London, 1692.

3. Secondary sources

Achinstein, Sharon. *Literature and Dissent in Milton's England*. Cambridge: Cambridge University Press, 2003.

Aitken, David. "Benjamin Keach: 'The Glorious Lover', An Analogue of Paradise Lost?" *BQ* 24 (1991): 132–135.

Arnold, Jonathan W. *The Reformed Theology of Benjamin Keach (1640–1704)*. Centre for Baptist History and Heritage Studies, vol. 11. Oxford: Regent's Park College, 2013.

Baines, Arnold H. J. "Innocency Vindicated; or, Reproach Wip'd Off." *BQ* 16 (1955–1956): 16–170.

_______. *The Signatories of the Orthodox Confession of 1679*. London, Carey Kingsgate Press, 1960.

Beddard, R.A. "The Restoration Church." In *The Restored Monarchy 1660–1688*, ed. J.R. Jones. London, Macmillan, 1986. 155–175.

Belcher, Richard P. and Anthony Mattia. *A Discussion of the Seventeenth Century Particular Baptist Confessions of Faith*. Southbridge: Crown Publications, 1990.

Boersema, Hans. *A Hot Peppercorn: Richard Baxter's Doctrine of Justification in its Seventeenth Century Context of Controversy*. Zoetermeer: Boekencentrum, 1993.

Broad, John, ed. *Buckinghamshire Dissent and Parish Life, 1669–1712*. Vol. 28. Bucks Record Society (1993): 63.

Brooks, James C. "Benjamin Keach and the Baptist Singing Controversy: Mediating Scripture, Confessional Heritage and Christian Unity." Ph.D. dissertation. Florida State University, College of Arts and Sciences, 2006.

Brown, Donald C. "To Sing or Not to Sing: Seventeenth Century English Baptists and Congregational Song." In *Handbook to the Baptist Hymnal*. Nashville, Tennessee: Convention Press, 1992.

Brown, Raymond. *Spirituality in Adversity: English Nonconformity in a Period of Repression, 1660–1689*. Studies in Evangelical History and Thought. Milton Keynes: Paternoster, 2012.

_______. *The English Baptists of the Eighteenth Century (1689–1815)*. London: Baptist Historical Society, 1986.

Burrage, Champlin. "Records of the Jacob-Lathrop-Jessey Church 1616–1641." *TBHS* 1 (1908–1909): 203–245.

______. *Early English Dissenters in the Light of Recent Research (1550–1641)*, 2 vols. New York: Russell & Russell, 1967 reprint.

Bustin, Dennis. *Paradox and Perseverance: Hanserd Knollys, Particular Baptist Pioneer in Seventeenth-Century England*. Studies in Baptist History and Thought, vol. 23. Milton Keynes: Paternoster, 2006.

Capp, B.S. *The Fifth Monarchy Men: A Study in Seventeenth-Century English Millenarianism*. London: Faber and Faber, 1972.

Carnes, James Patrick. "The Famous Mr. Keach: Benjamin Keach and His Influence on Congregational Singing in Seventeenth Century England." M.A. Thesis, North Texas State University, 1984.

Cathcart, William. *The Baptist Encyclopaedia*. 2 vols. Philadelphia: Louis H. Everts, 1881.

Coffey, John. *Persecution and Toleration in Protestant England, 1558–1689*. Harlow: Pearson Education, 2000.

Clear, Arthur. *The King's Village in Demesne or a Thousand Years of Winslow Life*. Winslow, 1894.

Clifford, Alan. "Benjamin Keach and Nonconformist Hymnology." In *Spiritual Worship*, Westminster Conference, 1985.

Copeland, David A. *Benjamin Keach and the Development of Baptist Traditions in Seventeenth Century England*. Lewiston: The Edwin Mellen Press, 2001.

Coult, Douglas. *A Prospect of Ashridge*. London: Phillimore, 1980.

Coward, Barry. *Oliver Cromwell*. London: Longman, 1991.

Culross, James. *Hanserd Knollys: A Minister and Witness of Jesus Christ*. London: Alexander and Shepheard, 1895.

Daniel, Curt. "John Gill and Calvinistic Antinomianism." In *The Life and Thought of John Gill (1697–1771): A Tercentennial Appreciation*, ed. Michael A.G. Haykin. Leiden: Brill, 1997. 171–190.

Darlington, Ida and James Howego. *Printed Maps of London, circa 1553–1850*. London: George Philip, 1964.

De Krey, Gary S. "The Politics of Belief." In *A Fractured Society:*

The Politics of London in the First Age of Party. Oxford: Clarendon Press, 1985. 75–120.

_______. "Revolution redivivus: 1688–1689 and the radical tradition in seventeenth-century London politics." In Lois Schwoerer, *The Revolution of 1688–9*. Cambridge: Cambridge University Press, 1992. 198–217.

Dix, Kenneth. *Benjamin Keach and a monument to liberty*. Dunstable: Fauconberg Press, 1985.

Dowley, T.E. "A London Congregation during the Great Persecution." *BQ* 27 (1977–1978): 233–239.

Evans, Nesta. "The descent of Dissenters in the Chiltern Hundreds." In *The World of Rural Dissenters*, ed. Margaret Spufford. Cambridge: Cambridge University Press, 1994.

Eveson, Philip H. *The Great Exchange: Justification by faith alone in the light of recent thought*. Day One: Bromley, 1996.

Fletcher, Anthony. "The Enforcement of the Conventicle Acts 1664–1679." In *Persecution and Toleration*, Studies in Church History 21, ed. W.J. Shiels. Oxford: Basil Blackwell, 1984. 235–246.

Foreman, H. "Some Seventeenth Century Baptist Educational Textbooks." *BQ* 30 (1983): 112–124.

Foster, John C. "Early Baptist Writers of Verse, Cheare, Bunyan, Keach." *TBHS* 3 (1912–1913): 95–110.

Garrett, James Leo. *Baptist Theology: A Four-Century Study*. Macon: Mercer University Press, 2009.

The General Biographical Dictionary: containing an Historical and Critical Account of the Lives and Writings of the Most Eminent Persons in Every Nation, 32 vols. A new edition revised and enlarged by Alexander Chalmers. London, 1812–1817.

Godfrey, W. Robert. "Millennial Views of the Seventeenth Century and Beyond." In *God is Faithful*. Westminster Conference Papers, 1999. 7–26.

Goldie, Mark. "Sir Peter Pett, Sceptical Toryism and the Science of Toleration in the 1680s." In *Persecution and Toleration*,

Studies in Church History 21, ed. W.J. Shiels. Oxford: Basil Blackwell, 1984. 247–273.

______. "The Hilton Gang and the purge of London in the 1680s." In *Politics and the Political Imagination in Later Stuart Britain*, ed. Howard Nenner. Rochester: University of Rochester Press, 1997. 43–73.

Greaves, Richard L. *Deliver Us from Evil: the Radical Underground in Britain, 1660–1663*. Oxford: Oxford University Press, 1986.

______. *Enemies Under His Feet, Radicals and Nonconformists in Britain, 1664–1677*. Stanford: Stanford University Press, 1990.

______. *Secrets of the Kingdom, British Radicals from the Popish Plot to the Revolution of 1668–89*. Stanford: Stanford University Press, 1992.

______. *Glimpses of Glory: John Bunyan and English Dissent*. Stanford: Stanford University Press, 2002.

Greaves, Richard L. and Robert Zaller, eds. *Biographical Dictionary of British Radicals in the Seventeenth Century*. 3 vols. Brighton: Harvester Press, 1982–1894.

Green, Ian. *The Christian ABC: Catechisms and Catechizing in England c.1530–1740*. Oxford: Clarendon Press, 1996.

______. *Print and Protestantism in Early Modern England*. Oxford: Oxford University Press, 2000.

Hanson, Brian L. with Michael A.G. Haykin. *Waiting on the Spirit of Promise: The Life and Theology of Suffering of Abraham Cheare*. Eugene: Pickwick Publications, 2014.

Harris, Tim. *London Crowds in the Reign of Charles II: Propaganda and Politics from the Restoration until the Exclusion Crisis*. Cambridge: Cambridge University Press, 1987.

______. *Politics under the Later Stuarts: Party Conflict in a Divided Society 1660–1715*. London: Longman, 1993.

______. *Restoration: Charles II and his Kingdoms, 1660–1685*. London: Allen Lane, 2005.

______. *Revolution: The Great Crisis of the British Monarchy, 1685–1720*. London: Allen Lane, 2006.

Haykin, Michael A.G. *Kiffin, Knollys and Keach: Rediscovering Our English Baptist Heritage*. Leeds: Reformation Today Trust, 1996.

Haykin, Michael A.G. and Jeffrey Robinson. "Particular Baptist Debates about Communion and Hymn-Singing." In *Drawn into Controversie: Reformed Theological Diversity and Debates Within Seventeenth-Century Puritanism*. ed. Michael A.G. Haykin and Mark Jones. Reformed Historical Theology, Vol. 17. Göttingen: Vandenhoeck & Ruprecht, 2011. 284–308.

Haykin, Michael A.G. and Steve Weaver, eds. *"Devoted to the Service of the temple": Piety, Persecution and Ministry in the Writings of Hercules Collins*. Grand Rapids: Reformation Heritage Books, 2007.

Hicks, Thomas Eugene Jr. "An analysis of the doctrine of justification in the theologies of Richard Baxter and Benjamin Keach." Ph.D. dissertation. The Southern Baptist Theological Seminary, 2009. Also available online: http://gradworks.umi.com/34/67/3467788.html.

Hill, Christopher. *A Tinker and a Poor Man: John Bunyan and his Church 1628–1688*. New York: Knopf, 1989.

______. *The English Bible and the Seventeenth-Century Revolution*. London: The Penguin Press, 1993.

______. *England's Turning Point: Essays on Seventeenth-Century English History*. London: Bookmarks, 1998.

Holmes, James Christopher. "The Role of Metaphor in the Sermons of Benjamin Keach." Ph.D. dissertation. The Southern Baptist Theological Seminary, 2009.

Horner, Barry E. *Pilgrim's Progress: Themes and Issues*. Darlington: Evangelical Press, 2003.

Howson, Barry H. *Erroneous and Schismatical Opinions: The Question of Orthodoxy Regarding the Theology of Hanserd Knollys (c.1599–1691)*. Leiden: Brill, 2000.

Ivimey, Joseph. *A History of the English Baptists*. 4 vols. London 1811–1830.

______. *The Life of Mr William Kiffin*. London, 1833.

James, Muriel. *Religious Liberty on Trial: Hanserd Knollys—Early Baptist Hero.* Franklin: Providence House Publishers, 1997.

Kevan, Ernest F. *London's Oldest Baptist Church.* London: The Kingsgate Press, 1933.

Keeble, Neil H. *The Literary Culture of Nonconformity in Later Seventeenth-Century England.* Leicester: Leicester University Press, 1987.

Kingdon, David. *Children of Abraham: A Reformed Baptist View of Baptism, the Covenant and Children.* Worthing: Henry E. Walter and Haywards Heath: Carey Publications, 1973.

Klaiber, A.J. "The Gospel Minister's Maintenance Vindicated." *BQ* 2 (1924–1925): 224–231.

Langley, A.S. "Seventeenth Century Baptist Disputations." *THBS* 6 (1918–1919): 216–243.

Lillback, P.A. "Covenant." *New Dictionary of Theology*, eds. Sinclair B. Ferguson, David F. Wright, J.I. Packer. Leicester: InterVarsity Press, 1988, 173–175.

Lipscomb, George. *The History and Antiquities of the County of Buckingham.* 4 vols. London, 1847.

Lumpkin, William L. *Baptist Confessions of Faith.* Valley Forge: Judson Press, 1959.

MacDonald, Murdina D. "London Calvinistic Baptists 1689–1727: Tensions within a Dissenting community under Toleration." Ph.D. diss., Regent's Park College, Oxford, 1982.

McBeth, H. Leon. *The Baptist Heritage.* Nashville: Broadman Press, 1987.

McGregor, J.F. "The Baptists: Fount of all Heresy." In *Radical Religion in the English Revolution*, eds. J.F. McGregor and B. Reay. Oxford: Oxford University Press, 1984. 23–63.

Malone, Fred A. *The Baptism of Disciples Alone: A Covenantal Argument for Credobaptism versus Paedobaptism.* Cape Coral: Founders Press, 2003.

_______. "Justification by Faith Alone in Contemporary Theological Perspective: A Critique of 'New Covenant Nomism.'" *Reformed*

Baptist Theological Review 1 (Jan. 2004): 105–132.

Martin, Hugh. *Benjamin Keach (1640–1704): Pioneer of Congregational Hymn Singing*. London: Independent Press, 1961.

______. "The Baptist Contribution to Early English Hymnody." *BQ* 19 (1961–1962): 195–208.

Mayor, S.H. "James II and the Dissenters." *BQ* 24 (1991): 180–190.

Muller, Richard A. "The Spirit and the Covenant: John Gill's Critique of the *Pactum Salutis*," *Foundations* 24, No.1 (January–March, 1981): 4–14.

Mullett, Michael. *Sources for the History of English Nonconformity 1660–1830*. British Records Association, 1991.

Murray, Iain. "Richard Baxter—The Reluctant Puritan?" In *Advancing in Adversity*. Westminster Conference Papers, 1991, 1–24.

Music, David W. "The Hymns of Benjamin Keach: An Introductory Study." *The Hymn* 34 (1983): 147–152.

Nettles, Tom J. *By His Grace and for His Glory: A Historical, Theological, and Practical Study of the Doctrines of Grace in Baptist Life*. Grand Rapids: Baker Book House, 1986.

______. "Benjamin Keach (1640–1704)." In *The Baptists: Key People Involved in Forming a Baptist Identity*. Beginnings in Britain. Vol. 1. Fearn: Christian Focus Publications, 2005. 163–193.

______. "Benjamin Keach, 1640–1704." In *The British Particular Baptists 1638–1910*. 3 vols. ed. Michael A.G. Haykin. Springfield: Particular Baptist Press, 1998. 1:94–131.

Newport, Kenneth G.C. "Benjamin Keach, William of Orange and Revelation, a Study in English Prophetical Exegesis." *BQ* 36 (1995): 43–51.

Nuttall, Geoffrey. "Another Baptist Ejection (1662): The Case of John Norcott." In *Pilgrim Pathways: Essays in Baptist History in Honour of B.R. White*, ed. William H. Brackney and Paul S. Fiddes with John H.Y. Briggs. Macon: Mercer University Press, 1999: 185–188.

Old Ordnance Survey Maps, Bermondsey and Wapping 1872: London Sheet 77. Newcastle-upon-Tyne: Alan Godfrey Maps, 1995.

Oliver, Robert W. "John Gill (1697–1771)." In *The British Particular Baptists 1638–1910*, 3 vols., ed. Michael A.G. Haykin. Springfield: Particular Baptist Press, 1998. 1:145–165.

Orme, William, ed. *Remarkable Passages in the Life of William Kiffin*. London, 1823.

Packer, J.I. "Baxter, Richard." In *New Dictionary of Theology*, ed. Sinclair B. Ferguson and David E. Wright. InterVarsity Press: Leicester, 1988. 82–83.

______. "The Doctrine of Justification in Development and Decline Among the Puritans." In *A Quest for Godliness: The Puritan Vision of the Christian Life*. Crossway: Wheaton, 1990. 149–161.

Parrett, J.K. "An Early Baptist on the Laying on of Hands." *BQ* 15 (1953–1954): 325–327, 320.

Payne, Ernest R. "Baptists and the Laying on of Hands." *BQ* 15 (1953–1954): 203–215.

______. *The Baptist Union: A Short History*. London: The Baptist Union of Great Britain and Ireland, 1959.

Pike, Godfrey Holden. *The Metropolitan Tabernacle: Or, An Historical Account of the Society, from its first planting in the Puritan era to the present time, with other sketches relating to the rise, growth, and customs of Nonconformity in Southwark, the Stockwell Orphanage, and the Pastors' College*. London: Passmore and Alabaster, 1870.

Porter, Stephen. *The Great Fire of London*. Godalming: Bramley Books, 1996.

Ramsbottom, B.A. *Stranger than Fiction: The Life of William Kiffin*. Harpenden: Gospel Standard Trust, 1989.

______. "The Stennetts." In *The British Particular Baptists 1638–1910*, 3 vols., ed. Michael A.G. Haykin. Springfield: Particular Baptist Press, 1998. 1:132–143.

Reid, Adam A. "Benjamin Keach, 1640." *BQ* 10 (1940–1941): 67–78.

Renihan, James M. *Edification and Beauty: The Practical Ecclesiology of the English Particular Baptists 1675–1705*. Studies in Baptist History and Thought, vol. 17. Milton Keynes: Paternoster, 2008.

______. "John Spilsbury (1593–c.1662/1668)." In *The British Particular Baptists 1638–1910*. 3 vols. ed. Michael A.G. Haykin. Springfield: Particular Baptist Press, 1998. 1:20–37.

Renihan, Michael T. *Antipaedobaptism in the Thought of John Tombes*. Auburn: B & R Press, 2001.

Riker, D.B. *A Catholic Reformed Theologian: Federalism and Baptism in the Thought of Benjamin Keach, 1640–1704*. Studies in Baptist History and Thought, vol. 35. Milton Keynes: Paternoster, 2009.

Royal Commission on Historical Monuments in England. Nonconformist Chapels and Meeting Houses, Buckinghamshire. London: Her Majesty's Stationery Office, 1986.

Short Title Catalogue 2, Early English Books, 1641–1700 (Wing).

Somerville, C. John *The Discovery of Childhood in Puritan England*. Athens: University of Georgia, 1992.

Spears, W.A. "The Baptist Movement in England in the Late 17th Century as Reflected in the Life and Thought of Benjamin Keach." Ph.D. diss., University of Edinburgh, 1953.

Spurgeon, Charles Haddon. *Autobiography, Vol.2: The Full Harvest, 1860–1892*. Edinburgh: Banner of Truth Trust, 1973.

______. *Lectures to my Students*. Pasadena: Pilgrim Publications, 1990.

______. *The Metropolitan Tabernacle: Its History and Work*. Pasadena: Pilgrim Publications, 1990.

Spurr, John. "From Puritanism to Dissent 1660–1700." In *The Culture of English Puritanism, 1560–1700*, ed. Christopher Durston and Jacqueline Eales. London: Macmillan, 1996. 234–265.

______. "Religion in Restoration England." In *The Reigns of Charles II and James VII and II*, ed. Lionel K. J. Glassey. London: Macmillan, 1997. 90–124.

Starr, Edward C. ed. *A Baptist Bibliography Being a Register of Printed Material By and About Baptists: Including Works Written*

Against the Baptists. 25 vols. Rochester: American Baptist Historical Society, 1952–1976.

Tames, Richard. *Southwark Past*. London: Historical Publications, 2001.

Taylor, A. *The History of the English General Baptists*, 3 vols. London, 1818.

Tolmie, Murray. *The Triumph of the Saints: The Separate Churches of London 1616–1649*. Cambridge: Cambridge University Press, 1977.

Toon, Peter. *The Emergence of Hyper-Calvinism in English Nonconformity 1689–1765*. London: The Olive Tree, 1967.

Trueman, Carl R. "Richard Baxter on Christian Unity: A Chapter in the Enlightening of English Reformed Orthodoxy." *Westminster Theological Journal* 61 (1999): 53–71.

[Trustees of Winslow Old Baptist Chapel?] *Winslow Old Baptist Chapel or Keach's Meeting House: a Short History and Guide, also Sermon, Poetry, Metaphors, and Allegories of Benjamin Keach, Pastor from 1658–1668.*

Turner, G. Lyon. "The Religious Condition of London in 1672 as reported to King and Court by an Impartial Outsider." *Transactions of the Congregational Historical Society* 3 (1907–1908): 193–205.

______. "Williamson's Spy Book" *Transactions of the Congregational Historical Society* 5 (1911–1912): 242–258; 301–319; 345–356.

Underhill, E.B. *Confessions of Faith and Other Public Documents Illustrative of the Baptist Churches of England in the 17th Century*. London: The Hanserd Knollys Society, 1854.

Underwood, A.C. *A History of the English Baptists*. London: The Baptist Union Publication Dept. (Kingsgate Press), 1947.

Underwood, T.L. *Primitivism, Radicalism, and the Lamb's War: The Baptist-Quaker Conflict in Seventeenth Century England.* Oxford: Oxford University Press, 1997.

Valentine, Theo. F. *Concern for the Ministry: The Story of the Particular Baptist Fund 1717–1967*. Teddington: Particular Baptist Fund, 1967.

Vaughn, James Barry. "Public Worship and Practical Theology in the Work of Benjamin Keach (1640–1704)." Ph.D. diss., University of St. Andrews, May 1989.

______. "Benjamin Keach." In *Baptist Theologians*, ed. Timothy George and David Dockery. Nashville: Broadman Press, 1990. 49–76.

______. "Benjamin Keach's *The Gospel Minister's Maintenance Vindicated* and the Status of Ministers Among Seventeenth-Century Baptists," *Baptist Review of Theology* 3 (Spring 1993): 53–60.

Verney, Margaret M. *Buckinghamshire Biographies*. Oxford: Clarendon Press, 1912.

Victoria County History for Bedfordshire. Vol. 1, London: Archibald Constable, 1904; Vols. 2 and 3, London: Constable, 1908 and 1912.

Waldron, Samuel L. *A modern exposition of the 1689 Baptist Confession of Faith*. Darlington: Evangelical Press, 1989.

Walker, Austin R. "Benjamin Keach (1640–1704): Tailor and Preacher." Annual Lecture of the Strict Baptist Historical Society, Friday, March 19, 2004.

______. "Benjamin Keach (1640–1704): Tailor Turned Preacher." In John H.Y. Briggs, ed. *Pulpit and People: Studies in Eighteenth-Century Baptist Life and Thought*. Studies in Baptist History and Thought, vol. 28. Milton Keynes: Paternoster, 2009. (This is slightly revised version of Annual Lecture of the Strict Baptist Historical Society, 2004.)

______. "Benjamin Keach and the 'Baxterian' Controversy of the 1690s." *Reformed Baptist Theological Review*, III:1 (January 2006).

______. "Benjamin Keach and the Protestant cause under persecution." Paper given at the 2nd Annual Andrew Fuller Center for Baptist Studies Conference. The Southern Baptist Theological Seminary, Louisville, KY. August 25–26, 2008. (http://www.sbts.edu/media/audio/andrew-fuller-center/07-plenary-session-6.mp3).

______. "Benjamin Keach: Cultivating corporate spirituality and church covenants." In G. Stephen Weaver Jr. and Ian Hugh Clary, eds. *The Pure Flame of Devotion: The History of Christian Spirituality, Essays in Honour of Michael A.G. Haykin*. Kitchener: Joshua Press, 2013. 363–382.

______. "Benjamin Keach: 'Much for the work of religion.'" In *The Faith That Saves*. Westminster Conference, 2004. 93–110.

______. "'Bold as a lion': The spirituality of Benjamin Keach," *Eusebeia: The Bulletin of the Jonathan Edwards Centre for Reformed Spirituality* 4 (Spring 2005): 17–46.

Walker, Rachel E. "Ordinary and Common Discourses: The Impact of the Glorious Revolution on Political Discussion in London 1688–1694." Ph.D. dissertation, University of Sheffield, 1998.

Wamble, Hugh. "Benjamin Keach, Churchman." *Quarterly Review* (April–June 1956): 47–52.

Watts, Michael R. *The Dissenters: From the Reformation to the French Revolution*. Oxford: Clarendon Press, 1978.

White, Barrie R. "Baptist Beginnings and the Kiffin Manuscript." *Baptist History and Heritage* 2 (1967): 29–34.

______. "William Kiffin—Baptist Pioneer and Citizen of London." *Baptist History and Heritage* 2 (1967): 91–103, 126.

______. *Hanserd Knollys and Radical Dissent in the Seventeenth Century*. London: Dr. Williams Trust, 1977. Friends of Dr. Williams's Library, 31st lecture, 1977.

______. *The English Baptists of the Seventeenth Century*. Didcot: Baptist Historical Society, 1996.

Whitley, W. T. "London Conventicles in 1683." In *Transactions of the Congregational Historical Society*, III (1907–1908): 364–366.

______. "Baptists and Bartholomew's Day." *THBS* 1 (1908–1909): 24–41.

______. "Ordination at Southampton, 1691." *TBHS* 2 (1910–1911): 65–66.

______. "Persecution at Lynn, 1698." *TBHS* 2 (1910–1911): 67–68.

———. *A Baptist Bibliography*. 2 vols. London: The Kingsgate Press, 1916, 1922.
———. "Loyal London Ministers, 1696." *TBHS* 6 (1918–1919): 183–188.
———. "Baptists in the Colonies till 1750." *TBHS* 7 (1920–1921): 31–48.
———. "London Churches in 1682." *BQ* 1 (1922–1923): 82–87.
———. *The Baptists of London 1612–1928*. London: The Kingsgate Press, 1928.
———. "Distressed Sion Relieved, 1689." *BQ* 5 (1930–1931): 227–331.
———. *A History of British Baptists*. Revised edition, London: The Kingsgate Press, 1932.
———. "The First Hymnbook in Use." *BQ* 10 (1940–1941): 369–375.
Wilson, Walter. *The History and Antiquities of Dissenting Churches and Meeting Houses, in London, Westminster, and Southwark*. 4 vols. London, 1808–1814.

4. *Other seventeenth-century Particular Baptist works on believer's baptism*

Note: Place of publishing is London in each case.

Cary, Philip. *A Solemn Call to all that would be owned as Christ's Faithful Witnesses, speedily and seriously, to attend unto the Primitive Purity of the Gospel Doctrine and Worship: Or, a Discourse Concerning Baptism*. 1690.
———. *A just reply to Mr J. Flavel's and Mr Whiston's arguments*. 1690.
Collins, Hercules. *Believers-baptism from heaven, and of divine institution, infants-baptism from earth, and human invention*. 1691.
———. *The antidote proved a counterfeit, or error detected, and believers baptism vindicated, containing an answer to An antidote to prevent the prevalency of Anabaptism*. 1693.

______. *The sandy foundation of infant baptism shaken: or an answer to (Frances Mence)...and is a full answer to (Michael Harrison), together with a narrative which contains the foundation of the controversy. To which is added a letter by a private hand (Richard Claridge) with a preface and an appendix containing 1. The pedigree of infant's habitual faith, 2. The judgement of learned men against it.* 1695.

______. *Truth and innocency vindicated: or an impartial account of the late proceedings between Mr Mence and Mr Collings concerning the salvation of infants by the imputation of Christ's righteousness.* 1695.

Coxe, Nehemiah. *A discourse of the covenants that God made with men before the law: wherein the covenant of circumcision is more largely handled and the invalidity of the plea for paedo-baptism taken from thence discovered.* 1681.

Danvers, Henry. *A Treatise of Baptism: Wherein, That of Believers, and that of Infants, is Examined by the Scriptures.* 1674.

______. *Innocency and Truth Vindictaed: Or, A short Reply to Mr. Will's Answer to a Late treatise of Baptisme.* 1675.

______. *A Rejoynder to Mr. Wills his Vindiciae.* 1675.

______. *A Second Reply in Defence of the Treatise of Baptism.* 1675.

______. *A Third Reply; Or, a Short return to Mr. Baxter's brief Answer to my Second Reply.* 1675.

Delaune, Thomas. *Truth Defended: or, a Triple Answer to the late Triumvirates Opposition in their Three Pamphlets, viz. Mr. Baxter's Review, Mr. Wills his Censure, Mr Whiston's Postscript to His Essay.* 1677.

______. *A Brief Survey and Confutation of Mr. Joseph Whistons Books of Baptism, A Just Reproof of the Clamorous Cavils of Mr. Obed. Wills, the Turbulent Appealer, Mr. Richard Baxter's Review of the State of Christian Infants Examined; and his Grounds for the Baptism of such to be Insufficient, and groundless.* 1676.

Gosnold, John. *Of the Doctrine of Baptisms, or, A Discourse of the Baptism of Water and of the Spirit.* 1657.

Kiffin, William. *A brief remonstrance of the reasons and grounds of those people commonly called Anabaptists, for their separation… or certain queries concerning their faith and practice propounded by Robert Poole, answered by W.K.* 1645.

______. with Benjamin Coxe and Hanserd Knollys, *A Declaration concerning the public dispute which should have been in the public Meeting-House of Aldermanbury, the 3rd of this inst. Month of Dec. concerning Infants-Baptism*. 1645.

______. with Hanserd Knollys, Daniel Dike, John Gosnold, Henry Forty and Thomas Delaune, *The Baptists answer to Mr Obed. Wills, his appeal against Mr Danvers*. 1675.

______. *A sober discourse of the right to church communion, wherein is proved by scripture that no unbaptized person may be regularly admitted to the Lord's Supper*. 1681.

Knollys, Hanserd. *The shining of a flaming fire in Sion: Or, A clear answer unto 13 exceptions against the grounds of new baptism (so called in Mr Saltmarsh his book, intituled, 'The smoke in the temple.' Also postscript, wherein some queries are propounded unto believers*. 1646.

Norcott, John. *Baptism discovered plainly and faithfully, according to the Word of God: Wherein is set forth the glorious pattern of our blessed Saviour Jesus Christ, the pattern of all believers in their subjection to baptism*. 1672.

Patient, Thomas. *The Doctrine of Baptisms, and the Distinction of the Covenants*. 1654.

Spilsbury, John. *A Treatise concerning the lawful subject of Baptism*. 1643.

______. *God's Ordinance, the Saints' Privilege Discovered and Proved in Two Treatises*. 1646.

______. *A Treatise concerning the lawful subject of Baptism 2nd ed., corrected and enlarged*. 1652.

5. *Digital sources*

More and more material by Benjamin Keach appears online on an irregular basis. These websites contain one or more of Keach's publications (accessed November 24, 2014).

The Digital Puritan
http://digitalpuritan.net/benjamin-keach/

Early English Books Online
http://quod.lib.umich.edu/e/eebo?key=author;page=browse;value=k

English Nonconformist Poetry, 1660–1700
http://www.pickeringchatto.com/titles/1294-9781851969654-english-nonconformist-poetry-1660-1700

Logos Bible Software
https://www.logos.com/product/40846/baptist-covenant-theology-collection
https://www.logos.com/product/45889/selected-works-of-benjamin-keach

Post-Reformation Digital Library
http://www.prdl.org/author_view.php?a_id=1413

INDEX

A Book for Boys and Girls, 148, 170
A Brief Discourse concerning Singing in the Public Worship of God in the Gospel-Church, 295
A Call to the Unconverted, 141, 165
A Defence of Gospel Truth, 351
A Discourse of the True Nature of the Gospel, 361
A Plea for the Nonconformists, 8, 186
A Second Argument, 192
A sober discourse of the right to church communion, wherein is proved by scripture that no unbaptized person may be regularly admitted to the Lord's Supper, 335
A Solemn Call...or a Discourse Concerning Baptism, 39, 327
A Vindication of the Protestant Doctrine of Justification from the Unjust Charge of Antinomians, 361
Abingdon Baptist Association, 56
Achinstein, Sharon, 141, 154
Act of Toleration, xxx, 12, 106, 191, 202–203, 339
Act of Uniformity, xxviii, 28, 46, 58, 70, 75, 76, 108, 153, 202, 313–314
Act to retain the Queen's subjects in their due obedience (1581), 66
Adams, Richard, 39, 204, 289,
Ainsworth, Henry, 40, 297, 335
Alleine, Joseph, 141
Allen, William, 39
Ames, William, 40, 335
An Alarme to the Unconverted, 141
An Apology for the True Christian Divinity, 181
An Argumentative and Practical Discourse on Infant Baptism, 316
An End to Discord, 351
Anabaptist, 2–4, 29, 37, 63, 64, 71, 183, 250–251, 318, 336, 341, 377
Anglican, Anglicanism, xxviii, 2, 5, 7, 8, 11, 22, 23–28, 33, 37, 40, 42, 50, 56–58, 75, 85, 92, 111, 124, 127, 134, 151, 162, 201–202, 204, 296, 312, 326, 330, 333, 344
Annesley, Samuel, 110, 162
Antinomian, Antinomianism, 3, 31, 166, 250, 345–348, 351, 352, 366, 371
Argyll, Lord, 129
Arminian, 22, 28, 39, 41, 87–95, 100, 146, 160, 191, 193, 216, 218, 259, 268, 331, 350, 353, 356, 366
Arnold, Jonathan, xviii, 352, 357, 362
assizes, xxx, 45, 46–53, 64, 72, 76, 109, 140
Athenian Mercury, 316

Athenian Society, 316
Aylesbury, xxi, xxviii, 29, 45, 52, 59, 62, 66, 67, 72, 81, 140, 224, 280, 312
Ayliff, John, 129

Bagwell, Samuel, 290
Bampfield, Francis, 7–8
Baptist Union, 221
Barclay, Richard, 181
Barrett, George, 204, 283, 288
Barton, William, 307
Bateman, Charles, 129
Bates, William, 196, 253
Bawdy house riots, 84
Baxter, Richard, xv, xxxi, 107, 141, 151, 165, 172, 177–178, 221, 250, 253, 271, 312, 316, 317, 337, 344–346, 348, 350–372
Baxterian, Baxterianism, 250, 271, 346, 351–363, 371
Bedford, Bedfordshire, 7, 24, 66, 173, 191–192, 288
believer's baptism, xviii, 5, 7, 9, 24, 27, 28, 32, 38–39, 41–42, 103, 152, 173, 311, 314, 316, 318, 319, 320–338, 376, 381
Bellarmine, Robert, 365
Berhamsted, 37
Bonham, Josias, 87, 172
Bonner, Edmund, 133
Book of Martyrs, 126
Bower, Richard, 65
Brine, John, 371
Brown, Moses, 227
Brown, Raymond, xxi, 24, 26
Buckinghamshire, xix, xx, xxi, xxvii, 6, 11, 15, 18, 20, 23, 26, 29, 30, 32, 36–37, 44, 45, 59, 62, 66–68, 75–81, 87, 88, 93, 105, 108, 140, 146, 173, 181, 183, 191–193, 214, 338, 349, 351, 380
Bunhill Fields, 376
Bunyan, John, xxix, 7–8, 23, 29, 66, 141, 144, 148, 165–167, 170, 173, 188, 191–193, 221, 303, 335, 348, 378
Burkitt, William, 316, 322, 326, 333, 336
Burnet, Gilbert, 114
Bustin, Dennis, xviii
Byfield, 87

Calamy, Benjamin, 186
Calvin, John, 40, 102, 121, 189, 335,
Cary, Philip, 39–40, 318, 327
Charles I, xxvii, 30, 33, 45, 46, 47
Charles II, xxviii–xxx, 8, 32, 45, 50, 54, 55, 56, 61, 67, 84, 92, 110, 111, 114, 115, 119, 125–129, 132, 133, 137, 200, 224
Charnock, Stephen, 196, 253
Cheare, Abraham, xv, xviii, 7–8, 206
Chesham, 37, 81
Child, John, xxx, 173, 191–196, 261
Children's Baptism from Heaven, 318
Chiltern Hills, 37
Chilton, George, 43–44
Christ Alone Exalted, 345, 353
Christ Church College, Oxford, 75
Christianismus Primitivus, 295
civil wars, xxvii, 14, 28, 29, 33, 36, 127
Clarendon Code, 202
Clarke, Adam, 187
Clarke, Samuel, xxxi, 271, 345, 349, 350–351, 358–362, 365
Clarkson, David, 253
Coffey, John, 28, 56, 108, 123, 134
Colfe, Mrs., 109
College, Stephen, 129
Collins, Hercules, xv, xviii, 7, 9, 86, 110, 134, 183, 185, 246, 288, 296, 309, 318, 319, 321, 381
Collins, William, 210, 215, 217, 219
Commonwealth, xxvii, 14, 28, 33, 36, 47, 50, 66
Compton, Robert, 124

Copeland, David, 8, 182
Cornish, Henry, 129–130, 200
Corporation Act (1661), 58, 202–203
Cotton, John, 147, 253
Council of Trent, 365
Counter-Reformation, 123, 136
Covenanters, Scottish, xxx
Coward, Mr., 363
Coxe, Nehemiah, 134, 206, 210–211, 215, 216, 221, 318
Cripplegate, 86, 94, 121, 285, 316
Crisp, Samuel, 345
Crisp, Stephen, 181
Crisp, Tobias, 345–346, 348, 351, 353, 361, 370
Cromwell, Oliver, xxvii, xviii, 22, 26, 28, 29, 33, 34, 35, 36, 50, 54, 57, 129, 300, 348
Cromwell, Richard, xxviii
Crosby, Thomas, xix, xxx, 9–10, 21, 37, 38, 41, 62, 67, 68, 72, 85, 87–88, 92–95, 107–109, 150, 177–178, 181, 183, 203, 209, 228, 229, 233, 234, 291–292, 293, 339, 341, 376, 384

Danvers, Henry, 183
Dawson, Thomas, 285
Declaration of Breda, xxviii, 54
Declaration of Indulgence, xxix, 68, 92, 125, 126, 143, 224
Delaune, Thomas, 7–8, 150, 172, 186, 206, 318
Dennis, Benjamin, 134
Devon, Devonshire, 7, 39, 67, 124
Disney, Henry, 75
Disney, Thomas, 19, 23–24, 43–45, 50, 70, 74, 75, 140
Dix, Kenneth, xxi, 232
Dorchester, 7
Drake's Island, Plymouth Sound, 7–8
du Moulin, Peter, 122, 201
Dungan, Thomas, 245
Dunscombe, John, 26
Dunton, John, 162, 250–251, 271, 376–377

Earl of Devonshire, 124
Earl of Shrewsbury, Danby, 124
Edict of Nantes, xxx, 126, 134
Edwards, Thomas, 313, 362
Egerton, John, 76
Elizabeth I, Elizabethan, 7, 36, 66, 126
Elwood, Thomas, 181
Essex, Earl of, 129, 200
Excell, Joshua, 318

Fairfax, Thomas, 29
Featley, Daniel, 313–314, 337
Felo de Se: or Mr. Richard Baxters Self-destroying, 178
Fifth Monarchy, 7, 46, 57, 64, 65, 85
First Conventicle Act (1664), xxviii, 45, 58, 65, 66–67, 75, 107
First London Assembly of Particular Baptists, xxx, 314
First London Baptist Confession of Faith (1644), xxvii, 4, 67, 215, 287, 314
Five Mile Act, xxviii, 59
Flavel, John, 40, 318, 340, 361
For a More full and firm Union among all good Protestants, 192
Forty, Henry, xxxi, 95, 96, 206, 250, 252
Fox, George, 179
Foxe, John, 126
Free Grace: or the flowings of Christ's blood freely to sinners, 30, 348
Freemans Lane, 94, 214, 225
Fuller, Andrew, xxiii

Gangraena, 313
Garrett, James Leo, xviii
Gaunt, Elizabeth, 129–130, 200
General Baptist, xxvii, xxviii, 8, 11, 19, 21, 23, 24, 28, 32, 33, 36, 37, 61, 64, 66, 68, 70, 87, 89, 94, 180, 181, 183, 215, 216, 218, 295–296, 298, 311, 379

Gill, John, xxiii, 11, 103, 371–372
Glassius, Salomon, 186
Glorious Revolution, 114, 119, 122, 124
Goat Street church, 218, 225–229
God's Terrible Voice in the City, 141
Godfrey, Edmund, 127
Goodwin, Thomas (the younger), 361
Goodwin, Thomas, 107, 196, 253
Gospel-Truth Stated and Vindicated, 346, 351
Grace Abounding to the Chief of Sinners, 165
Grantham, Thomas, 295
Great Brickhill, 24, 26, 28
Great Ejection, xxviii
Great Fire of London, xxviii, 83, 84, 114, 226
Great Plague, xxviii, 58, 62, 83, 84, 89, 114, 203
Greaves, Richard, xxi, 57, 65, 85, 107, 124, 127, 129
Green, Ian, xxi, 144, 152
Greenhill, William, 28
Grove, Jane (Keach's first wife), xxviii, xxix, 61, 62, 70, 92–93, 179
Gunpowder Plot, 126
Gurnall, William, 187

Halliwell, Richard, 283, 288
Harris, John, 39, 204
Harrison, Edward, 107
Hartnoll, John, 61, 71
Helwys, Thomas, 19
Hertfordshire, 44, 93, 192
Hewling, Benjamin, 129–130
Hewling, William, 129–130
Hicks, John, 129–132
Hicks, Thomas, 181
High Wycombe, 181
Hill, Christopher, 13, 121
Hilton Gang, xxi, 111
Hilton, John, 111
History of the Puritans, 341
Hobson, Paul, 29, 348
Holland, xxxi, 21, 23, 126, 136, 183
Hollis, John, 392–393
Hollis, Thomas, 392–393
Holloway, James, 129
Holmes, Abraham, 129
Horselydown, xxix, xxx, 15, 92, 185, 214, 224–228, 233, 245, 271, 280–284, 288–293, 294, 296, 298, 334, 341, 344, 362, 363, 366, 375, 382
Housel, Zachary, 363
Huguenots, 126
Hyde, Edward, Lord Chancellor, 45, 67
Hyde, Robert, Lord Chief Justice, 45–47, 51–52, 64–65, 139
hyper-Calvinism, 256–257, 371, 372

Independent(s), 8, 24, 27, 28, 33, 36, 40, 56, 57, 85, 103, 121, 151, 179, 214, 218, 234, 238, 296, 300, 318, 324, 335, 351, 361, 380, 382
Ives, Jeremiah, 181
Ivimey, Joseph, 45, 202, 204, 215, 216, 219, 225, 226, 257, 377

James II, xxix, xxx, 7, 85, 124–126, 128, 133, 134, 136, 137, 196, 198, 200, 379
Jeffreys, George, 8, 128–129, 130, 133, 134
Jessey, Henry, 56, 173
Jesuits, 134
Jones, James, 109, 134, 192, 194
Justice Reading, 109

Keach, Anna, sister, 19

Keach, Benjamin,
- adopts Calvinistic theology, xxix, 39, 87–95, 99–103, 146, 158, 160, 191, 196, 218, 256–257, 262–269, 379, 385
- as a General Baptist, 23, 28, 32–33,

37, 41, 68, 70, 87, 89, 94, 215, 218, 298, 311, 379
baptism of, xxvii, xxviii, 19, 24, 37–38, 311
believer's baptism, xviii, 15, 19, 21, 28, 37–42, 96, 152, 178, 189, 311–341, 378
birth of children, 62, 86, 112, 228
birth of, 15, 70
catechisms of, 9, 139–171
character of, 5–11, 54, 76–77, 207, 229–234, 287–289, 376–377, 386–387
chronology of, xxvii–xxxii
conversion of, 13–42, 88, 311
covenant of grace, 89, 95–103, 196, 251–262, 321–322
death of, xxxii, 1, 6, 12, 375–376
dream of, 63
education of, 19, 75
encouragement of literacy, 147–154, 188
fined, 52, 108
hymn books of, 9, 294
imagination of, 166–167, 169, 378
imprisonment of, 6, 52–53, 68, 72–73, 93, 280, 383
justification by faith, free grace, xv, xviii, 21–22, 30–31, 33, 40, 42, 96, 101, 158, 251, 253, 255, 276–277, 306, 328, 343–373
laying on of hands, 9, 172, 183–185, 207, 244, 399–400
leadership of, 8, 67, 375, 378
living in Winslow, 19, 23, 44, 46, 47, 50, 52, 61, 62, 70, 73, 81, 89
Lord's Supper, 189
maintenance of ministers, 9, 188, 208–214, 287
marriages of, xxviii, xxix, 61, 70, 93, 112, 181
moves to London, xxix, 6, 59, 71, 73, 76, 81, 83–85, 105, 146, 171, 225
Neonomian controversy, xxxi, 344–346, 348, 350, 353, 361, 362, 365, 371, 373, 381, 382
ordination of, xxix
pilloried, xx, xxviii, 6, 52, 53, 62, 81, 140, 224, 280, 383
poetry and hymns of, 9, 72–73, 77, 112–123, 137, 154–162, 174–175, 198, 296, 303–309
preaching of, 9, 37, 50, 66, 70–71, 112, 142, 171–173, 175–177, 196, 223–247, 249–277, 375, 385
promotion of practical godliness, 142–143, 152–156, 162–170, 171, 207–208, 221, 230–231, 267–268
Russen's accusations, 2-6, 8, 229–230, 314, 315, 338–339, 364, 376, 391–393
singing of hymns in church, xvi, xx, xxx, 9, 218, 227, 244, 279–309, 327, 344, 363, 399–400
sufferings/persecution of, xix, xx, 6, 12, 46, 50–59, 63, 68, 72, 76, 92, 106, 108–117, 136, 190, 212, 224, 280
theologian, 8, 9
trial of, 21, 46–54, 66, 81, 312
upbringing in Buckinghamshire, xix, 6, 70
view of paedobaptism, 21, 33, 38–42, 47–52, 53, 217, 311–341
view of Revelation, 199–201, 379
view of the Bible, 14, 64, 169, 182, 188–191, 222, 240–241, 249–277, 299
view of the papacy and Catholicism, 106, 117–137, 157, 171, 197–201, 379
will of, 145, 153, 214, 247, 228, 375, 389
writings of, 9, 12, 108, 112, 139–170, 182, 186–190, 214, 249–277, 296, 343

Keach, Benjamin, grandson, 247
Keach, Elias, son, xxi, xxviii, xxx, xxxi, 62, 92, 95, 228, 229, 232, 242–247, 400
Keach (Stinton), Elizabeth, daughter, xxix, xxx, 95, 228, 389
Keach (Green), Hannah, daughter, xxviii, 62, 92, 95, 179, 228–229, 363, 376, 389
Keach, Henry, brother, 19, 43–44, 70
Keach, John, father, 15, 17
Keach, Joseph, brother, 19, 70
Keach, Josiah, brother, 19
Keach, Joyce, mother, 15
Keach, Maria, sister, 19
Keach (Enby), Mary, daughter, xxviii, 62, 92, 95, 228, 389
Keach, Rachel, daughter, xxix, 95, 228, 389
Keach (Crosby), Rebecca, daughter, xxx, 95, 203, 228, 389
Keach (Stinton), Susannah, daughter, xxix, xxxi, 95, 227–228, 389
Keeble, Neil H., xxi, 140, 148, 165, 168
Keith, George, 181
Kethe, William, 307
Kiffin, William, xv, xviii, xix, xxviii, xxxi, 11, 39, 56, 67, 69, 73, 86, 107, 110, 130, 174, 181, 204–206, 251, 281, 288, 289, 318, 335
Knollys, Hanserd, xv, xviii, xix, xxxi, 7, 8, 11, 67, 86, 94, 107, 110, 147, 149, 150, 181, 199, 203–206, 216, 221, 251, 281, 283, 296, 318
Kreitzer, Larry, xviii

L'Estrange, Roger, 108, 140
Lark, Sampson, 129, 130
Lathrop, John, 173
Leader, Esther, 283–284
Leader, Luke, 281, 290–292
Leader, Mary, 281, 290
Leighton Buzzard, 26, 44, 75
Lincolnshire, 75
Lisle, Lady Alice, 129–130
Lollards, Lollardy, 37–38, 121
Long Parliament, 33
Louis XIV, xxix, xxx, 125–126, 133
Lower Dublin Baptist Church (Pennepek Church), 246
Lumley, Lord, 124
Luther, Martin, 3, 40, 64, 121, 136, 335, 351, 365
Lyme, 130

MacDonald, Murdina, 8–9, 209–210, 284, 286,
Man Made Righteous by Christ's Obedience, 351
Man, Edward, 204, 283
Manton, Thomas, 105–107, 196, 221, 253
Mark Lane Independent Church, 186, 361
Marlow, Isaac, xxx, 227, 282–286, 288, 292, 295, 298–302, 308, 381
Marshall, John, 217
Mary I, 36, 126, 133, 134
Mary II, xxix, xxx, xxxi, 6, 9, 91, 119, 135, 136, 196, 198, 199
Mary of Modena, 125
Mason, John, 294, 307
Massachusetts, 147
Maze Pond church, 218, 284–286, 290
Mead, Matthew, xxi, xxviii, 24–28, 31, 33, 39, 86–88, 110, 311, 318, 379
Mennonite, 4, 19
Metropolitan Tabernacle, xvi, 10, 11, 221
Milden, 316, 326, 336
Milton, John, 166–167, 300, 303, 378
Monk, Thomas, 67–68
Monmouth uprising, xxx, 128–132, 134, 198, 200, 379
Moore, John, 392–393
Moore, Mary, 246–247

Moorfields, 84
Morgan, Robert, 318
Murray, Iain, 350, 366
Music, David W., 306–307

Neal, Daniel, 341
Nelthrop, Richard, 129
Neonomian controversy, xxxi, 344–346, 348, 350, 353, 361, 362, 365, 371, 373, 381, 382
Nettles, Tom, xvii, 256, 257
New England, 147, 154
New Model Army, Parliamentary Army, 29, 30, 33, 36
Newgate Prison, 7–8, 186
Newport Pagnell, 29–30, 81
Newton, John, 303
Nonconformist(s), xxviii, xxx, 28, 39, 50, 55, 65, 66, 68, 85, 107, 114, 115, 124, 140, 143, 148, 151–153, 162, 169, 186, 196, 197, 201, 202, 204, 221, 312, 316, 317
Norcott, John, xxix, 86, 87, 165, 172, 173–177, 183, 249, 318
North Marston, 71
Northamptonshire, 87

Oates, Titus, 127
oath of allegiance, 7, 56, 65, 75, 202
Olevianus, Caspar, 102
Oving, 71
Owen, James, 318, 319, 322, 325, 332, 337, 338
Owen, John, 40, 107, 110, 121–122, 151, 195, 196, 221, 253, 335, 364, 365, 378

paedobaptist, xviii, 5, 40, 152, 178, 319, 320, 322, 328, 330, 333, 335, 344, 379, 381, 391
Packer, J.I., 366
Paradise Lost, 166
Particular (Calvinistic) Baptist, xv, xvi, xix, xxiii, xxvii, xxx, xxix, 2, 4, 6, 7, 8, 11, 21, 29, 32, 37, 39, 40, 65, 67, 69, 85, 86, 87, 92, 94, 100, 103, 107, 109, 110, 124, 130, 134, 145, 149, 150, 151, 162, 172, 173, 181, 183, 185, 191, 192, 204–214, 215, 218, 219, 224, 228, 234, 246, 251, 271, 280, 292, 296, 307, 308, 312, 313, 315, 321, 335, 339, 341, 344, 351, 362, 363, 371, 375, 377, 378, 381, 393
Partridge, Susannah (Keach's second wife), xxix, 93–95, 181, 203
Patchell, John, 129
Patrick, John, 307
Penington, Isaac, 181
Penn, William, 181
Petto, Samuel, 253
Petty France, 215–216, 251
Philadelphia Baptist Association, 147, 246, 247, 400
Philadelphia, 147, 245–247
Pilgrim's Progress, xxix, 141, 144, 165, 166
Pinners' Hall, London, 2, 315, 346, 351, 353, 393
Plant, Thomas, 134, 181, 192
Plymouth, 7, 288
Poole, Matthew, 253, 330, 351
Popish plot, xxix, 112, 127
Powell, Vavasor, 296
Presbyterian, Presbyterianism, 8, 36, 40, 58, 85, 105, 109, 121, 130, 151, 179, 214, 238, 296, 300, 312, 317, 324, 331, 335, 350, 351, 361, 366, 371, 380, 382
preterition, 264
Pride, Thomas, 33
Pride's Purge, 33
Protestant, Protestantism, 10, 28, 39, 73, 118–129, 133–137, 152, 162, 171, 198–202, 206, 218, 219, 221, 222, 312, 330, 365, 379
Puritan(s), 36, 40, 56, 58, 105, 106, 127, 145, 156, 168, 176, 196, 253, 312, 344, 351

Quaker, Quakerism, xv, 3, 8, 57, 66, 76, 85, 111, 172, 177–185, 229, 261, 299, 363, 376
Queen Anne, xxii, 1

Reading, 56
Reformation, 23, 63, 121, 124, 136, 300, 335, 372
Restoration period, 14, 55, 57, 59, 110, 140, 141, 144, 169, 204, 245, 312
Rickmansworth, 93
Rider, William, xxvii, 11, 89, 183
Riker, David, xviii
Rippon, John, 11
Roberts, John, 108, 145, 194, 214, 389, 392, 393
Roberts, Prudence, 145, 214, 389
Roman Catholic Church, Catholicism, xv, xxix, xxx, 8, 39, 40, 41, 92, 111, 117, 121, 122, 124–127, 133–137, 143, 157, 189, 198–201, 300, 335, 344, 355, 359, 365, 379
Rothwell, Mr., 318
Rumbold, Richard, 129
Rump Parliament, 33
Russell, Edward, 124
Russell, John, 19, 37–38
Russell, William Lord, 129, 200
Russen, David, xxxii, 2–5, 7, 229, 314, 315, 338, 364, 391–393
Rutherford, Samuel, 345
Rye House Plot, xxx, 110, 128, 129
Ryswick, Holland, xxxi, 252

Sabbath, 229, 363–364, 382, 399
Salisbury, 7
Saltmarsh, John, 30–32, 348
Sancroft, William, Archbishop of Canterbury, xxix, 45, 111, 202
Sandford, Edward and Ann, 227, 281, 282, 291–293
Savoy Declaration of Faith, xxviii, 103, 121, 151, 215, 218, 252, 351
Scripture Justification, 271, 351, 362
Second Conventicle Act (1670), xxix, 7, 45, 65, 70, 106–111, 127, 136
Second London Assembly of Particular Baptists, 100, 204–214
Second London Baptist Confession of Faith (1689), xxix, 9, 100, 103, 185, 214–222, 240, 244, 247, 252, 264, 319, 328, 351, 365
Separatist(s), 19, 36, 56, 67, 312, 335, 339, 380
Seventh-Day Baptist, 7, 179, 228–229, 315, 363, 383
Shadwell, 27, 85, 86, 89, 94, 173, 193, 225
Sheldon, Gilbert, Archbishop of Canterbury, xxviii, 45, 56, 75, 85, 111
Shepton Mallett, 130
Sherborne, Dorset, 7
Shute, Gyles, 24, 217, 318–319, 322, 329, 337, 381
Shute, Hannah, 24
Sidney, Henry, 124
Skidmore, Henry and Elizabeth, 93
Smyth, John, 19
Smythies, William, 316
Socinianism, 179–180, 355
Solemn League and Covenant, 58
Some Brief Remarks, 288, 292
Somerset, 130, 393
Soulbury, 26, 43, 70
Southwark, xx, xxvii, xxix, xxxii, 1, 82, 108–111, 112, 121, 145, 172–174, 192, 214, 217, 218, 220, 224–227, 284, 285, 293, 344, 375, 376, 389
Spilsbury, John, 174, 318, 321
Spitalfields, 193
Spurgeon, Charles Haddon, xiv, 11, 187, 221, 222, 226, 259, 260, 261, 339–341, 377
St. Bartholomew's Day massacre, 126
Stapleford Mill, 43, 70

Steed, Robert, 39, 283, 288
Stennett, Joseph, xxi, 1–9, 11, 179, 228–229, 314, 315, 363, 364, 375–376, 382, 384, 391–393
Stepney, 24, 26, 86, 318
Stinton, Benjamin (married Keach's daughter Susannah), xxxi, xxxii, 21, 227–228, 341, 389
Stinton, Mary, 227
Stinton, Richard, 227
Stinton, Thomas (married Keach's daughter Elizabeth), xxx, 228
Stoke Hammond, xxvii, 15, 18, 19, 20, 24, 26, 38, 42, 43, 44, 50, 70, 74, 75, 140, 311
Strafford, Thomas, 46, 76
Strange, Nathaniel, 65
Suffolk, 316
Swanbourne, 71
Sydney, Algernon, 129
Synod of Dordt, 21

Taunton, 130, 216, 393
Test Act, 125, 202–203
The Almost Christian Discovered, 27
The Book of Common Prayer, 8, 46, 48, 51, 56, 58
The Christian in Complete Armour, 188
The churches Glory: Or, the Becoming Ornament: being a Seasonable Word, tending to the Provoking, Encouraging and Perfecting of Holiness in Believers, 87, 172
The Dippers Dipt: Or, The Anabaptists duck'd and plung'd over head and ears, at a disputation in Southwark, 313
The Glory and Ornament of a True Gospel Constituted Church, 232, 242
The Heavenly Footman, 188
The Narrative of the Proceedings of the General Assembly, 206
The New England Primer, 147
The Occasions, Causes, Nature, Rise, Growth and Remedies of Mental Errors, 361
The Park, 376
The Philadelphia Confession, 400
The Purity of Gospel Communion, 292
The Quakers Quaking, 181
The Scripture Gospel Defended, 346, 353
The Standard Confession, 32
Thirty-Nine Articles, 56, 202
Tilenus, Daniel, 330–331
Tingewick, 62
Tombes, John, 178, 322
Tong, Israel, 127
Tooley Street, 89, 92, 220, 224–226
Torbay, 125
Tower Bridge, 94, 225
Traill, Robert, 361–362
Treaty of Dover, 125
Treaty of Ryswick, xxxi, 252
Tredwell, John, 316, 336–337
Truth Cleared: Or, a brief Narrative of the Rise, Occasion, and Management of the present Controversy concerning Singing in the Worship of God, 282–286
Tyburn, 130
Tyndale, William, 14

Underwood, T.L., 180
Ursinus, Zacharias, 102

Vaughn, James Barry, 19, 166–167, 233, 256–257, 297–298
Veale, Edward, 351
Venner, Thomas, 7, 57, 65, 68
Vincent, Nathaniel, 109
Vincent, Thomas, 83, 141

Walcott, Thomas, 129
Waldensians, 300
Walters, Lucy, 132
Walton, Elizabeth, 26

Wapping, xxix, 7, 86, 87, 110, 111, 172–174, 183, 246, 318, 381
war with France, xxx
Watts, Isaac, 234, 303
Watts, Michael, 83, 85
Webb, John, 393
Wesley, Charles, 303, 304
Wesley, John, 366
Westminster Confession of Faith, xxvii, 102, 151, 214, 218, 252, 350, 351
Whinnell, Thomas, 216
Whitehead, George, 111, 181
Whitley, W.T., 85, 89, 92, 227
Wilkes, Luke, 23, 44–45, 50, 70, 75
Wilkinson, Richard, 392–393
William of Orange (William III), xxii, xxix, xxx, xxxi, xxxii, 1, 6, 9, 39, 90–91, 119, 124, 125, 135, 136, 196, 198–200, 202, 221, 250, 379, 384
Williams, Daniel, xxi, xxxi, 345, 347, 350–351, 353, 355–359, 365, 367
Williamson, Joseph, 65
Winslow, xxviii, 19, 23, 24, 32, 37, 44, 46, 47, 50, 52, 61, 62, 66, 68, 71–73, 78–81, 87, 89, 140, 280, 311
Wycliffe, John, 121

Zwingli, Ulrich, 189

Benjamin Keach's writings

"The Blessedness of Christ's Sheep," 262, 269
A Counter-Antidote, 318
A Feast of Fat Things, 294
A Golden Mine Opened: or, The Glory of God's Rich Grace Displayed in the Mediator to Believers, xxxi, 73, 95, 214, 225, 262, 346
A Medium Betwixt Two Extremes, 250, 346, 351, 358, 362, 371
A pillar set up, 92
A Short Confession of Faith, xxxi
A Sober Appeal for Right and Justice, 284
Antichrist Stormed: Or, the Mystery Babylon, the Great Whore, and Great City proved to be the present Church of Rome, 136, 199–201
Believer's Baptism, 318
Christ Alone the Way to Heaven, xxxi, 271, 351
Darkness Vanquished: Or, Truth in its Primitive Purity, 172, 183
Distressed Sion Relieved: Or, The Garment of Praise for the Spirit of Heaviness, xxx, 72–73, 77, 119–120, 123, 131–133, 199
God Acknowledged: Or, the True Interest of the Nation, 250
Gold Refin'd: Or, Baptism in its Primitive Purity, xxx, 316, 324, 332–333
Gospel Mysteries Unveil'd: Or, Exposition of all the Parables, xxxi, 250
Instructions for Children, 143, 146–147, 150–152
Keach's Covenant, 395–398
Laying on of Hands upon Baptized Believers, as such, Proved an Ordinance of Christ, xxxi, 184
Light broke forth in Wales, 318

Mr. Baxter's Arguments for Believers Baptism, 177–178, 316
Pedo-baptism Disproved, 316
Sion in Distress: Or, the Groans of the Protestant Church, xxviii, 72–81, 112, 113, 122, 127, 137, 197, 379
Some Passages of the Fearful Estate of John Child, 191
Spiritual Melody, xxxi, 294
Spiritual Songs, 294
The Articles of Faith, 242–247, 320, 321, 400
The Ax Laid to the Root, 316
The Breach Repaired in God's Worship, xxxi, 292, 295, 297, 298, 301, 302
The Child's Instructor: or, A New and Easy Primmer, xxviii, 43–44, 47, 73, 89, 107–108, 139, 146, 268
The Child's Delight: or, Instructions for Children and Youth, 143, 146, 150, 152
The Counterfeit Christian: Or, the Danger of Hypocrisy, xxxi, 269, 272–276
The covenant and catechism of the church…meeting…in Southwark, xxxi, 395–398
The Display of Glorious Grace: Or, the Covenant of Peace Opened, xxxi, 89, 250, 252–259, 268, 272, 346, 355, 362,
The Everlasting Covenant, xxxi, 250, 252, 346
The Glorious Lover: A Divine Poem, Upon the Adorable Mystery of Sinners Redemption, xxix, 143, 158–161, 166–170, 276
The Glory of a True Church, and Its Discipline Display'd, xxxi, 232, 234, 240,
The Gospel Minister's Maintenance Vindicated, 188, 208–209
The Grand Imposter Discovered: Or, the Quakers doctrine weighed in the balance and found wanting, 172, 180, 182
The Great Salvation, 257–261
The Jewish Sabbath Abrogated: or, The Saturday Sabbatarians confuted, xxxi, 364
The Marrow of True Justification, xxxi, 250, 346, 354, 358, 362, 367
The Progress of Sin: Or, the Travels of Ungodliness, xxx, 143, 148
The Rector Rectified and Corrected, 316, 336
The Travels of True Godliness, xxx, 8, 143, 162, 163, 165, 169, 250, 352, 353
To All the Baptized Churches and faithful Brethren in England and Wales, Christian Salutations, 215, 280
Tropologia, a Key to open Scripture Metaphors, together with Types of the Old Testament (Types and Metaphors), xv,xxv, xxx, 172–173, 177, 186–191, 196, 210, 230, 231, 249, 272, 296, 297, 300, 316, 321, 329
War with the Devil: or, The Young Man's Conflict with the Powers of Darkness, xxix, 143, 144, 154, 155, 157, 158, 162, 170, 250, 276

Other titles available from Joshua Press…

Great themes in Puritan preaching

Compiled and edited
By Mariano Di Gangi

DRAWING FROM a gold mine of Puritan writings, this book provides a taste of the riches of Puritan theology and its application to life. This title will whet your appetite and stir your faith to greater views of Christ, his Person and his work.

ISBN 978–1–894400–26–8 (HC)
ISBN 978–1–894400–24–4 (PB)

The voice of faith

Jonathan Edwards's theology of prayer

By Peter Beck

EXPLORING THE sermons and writings of Jonathan Edwards, Dr. Beck draws a comprehensive picture of his theology of prayer and why Edwards believed God would hear the prayers of his people. Interspersed are three external biographies that set the historical and theological scene.

ISBN 978–1–894400–33–6 (HC)
ISBN 978–1–894400–32–9 (PB)

Visit us online at www.joshuapress.com

MATTHEW BARRETT

The GRACE of GODLINESS
An introduction to doctrine and piety in the Canons of Dort

The grace of godliness

An introduction to doctrine and piety in the Canons of Dort

By Matthew Barrett

BARRETT opens a window on the synod's deliberations with the Remonstrants and examines the main emphases of the canons, with special attention on their relationship to biblical piety and spirituality.

ISBN 978-1-894400-52-7 (PB)

Searching for truth

Discovering the meaning and purpose of life

By Joe Boot

BEGINNING WITH a basic understanding of the world, Joe Boot explains the biblical worldview, giving special attention to the life and claims of Jesus Christ. He wrestles with questions about suffering, truth, morality and guilt.

ISBN 978-1-894400-40-4

Other titles available from Joshua Press…

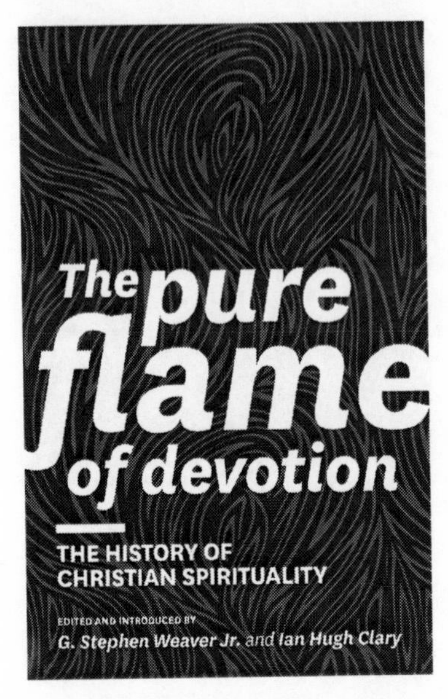

The pure flame of devotion

The history of Christian spirituality

Edited and introduced By G. Stephen Weaver Jr. and Ian Hugh Clary

THIS VOLUME is meant to ignite your interest and understanding of key time periods and pivotal people from various eras of church history.

ISBN 978–1-894400-55-8 (HC)
ISBN 978-1-894400-54-1 (PB)

Social justice through the eyes of Wesley

John Wesley's theological challenge to slavery

By Irv A. Brendlinger

THIS BOOK brings to light John Wesley's convictions about slavery and demonstrates how his theology compelled him to work to abolish it—writing, supporting and interacting with key players in the anti-slavery movement.

ISBN 978-1-894400-23-7 (PB)

Other titles available from Joshua Press…

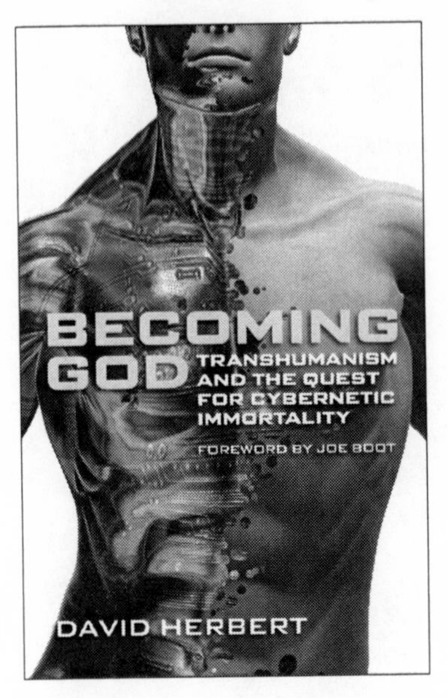

Becoming God

Transshumanism and the quest for cybernetic immortality

By David Herbert

AN ANALYSIS of the philosophic and scientific roots of this growing movement, this book also profiles the key world figures—Ray Kurzweil, Aubrey de Grey, Kevin Warwick, Natasha Vita-More, and others. A great introduction to understanding transhumanism.

ISBN 978-1-894400-58-9 (PB)

The key to understanding origins

The underlying assumptions

By David Herbert

BEGINNING WITH the religious nature of man, Dr. Herbert shows how a belief in either naturalism or supernaturalism, determines what your position will be. He examines the basic tenets of each and opens the subject up for investigation.

ISBN 978-1-894400-53-4 (PB)

Deo Optimo et Maximo Gloria
To God, best and greatest, be glory

www.joshuapress.com

CPSIA information can be obtained at www.ICGtesting.com
Printed in the USA
BVOW07s0128140115

383169BV00004B/181/P